# Let Me Set the Scene

The years 1956–1976 are perhaps the most important in what has come to be called the Renaissance of English theatre and drama in the late twentieth century. The companies most involved in this revival were the English Stage Company, the Royal Shakespeare Company, and the National Theatre. It is a special privilege, therefore, to have a first-hand account of the day-to-day workings of these companies as told by Michael Hallifax, who was responsible for much of the day-by-day operation of each of these companies at crucial times in their development. Mr. Hallifax's account ranges through the daily routine of keeping a multi-production repertory running smoothly, hiring personnel and supervising actors' auditions, touring (including not only within England but also throughout Europe and in the United States and Canada), hosting other companies from throughout the globe during an annual World Theatre Season in London, working with leading actors of the British theatre, arranging theatre attendance by members of the Royal Family, and planning various ceremonial occasions.

Assisting George Devine, Peter Hall, and Laurence Olivier, Michael Hallifax was at the very heart of the most influential companies in England, and his account of administering many of the decisions that made the theatres so effective brings us as close as we are apt to come to the inner life of these companies over two decades of greatness. It is a book that everyone who is interested in theatre should read.

OSCAR BROCKETT

Michael Hallifax's book gives us a unique insight into the running of three of England's finest theatrical institutions and he shares with us his memories of working with the great directors who ran them. That Mr. Hallifax was the man chosen to run backstage by all three is an extraordinary tribute to his character and ability. His organizational gifts, transparent honesty, and an impressive command of detail are all apparent in his memoirs. He has a touching and delightful relationship with his bosses, especially Sir Laurence. He also has an eye for acting and there are enjoyable anecdotes and character studies to prove it. *Let Me Set the Scene* is a fascinating look behind the scenes and a valuable addition to theatrical history. It deserves a place on the bookshelves of theatre buffs everywhere.

DAME JOAN PLOWRIGHT

# Let Me Set the Scene

Twenty Years at the
Heart of British Theatre
1956 to 1976

## MICHAEL HALLIFAX

*Recalling Great Actors, Great Events, Great Plays*

ART OF THEATER SERIES

A SMITH AND KRAUS BOOK

Published by
Smith and Kraus, Inc.
177 Lyme Road, Hanover, NH 03755
www.smithkraus.com

First edition: April 2004
9 8 7 6 5 4 3 2 1

*Cover and text design by Freedom Hill Design, Reading, Vermont*
Cover photograph by Gordon Goode, taken on the stage of the Royal Shakespeare Theatre, 1962. From the left: Patrick Donnell, general manager, Stratford; John Goodwin, publicity, Stratford and Aldwych; John Wyckham, technical administrator, Stratford and Aldwych; Abd'Elkader Farrah, associate designer, Stratford; Michel Saint-Denis, director; Peter Hall, managing director; Peter Brook, director; Clifford Williams, associate director, Stratford; Michael Hallifax, manager, Stratford; Eduardo Milano, catering manager, Stratford; Maurice Daniels, repertory manager, Stratford; John Roberts London general manager, Aldwych.

Library of Congress Cataloging-in-Publication Data
Hallifax, Michael.
Let me set the scene : twenty years at the heart of British theatre, 1956 to 1976 /
Michael Hallifax. —1st ed.
p. cm. — (Art of theater series)
ISBN 1-57525-330-5
1. Theater—Great Britain—History—20th century. 2. Hallifax, Michael.
I. Title. II. Series.
PN2595.H34 2003
792'.0941'09045—dc21
2003045480

# ❦ CONTENTS ❦

# ❦ FOREWORD ❧

Michael Hallifax remains a charming enigma. I have known him for over forty years and worked with him for much of that time. He presents an elegant figure to the world — tall, slim, and always immaculately turned out, as he picks his way through the mess and muddle of backstage life. You would think him an eminent diplomat touring a world that must be utterly foreign to him. But you would be wrong. Michael loves the muddle and the mess. They give him something to minister to.

He is a consummate professional, and his life has been all backstage as assistant stage manager, stage manager, stage director, company manager, production manager, contracts manager, repertory scheduler, theatre manager, and actors' friend. He must have done every one of the named and unnamed behind-the-scenes jobs that have ever been thought of. He is the dependable man that makes theatre possible.

Michael Hallifax is even-tempered, yet I have heard him raise his voice to an alarming heat when faced with unprofessional behaviour. He is fair-minded to a fault; yet I have known him to express dislike of somebody's work with energetic asperity. He would have been good casting as an ambassador or a well-balanced headmaster, who was urbane, yet occasionally surprising. Instead, he chose the theatre, and his life in it has been pursued with the private, yet fervent zeal of a priest.

But there remains a mystery. He has shown an unmatchable instinct for knowing where the next important development in the British theatre is going to occur. Some sixth sense tips him off, and he changes jobs in good time to help the next revolution.

Immediately after the Second World War, all the exciting innovations in the theatre were coming from the near-monopolistic H. M. Tennent, Ltd, which not only maintained the great stars like Gielgud,

Richardson, Coward, and Ashcroft in provocative work, but encouraged new and original geniuses like Peter Brook. The young Michael Hallifax was working for them.

In 1948, Tony Quayle began a renaissance that amazed at Stratford-upon-Avon when he directed the Shakespeare Memorial Theatre (the Royal Shakespeare Company had yet to arrive). Wonderful productions and wonderful performances were the result. Michael Hallifax was there.

In 1956, George Devine changed the shape of British Theatre when he turned the Royal Court Theatre into a home for writers. Michael Hallifax was his general manager.

In 1960, I founded the Royal Shakespeare Company and created an ensemble that played at Stratford-upon-Avon and at the Aldwych Theatre in London. Michael Hallifax was with me.

In 1963, Laurence Olivier founded the National Theatre company. Michael was there to help.

In 1976, as director of the National Theatre, I took the company into the new buildings on the South Bank. Michael was in charge of planning and scheduling.

What is his secret? Theatre, like every other worthwhile discipline, depends on a fastidious attention to detail. Michael has always provided that concentration. I don't know how he has remembered all these tiny events. (The difficulty of loading a gas cooker for *Look Back in Anger* into a taxi is particularly treasurable). But he remembers event after event and all the minutiae of a full life in the theatre. He tells us up front that we're going to have "no spicy goings-on," and while there is the occasional quick revelation (he leaves the Royal Court because he is tired, but also because he found it too "political"), he keeps his word. It is no wonder that such a professional should be discreet. But it is often not difficult to read between the lines.

*Sir Peter Hall*

# ❧ INTRODUCTION ❧

When I was the London manager for the Royal Shakespeare Company at the Aldwych Theatre, London, a movie company used the theatre for location filming of *The Deadly Affair*. The stars were Simone Signoret and James Mason, and I spent some time chatting to them when they were waiting in the dress circle for their call.

It was that enjoyable encounter I always had in mind when, during Sir Laurence Olivier's ten-year reign as director of the National Theatre of Great Britain, he would put forward the name of a movie-actor friend for a role in a forthcoming National Theatre production. The actor was James Mason. When his name was mentioned, the reaction of those of us who were present would be the same. "Oh, yes. James Mason. Great in films, but when did he last work in the theatre?"

Because of the recurrence of his name, I was particularly interested, many years later, to see copies of his autobiography in all the bookshops. It wasn't long, however, before I noticed that these copies being offered at a discount so soon after publication. I wasn't really surprised for the reviews of the book had been tepid. The main objection was that James Mason himself and all those about whom he spoke were too nice. There was no scurrilous gossip. No dirt. No scandal. Yet he had had a long career in films, but that wasn't enough to sell the book.

I had the fate of that book very much in mind when I decided to accept Sir Peter Hall's challenge to write about my theatre experiences. He reminded the assembled masses at the wonderful affair organised for my last day at the National Theatre that I had helped George Devine set up the English Stage Company at the Royal Court Theatre, I had worked at Stratford-upon-Avon and at the Aldwych Theatre, London, for the Royal Shakespeare Company when he himself was the managing director, and I had worked with Sir Laurence Olivier for the

National Theatre at the Old Vic. It was then that Sir Peter said I should write about these three great companies and although I commented that I had never kept a daily diary, I would do my best to recall people and plays and unusual events during the twenty-year span those companies covered.

It was some years before I started to write, though I knew before I set down the first words that my book would not be filled with gossip. Not that I would be suppressing news of some spicy goings-on, simply that I wasn't aware of any. That wasn't my world: mine was far more interesting. From stage management I moved into company management before easing into administration, and these fascinating posts kept me in touch with actors and all branches of staff, backstage, front-of-house, and workshops — and what marvellous people to be amongst. No wonder I can say that my world was an absolutely marvellous one.

I have, without doubt, had a most satisfying life; though, as always, the good times have been sprinkled with the not-so-good. But when a show has suddenly folded or when a hoped-for job hasn't materialised, I could always fall back on the wise words of Elizabeth, my wife. "Don't worry," she'd say. "It'll be for the best." And it always was for the best, even though the best might not appear immediately.

As I write that, I think of the days when I went to the Royal Academy of Dramatic Art to talk to the stage management course about touring overseas. This was during the 1960s, so my days at the Royal Court were some way behind me. When one group heard of my involvement with George Devine and the Court, I was asked whether it had been great to know we were making theatre history. I was taken aback, and I am sure now I should have told them what they were wanting to hear. Instead, I found myself saying, "Oh, heavens. I'm absolutely certain that none of us at the Court had thoughts of anything like that. All I knew was that I had a job, and this meant I was actually being paid. I considered myself lucky indeed that, after the first few rocky months, it looked as though those wage packets would continue to arrive. The fact that the work for which I was being paid was the most wonderful in the world was a great, big, glorious bonus."

So I have written about that bonus at the Court, and the many bonuses that followed, up until the last days of the National Theatre at the Old Vic and the move to the new building on the South Bank. Every now and then, glimpses of life before the Court slipped in, but I felt that the concentration should be on the big three, with a few lines on what now seems like an eighteen-month sabbatical as manager at the Comedy Theatre.

I have really enjoyed writing this book in which I have, every now and then, spent a little time explaining a custom, a title, or a duty that has become obsolete or simply out-of-date. It is quite understandable if a theatre no longer employs a linkman, but because I am interested in the reason for such a fascinating form of employment all those years ago, I have commented on him. And others.

Finally, I offer my sincere thanks to Sir Peter Hall for kick-starting my book writing, to my elder son, Guy, who nobly volunteered to be my U.K. editor, and to Michael York, who put me in touch with my U.S. publisher, Marisa Kraus of Smith and Kraus. Without her help and enthusiasm, I would not have had to write this introduction, since there would have been nothing to introduce.

*Michael Hallifax*

# Act One
## The English Stage Company 1956 to 1959

George Devine, as artistic director of the newly formed English Stage Company, sets up a Writers' Theatre in London at the Royal Court Theatre, Chelsea. New plays and revivals of classics are planned. A slow start but after six months, with the premiere production of *Look Back in Anger* and a revival of *The Country Wife*, the company is firmly established. Sir Laurence Olivier plays Archie Rice in *The Entertainer*. *Look Back in Anger* plays on Broadway. Samuel Beckett's *End-Game* and *Krapp's Last Tape* are given their first British productions.

### Scene 1 ❦ The Royal Court Theatre, 1956

The curtain rises to show the façade of the Royal Court Theatre in Sloane Square. The Square, or more accurately, the Rectangle, with its trees, its central fountain, and, just across the road from the theatre, its steep steps leading down to the "Ladies," as the discreet notice says, is in the Chelsea area of London and is about three miles from Piccadilly Circus.

Since it is 1956, Chelsea is still very much a backwater, even though the Square is the meeting place of six roads, four of which are important urban roads, while the other two each lead to a warren of streets filled with imposing five-storey Victorian or Edwardian mansions.

The Royal Court Theatre sits at the eastern end of the Square almost cheek by jowl with the Sloane Square District Line railway station. The proximity of the Tube, as it is incorrectly called since it does not burrow underground as does the real Tube, was of enormous benefit to the theatre's patrons, as were several bus routes that literally passed the door and stopped close by.

1

It was the District Line that I used for my journey from Hammersmith to Sloane Square for a meeting with George Devine. On the journey, I remembered his words when I went to his dressing room to bid him good-bye at the end of a three-week season at the Shakespeare Memorial Theatre, Stratford-upon-Avon. It was just before Christmas 1955. "Have a good rest at Christmas, Michael. I think the new company will keep us quite busy in the New Year. So let's meet at the stage door of the Royal Court at ten o'clock on Monday the eighth of January."

George Devine was the artistic director of the newly formed English Stage Company that was at first scheduled to take over the Kingsway Theatre. This small theatre in Great Queen Street, not far from the New London Theatre and the Theatre Royal, Drury Lane, had been closed for some years due to extensive damage, such as the stage being open to the sky, caused by enemy action during the 1939/1945 War — now curiously referred to as the Second World War. (There was no First World War, except in retrospect. The expressive title for that terrible conflict of 1914 to 1918 was the Great War.) The dilapidated state of the theatre suited George Devine, and the plans he made for his new company were based on the Kingsway and the manner in which it was to be restored to use. All was going well and encouragingly when the English Stage Company's council (another term for a board or committee) learned that the high costs of rehabilitating the theatre had risen to such an alarming extent that the ten-strong council, of whom only one, Alfred Esdaile, was a theatre man, told George that he must forget the Kingsway. They added that there appeared to be no alternative at that time.

Some months later, when I was talking to George while on tour with his production for the Shakespeare Memorial Theatre of *King Lear,* he told me how shattered he had been by this news. Perhaps it was as well that he had not only the direction of the play but also the role of Gloucester to take his mind off the problems he was encountering while forming a company that was seemingly teetering on the brink of extinction.

However, Alfred Esdaile controlled a second theatre in addition to the Kingsway, and a new base for the English Stage Company was only found when he announced that, in place of the Kingsway, he was now willing to offer the company his other theatre, the Royal Court. His offer was immediately accepted.

This compact theatre, seating about four hundred, was built in 1888. On one side, there were a few shops and a pub, while on the other was a lane dividing the theatre from the station, which led to an open space at the back of the building. A few cars could be parked in this space, but its main use was in giving access to the narrow dock doors and also to a flight of iron stairs that served as the fire escape for the two upper levels of the building. The theatre was going through a quiet patch after several years of success with revues presented by Laurier Lister. He had left a memento at the stage door where there was a huge coir mat clearly marked with the initials L. L. But if the little Chelsea theatre in L. L.'s time had been buzzing with the pleasure of packed houses and enthusiastic audiences, it had certainly lost that feeling by the time we moved in.

I reached the stage door just before ten o'clock. I was as exact with my timing as George had been with his instructions to me. As the saying goes, "Once a stage manager, always a stage manager," and George's stage management training always meant that instructions were very detailed and very exact. I was a stage manager myself and had been for many years, so I always appreciated that exactness, and I used him as a model for this and many other excellent stage manager traits he had retained. One of his habits I did not have was his pipe smoking. This he seemed to do almost continuously, but I reckoned, apart from the obvious pleasure it gave him, perhaps it was a way of calming his nerves. They were going to be stretched to breaking point and beyond in the next ten years.

As we climbed the stairs to the offices, George explained that we were not going to have the run of the whole theatre at first. On the stage was a production by Sam Wanamaker (with whom I had worked a few years previously) of *The Threepenny Opera,* which would be playing there until the end of February, while we were allocated the offices on the floor above the upper circle foyer. These faced Sloane Square, not that there was a view of the Square from any of its windows, for they were all set too high in the wall. The floor above our offices was rented to Clement Freud, where he ran a very successful nightclub.

There was a separate stairway to reach the club with its entrance set into the side of the building at the start of the lane. This meant that the closing of the theatre after an evening performance did not affect those going to the club.

As we crossed the upper circle foyer on the way to the final flight of stairs, I thought how lucky I had been to have worked twice with George Devine before word of his new company became public knowledge. I first met him when I was the stage manager of Tennent Production's presentation of Henrik Ibsen's *Hedda Gabler*. He played Tesman to Peggy Ashcroft's Hedda, and although Miss Ashcroft's series of superb performances (one of which, *The Deep Blue Sea*, I had seen two years previously) was well known to me, I had never heard of George Devine. It didn't take long into the rehearsal period to be certain that Miss Ashcroft's Hedda was going to be another stunning performance, while at the same time I was as sure that Mr. Devine's Tesman was also going to be wonderful. Newspaper critics wrote of his performance as "bumbling," "loveable," and a "bear of a man." All suited his Tesman splendidly — and come to think of it, except for the "bumbling," the man himself as well. His makeup gave him the appearance of the playwright (often referred to jokingly as Henry Gibson) with side-whiskers and small spectacles, the only difference being that Henrik Ibsen's hair was white, whereas George's was grey, veering towards white.

We returned from Oslo, the final date of the *Hedda* Continental/Scandinavian tour, by sea to Newcastle-upon-Tyne and from thence by train to London. I was coming back with no job in view, and although I was quite used to that situation, I was not prepared for the situation I found at home in Barnes where my wife, Elizabeth, and both boys, Guy and Clive, were deeply into mumps.

A week later, I got a phone call from Patrick (Paddy) Donnell, the general manager of the Shakespeare Memorial Theatre at Stratford-upon-Avon, asking if I were free to become the stage manager of a six-month tour of *The Tragedy of King Lear*. Sir John Gielgud would be playing Lear and the play would be directed by George Devine, who would also be playing Gloucester. Patrick Donnell added that he would also be with the tour as manager and stage director. At once I said that I would very much like to accept the offer, although, as I was saying this, I was only too aware that with Elizabeth extremely poorly upstairs, I might easily go down with mumps during the first weeks of rehearsal. However, by the time rehearsals started at the Scala Theatre, the family had recovered and mumps was not passed on to me.

It was while we were playing *King Lear* at the Opera House, Manchester, some months later, that it became common knowledge that George Devine was setting up a new company that would be based in London and would be titled the English Stage Company. That evening I screwed up my courage and went to his dressing room to ask if I might be considered as his stage director. He grunted while getting on with his makeup, but he didn't say anything, so I took his reaction, if a grunt can be counted as such, as a hopeful sign.

Shortly after this, George asked me to come to his dressing room one evening to meet Mr. Greville Poke, the secretary of the Council of the English Stage Company. Mr. Poke asked a few general questions about my theatre career, but since his reaction had given me no clue as to whether I had impressed him or not, I was quite surprised the following evening when George said that Mr. Poke had approved my application. He then swung round in his chair to face the mirror and, continuing his makeup, added, "Better the devil you know . . ." and the job was mine.

## Scene 2 ❧ The English Stage Company's first stage director

Now, three months after George was given the go-ahead to engage me as his stage director, here, unbelievably, he and I were at the Royal Court Theatre. At that time, a stage director was the equivalent of what became a company manager: in overall charge of the acting company and dealing with its business side. All the preliminary work of setting up the production, such as casting, negotiating contracts, arranging a pre-London tour, and so on, would be carried out by the management, who would pass on the necessary instructions and details to the stage director. With a touring production — and most plays would tour before going in to the West End — the stage director would light the show at each date. He might also have lit it at the first date if the producer of the play (not then termed the director) had not wished to do this. The credit for the producer in the programme would be: "Produced by —"

The stage manager would be responsible for the smooth running of performances and answerable to the stage director. He might take understudy rehearsals, but that job would normally fall to the stage director: the stage manager would more often than not be an understudy. If the management felt generous or if stage management obviously needed extra help, an assistant stage manager would be engaged. He or she would certainly be an understudy, in fact would be engaged with understudy capabilities in mind rather than stage management skills. There was no such position as deputy stage manager.

During the 1950s, it was found that when a deal was made with American management or an impresario, the titles for the various British grades, from producer to assistant stage manager, did not accord with those used in the United States. Since those on the other side of the Atlantic seemed to fit the holders of the various appointments more clearly, slowly the change to the American use of titles came about. A play would be produced by the producer, but it would be put onstage by a director. The stage director became the company manager but often he or she would also be the stage manager, thus was born the company and stage manager position. The deputy stage manager appeared and slotted in more or less where the stage manager used to be, and only the assistant stage manager stayed unaltered.

These changes did not feature in George Devine's world in 1955, so he automatically referred to me as his stage director. As the number of stage management teams working for me at the Court increased — as many as five at one time — George invented a new title for me, general stage director. This didn't alter my salary, nor would I have considered that it should. From the start, I was paid what I considered the very generous figure of £18 a week.

During early discussions with George, he had told me that he would in time be employing a general manager "who will deal with all the front-of-house and the business side, while you will be in sole command of everything that happens the other side of the curtain. You will be responsible only to me."

## Scene 3 ❧ Preparing for the English Stage Company's initial productions

Even as we threaded our way through to the foyer of the Royal Court Theatre, I had the feeling that I was actually in George's own theatre, and it wasn't long before I realised that all those who worked for him had exactly the same feeling. We reached the offices where he pointed to the first door and said, "That's Clement Freud's office so, as you will realise, he is reasonably close to his nightclub." He pointed to the ceiling, "That's it up there." George moved on into a short narrow corridor with two doors on the left. He opened the first saying, "This will be Tony Richardson's, the next will be mine, and at the end will be the General Office." Tony Richardson, whom I had yet to meet, had been appointed assistant artistic director, but he was currently busy directing *Othello* for television.

I looked briefly into the three rooms before settling in George's, where he sat behind a small desk and started lighting a pipe. "We've got a lot to do and not much time to do it," he said, puffing the while. "So let me go through a list of jobs I want you to get on with at once. I have been making a little progress in the formation of an acting company, but we need to hold auditions now that we are back in London, and I want you to join me in the stalls when we start next week. Now that you will be with me, we will need someone to check in those who come to audition, as you did at the Palace Theatre last summer. We'll call him the stage manager, for this will give him some authority. So please get hold of John Osborne who has absolutely no money, and get him to come along and be our stage manager on a day-to-day basis. We can pay him ten shillings a day. You'll find him on a boat moored at Chiswick."

## Scene 4 ❧ Meeting John Osborne, August 1955

My first meeting with John had been at one of the auditions during the London Season of *King Lear* at the Palace Theatre on Cambridge Circus. I had called in on George in his dressing room one evening when he unexpectedly asked, "Would you like to be my stage manager next week when I am holding auditions on the stage here? I can't pay you anything, but I would be very grateful if you would do this." I had often done this when I was working for Tennent's — again for no extra payment on my £14 a week, since it was considered part of one's job — so it was no problem to do what George wanted. My duties were to greet the actors and show them to a row of chairs I had arranged in a convenient corridor. There I had to try and put them at their ease (not a simple matter), and then, when the actor on stage had finished his or her audition, to be ready to lead the next contender to be introduced: this had to be given very clearly so that George did not have to ask for the name to be repeated. Back to the corridor, for the routine to start again. I was always very careful to tell all of them that only George Devine was in the very centre of the inky blackness of the stalls and that, as an actor, he understood well the effect nerves have on a fellow actor at such ordeals.

This approach was very different from the Tennent days when Daphne Rye was responsible for casting for Hugh Beaumont. Mr. Beaumont, "Binkie" to his friends, was the managing director of H. M. Tennent, Ltd. and a powerful figure in the world of London theatres. This was especially true during the 1950s when it would not be unusual for there to be seven Tennent productions playing at the same time in the West End. When one looked at Tennent programmes, one would be struck by how often the names of many actors would appear over the years. This was because Binkie and Daphne had built up a large company of actors on whom they could rely, and not only for small parts and understudies. Many an actor had an almost permanent job, moving from play to play in the same way, fortunately, that I experienced on the stage management side.

Daphne Rye was respected and liked and feared for she had, as with Binkie, so much power. She was a lovely large jolly lady for whom auditions were organised and to which she came, sweeping in to the stalls with an entourage of several merry young men. Certainly, like George, she would sit out in the darkness, but she and her friends would carry on a lively conversation between the departure of one actor and the arrival of the next. All too often, as a trembling young man stepped onto the stage, he would be greeted by a roar of laughter from the pitch-black stalls. This in no way was connected with the appearance of the actor but was simply part of the general merriment out there — but how was the actor to be sure of this? Many were certain that their flies were not buttoned up (no zippers, then), but standing alone on a large stage in a blaze of lights, checking that area of dress was unthinkable.

With George in the stalls at the Palace Theatre and myself as his stage manager, there were no hoots of laughter at these auditions. I was working my way steadily down the audition list that George had provided until I reached the name of John Osborne. He was just another young actor, among many that morning, and the name meant nothing to me. When he came along the corridor to await his turn to audition, I saw a tall young man, with thick wavy hair and a long thin face. Most of those who had already been seen by George had been quiet and reserved, and although I talked to all of them, I felt their side of the conversation was rather guarded. Were they wondering if I would give reports to George or was it a case of wanting to get the torture over?

John was the exception, and I soon realised why. He told me that one of his plays, *Look Back in Anger,* had been accepted by George and Tony Richardson for the English Stage Company, and it would be presented during the first season. However, he added that he also desperately wanted to join the company as an actor. I had enjoyed talking to him, and presumably because of his telling me about his play, out of those who came to audition over two days at the Palace Theatre, I remembered him the most clearly. I was therefore very pleased all those months later to know that we were able to put a little work his way while he was waiting to join the company — for George had indeed engaged him. His first job was to understudy the role of Jimmy Porter in his own play.

## Scene 5 & Further instructions from George Devine

"We will be playing in repertoire as they do in Stratford," George continued. "This means that we must get as many productions onto the stage as quickly as possible after April 2, which is the day on which we open our first play, *The Mulberry Bush* by Angus Wilson. We will refer to this as the Wilson, for it is going to be a writer's theatre, so all the plays will be called by the name of the playwright. Opening a week after the Wilson will be Arthur Miller's *The Crucible,* which, of course, will be known as the Miller. Each will have an invited audience dress rehearsal on Monday, opening the next night.

"However, for the following two productions, *Look Back in Anger* (the Osborne) and then the double bill of Ronald Duncan's *Don Juan* and *The Death of Satan* (the Duncans) each will be given dress rehearsals on Monday and the Tuesday with the opening on the Wednesday.

"The public must be made aware that, once we get going, in any one week, they will have the choice of two plays, playing half a week each. This also means that at the start we will be rehearsing two productions at the same time, so I want you to find out what chance there is around here of some reasonable rehearsal rooms at reasonable rates. And don't forget to work out how many you will need on stage management and start interviewing straight away. I will leave you to draw up a short list, but I would like to meet those in whom you are particularly interested so that we may discuss them before you finally offer contracts.

"Until we can set up our own workshops, we must get the small amount of scenery most productions will need built outside the theatre, so please find a firm who could do this. At the same time, please get several quotes for someone to clean and then polish the stage floor. We cannot afford the usual painted stage cloths, so we will either just use the wooden floor, or we will put down rugs or small carpets if they are vital.

"Because I want an apron stage, the orchestra pit must be boarded over — but done in such a way that should we want to use it at any time, all we will need to do is to remove the cover. However this cover must match up as near as possible with the stage floorboards. And, of course, the footlights must go and their trough filled in, again matching all the boards."

George then spoke of wanting assemblies. He had adopted the term used by the Shakespeare Memorial Theatre at Stratford-upon-Avon where, far downstage on each side, there were wide entrances, reached from good-sized offstage spaces. These spaces provided the area necessary for crowds, and especially armies, to assemble out of sight of the audience, yet close enough for the leading members of those assembled to appear onstage within moments. The sudden eruption of a mob yelling and shouting as they raced onstage was always wonderfully stirring. "For us," George continued, "it will mean removing the stage boxes so that the empty spaces that will be left can be turned into assemblies. This will give us entrances, downstage of the proscenium arch on both sides, opening onto the apron stage. I am hoping that when you raise the floor of the boxes to the level of the cover of the orchestra pit, you will find there is enough headroom inside for the actors to be able to stand upright while waiting to enter.

"On the level directly above these assemblies are, of course, the circle boxes, but I am sorry to say we cannot allow them to be used as such since we will need as much lighting from the front-of-house as Mr. Esdaile, whom you will remember owns the theatre, will allow. As with many theatre owners, he doesn't want the circle front to be hidden behind a row of lamps. The circle boxes will be excellent places for reinforcing the light we get from the front-of-house and the perches, so please prepare them with the necessary supports for lanterns to be hung there.

"Then I want you to take down the house border and, yes, I know, all the lamps used over and around the stage will be visible to the public. But audiences know that the light on stage has to come from somewhere, so they are going to see where that somewhere is for once.

"Finally, the only permanent staff we have here are Mr. Esdaile's, and we are contracted to employ them, so get to know them and make them realise the sort of theatre this will become. They may find their quiet life will be badly disrupted since the building will be alive and busy all day and every day — including many Sundays — so there may be some opposition. Off you go now, but let me know how you are getting on, and of course come and see me if there are any problems you would like to discuss."

What he forgot to add at that time, although he sprang it on me a few moments before the public dress rehearsal of *The Mulberry Bush,* was a request for me to go onto the apron stage to remind the audience that they would be watching a dress rehearsal. I was to emphasise that if the director felt the need to make an alteration during the evening, then he would be stopping the rehearsal. I would have liked a few moments to consider what I had to say, but there was no time. Even though I had been working on and around the stage all day, I was respectably dressed in a suit, and my shoes only needed a quick buff up and I was ready to appear before our first audience looking reasonably presentable. Even if those sitting out front didn't mind how I looked, I minded.

## Scene 6 ℘ Completing the backstage team

It was very clear that one stage management team could not possibly cope with what George's plan for a repertoire of plays would entail, so I went to his little front-of-house office and told him that we would need two sets of stage management and I showed him a work pattern I had developed for them. At once he said that of course we must employ that number.

But there was another request I had to put to him, and I chose this moment. "I hate to mention this, Mr. Devine," I said, "but I have a feeling that the two teams of stage management are going to find it very difficult to deal with what will be extremely busy days. I feel that they will not be able to give of their best unless they are all fully committed to stage management and are not actors filling in time until they can get an acting job. Will it be possible for them not to be used as extras or small part players?" Then, chancing my arm, "And also could they please be free from understudying?" George only thought for a moment, and then said. "Yes, you're right. Let's do that." This was success indeed, so I pressed on, "Since I also seem to have become the production manager, as well as the stage director in charge of the two stage management teams, and since there is no backstage staff during the day, with four productions to be staged within six weeks, it is going to be tricky for me unless I have the help of a full-time stage carpenter. Do you think the budget would stretch to such a person?" "Have you anyone in mind?" asked George. "Yes," I said. "When we were at the Palace Theatre with *King Lear* in the summer, I got to know the staff very well and amongst them was a young chap from Australia. He knew about the English Stage Company and begged me to remember him if the project actually took off and we were looking for staff. Well, it has taken off, so I would very much like you to meet him for I think he is exactly the sort of person we want here. His name is Kevin Maybury, and he can come along to the Court at any time you say."

I made the necessary arrangement for the meeting that, unusually for George, took place at the back of the circle. I left them together and went to my office, apprehensive but knowing that Kevin would acquit himself well. The conversation between them lasted a long time, but finally Kevin appeared saying he was not sure what the outcome would be. I said that I would let him know just as soon as I had any news, but Kevin said he would go and have a coffee and then come back to my office. I went straight up to George's office. He looked up without any expression on his face, so I was forced to say, after a moment's hesitation while I waited for him to speak, "Do you think Kevin would be an asset to the company?" As often happened, George surprised me. He took the pipe out of his mouth and said, "I think he will do admirably. Get him to start as soon as he can." He smiled, down went the head and back went the pipe.

With dear Miss Pickford ("Picky" to everyone, of course) as wardrobe mistress, John Recknell as chief electrician (both of whom had been working at the theatre for Mr. Esdaile), Peter Theobald as the lighting board operator and a truly remarkable group of four part-time stage hands (Bob and Ted Bolton, Percy Tweedale, and A. W. Davies) who, for some years, had worked at the Court whenever they were required and daytime jobs permitted, the backstage team was complete.

It was going to be hard work and long hours, but we all felt that we were for the first time not working for a firm but for one man whom we respected and trusted and that was a wonderful feeling. For myself, however paternalistic, supportive and caring those at the top at the Shakespeare Memorial Theatre had been during the past six months tour with *King Lear*, the atmosphere at the Royal Court was subtly different. Everything we did was for Mr. Devine (as all of us working backstage called him) and his theatre. We had to make the theatre successful, not because we would be out of work if it weren't, but because we would have somehow let him down.

## Scene 7 ✑ The English Stage Company takes over the Royal Court Theatre, March 1956

March 1956 was certainly an all-systems-go month. Two productions were in rehearsal in rooms close to Sloane Square; in fact one, a Parish Hall in Pavilion Road, was the other side of the Square to the theatre so, although it had a depressing atmosphere, its nearness almost made up for its downside. The second rehearsal room was in Bourne Street, a narrow road, fully stocked with cottages, that ran parallel to the back of the theatre. This room was light and airy, but the acoustics were not good. I never enjoyed having to go there for I was so conscious of this defect. Much later, I started using a good-sized room in a building at World's End that faced the first of the two sharp bends in the King's Road. The fact that it was a bus journey away from the theatre had made it unacceptable in those early days. However by the time I needed to use that particular room, our workshop in Park Walk was also in operation, and they were only a few minutes apart. Both the workshop with its romantic weather-board construction and the building on the bend in the road are now long gone. Sad about the workshop (Tony Richardson used it for a scene in his film *Saturday Night and Sunday Morning*), but anyone was welcome to the other.

Back in the theatre, the stage floor had been given a face-lift, and its wonderful boards revealed a beauty that had not been displayed for a very long time. The firm that fitted the three large panels, which now covered the orchestra pit, did a good job doing that and the filling in of the footlights trough.

At the same time, the assemblies were constructed, and this "little" job proved more tricky than I had thought. Certainly there was just about the right amount of headroom once one was on the raised flooring of what had been the boxes, but the difficulty was the getting there. The height of the door that led into the original box from the front stalls was fine for that purpose but very low when it became the start of a short flight of steps up to the raised floor. Stepping up to the assembly was not as potentially lethal to an actor's head as leaving. Ducking while moving downwards is not an easy manoeuvre: You either duck too late so that you crack your head when it meets the top of the door-frame, or you don't duck far enough with a similar painful consequence.

The two stage management teams were hard at work, and I used to visit them in their rehearsal rooms as often as possible. In the main, I stayed around in the ever-busy theatre. My base was mercifully on ground level. It was very conveniently placed just round the corner from the stage door (the one with the Laurier Lister mat) and just off the landing where the stairs went up to the four dressing rooms and down to the stage. At the top of the stairs lay the wardrobe and the accounts office. It would have been great if I could have been the sole occupant of the little office, but it also had to house stage management. Very quickly we realised the room had another drawback that we all had to accept: It was on the only direct route from backstage to front-of-house without going outside or through the auditorium.

There was no window to the room — big snag — but there was, curiously, a third door that opened onto a short, narrow empty space at the end of which was a suitably small window. It looked as if there had been a washbasin or a lavatory there. Once when George was passing through, I stopped him and asked if he thought I could get Mr. Esdaile to agree that the wall should be taken down. I didn't feel I needed to point out that our overcrowded little room could be given three feet more depth, as well as making it possible for us to get some air. He looked at this odd space and then said no. I realised at once that any little extra that would mean spending money was not the sort of subject to be brought up at this time. I must wait for better days. It was a long wait but eventually I got permission. It made an enormous difference to the room, but by then the desperately busy early days, when we had so badly needed the space and especially fresh air, were long behind us.

## Scene 8 ◎ The initial production team for the English Stage Company

While the preparations were galloping apace at the Royal Court from the beginning of 1956, there was other activity, intimately connected with the new company, taking place elsewhere. George Devine's wife, Sophie, was one-third of the brilliant theatre design team called "Motley," her partners being her sister Margaret ("Percy") Harris and Elizabeth Montgomery. Elizabeth was in America, so, since George had arranged for Motley to design the sets and costumes for the first production and the costumes for the second, this work was carried out by Sophie and Percy.

At the start, the idea was that the setting for every production would be as simple as possible. It was also planned that every actor would be fitted with a basic costume for use in period productions, to which could be added the extras necessary for any of the characters he or she had to play. Arrangements were made for a workroom in George and Sophie's riverside home in Lower Mall, Hammersmith. Stephen Doncaster, in charge of wardrobe, and Wendy Turner, his more-than-able assistant, set up their department there. Stephen was also to design the sets for our second production, Arthur Miller's *The Crucible*. These turned out to be brilliant and economical, while this play would be the first time Sophie's basic costume design would come into use.

Jocelyn Herbert and Clare Jeffery were also part of the production unit, with Jocelyn designated scene painter and Clare, properties. Their workroom was under the stage at the Court, so down I went to see that they were all right. Their first tasks were to make a leafless mulberry tree (rather than the bush of the title) and a garden statue for Angus Wilson's *The Mulberry Bush,* and a large log for *The Crucible.*

I told Jocelyn and Clare to put in their expenses, plus all receipts, each week when they would be reimbursed. If they had to pay out a lot before the week was up, then they must not wait for the end of that week but submit them at once, and I would arrange immediate reimbursement. They must not make themselves short of cash through paying for items for the theatre.

At the end of the first week, I had to go down to see them, taking the pieces of scrap paper, littered with odd sums and a few receipts, that they had kindly put on my desk. I said I would sort this lot out but in future the figures must be presented in a way that first myself and then Frank Evans in accounts could understand and justify.

I then demonstrated how they should claim. I explained they must use a petty cash slip, starting with the date, followed by the name of the supplier, the type of goods bought, and the cost. To make it clear, I then started to write out an imaginary claim on one of the slips I had brought with me, and said, "Now suppose you had bought some material from . . ." I paused as I thought of a name for a fictitious shop. With Peter Jones, the big store across the Square from the theatre, in mind, I said, "Let's call it Petra Janes. Now, you write this name at the top of the page," and so I pressed on with the lesson. Yes, they both understood perfectly, and I would be amazed at how neat and well organised their expenses would be next week.

They certainly showed terrific improvement, but Clare had let the name of my invented shop go to her head. Every item she had bought from a variety of shops in the locality were all entered on the petty cash slip as having been purchased at that well-known Chelsea store, Petra Janes. Never mind, it was soon put right, and by the following week, their expense accounts were models of perfection.

## Scene 9 ◈ Greville Poke

Very soon after moving into my office, Greville Poke, whom I hadn't seen since our dressing-room meeting in Manchester, began writing me letters. They came in small manila envelopes, and they were typed on a small piece of headed paper. They all contained a question such as, "Have you thought about first-aid boxes?" Thus they were all eminently sensible and often they touched on a subject such as the first-aid boxes that had simply not entered my mind, but I found them, all of them, extremely irritating. They arrived with infuriating regularity and nearly always when pressure had reached one of its many peaks, so that there was no time to concentrate on anything other than the current production. But perhaps what irritated me the most, apart from knowing that he was absolutely correct, was that they were never signed by Greville himself. The signature of a secretary, presumably, looked like "G. Pavitt," and I loathed G. Pavitt with a deep, totally unjustified loathing. I am sorry to say that really the culprit was Greville for wording his little letters in such an abrupt and rude manner and not even bothering to sign them — that was the last straw.

## Scene 10 ◈ Working in and around Chelsea

When I knew that I was to work for the English Stage Company in Chelsea, I was delighted. Living in Barnes, a leafy suburb in southwest London and only about four miles from Sloane Square, getting to and from the Royal Court Theatre posed no problem. The theatre that might have housed the new company, the Kingsway, certainly would have done — even if it were only a matter of fares and length of travel time. But coming to the Royal Court in December 1955 to have a first look around the theatre with George, Percy, and Jocelyn, Chelsea looked a very depressing place. I certainly had often passed through this part of London on the top of a bus but never to stop, since it offered nothing that couldn't be found in more congenial surroundings elsewhere. The grandest shop was certainly Peter Jones, which, in those days, had a curious wing at the end of the store furthest from Sloane Square that stuck out into the King's Road. This part of the main building forced traffic into one lane each way — not that there was all that amount of traffic. The shops otherwise were very old-fashioned and of little appeal.

There was one coffee shop called *Guys and Dolls*. Forty years later, it still has G & D over the door, but this was opposite the Duke of York's Barracks, too far down the King's Road to be of any use. However, in Holbein Place, not more than two minutes walk from the theatre, was a tiny sandwich bar, a real hole-in-the-wall, that dispensed tea, coffee, sandwiches, and that delicious mixture of dough and dried fruit called Chelsea buns. Appropriately, this endearing little place was called The Chelsea Bun. It was run by the owner, a lady we all called Mrs. Bun, even though, for some reason, she didn't like this name. This became our green room, our second office, the place to sort out problems and the place where we could be away from the theatre for a few moments. A real metropolitan oasis.

When I went searching for furniture for a production, I had to get it transported to the theatre by the shop's own transport, or I would have to engage a van or taxi. But one morning, very early in our days at the Court, I was fortunate to have bought a considerable amount of furniture from a small shop in the far reaches of the King's Road. This shop was one of several in that part of the road where prices were dramatically lower than in similar shops nearer to Sloane Square. When I mentioned my problem of getting what I had bought to the theatre, the owner said he would bring it all along later that day.

During the afternoon, he arrived in a taxi but not a hired one for, to my surprise, he told me he owned it. When we had unloaded, he said, "You need transport of your own, son." Then, with a gesture towards the taxi, he went on, "Would you like to buy this?" At home in Barnes that evening, Elizabeth agreed that I should accept the offer, so for £25 we became the owners of a 1936 dark blue Beardmore London taxicab. Of course, it had no meter, but it did have a very spacious rear passenger compartment that would indeed be very useful. Then I found it had an added advantage. Half the roof over this area folded back, which meant that I could load long items, such as the bed for *Look Back in Anger.* After folding the roof, I stood at the back of the taxi, lifted the piece over the folded roof, and slid it forward until its front end met the partition that divided the passengers from the driver.

Apart from the windscreen, a fixed roof over my head, and the glass partition behind me, as the driver of this taxi I had no shelter from the elements. Rain, sleet and snow could happily attack me from either side. On my left, the space was completely open for, in its real taxi days, this was the compartment for luggage. I used this space for a multitude of props and furniture, and again for *Look Back,* I was easily able to transport a gas cooker by placing it beside me and strapping it in securely. On my right, there was a half-door, but between the top of this door and the roof, there was nothing. Excellent though for making vital hand signals, and hand signals it had to be, for there was no other way of indicating my intentions.

It wasn't too easy driving the cab when it was raining or snowing for the tiny windscreen wiper was operated manually by the driver. With one hand busy with the gear lever and the other on the steering wheel, the wiper had to be given a quick flick whenever I judged it would be reasonably safe to take a hand off the wheel.

Our taxi was often hailed, once by a bowler-hatted young man who, in spite of heavy rain, waved a furled umbrella at me. "Taxi!" he yelled. "Sorry, I'm not a taxi," I called back. "Well, you ought to be," he shouted after me. Another time, Elizabeth was sitting on the tip-up seat directly behind me so that we could chat through the very small gap the sliding glass panel, between driver and passenger, allowed, when a man called out, "Engaged?" I glanced back briefly at Elizabeth and then turned to the man and answered, "No, married."

When Joan Greenwood joined us for an all too brief initial stay, she happened to be leaving the theatre after an evening performance at the time I was driving out of the theatre's yard. I pulled up and offered her a lift. She accepted at once. I was about to open my little door to see her safely into the cavernous passenger compartment when she rushed round the back of the taxi and leapt up into the luggage space in the front. "I don't think you will be safe there," I said as she crouched down beside me. "Oh, don't let's bother about safety," she said in her deep, croaky voice. "This is far too exciting." Off we went down the King's Road with this tiny person giving whoops of joy every time we swept round a corner or swerved to avoid a jaywalker. No one else ever graced the luggage space again.

## Scene 11 ⚭ The English Stage Company and its first audiences, 1956

I wish I could report that from the start the English Stage Company was an enormous success, but to say that would be far from the truth. On Tuesday, April 2, 1956, *The Mulberry Bush* opened the season and certainly the play chosen showed clearly what George had meant when he spoke of his theatre being a Writers' Theatre. But the notices in the press only indicated that here was a play of the type often seen in the West End — a drawing-room drama — but it did not compare well with those already playing in the many theatres along Shaftesbury Avenue nor did it have the added advantage of well-known star actors. Certainly at the Royal Court, the names of Gwen Frangcon-Davies, Rachel Kempson, and perhaps Agnes Lauchlan could catch the eye, but it would be very doubtful if the remainder of the young cast would be known at that time. A month later, when John Osborne's *Look Back in Anger* joined the repertoire, four of the cast of *The Mulberry Bush* would be seen again — Alan Bates, Kenneth Haigh, Helena Hughes, and John Welsh.

Although Arthur Miller's *The Crucible*, opening a week after *The Mulberry Bush*, fared better at the box office, the notices weren't such as to make the public wonder where on earth this Royal Court Theatre could be found before they rushed to book tickets. Tony Richardson's first production for the company, *Look Back in Anger*, got mixed reviews, most of which were against the play and the unlikeable main character, Jimmy Porter, very well played by Kenneth Haigh. However, Kenneth Tynan, the widely read and brilliant drama critic of the *Observer*, one of the Sunday broadsheet newspapers, was stoutly for the play and gave it an excellent review that was later quoted in the theatre's programme for our fifth production, Nigel Dennis's *Cards of Identity* (the Dennis). The introduction to the quotes was curiously worded. It was headed "*Look Back in Anger* by John Osborne," followed by, "What the Press says." Those words certainly prepared one for a series of quotes from various newspapers and other publications, as was the normal practice. But not at the Court. Our press representative, for there was no press office, then set out six quotes, with the number of lines per quote ranging from one to three. Very good they were too. But they were all taken from the Tynan piece in the *Observer*.

Whatever the notices, the real problem lay with the number of productions that George was determined should come tumbling in as close together as possible so that he might build a strong repertoire. The system he wanted was akin to an archer having as many arrows as possible in his quiver. George's quiver was his repertoire, and the arrows were the productions that were available to him at any one time. By the end of June, he had hoped to have five arrows in his quiver so that he could offer his public that number of productions every week, and on different days from one week to the next. Sadly, because of the lack of plays that attracted the public, George's initial repertoire was never able to provide him with more than two plays, so he used those in the most interesting way he could by making the changeover midweek. This meant that, for example, week one would play *Look Back in Anger* on Monday, Tuesday, and Wednesday and then change to *The Crucible* for Thursday, Friday, and Saturday. Week two would retain *The Crucible* for Monday, Tuesday and Wednesday, then *Look Back in Anger* would complete the week, and so on.

Londoners were not used to such a style of presentation unless the theatres using this system had a known speciality, such as Shakespeare at the Old Vic or opera and ballet at the Royal Opera House. In the West End, a play stayed in one theatre, playing eight performances a week, for as long as it drew the public. When it was no longer advertised, the public knew that it had finished its London run and was probably carrying out a post-London tour. That made sense, whereas the Royal Court's mad arrangement, as the public saw it, where one never knew what play was on from one day to the next, was beyond understanding.

One of our neighbours in Barnes was the actor/playwright John Whiting who said he was forced to telephone me for help in getting tickets since he wanted to see *Look Back in Anger*, but whenever he had a free evening, the play was never on. "Is it a ghost play?" he asked. And well he might. After *Look Back* opened on Tuesday, May 8, 1956, it gave three more performances (two on the Wednesday and one on the Thursday), and then, because of the opening of *Don Juan* and *The Death of Satan*, and because *The Mulberry Bush* and *The Crucible* were still in the rep and needing performances, *Look Back* didn't return to the stage until Thursday, May 24. A two-week gap is no way to settle a play into a repertoire, however understandable the reason.

I can only presume that George and Tony decided that *The Mulberry Bush* would not be strong enough to withstand the gaps between the few short blocks of performances it was allocated immediately following its opening, for it was withdrawn on Saturday, May 19. It had given a creditable thirty performances, but even so, the feeling was that more had been expected of it. Although no one in the company seemed to think that *Don Juan* and *The Death of Satan* would draw the crowds, I cannot imagine that anyone foresaw their dramatically early demise, for they were taken off on Saturday, May 30, after only eight performances. This left their further eight performances, scheduled for June, to be shared between *The Crucible* and *Look Back in Anger*, which added to the performances already announced for those two productions. I don't think John Whiting would have had any difficulty in catching *Look Back in Anger* during that month.

## Scene 12 ❧ Giles Corey, lost and found

Soon after *The Crucible* opened at the Court on April 9, 1956, George Devine received a cable from Arthur Miller's agent in America who said that he understood that George had cut the character of Giles Corey from the play without the author's permission. The cable continued by saying that Mr. Miller had given instructions to his agent that this character was to be reinstated immediately otherwise the licence for the presentation of the play would be withdrawn. George sent for Peter Duguid, an actor whose work he knew well, who came from Scotland at once and with a short rehearsal, which was all that was necessary for the small role, he was put into the play and nothing more was heard from Mr. Miller. On the day of the rehearsal for Peter, John Welsh, who was cast in all seven initial English Stage Company plays, had to attend rehearsals of three productions plus the one for *The Crucible*. Getting him to two rehearsal rooms (the two Duncan plays were not rehearsed in the same place), then to the rehearsal of *Look Back in Anger*, before returning to the Court for *The Crucible* required almost split-second timing. George and Tony had to work out their rehearsal schedules carefully and then, not so easy, stick to them. This type of exercise suited the ex–stage manager, George, more than the maverick, Tony.

## Scene 13 ❧ *Look Back in Anger:* *Picture Post* **and the BBC**

In June 1956, with two plays (*The Crucible* and *Look Back in Anger*) left in the repertoire and struggling to survive, *Picture Post* sent a reporter, Robert Muller, with a photographer, to interview the *Look Back in Anger* company. There was the promise of a spread in this extremely popular weekly magazine. Robert wrote a sympathetic, supportive, and upbeat article, accompanied by several photographs. This was a miracle and one that the cast was lucky to be given, for on the day of the *Picture Post* visit, I spent some time trying to stop Kenneth Haigh, who played Jimmy Porter, retiring to his dressing room, while at the same time not letting Robert leave, which he had every reason to do. I have no idea what caused such behaviour or why Kenneth's attitude was surly, unresponsive, and uncooperative when the interviewer was asking reasonable questions and giving all signs of wanting to help the play and the English Stage Company as much as he could.

The arrival of the edition that carried the interview certainly helped morale throughout the theatre to say nothing of increasing the box office figures for *Look Back*. Its first surge was not all that tremendous, but a surge nevertheless. In his article, Robert Muller referred to the company as "The Good Companions," which is the title of a 1930s play by J. B. Priestley, which concerns a struggling theatrical company that calls itself The Good Companions. This play experienced more success later when it was made into a film starring the immensely popular Jessie Matthews and John Gielgud.

The use of "The Good Companions" as the title for the *Picture Post* article was a case of déjà vu for me. In 1939, I was an assistant stage manager with a repertory company at the handsome King's

Theatre in Hammersmith. We too had a visit from a reporter accompanied by a photographer resulting in a full-page, illustrated article in the *Daily Mail* under the heading "The Good Companions." For myself, the article was a page of embarrassment for the bulk of the long article was divided between an interview with Arthur Camp, the chief electrician, and an interview with leading actor Esmond (Teddy) Knight, in which he mainly spoke about me. He finished by saying that he knew I would be a big noise in the theatre one day. The actors were very upset at the lack of interest in them for they were dismissed early in the piece, although there were two or three photographs of some. It was my bad to luck to return from a prop-buying jaunt that morning to find the whole company assembled on the stage apparently all reading newspapers. Enid Sass, one of the leading actresses, put down her paper, stared across the stage at me, and then asked with utmost sarcasm, "A big noise? Are you going to be a call boy all your life, dear?" It was a little while before I saw the article and associated Enid's snide remark, with regard to part of my current job, with Teddy's forecast of my future.

Looking back, I don't think I would have liked to have been a call boy all my life, although many men became call boys and stayed in this important position for very many years. Call boys were the most wonderful breed of theatre employees. They were very often ex-dancers who just loved the theatre, its atmosphere, its people, and, in winter, its warmth. At the start of a week on tour, the stage manager gave the call boy a book that showed the calls for the cast. Each page of the call book had a separate call, such as:

Call No. 7
"I really think it is time we went indoors now."
Miss Nellie Bowman
Dressing room no. 2

The (invented) line cue given above would have been chosen by the stage manager. He had to reckon firstly, how long it would take the call boy to reach the appropriate dressing room once the actor on stage had reached these words; secondly, how long the artist would take to make his or her way to the stage; and thirdly, how long the artist would take to be in the wings ready to make his or her entrance.

When one was on a tour that only stayed in each town for a week, the call book had to be redone at each place, for, of course, the dressing rooms — let alone their occupants — would be different at each theatre.

The cue would be marked in the prompt script, and when it was reached, the stage manager would nod at the call boy and off he would go, at speed but silently. He would arrive at dressing room number 2. Knock knock. "Your call, please Miss Bowman." From within, "Thank you, Jim." At ninety miles an hour, Jim speeds back to his seat beside the stage manager in readiness for call number 8. At the next performance on the following evening, a good call boy would stand up just before the cue came. This was to show how closely he had listened and how well he had got to know the play at his first hearing. They were amazing, those likeable people, and it was sad that, unwittingly, Tannoy, or other types of sound systems, took away their jobs. (The name Tannoy is a hangover from the Second World War when most airfield huts, beside which the fighter pilots' craft were parked, had a loudspeaker with its commercial name, Tannoy, fret-sawed in a curve across its face.)

Returning to *Picture Post* and the seemingly imperturbable Robert Muller, his excellent article arrived on the newsstands at exactly the right time for the English Stage Company. During June, George had gravely told me that it looked as if the company would not last beyond July, but he made this prediction just before the public read the article in *Picture Post*. Whatever dire thoughts George may have had, we went ahead with the next production, Nigel Dennis's *Cards of Identity*.

But in spite of its leading player being the very popular Joan Greenwood, and in spite of a wonderfully funny and fascinating Act I that made one look forward to the other two acts, the momentum was not maintained, and the play ran out of steam long before the final curtain.

In addition to Joan Greenwood, the play gave the first chance for the public to see Joan Plowright in a comedy role. She joined the company to play Mary Warren in *The Crucible*, followed by small roles in both *Don Juan* and *The Death of Satan*, so the part of Miss Tray in *Cards of Identity* was a revelation. Her first entrance was unforgettable. She was ushered onto the stage but was then left alone since the doctor, with whom she had an appointment, had to be told of her arrival. She gave surreptitious glances around the room and was obviously very ill at ease and not sure what was expected of her. Yet even just standing still in the middle of Alan Tagg's excellent set caused the audience to start laughing, and when she suddenly began to sing a few lines of "Love and Marriage," the audience exploded.

At this time, the BBC was transmitting on television a weekly programme of a twenty-minute live extract from a West End show, and one of these programmes was allotted to *Cards of Identity*. I could only think how lucky it was that the Royal Court was considered West End. The fixed positions for the cameras and the additional lighting had been worked out several days in advance, but even so it took most of the actual day to connect all the pieces of equipment. The actors were asked to try to forget that there were cameras in the auditorium and certainly the performances came across as they had done on previous evenings. The BBC allowed the company to choose which part of the play should be televised, so George and Tony Richardson, its director, chose the excerpt. Maybe their choice was not the best for television, or maybe the extra lighting, so brilliantly white it made the auditorium as bright as the stage, did not help either the actors or the audience. Sad to say the scene failed to come over well and on August 22, *Cards of Identity* gave its fortieth and final performance. Still, with a box office of nearly 50 percent, it was by no means a failure. It was just not the roaring success the company needed.

So ended, until May 14, 1957, the repertory system at the Royal Court. Now it was left to *Look Back in Anger* on its own to keep the theatre open until Saturday, October 27. This run of nine and a half weeks, which meant seventy-six performances, shows the strength of its appeal, boosted by the *Picture Post*, to the public. This appeal was given a further tremendous boost early in the penultimate week of its solo run. The BBC had come on the scene again with its second offer of a twenty-minute extract to be televised live from the theatre. The play that had been chosen was *Look Back*, and the date would be Tuesday, October 16. Once more the choice of which scene should be televised was handed over to the company, and once more, as with the *Cards of Identity* extract, it was Tony, again the director of the chosen play, and George, this time assisted by myself, who discussed which section of the play should be chosen. Tony was determined it should be the opening of Act II, Scene 2, when we meet John Welsh as Colonel Redfern for the first time. The Colonel is the father of Jimmy Porter's wife, Alison, played by Mary Ure. George and I both agreed that Jimmy Porter must appear in the extract, and we were concerned that there was no sign of him in the scene Tony had chosen. In the end, Tony's choice prevailed, mainly because I think he would have vetoed the project if he didn't get his way.

The scene he chose proved to be the turning point for the English Stage Company in 1956. The effect on the box office was magical. At once, the phones started ringing and queues formed at the theatre. I was astounded at how many people had seen the telecast and what a wide spectrum of the public came to see the play. At last, young people were attracted, and it was exciting to find them in the bars and corridors and to guess from their slightly bewildered behaviour that they were in a theatre, as opposed to the other extremely popular form of entertainment, the cinema, for the first time.

But if this new young public, as well as seasoned theatregoers, wished to see *Look Back* and couldn't get in to the Royal Court, they had a chance at the Lyric Theatre, Hammersmith, for the production moved there, opening on Monday, November 5, for a three-week season that ended on Saturday, November 26. Two days later, in a set specially designed for television, a ninety-minute version of the play was put out live over the commercial TV channel by Granada, a company based in Manchester.

Ever since we had opened, the evening performances, except for Saturdays, started at 7:30 PM, but at the beginning of September until *Look Back* finished its run at the end of October, curtain up was at 8:00 PM. Backstage, we could just take the 8:15 PM start for a Saturday evening second house, for it followed on comfortably close to curtain down on the 5:00 PM first house, but that extra half-hour for the five nights leading to the Saturday 8:15 PM curtain up was not welcomed. We were all greatly relieved when the next production saw the return to 7:30 PM.

Not only was *Look Back* the pioneer of a new curtain up time, but it was also during its run that the theatre's auditorium became a no smoking zone. Nothing in the programme for its predecessor, *Cards of Identity*, about no smoking but from August 29, the *Look Back* programme sneakily slipped in a charming paragraph that neatly made it appear that its new order had always been the norm at the Royal Court. The sentence read: "Patrons are reminded that Smoking is not permitted in the auditorium." The cheek of the notice, with its smug verb *reminded*, is compounded by the vital word *smoking* being given a capital *S*.

## Scene 14 ❧ Percy Harris's permanent surround for the Royal Court Theatre

Once *Look Back in Anger* had gone down the road to Hammersmith, its place at the Court was taken by Bertolt Brecht's *The Good Woman of Setzuan*. In autumn 1956, his company, the Berliner Ensemble, played a season at the Palace Theatre in London. The reports that reached us at the Court indicated that audience reaction was the same as mine when George had organised a visit to Brecht's theatre in East Berlin. We were in that shattered city as part of the Shakespeare Memorial Theatre's 1955 European Tour and on a free evening, George invited me to join a party to go into the eastern sector, not only to see a company about which we had heard so much, but actually to see them playing in their own famous theatre.

There was no Berlin Wall, so it was only a case of a taxi ride, passing through a militarily manned checkpoint, and then our party, which included Percy Harris, was making its way through the crowded foyer, handing our coats to a willing staff manning a cloakroom of such a size as I had never seen before in any theatre, and so into the auditorium. The understandably shabby theatre was packed, but somehow we had been found excellent seats in the third row centre of the stalls. I had a not very original feeling that the true occupants had been displaced to make way for our party.

Not understanding a word of *Mutter Courage und Ihre Kinder* didn't stop me having a wonderful evening. It was the staging that astounded me: it was so inventive and yet so simple. There was no rake on the stage that housed a huge revolve, which turned absolutely silently and which was enclosed by a vast cyclorama. I say that it was enclosed, but there must have been a reasonably large opening upstage centre, masked from the front by a canvas panel several feet downstage of the opening. At the end of a scene, the revolve, if not already in use, would turn, and actors, props, and any piece of scenery not wanted for the next scene would disappear behind the cloth but would not reappear on the other side. However, from that other side would come actors, a gate or a fence, and so on ready for the next scene. They were not on the revolve in any haphazard way, but every person and every piece was placed so that when the revolve stopped, they were in the correct positions for the start of their scene.

In this production, the revolve could be used to stunning effect, especially when Helene Weigel, as Mother Courage, was stoically pulling her cart. Once she and cart reached downstage centre, the revolve started turning, but because she was walking against it, she remained downstage centre, while small pieces of props and scenery, having been placed on the revolve when screened by the panel, passed her, all adding to the effect of her travelling. I mention all this because in Stratford-upon-Avon, where the 1955 *King Lear* tour finished with a three-week season at the Shakespeare Memorial Theatre, Percy Harris came down from London to the small hotel where George was staying and set up the model of the Royal Court Theatre so that we might see her design for a permanent surround for its small stage.

At once I noticed that she had sensibly adapted all that we had seen on and around Brecht's stage, for there was the cyclorama with its break upstage centre, downstage of which was the masking panel. Here could have been the first difference from the scenic design for the Theater am Schiffbauerdamm, for Percy's panel could be flown, thus allowing an audience a view through to the back wall, if the designer wished this. Then we saw there was another difference in the cyclorama, for Percy had made a break halfway down each side to allow for entrances there. These were in addition to further entrances from the prompt and opposite-to-prompt corners. Thus the tally of entrances available on each side at the Court — including the assemblies — was a very useful four.

When the canvas for the panels arrived, Kevin and I quickly (but painfully, since one could not stand upright in the grid, and therefore all spot-lining and other work had to be carried out whilst kneeling uncomfortably on a joist) hung the flying cloth and the four panels. The latter fitted well, with curved iron tubing top and bottom. The amount of space at each entrance was good, but Percy was not happy with the texture and decided that the material should be softened in appearance.

Next day, she gave me the name of a firm based in Northeast England where they made, if that's the correct verb, nets for fishing boats. I phoned them at once and was able to order netting with the small mesh that Percy decided was necessary to lessen the glare of the cloths. Sure enough, the effect with the netting was exactly right but not without a cost: The netting would not lie close to the canvas, and although this didn't detract from the effect Percy wanted, it did make the setting and striking of rough-textured pieces very difficult and time wasting. If *The Mulberry Bush* in our first production had indeed been a bush, it would have helped us, but it was a large leafless tree that managed, as with many inanimate objects, to have a life of its own. If there were a chance for its spiky twigs and branches to get caught up in the netting, it took it. This hazard applied also to members of the cast. It was all too easy for an unwary actor to leave the safety of the wings little knowing that the netting was in wait to catch, for example, a button or a buckle. The ensnaring only took a second, but trying to disengage took the poor actor an agonising number of seconds.

## Scene 15 ⊕ Initial designs at the Royal Court Theatre

*The Mulberry Bush* setting by Motley consisted of a manageable piece of scenery depicting part of the drawing room of a country house, which contained a French window through which one could see the mulberry tree. For Act II, this piece of scenery was reversed, so that the action of the play could move into the garden, with the exterior of the French window flanked by short pieces of wall in the background, while the tree and the splendid statue (Jocelyn and Clare's work at last brought up from under the stage) came into their own. For Act III, it was back to the interior, so for the second time in the course of a performance, the tree had to be moved from one side of the upstage area to the other, and it was these moves that started us cursing the netting for its ability to cling to passing objects yet its inability to cling to the canvas panels.

*The Crucible's* setting by Stephen Doncaster consisted of a large wooden frame containing ceiling beams. Once hanging above the acting area, this frame could be angled to denote a change of location, so it was not until *Look Back in Anger* that anything resembling an actual set appeared. Alan Tagg produced his model of a room, which almost filled the whole stage to which my immediate reaction was, "But scenery is not allowed." There was a pause before Alan in his quiet voice replied, "The walls of the room are not high, but they are high enough to allow a window, which must be practical. Jimmy Porter has to shout at the church bells out of that window, which he then shuts, resulting in the volume of the bells being legitimately reduced. Any other way would be implausible."

Thus scenery crept onto the Court stage. It certainly didn't creep into the scene dock whose size was in proportion to the remainder of the backstage area — desperately small. This meant that, as the number of sets increased, so the scene dock had to be very carefully stacked, but in spite of that care and planning, during a changeover it often entailed spending time we could not spare taking out one or two sets in order to reach the one that perforce was at the back of another pack.

## Scene 16 ❧ The Berliner Ensemble visit the English Stage Company

Who can forget the extraordinary sight of the system used to get a hot meal to the members of the Berliner Ensemble, at that time playing in the West End? The company had been invited by George to come to the Court on a Sunday evening in November 1956 for an entertainment and then a meal. The food was cooked in the kitchen of Clement Freud's club at the top of the building and put onto plates. These then were sent via a human chain down a flight of stairs, along a corridor, through the bar at the side of the building into the dressing-room area, and down the stairs to the stage. It worked brilliantly: The food was very good and remarkably hot, and the German company, sitting in the stalls, was very impressed and well fed.

In spite of the fact that we were all very aware that Bertolt Brecht, the founder of their company, had died only a few months previously, it was a good evening. As ever with foreign visitors, it was a pity we couldn't chat with every member because of our inability to speak German, but we knew that they appreciated all that George had arranged on their behalf, and we were sure also that they felt the warmth of our welcome.

## Scene 17 ⌖ Activity in the theatre, autumn 1956

With the seventieth anniversary of the opening of the Royal Court Theatre only two years away, it was not unnatural to find weaknesses in
the building. The area needing the most urgent attention was the auditorium ceiling, including the dome, and work was started on this during autumn 1956. To carry out the work, the upper circle had to be
closed from mid-October to mid-December. While we were preparing
for this work, George announced that it would be possible to pay for
a designer to put forward ideas for a new colour scheme in the auditorium. He had two or three designers in mind who might like the challenge and enjoy the work, so would I please contact them and take them
around — separately, of course.

The colour scheme suggested by Terence Conran I liked very much,
and I also liked his idea of having a huge photographic blowup of a
Chelsea scene that would be hung on the curved back wall of the foyer.
But I also liked what Alan Tagg put forward, and it was his scheme
that finally was chosen. This work, which entailed painting the auditorium walls a dark grey and the velvet on the circle fronts changing
to coral, was carried out simultaneously with the work on the ceiling.
By the time *The Country Wife* opened in December, the ceiling was
completed, the upper circle was reopened, and the auditorium looked
smart and clean. Same old seats.

George was not satisfied that the theatre was being used to the full,
so he made an arrangement with the English Opera Group that they
would present weekly concerts at lunchtime on Thursdays and monthly
concerts on Sunday evenings. This meant that stage management members who, at the end of October had put the setting for *The Good
Woman* on the stage, thinking it would stay there for its run, found
themselves having to clear the stage for the concerts. The Thursday concert on December 13 (Barry Tuckwell, horn, and Robin Harrison,
piano) came on the day after the first night of *The Country Wife*, so no
coming in late the following morning for the stage management. A
ticket for a Thursday concert was two shillings, but the Sunday concert on December 16 (Peter Pears, tenor, with the Purcell Singers under

their conductor, Imogen Holst) was twelve shillings. The same amount was charged for the Sunday concert on January 20, 1957, when Peter Pears was accompanied by Benjamin Britten.

On Sunday evening, November 18, 1956, Arthur Miller came to the theatre to be one of the panel for a symposium, chaired by Kenneth Tynan. The panel was seated on the forestage in front of the pinoleum curtain, which was replacing the house curtain for the production of *The Good Woman of Setzuan*. I had never come across this type of material before, which seemed to consist of short lengths of a reedlike substance. These reeds were attached to each other horizontally in the manner of a venetian blind. The resulting strips were then placed side by side to produce the actual curtain. One of the advantages of this material was that it had the same characteristics as gauze in that when lit from the front, it presented itself as a solid wall, but lit from the back, it became transparent. Thus when one was on a darkened stage, it was possible to study the audience, knowing that one couldn't be seen. On the evening of the discussion, I used this method of secretly looking out front because I had heard a heightening of the sound from the audience just before the symposium began. I soon saw what had caused this increase of noise front-of-house. Being guided towards the first seat of the front row was Mrs. Arthur Miller or, as she was perhaps better known, the famous film actress Marilyn Monroe.

At the end of the evening, I was on the side of the stage waiting to clear the furniture from the forestage, when Kenneth Tynan came importantly through the pass door. He was leading the Millers away from the crowds who would doubtless have overwhelmed them if they had left by the front-of-house. I had not met Ken at that time, although I knew him as being the real champion from the ranks of the press of *Look Back in Anger*, so he naturally rushed past me with his protégés in his wake. In spite of the hurry, I was able to say good evening, first to Arthur Miller and then to Miss Monroe. She was simply dressed and with apparently no makeup but looking sweet and demure. She gave me a bewildered smile, murmured something, and walked hurriedly on to keep up with her escorts.

## Scene 18 ❦ The end of 1956 and the start of 1957

If *Look Back in Anger* was looking as if it could help the English Stage Company stay afloat, then surely Peggy Ashcroft (or Dame Peggy Ashcroft, as she had recently become) playing the role of the Good Woman herself, must surely set us firmly in the black and establish us as more-or-less permanent incumbents of the Royal Court Theatre. But Brecht . . . ? In spite of the acclaim that greeted the Berliner Ensemble's very recent visit to London, there seemed to be as much against, as there was for, a successful run of *The Good Woman of Setzuan*. At least it had not featured in the Ensemble's repertoire in London.

It was decided that the production should not open cold at the Royal Court, so it was booked into the Theatre Royal in Brighton for a week, then another week in Oxford before opening on the last day of October in Sloane Square.

Dame Peggy gave great performances in the dual roles of Shen Te and Shui Ta, and the large cast of twenty-seven actors and the small onstage band put over the play and the songs to the manner born. But in spite of a box office of nearly 60 percent for its forty-six performances, as with *Cards of Identity*, it wasn't the huge success the company still needed to complement the acclaim now heaped on *Look Back in Anger*.

That success came immediately after the Brecht with a stunning revival of Wycherley's *The Country Wife*. This played sixty performances with a 90 percent box office, so this homegrown production was exactly what the public and the company wanted. The majority of the cast had been with the English Stage Company during its rep days, but there were some newcomers, including Laurence Harvey, who very successfully played Mr. Horner. The joy of the production, however, was Joan Plowright as Margery Pinchwife. It was the kind of occasion that made one think that she must have been born to play this part at this time in this production.

In addition to playing Pinchwife, George Devine also directed the play with great pace and élan in a brilliant black-and-white setting by Motley. Percy Harris introduced our workshops to thick, clear plastic, which she used extensively, especially for chairs. The plastic was cut out in chair shape and then the outline of what would have been wood was painted in black onto the plastic. Each chair took up far less room on stage than the real piece of furniture would have done, and one could see through the furniture apart from the black outlines.

*The Country Wife* transferred to the Adelphi Theatre in the Strand at the beginning of February 1957, where, in that large and wide theatre (it is large and wide at all times, but coming in from the Royal Court it seemed excessively large and wide), it had a good run. This transfer allowed us at the Court to mount another production: Carson McCullers's *The Member of the Wedding*, in which Geraldine McEwan touchingly played the little girl Frankie Addams. There were many newcomers in the cast, since so many of the original company had now moved to the Adelphi. Tony Richardson directed this with an extremely effective and evocative standing set by Alan Tagg. Sadly, the play was not a success. It gave just under forty performances that brought in just under 40 percent at the box office, yet it was well directed and well played. One can find excuses for a play's failure to attract the public, and they could probably all apply to the Carson McCullers play. It was the subject matter or the weather or the time of year or the apathetic press. But in the end, one just had to accept that it was not liked by the public.

So Alan Tagg's Spanish moss was taken down, and in its place we once more put up the set of *Look Back in Anger*, which was rapidly becoming the "if in doubt" production. By now, Richard Pasco was playing Jimmy Porter, having very successfully taken over the role from Kenneth Haigh in October, and Heather Sears had replaced Mary Ure as Alison. It was good that Alan Bates and Vivienne Drummond were still in the production with both still giving their remarkable performances — true, honest, and totally believable. However, Richard wasn't the only Jimmy Porter when *Look Back* returned to the Court on March 11, for Alan Dobie was playing the role in the touring company that opened in Cambridge on February 25.

March 1957 was a busy month at the Court. Although we were all geared for the rehearsals and then the opening early in April of John Osborne's second play, *The Entertainer*, George had invited a French company to appear for the week before the most eagerly anticipated first night or premiere. Thus it was that on April 2, the exact (from the date point-of-view) anniversary of the English Stage Company's opening production, two plays by Samuel Beckett were presented on the stage of the Royal Court Theatre. It was a grand occasion, being a Gala Performance for which the popular actress Phyllis Calvert had "kindly arranged for the selling of programmes." The result of her "arranging" meant that the programmes sellers were also well-known actresses, the full roster being Faith Brook, Judy Campbell, Rosalie Crutchley, Rachel Kempson, Sarah Lawson, Anna Massey, Geraldine McEwan, and Marjorie Stewart.

The plays were *Fin de Partie* and *Acte Sans Paroles,* and they were presented in that order. The actors were not part of a French company, but actors cast for those particular plays with Roger Blin, who played Hamm in *Fin de Partie,* also directing the play. As the title indicates, *Acte Sans Paroles* was a mime play, in which Deryk Mendel played the only character in addition to directing.

George brought Samuel Beckett down to the stage while we were setting up his plays, and it was there that George enquired, "What is your translation of *Fin de Partie,* Sam?" This question brought the reply, in a lovely Irish accent, "It is 'end game,' a phrase used in a game of chess." They then went on to discuss chess, a game about which I knew nothing, and at that moment, I hadn't the time or the inclination to change that situation. Samuel Beckett was a name known to us through Peter Hall's production of Sam's first play *Waiting for Godot,* in a translation from the French by the playwright. This was at the Arts Theatre in 1955, while some of us also knew that the first presentation of that play, in French, was in 1953, when the director was Roger Blin.

## Scene 19 ⟨⟩ A day in the stage director's life at the Royal Court Theatre

As the months went by, so the tasks that fell my way became more clear and more plentiful. First and foremost, I had to make sure that the two stage management teams — that would increase to five when our touring and Sunday nights without décor productions were in full swing — had all that they needed to make rehearsals and performances run as smoothly as possible. In this area, I was enormously helped by Kevin Maybury, who was always cheerful and indefatigable. Between us, we would ensure that we had enough stagehands for the various shows, getting in extra staff, mostly students, as necessary. Many of the students worked so often with us that they became almost as semi-permanent as the original quartet. Speaking of our original quartet, it was one of that foursome, Alf Bolton, who gave a neat answer to a visitor who had dropped in to see us during an overnight strike and fit-up. The question asked was whether the coffee stall in the Square would still be open. Without a pause, Alf replied, "Oh, yes. You can get a cup of coffee or a guardsman there at any time of night."

Talking of pickups, when I drove around in my taxi buying furniture and props, I often used to pick up, at bargain prices, a useful table or chair or a mirror either to replace or to add to the furnishings in the few dressing rooms. It was the appalling lack of such necessities that I spoke about to George very early on, and I asked if I might start to improve the rooms. "You certainly must do," he said. "Just spend as little as possible." With the invaluable help of the taxi and a good supply of little shops selling junk (junk to some but treasures to me), the dressing rooms soon had a feeling of friendliness and a faint air of comfort. It wasn't long before I became well known to the owners of the many shops I haunted as I searched up and down the further reaches of the King's Road for exactly what a designer wanted for his or her set, and several would let me know if they had seen something that they knew was on my list.

## Scene 20 ❧ *The Entertainer* at the Royal Court Theatre

"Do we call this play Osborne Two?" I asked George when it became known that in April 1957 we would present John Osborne's second play for the company. The brave new style of referring to a play by the author's name was sliding away. Erosion started with *The Country Wife*, which was apt to be known by that title rather than as the Wycherley, though we had certainly used McCullers, which was neat and sharp in contrast to *The Member of the Wedding*, which somehow didn't flow too well. I felt this second Osborne might see the end. I was wrong. "Yes, it is Osborne Two," said George.

If *Look Back in Anger*, Dame Peggy Ashcroft in *The Good Woman of Setzuan* (in spite of its not being totally successful), and Joan Plowright and Laurence Harvey in *The Country Wife* had helped put the English Stage Company very firmly on the theatrical map — not forgetting that the Royal Court Theatre itself was also a beneficiary — then *The Entertainer* set the seal.

During our first summer at the Court, I had looked in on George in his dressing room during a performance, and to my amazement, there was Sir Laurence Olivier sitting in a reasonably comfortable armchair — in fact, the only armchair. We chatted briefly, and then Sir Laurence asked if it was possible to get into George's dressing room without coming in through the theatre's main entrance on Sloane Square. "It's the press, you see," he explained. "I only live round the corner as you know [no, I didn't] so I will probably be dropping in to see George quite often, and if the press see me, they'll invent all sorts of ridiculous reasons as to why I am here." "That's easy," I was able to reply. "If you leave Bourne Street through a gap in a row of small houses, as I'll show you, you'll come out in the middle of a group of cottages. At the far end of their central path are steps leading up to the back of the theatre where there is a fire escape. Go up its iron stairs to the first floor, and I will give you a key to the door on that level. This door opens on to the short corridor that leads directly to this room." All this was arranged, and from then on Sir Laurence was certainly very often in the theatre, although I am sure the company was mainly unaware of his presence. But now, a few months later, wonder of wonders, he was going to be here as the leading actor in the newest John Osborne play, and the interest from public and press was intense.

I was very pleased that Alan Tagg was once again the designer. He had already designed three of our productions (*Look Back*, *Cards of Identity*, and *The Member of the Wedding*), and I liked working with him very much, even if he did drive me demented at times. Although he knew exactly what he wanted in the way of materials, furniture, and props, when we went into a shop or furniture store, he wasn't always able to find something that satisfied him totally, nor was he able to let me know whether what I was showing him meant that I was getting "warm" or whether, as was usually the case, I was still "cold." I have to say that it was myself, rather than a shop assistant, who would be holding up the material or pointing to pieces of furniture, for most assistants could take so much of Alan's indecision, and then they would fade away. It was always wise not to think a piece was chosen when Alan, having studied it for a long time, would say "Yeeeeees," for without doubt this word would be followed by, "But perhaps we could find . . ." and we were off again. I knew the end result would be as perfect as availability and budget would allow, but the end was so often a long time a'comin'.

Lack of time meant I was seldom able to watch any of the rehearsals for *The Entertainer*, but when I had perforce to call in to check something with its director or stage management, it was interesting watching the way Sir Laurence, one of the greatest actors of his time, and Tony Richardson, the brilliant young director, treated each other. Although he would never for a moment have admitted it, I felt sure that Tony was thinking "Sir Laurence's standing in the profession and his experience in an enormous variety of roles are immense, so how do I, with a good but limited standing and increasing but not a vast range of experience, get him to do something that is different from what he has decided he should do at a certain point?"

From the opposite angle, Sir Laurence, again I felt sure, was working out how he could get his way without removing the authority of this young man, who obviously knew what he was doing. For the remainder of the cast, Tony's direction was fine, but he didn't seem always to appreciate not only what his leading player was aiming at but also what he had to achieve that would make him feel comfortable in the role. Thus it was that rehearsals were littered with questions such as, "I wonder, Larry, if you would like to try a slight variation on what you are doing so marvellously in that scene?" This would be followed by details of his suggestion. Next would come from the other side, as it were, words such as, "Yes, that's good [a slight pause], but I wonder whether it might help the scene if as I start that long speech, I could . . ." and an idea for a slight variation would be put forward. This would be considered by Tony and then accepted. So between them, neither lost face, and Sir Laurence played it exactly as he had planned. Tony always called Sir Laurence, "Larry." To us, he was "Sir Laurence" or just "Sir."

There were two big problems among the many that presented themselves during rehearsals and during the construction of the set. The Lord Chamberlain, in his role as censor of the words and actions of all plays presented to a public audience, having read the script put a veto on one scene that caused much fury on John Osborne's part. In the scene in question, a black girl danced on a coffin that was covered by a Union Jack. In no way, decreed the Lord Chamberlain, was the national flag to be treated in that way. His letter also mentioned the appearance of a nude woman, Gorgeous Gladys, who would, he understood, be depicted as Britannia during one of Archie Rice's music hall numbers. The Lord Chamberlain let it be known that even though this was the Royal Court and not the Windmill Theatre, if an actress were to appear nude on the stage, then, as at the Windmill, she would not be allowed to move. Linking, in any way, the Royal Court with the Windmill (where tableaux filled with nudes were the order of the day — all day and every day) added to John's initial fury. After much venom was hurled around, the dancing on the coffin scene was, at the last moment, cut from the production. In fact, it was such a late decision that the character and the actress playing her were named in the original programme.

As far as the appearance of Gorgeous Gladys was concerned, it was accepted that she should indeed be a seated, immobile Britannia. But, and this had nothing to do with the Lord Chamberlain, there remained the question as to who was going to appear in this part. Vivienne Drummond, who took over the part of Helena (pronounced Hellena) from the actress Helena (pronounced Heleena) Hughes during the first run of *Look Back in Anger* and then played in *The Member of the Wedding*, would be perfect casting, but she turned it down. Sir Laurence was told of her decision, whereupon he asked if he might talk to her. A quarter of an hour later, we were told that Vivienne would be playing Gorgeous Gladys — I nearly wrote that she would be very happy to appear as Gorgeous Gladys, but that would be far from the truth.

A year after the orchestra pit was covered, those covers came off for *Acte Sans Paroles* and stayed off for *The Entertainer*, both productions needing the pit to house a small band — three musicians for the Beckett mime play and five for *The Entertainer*. As soon as the pit was open once more, it struck me that the assemblies could no longer be used as such, so why not reinstate the stage boxes? The theatre was obviously going to be sold out for a play written by the now well-known John Osborne and starring Sir Laurence, so here was an easy way of adding eight seats — and commensurate revenue — at each performance. As soon as George gave his permission, Kevin built the two curved fronts, while my contribution was to buy the necessary coral velvet to cover the tops, as well as material for curtains, pelmets, and tiebacks. In the box office, Albert Rouse, the manager, started selling the extra seats, which proved to be exceptionally easy.

John Osborne had written his play as if the audience was in a music hall with each scene being numbered, whether the setting was the sitting room of seedy theatrical digs or on the stage of the local Music Hall where Archie Rice, the role to be played by Sir Laurence, was performing. Tony and John wanted each side of the proscenium arch to be fitted, as in all music halls, with a framed, glass-fronted box within which the numbers of each act, or turn, would be shown in lighted figures. At a music hall, this system helped those members of the audience who decided that a drink in the bar would be more acceptable than the next turn. When they felt it might be time to check on the progress of the evening's entertainment, they would re-enter the auditorium, look at the number displayed in the proscenium arch box, check that number in the programme to see which turn it was, and then make up their minds whether to return to their seats or to go back to the bar.

The programmes for *The Entertainer* at the Royal Court were to reflect this idea, so that not only was each of Archie Rice's scenes in the music hall given a title and a number, but also the scenes in the lodgings would be allocated numbers, but this time the names of the characters, who would appear in the various scenes, would be added. The programme detailed a total of thirteen turns, with music hall scenes alternating with scenes in the digs.

Worrying about how we would re-create the lighted numbers on the proscenium arch, I went at once to John Recknell, the chief electrician, and put this to him. I dreaded to think what John might say, since he was the one member of the Esdaile staff who had reacted to the new company in the negative way that George had forecast. To my surprise and delight, John actually brightened and said he was sure he knew exactly where in the theatre he could find such equipment, and he would look them out and start wiring them up. This was wonderful and totally unexpected news. I had never imagined that the Royal Court had once housed a music hall, but John was even able to point out the marks on the proscenium arch where the boxes had been fixed. It was not an easy job, but he worked diligently on his project, and by the time we came to put the set on the stage, he was able to fix the boxes to the proscenium arch and show us that the lighted numbers worked splendidly.

The effect on all of us when the five-piece orchestra could be heard tuning up and then playing in the pit was magical. William Blezard led them brilliantly, making the five of them sound exactly like any orchestra in any music hall. Honor Blair had been engaged to teach Sir Laurence the tap steps and movement for his music hall act. Not only was she always on hand during rehearsals, but once the play had opened, she came to the theatre before every performance to check Sir Laurence as he went through every number and all his routines.

The first night of the play went very well, although the tremendous enthusiasm in the audience after Act I was not maintained throughout the rest of the evening due to the darker side of the story emerging. But the very end of the last act was so moving that the reception when the curtain fell was deafening. There was no doubt where the theatre-going public would be aiming in the next few weeks.

The penultimate scene of the production was played in front of a painted cloth with Archie Rice reprising John Addison's haunting number "Why Should I Care?" Behind the appropriately tatty music hall cloth, all the staff were working flat out: on the stage, from which all props and furniture had to be cleared and placed against the side walls, while in the flies, all cloths, legs, and borders had to be flown as far out of sight as possible. It was a rush for all of us, but it always got done, so that when the music hall cloth was flown out, the audience could see to the back wall of the theatre over a totally empty stage except for Archie, who, having finished his number, turned and, as he moved upstage, was joined by his wife, Phoebe, extremely well played by Brenda de Banzie. She came out from the opposite-to-prompt corner, and arm-in-arm, the two walked slowly towards the up-left corner of the stage (to the scene dock, in fact), with the band still playing "Why Should I Care." A follow spot — the one remaining light — closed on them until only the backs of their heads were lit, and then — blackout.

I often used to go from my office to the circle box (now filled with lighting equipment) — from where I could see but not be seen — down onto the stage and the orchestra pit, and then across to the stage box and the first few rows of the stalls. It was from this vantage point that I could watch the dramatic and moving scene when Sir Laurence's character is given a telegram that tells him his soldier son Mick had been killed in action. Here, John Osborne used the very recent real-life 1956 crisis in Suez, as the occasion during which and the location where Mick would die. Archie Rice read the telegram, uttered a howl, and then slowly walked diagonally across the stage to the base of the stage-right proscenium arch. There he leant back upon it before slowly sliding down until he was slumped on the floor.

One evening during this scene, I noticed a man in the stage box sitting right forward so that he was as near the stage as he could possibly get. But his obvious enjoyment of the play turned sour when, to his horror, he saw that this great actor was, without saying anything, crossing the stage and aiming straight for him. I could see this poor fellow was desperately deciding what he should do, then, with mind made up, he very, very slowly put his hands under the seat of his light gilt chair, very, very slowly lifted it, and very, very slowly he and chair backed into the darkness of the box.

But it wasn't the end of his torment. When he must have felt safely hidden away, further horror. There on the coral velvet cover of the box front was his programme. Would this distract Sir Laurence? Should he move it? Yes, he should, and so a hand and then an arm came out of the shadows at a very low angle. The hand reached up to the box front and very, very slowly pulled the offending white object back into the blessed anonymity behind the box curtains.

## Scene 21 ⊘ Gorgeous Gladys appears in
### *The Entertainer*

Vivienne Drummond as Gorgeous Gladys playing the role of Britannia in one of Archie Rice's music hall scenes was very brave about baring all, but she was determined that as few persons backstage as possible would be able to see her. Alan Tagg arranged that she sit on a stool on a three-foot-high triangular rostrum, which was enclosed by a book flat at the back. At the front, a pair of black velvet tabs would be opened just enough to expose the rostrum, and so by sitting well back in the triangle, Vivienne was therefore visible only to the audience and not to peeping eyes in the wings.

During the few seconds of her scene, she sat quite still, apparently gazing into the far distance, but actually to within a few inches of one side of the book flat. I felt that she took comfort in the thought that if she couldn't see anyone, then no one could see her. She steadied a shield, placed on the rostrum beside her, with her right hand and held a trident with her left, thus more or less reproducing the posture of the lady featured on the backs of the old copper pennies.

Shortly before her cue to take up her position, Betty, her dresser, would bring Vivienne, covered with a wrap, down to the stage. In the gloom, I would meet them and lead them along the narrow, dark corridor, formed by the back of the music hall cloth and the black tabs, to the front of the rostrum. There, Vivienne would take off her wrap, hand it to Betty, and take my hand, and I would help her onto the rostrum. When seated, I would give her the trident and shield, and she would take up her pose, while Betty and I would race to the wings. Time was short for this move.

At the end of the scene, the system went into reverse, with my helping Vivienne down and Betty enveloping her in her wrap and hurrying her offstage. Only when they were seen to have reached the safety of the wings was the rostrum and props, the stool and the book flat speedily struck and the black tabs opened. One evening, however, when Vivienne put out her hand so that I could help her down, she missed my hand and instead put a finger neatly into one of my eyes. When she had left the stage, I turned in the wings to be faced by one of the faithful stage staff, Ted Bolton. He looked at my streaming eye, shook his head in mock disbelief, and whispered, "There you are, Mr. H. We knew you'd go too far one night."

## Scene 22 ❧ *The Entertainer* at the Palace Theatre, Cambridge Circus, London

In September 1967, *The Entertainer* opened at the Palace Theatre. The little settings that fitted the Royal Court had to be enlarged to fit the much bigger stage of the Palace. This Alan Tagg cleverly achieved so that the audience, when looking at the sitting room of the lodgings, in which so much of the action took place, did not wonder how on earth these tawdry digs had such a large room.

Alan was able to provide Tony Richardson with a trap (Tony was very partial to having the use of a trap), and thus the audience was able at times to see a character enter or leave by way of a flight of upstage stairs. Not all the time, however, for Alan positioned a painted gauze panel as the back wall of the room, which, as with the pinoleum of *The Good Woman,* when lit from the front gave the impression that it was solid. When it was necessary for the audience to see someone coming up the stairs or when a scene had to be played on the landing, the lighting was reversed, with the gauze panel being lit from the back, which made it transparent.

Only Sir Laurence, Brenda de Banzie, George Relph, and Richard Pasco had played in the original production but of the four newcomers to this cast, two, Joan Plowright and Robert Stephens, had joined the English Stage Company at its inception, both playing in the second production, *The Crucible.* By the time *The Entertainer* opened in the West End, one would think that all eight actors had been together for a long time.

The changes in the settings did not seem to faze any of the cast, but once more I felt that the wide open spaces owed the production nothing, though I doubt if any of the audiences would have felt that a smaller space would have benefited the play. Happily, the auditorium at the Palace Theatre is remarkable, for although the theatre seats 1,400, they are spread over four tiers with each tier built well forward. In this way there is a warm, wraparound effect, and I am sure this helped every member of the audiences that packed in during *The Entertainer's* visit to enjoy the play.

I called in on the company at the Palace as often as possible, and on three occasions I was onstage at the end of the performance (no rushing up to the flies for me in this theatre to help clear the stage of hanging cloths, and so on for the last scene), which involved me by chance in leading three separate guests to Sir's dressing room. The first was Somerset Maugham, whom I heard tapping gently on the pass door. He was a tiny man with more than his fair share of old-age lines and wrinkles on his sharp face.

The next was the ravishingly attractive Elizabeth Taylor. She was dressed to be seen, and one certainly couldn't miss her. She simply glittered: jewels, false or real, seemed to have been placed wherever there was a blank space — even the heels of her shoes were ablaze. A week later, Vivien Leigh came round after a performance. An absolute stunning beauty, wearing an ankle-length fur coat but no jewellry in sight. She didn't need any glitter to be noticed.

Once, during a visit to the Palace, Sir Laurence invited Elizabeth and myself to drinks in his dressing room after the evening show at the end of the week. When I told Elizabeth, she commented that at last she would be able to tell him the story of her mother and one of his performances as Richard III. It was when he was with the Old Vic Company at the New Theatre (now the Albery) in St. Martin's Lane, during the Second World War.

Sure enough, Elizabeth found her chance and recounted to Sir Laurence how her mother braved the unreliable wartime train service to travel down from Leeds early one morning to be in time for a matinee. She only just made it, for she and Elizabeth reached their seats as the houselights were lowered, so there was no time for her mother to look at the programme. When the curtain rose, Sir Laurence, as Richard, was standing centre stage. With a shoulder-length wig of black, greasy hair, white face, and long thin nose and costumed in doublet, hose, and a short cloak, the actor began, "Now is the winter of our discontent . . ." At the end of the speech, Elizabeth's mother turned to her and whispered, "That chap's good. Olivier'll have a bit to do to come up to his standard."

Sir enjoyed this tale a lot, but not to be outdone, he immediately said, "Oh, you must have been the little girl in a box one matinee." Although Elizabeth denied this, he pressed on with his story of this little girl who, he said, spent the whole matinee almost falling out of the box so that she wouldn't miss anything. "And you know what it is," he went on, "an actor has to direct a soliloquy to someone in the audience, or some object in the auditorium, so that particular afternoon I directed all mine to this child. When I had given the speech [and here he rattled off several lines of the play before he continued the story], I flung my cloak over my shoulder and hobbled offstage, only to hear a piping little voice following me into the wings saying, 'Mummy, what's the funny lady going to do now?'"

## Scene 23 ⊗ Photographs of the productions at the Royal Court Theatre

We had many photographers to take pictures of the various productions for press and publicity purposes, such as Julie Hamilton and David Sim, but with *The Entertainer*, someone new appeared — Tony Armstrong-Jones. Not only was he new to us, but his style, too, was new. Both Julie and David were much more free and easy and much quicker than the two respected members of the old school, Houston Rogers and Angus McBean, both of whom photographed a production apiece (*Look Back in Anger* and *The Country Wife,* respectively) at the Court, but our newest photographer said he did not want a photo call as such, where the actors came in especially to have photographs of various scenes taken. He said he would attend a dress rehearsal, and the actors were to play the scenes as if he weren't there — but "there" he certainly was. He was up on the stage with the cast, weaving his way in and out and taking pictures at great speed and from all angles. The results were wonderful and unusual, and the company was grateful that they could use the photo call as another dress rehearsal rather than having to give up several hours of their all-too-short rehearsal time to be photographed. Up until now, a photo call had always entailed much time being spent on lighting each carefully selected scene and arranging the correct pose for the actors. The results were fine as records, but they usually lacked life and reality, while reactions, such as horror or surprise, would often turn out to be greatly exaggerated.

## Scene 24 ⊗ The English Stage Company in 1957, after *The Entertainer*

Once more it almost seemed that George Devine had decided that those working backstage had not enough to do, for he allowed the excellent stage designer Carl Toms to design a splendid setting for Ronald Duncan's English adaptation of Jean Giraudoux's *The Apollo de Bellac* as if it were to sit unmoved on the Royal Court stage for the rest of time. It had a large staircase, a practical upper floor, and a monster of a chandelier. I objected, of course — not only was the setting excessively large, it was one half of a double bill — but equally, of course, my objections were overruled. The other half was *The Chairs*, which gave Jocelyn Herbert her chance to design a play rather than paint other designers' scenery. Her remarkable design for this amazing play seemed to find Jocelyn experimenting and being surprised and, I hoped, encouraged by the results, all at the same time.

Compared to the lavish *Apollo*, Eugene Ionesco's *The Chairs*, in Donald Watson's translation, had a rough-and-ready feel to it, and for all of us, when we were setting up, it was a type of set we had never come across before. Some even felt that it was one they never wished to come across again. The walls were indicated by ropes hanging from a curved metal bar, while between the ropes were hung squares of canvas painted in various colours. It certainly presented problems, quite apart from having to strike the *Apollo* set before we could start this one. *The Chairs* needed two practical doors through which, during the play, on one side George Devine and on the other Joan Plowright had to pass in and out, collecting chairs from offstage and setting them, as if for a meeting, onstage. There were also two windows and a vital, practical, golden double door upstage centre.

Getting a door to work smoothly — especially when it has a two-way hinge, as had each of the single doors on each side of the set — is bad enough at the best of times, but the lack of space and the speed necessary to make the change within the time span of the interval or intermission (although this had been especially extended to twenty minutes) made this change very tricky indeed. Even when the set was ready, there was then the difficult task of stacking the chairs offstage in a space that hardly allowed for one chair, let alone many times that number. Space also had to be allowed for the stagehands to pass the chairs to George and Joan, but to do it such a way that it looked as if the two old people really were collecting the chairs themselves.

*The Chairs* was, for me, a joy. Beautifully directed by Tony Richardson and most brilliantly played by Joan and George. It had not been difficult during rehearsals to imagine how the avuncular, white-haired George would look aged ninety, but Joan was not so easy. However, seemingly without difficulty, down onto the stage came this querulous, little old lady, and between them, they were absolutely wonderful. The dexterity with which they handled the chairs was amazing. And that extraordinary setting seemed totally correct for what went on within it. If only more of the public could have experienced my enjoyment, but its thirty performances only brought in a box office figure of 33 percent. Could it be that the double bill caused the public to think twice about coming to see it and, on reaching the second of those two thoughts, decide against it? Or could it be that both plays in this double bill were written by Frenchmen and was there, in these early days, too much reliance on plays that originated overseas? Out of the first fourteen plays (I am not counting Samuel Beckett's mime, *Acte Sans Paroles*), only eight were homegrown.

## Scene 25 ❧ Sunday nights: productions without decor

Adding to the travails attached to the double bill, George decided he wanted to help young authors and to encourage young directors, so in May 1957 we presented the first of our Sunday night "productions without decor." These were to be so basic that the title of the season was not even granted capitals for its initial letters. The productions for the first season were given to Peter Coe, John Dexter, and Lindsay Anderson. Peter was the first of the trio, and he directed *The Correspondence Course* by Charles Robinson. John followed with Michael Hastings's first play, *Yes — and After,* which brought a lot of publicity for the playwright, but which did me no favours. Because Michael and I share initials and first names and both our surnames are linked to English towns (even though mine is spelled with two *l*'s), and because of the publicity heaped on him due to his youth and ability as a playwright, from then on and for a considerable time, business telephone calls to me would invariably start, "Is that Michael Hastings?" "No, it's Michael Hallifax." [pause] "Ah. Yes. [pause] Well, Mr. Hastings, I wonder if . . ."

Lindsay rounded off that first season. He bravely came with a play by Kathleen Sully, *The Waiting of Lester Abbs,* and a cast of twenty-three. It was fortunate Kathleen's play involved so many characters, for it seemed the majority of the profession, no matter in which part of the theatre their talent had taken them, wanted to appear in Lindsay's production. Among the twenty-three were actors Ian Bannen, Alfred Burke, and Robert Stephens; playwrights Michael Hastings and Alun Owen; and director John Dexter.

The autumn saw two more Sunday nights, the second of which was *A Resounding Tinkle* by N. F. (Wally) Simpson, directed by William (Bill) Gaskill. Four months later, this play, in a double bill with Wally's *The Hole,* was given a production as part of the main season. Bill Gaskill directed both productions wonderfully well, and I loved both of them. I still recall with great pleasure the seriousness with which Wendy Craig, as Middie Paradock in *A Resounding Tinkle,* considered giving spectacles to eagles because she was worried whether they could see their prey on the ground from the height at which they flew.

## Scene 26 ❦ Touring from the Royal Court Theatre, 1957

But George hadn't finished with the amount of work he could find for us simply by putting in a few Sunday nights. In July, I took two plays — *How Can We Save Father?* by Oliver Marlow Wilkinson, directed by Peter Wood, and *Purgatory* by W. B. Yeats, directed by John Dexter — to the Devon Festival. They were to be played as a double bill (yet another) in Barnstaple and Exeter. *Purgatory* may have been the title of the second play, but it was also the absolutely correct word for that tour. There was no checking out a theatre in advance of a visit at that time, so I was more than a little put out to find that the local stage manager in Exeter had overlooked letting me know that the theatre was mainly used as a cinema. This meant that there was no theatre-going audience who might, just by chance, have decided to risk coming to a performance, and also that there was a tall, immovable cinema screen set about halfway upstage and stretching almost from wall to wall. The final straw was that this accursed screen curved downstage at each end, thus managing successfully to prevent my using any of the bars I needed to support scenery or hang lamps.

Another brief tour took *Look Back in Anger* to Russia in August, followed by New York in September. George had allowed me to get in a special stage management team for each Sunday night, and from one of these, I picked Donald Ross to go to Moscow as the manager of the company, since my being there would have taken me away at an impossibly busy time. When Donald came back, he accused me of knowing how awful it would be, and he was sure this was why I had engaged him. He reported that they didn't fly to Moscow direct but to Leningrad from whence there was a long train journey south. When they arrived in the capital at last, they found that the hotel allotted to them was not in the centre of a very crowded and an excessively hot city but a long way out of town. To add to their unhappiness, all they seemed to get to eat were sausages and onions.

My sorrow at losing *The Chairs* proved to be short-lived, I'm glad to say, for at the beginning of August, when *Look Back* was off to Russia, it returned to the Court for just one week. This time with a new partner, *How Can We Save Father?*, following its preliminary showing at what for me had proved to be an unhappy Devon Festival.

## Scene 27 ✆ *Look Back in Anger,* the Lyceum Theatre, New York, 1957

On September 23, 1957, I was sent to New York to join the *Look Back in Anger* Company during their last week of rehearsals and to stay not only for the first night but for the second night as well. An American stage manager, Hal Stone, with an assistant, had to take over the production, and my main job was to ensure they could run the show exactly as it had been run by the English stage management.

David Merrick, who was presenting the show, had either only got American Equity's permission for four of the original five members of the cast to play in New York, or it may have been that the role of Colonel Redfern was counted as a small part and therefore Mr. Merrick could save money by employing a local actor. Thus it was that Mary Ure, Kenneth Haigh, Alan Bates, and Vivienne Drummond had had to say good-bye to the ever-dependable, excellent John Welsh, who had created the role, and now were to be joined by Jack Livesey, an Englishman who had been living in the States for some years and who possessed a green card, which entitled him to work there. Jack's brother also was an actor, well known on the London stage and in British films, Roger Livesey.

Besides the cast, the only others allowed to go over with the show were Tony Richardson, the director, John Osborne, the playwright, and myself. I was booked into the Piccadilly Hotel, which was on the opposite side of Times Square to the theatre in which *Look Back* would play, the Lyceum on 45th Street.

During the first half of the 1950s, various theatre jobs had meant my making many journeys by air, but these were either reasonably short flights or, on the longer journeys, the plane was forever dropping down for a short stop en route. So the flight to New York was the longest nonstop I had experienced. All went well until we were, so my charming neighbour, a Texan, told me, in the Boston area. Suddenly the plane gave the most almighty lurch that made me grip the armrests. The Texan seemed totally unmoved, and although I feared there might be more of the same, I stopped worrying when he announced, in his delicious drawl, "We've just been struck by lightning." Like him, presumably, I decided we weren't going to be hit a second time and anyway, we must be very near the end of the journey. While my neighbour had been chatting on during the flight, my mind went back once more to the Second World War when, for a magical period during the Italian campaign, I had been attached as an interpreter to the Free French Forces, the Corps de Poursuite. The interpreter for the American forces was a Texan, and not only did he have the same slow and deep voice as my plane companion, but he also spoke French as if he were speaking American but using unusual words. "Bonn Jewer, monn Gen-er-arle," he would say, and Général Juin, the commander-in-chief of the Corps de Poursuite, would twinkle, bid us both good morning in English but from then on the business of the day was conducted in French.

To arrive in New York for the first time was as exciting as I had known it would be. However prepared I was, by having devoured pictures of that unbelievably tall city and even having an excellent aerial photograph covering most of Manhattan on my bedroom wall when in my teens, I was not prepared for the height and the density of so many of the buildings, beside which small shops, even some of one floor only, were nestling. The centre of my world for the next few days was Times Square, where it was most satisfying to see smoke coming out of the mouth of someone smoking (was the cigarette a Camel?) as depicted on a vast hoarding or billboard on one side of the Square. It wasn't a clean, smart city, but it certainly was alive, and although the surface of the roads I crossed was in a poor state, that didn't deter the yellow cabs racing along at frightening speed.

The first night I slept fitfully, and it was on one of my awake patches that I realised I had no clock and no watch. How was I going to know the time, for, of all days, I mustn't be late for the morning's rehearsal. My mind cleared enough to realise that all I had to do was to phone down to reception. This I did and was told it was 4:27 AM. Great. I must have dropped off, for when I was next aware that I was in a strange room, there was faint light in the direction of the window. I called reception. "Ten minutes of six." Curious way to tell the time, I thought, but thanks. From then on, I could doze no more, and soon reception was obviously beginning to lose patience with my phone calls. I opened the curtains and found it was a beautiful day, and the sun was up. Then I discovered a ploy that was going to save me endlessly phoning down for a time check. If I opened the window to a certain angle, I could see the reflection of a clock that appeared to be on the side of some building. It was not near but the sun shining on the face of the clock made the hands stand out reasonably clearly. Fantastic luck. There had to be a snag and there was. In fact, there were two. Firstly, the two hands seemed to be almost of the same length, and secondly, because I was gazing at a reflection — and, however far I leaned out of the window, I could not see the actual clock — I then had to work out whether the time was, say, twenty to seven or twenty-five to eight.

I went down to breakfast at what turned out to be a reasonable time — I had checked with the first person who got into the lift — and was directed to the café on the ground floor of the hotel. It was not a large room, full to the brim with customers, and was a scene of intense activity. I noticed a seat being vacated at the counter, so I made for it smartly and slipped onto it gratefully. It seemed to be a good place to see what I could order and what others were eating. Before I had time to take stock, let alone check out a huge board behind the counter that showed what was on offer, one of several assistants saw me and shouted something in my direction. I couldn't understand what he was saying, but I presumed by his attitude, which was of the "two-seconds-and-then-you've-had-it" variety, that he was testily waiting for my order. Whatever I ordered brought forth what seemed like a string of alternatives, most of which I found impossible to decipher.

I was on the point of leaving un-breakfasted, when I heard my name called, and there was Kenneth Haigh standing in the doorway. It turned out, although unbeknownst to me, that he was staying in the same hotel. It looked as if I was going to get breakfast after all, especially when the man next to me upped and left and Ken took over his seat. At once he explained that everyone in New York was in a hurry, and that the sooner a customer was fed, the sooner he left and another order could be taken. "No cosy old-world chat over a cup of coffee is permitted here," Ken added, after he had interpreted and given my order, which, modest though it was, arrived with indecent haste. It was also with indecent haste that we finished our meals and left the frenetic room.

Later, he guided me to the building in which the company was rehearsing. It was plainly a building that seemed to consist solely of rehearsal rooms and to reach our particular room, we had to thread our way amongst dancers from a new musical, *West Side Story*, that, like ourselves, was just about to open on Broadway. These dancers, spread along a corridor, were lolling back against the wall, standing in small groups, or sitting with their backs to the wall and their legs spread out in front of them, so picking one's way carefully was essential. All were in a state of total sweaty exhaustion. It would have been more pleasant if there had been a window or some air-conditioning. Wherever one went around the city, one couldn't fail to see poster after poster announcing the imminent arrival of this new musical — the gloriously infectious picture of an attractive laughing girl running past ash cans on a New York sidewalk with a similarly happy young man appearing to have almost caught up with her, for his outstretched hand is just making contact with hers.

The *Look Back* company were all in good heart, and Jack Livesey seemed physically perfect as the Colonel, although I was very sorry for him having to join a group who had been together for such a long time in this and other plays. Tony Richardson was bubbling over with life and really enjoying himself. He didn't even complain of the difficulty of concentrating in the rehearsal room allocated to the company because of the sound of singing and finger-clicking that came through the wall.

After rehearsal, I went to the Lyceum Theater on 45th Street, and from then on I was at the beck and call of all those working on the stage. "Hey, Michael, does this go this way round or that?" There was no "Mr. Hallifax" here, nor even "Mr. H," as the Royal Court stage hands addressed me. There was a good feeling in the theatre as we built the set. It had looked so right at the Royal Court, but, like *The Entertainer* at the Palace Theatre in London, it became small and insignificant on the Lyceum stage, which was very wide, and the proscenium arch was very high.

Tony had been very excited for once again, as with *The Entertainer* at the Palace, he had been told that it was possible to provide a trap a few feet beyond the upstage door of the set. However, there was no way the walls of the set could be transformed from solid to see-through, so the trap must be as close to the upstage centre door as possible, which would enable not all but certainly many of the audience to see a character taking a step or two either coming up or going down an actual staircase. He was sure this would make all the difference to many of the entrances and exits. But for those entrances that wouldn't involve the stairs, there was a snag: there was no way of reaching that upstage door without being seen by patrons in the two balconies. From those high positions, one could see over the tops of the downstage flats on stage left, and even if the actors walked as close to the flats as possible, they would still be seen. There was only one way to overcome this. A small overhang, covered in black velvet, had to be attached to those stage-left flats, which would mean an actor could leave the prompt corner and walk confidently round to the upstage entrance under the little roof knowing he couldn't be seen en route by any of the audience. Although I continued to admire what was placed on the stage at the Lyceum, I could never get over how tiny the set appeared, looking lost and a little sad in the middle of that great opening.

Not knowing the union rules in New York, I was severely reprimanded when, noticing that the ironing board had been set a few inches too far upstage, I automatically started to place it where it should have been, but I was immediately told that I wasn't allowed to touch, let alone move, scenery, furniture, or even a prop. After eighteen months at the Royal Court where I helped where help was needed, whether it was opening a trap or pulling on a hemp rope in the flies, I found this stricture exceedingly difficult to remember to obey. This didn't stop me being sent out to buy whatever was needed when it was something that only I would know exactly what Tony wanted.

One of these items was a gas cooker. I was told that I might possibly find one in a scrap yard — although I couldn't believe such a place existed in the middle of New York. Bravely I went alone, hoping the cab I hailed would have a friendly, helpful driver. The first cab I hailed, which actually swung across to collect me, proved to have such a person, although I knew that he thought he had a real nutter in the back of his cab. After a worryingly long ride, we stopped outside a likely looking yard, and on reading a huge notice board outside advertising what might be found inside, it all seemed too easy. I was soon disillusioned when I was taken to where cookers were stacked as I had seen cars piled up in similar scrap yards. Unfortunately, none of them looked like an English gas cooker, and most of them, and I suppose I shouldn't have been surprised at this, were unbelievably bigger than the one John Osborne and I had chosen in London. Knowing that there was nowhere else to go, I chose the least offensive, prayed it wouldn't stick out too far into the set, and returned to the theatre, only to be presented with another errand later that evening. A very worried Hal came to me and said that Tony didn't like the dictionary he had produced, so would I please go out to a local bookshop, which he assured me was only a couple of blocks away, and buy one that would be acceptable.

"But it's far too late to go this evening," I said. "It must be nine-thirty at least." Hal looked surprised for a moment but then said comfortingly, "Don't worry. The bookstore won't close until eleven o'clock at the earliest." I went out of the stage door into the badly lit street at the back of the theatre, and it wasn't long before I came across the bookshop Hal had suggested. I saw an assistant, so I went up to him and asked where I might find the dictionaries. "You might find the what?!" he asked, very loudly. "The dictionaries, please," I repeated. The young man turned to another assistant lolling nearby. "Hey, Steve, come and listen to what this guy wants!" The second young man strolled across, and once more I gave my request, only to realise, rather belatedly, what was causing the fun. So I obligingly said the word dictionaries several times, while the assistants enjoyed themselves trying to copy my accent. At last I said, "Well, where are they?" to which the first young man, genuinely mystified, asked "Where are what?" At last, amidst great hilarity, my new friends showed me where dictionaries were stacked. I chose one, gave it to Hal who gave it to Tony who didn't approve. Nor did he approve, as I knew he wouldn't, of the gas cooker, but he accepted my assurances that it was this or nothing, and one soon got used to the monster up in the corner.

## Scene 28 ❧ Preview and premiere of *Look Back* on Broadway, October 1957

All went well at the theatre until the second scene of Act II at the first preview. Hal had told me that he and his assistant were now feeling quite confident that they could run the show without my being in the background, so I had arranged for a seat in the stalls. In spite of the fact that the original quartet of actors were playing to an American audience for the first time, they were firmly in place and as excellent as ever in Act I and also at the start of Act II, but when we reached the second scene, which is when Jack Livesey as Colonel Redfern first appeared, the smooth flow of the play changed. In the middle of one of Jack's speeches the poor chap dried — although, since this was in New York, I suppose I should have written "went up." There was a very long pause with nothing happening on stage or off until at last a prompt of only one word whispered its way across the set, taking in the auditorium, it seemed, en route. Jack picked up the word and said it, but nothing followed. Another agonising pause until another prompt, slightly louder, but again only a single word. Once more Jack took the word and said it, but once more it was followed by silence. At last, a prompt came consisting of several words, and once more he repeated them, but when he had used them all up, silence followed. It was obvious that none of them was of any help to him; in fact, none of them even had any meaning for him. Jack didn't stay where he was, but walked over to the prompt corner and was seen to indicate that he wanted to look at the prompt script. Bravely he took his time, studied the script, handed it back, and returned to the centre of the stage. A slight pause and then he continued from where he had last dried and from then on, although I think everyone in the audience was waiting for a repetition of the horror that had gone before, shakily reached the end of his scene. On his behalf, I felt like rushing along to Times Square — it was closer than the river — and throwing myself under a passing bus.

Nothing untoward happened on the first night, which was played beautifully by all the cast but without marked response from the audience. In the first interval, I was told this was what happened in New York on these occasions, for no one in the audience would want to express like or dislike in case they chose a reaction not reflected in the notices the next day.

## Scene 29 ❧ After the premiere of *Look Back in Anger*

Every company needs a leader, and Tony was our out-and-out leader. He knew all about New York and arranged outings whenever possible. For instance, he took Ken and Alan to a health club where, as Alan reported later, totally naked they were hosed down with vicious jets of water because Tony said it would be very good for them and they would lose pounds. He also arranged seats for *Bells Are Ringing,* which starred the incomparable Judy Holiday, an outing in which luckily I could join. He was at his best on the morning of the first night or, as it is called in the States, the premiere. "David Merrick has invited us all to join him at Sardi's after the show, but before we go there, we will all meet in the bar next to the stage door," Tony exultantly informed us. "The first notice to come out will not be in a newspaper but over the air. Mary, you and Vivienne will want to tart yourselves up before we go to Sardi's, so the rest of us will go to the bar, and you two can join us when you are ready."

Tony collected Kenneth Haigh, Alan Bates, John Osborne, and myself (Jack had gone off separately with his wife), and we dutifully followed him to the bar, which proved to be excessively gloomy and depressing. But, as Tony had said, there on the counter was a large, dark brown, Bakelite wireless set, and it didn't seem too long before Tony, who had been practically sitting on the wireless, said, "Here it is." We clustered round and heard the critic being introduced after which he started, "Well, I have just been to the worst play I have seen for a very long time . . ." or words to that effect. Then on he went, seemingly finding it impossible to say anything good about anything or anyone. Whatever words he used, they weren't the sort of words one remembers, or one wants to remember, being said about a play with which one is happily and proudly associated. But whatever his actual words, they, needless to say, depressed us hugely, and when Mary and Vivienne came in, looking absolutely wonderful (it may have taken a long time, but the result was worth every minute), they both said in unison, "What on earth's the matter?" We all tried to tell them at the same time, but over the top of all our explanations came Tony's voice telling us that it was time we went over to Sardi's. "It's only just over Times Square so we won't take a cab, we'll walk," he announced firmly. Since all the company were quite sure by now that the play would be off by the weekend, if it got that far, economy was more than wise. Tony set off with Mary, Vivienne, and Kenneth, while Alan, John, and I followed.

On the way, I did what I had done so often over the years and that was to try and cheer up the one who had been hurt by comments or by notices. John had not been so much hurt by the critic we had just heard as battered by him. "Don't worry," I said to him. "After all, we've only heard one critic. There are still the papers, and I'm sure they won't be reacting in the sour way of the man on the radio. Who is he, anyway? Ignore him." John heard me out then said, "Well, it was a sellout in Leatherhead last week, anyway!" The thought that an excellent, though small, repertory theatre in Surrey had done wonderful business with his play cheered us up during the rest of our walk along the gloomy backstreet behind the theatre, and then we were in Times Square, which was ablaze with lights. Perhaps the contrast between the dark street that housed the grimy backstage wall of our theatre and the brilliantly lit Square was telling us something. Continuing to follow our leader, we soon found ourselves outside the famous Sardi's, the only place, Tony told us, to which everyone who was anyone had to go for supper after a first night.

## Scene 30 ℰ Sardi's Restaurant, New York

Tony, of course, organised our entrance into the restaurant: he led Mary and Vivienne, then Kenneth and Alan, and finally John and myself. As soon as Mary and Vivienne appeared — and it looked as if they had been especially chosen to be a complete contrast, with Mary pretty, petite, blonde, and appearing shy and Vivienne handsome, tall, dark, and exuding confidence (although I knew she didn't feel it) — the diners, who had turned in their seats to see the latecomers, immediately applauded. This took the dejected company completely by surprise and cheered all of us instantly. Tony pressed on and led us expertly to a long table against a wall around a corner at the further end of the room. Already seated were David Merrick, his assistant, David Pelham, his general manager, Jack Schlissel, Jack Livesey and his wife, the two understudies, and the stage management team. Tony arranged the seating quickly and neatly, and I found myself with Hal Stone, the stage manager, his wife, Toni, his assistant, and the two understudies, all safely tucked away in the further reaches.

Drinks were ordered, but our spirits, lifted by the opening applause, soon fell for we were all waiting for two events — the arrival of food and the arrival of the morning's newspapers. A further drink would have helped, but no more of that was seen after the first splurge. Time went by desperately slowly. Although we were starving, our little group down at the cheap end were enjoying ourselves, but I couldn't say the same for those at the expensive end. At last word reached us that David Pelham was going out to collect the papers, but once more it seemed an extremely long time before he reappeared. When he did, our hearts rose. He arrived with a huge smile that seemed to say it all. He put a great bundle of papers on the table, picked up the top copy, and held it open so that we could all see the headline: "Look Back Lights a Bonfire on Broadway!"

At once, menus were passed round, and certainly at our end, we gazed at all the tempting dishes on offer, but by that time we were far too tired to think of eating and soon we were thanking Mr. Merrick for a wonderful evening and setting off towards our various hotels or homes. Luckily, Sardi's and the Piccadilly were near neighbours.

## Scene 31 ❧ Final days with the *Look Back* Company, New York

The next day, there was no call, so I didn't meet the company until the evening, and I was able to wander round the shops, hoping I could find something I could take back for Elizabeth and the boys. Maybe I was just unlucky, but I found the attitude of the shop assistants from whom I sought help or advice was surly and uncaring — and our exchanges were always brief to the point of rudeness. It wasn't until I had made my way down Broadway to Macy's that I found someone who was kind, took time, and was extremely helpful. Pleased with my purchases, I went to the theatre to check whether Hal had any last-minute questions, but there was nothing else for me to do other than to say good-bye to everyone. This included a big guy on props whose name was Ralph. During the fit-up, he told me that he was an enormous (I could understand that adjective, as I studied his large, comfortable frame) fan of Oscar Wilde. "I've learned the whole of 'The Ballad of Reading Gaol,'" he told me with pride. I expressed surprise and true admiration. At the same time, I was wondering if he would appreciate being told how we in England pronounced the final two words of the title of the ballad or whether he would take exception. Since he was such a very likeable man, I decided not to say anything but continued to savour his Reading being pronounced as it is written and not as Redding, and his gaol becoming goal as in football, not jail as in prison.

Tony thanked me for all that I had done and gave me a long-playing record of *Bells Are Ringing*, which I managed to get safely home, although we had no record player. Several of the cast asked me when I was going back to London, to which I replied that I was leaving the stage door at three-thirty the following afternoon.

The reaction of the audience at the second performance was one of those chalk-and-cheese affairs compared to the previous one. "There you are," said Hal as we stood beside the stage and heard wonderful laughter coming from a packed house. "They know that this is a hit show and are treating it as such." As a farewell present, Hal had given me one of his fibre-tip pens. I had been admiring these useful objects, which had not yet reached England, because they wrote with broad strokes and would certainly be excellent for writing notices, such as on the board at the stage door at the Court, where it would be effortlessly eye-catching. There was also a good chance that writing with a pen would save typing errors such as I once saw on a call sheet on the board at the Shakespeare Memorial Theatre. The call was for *Othello*, but the key for one letter had not been struck, so the notice was cheerfully headed *O hello*.

By the time I left New York, Mary and John were the toast of the town, which made it all the more amazing when, just as I was going out to a waiting taxicab at the stage door, Mary and John appeared, slightly out-of-breath. "Oh, we thought we might have missed you," said Mary. "We wanted so much to wish you a safe journey and to say thank you for everything." At this, they each gave me presents, kissed me, and I went off in the cab. A great way to end a visit that was so very unlike my life at the Court.

## Scene 32 ◎ English Stage Company's productions, at the end of 1957

November saw the arrival of William Faulkner's play, *Requiem for a Nun*, directed by Tony Richardson and with the leading roles played by a husband-and-wife team from America, Zachary Scott and Ruth Ford. We hadn't heard of the latter, but the former was known through films. He proved a delightful person and the first I had come across who exercised the remarkable American facility of remembering, forever it seemed, the names of those to whom he was introduced. Ruth was rather grand and had every reason to be on many counts, especially for the fact that William Faulkner wrote this play for her. She was the star, even though we didn't acknowledge such a being — unless, of course, he happened to be an actor named Laurence Olivier.

There was a small bar between front-of-house and the dressing rooms that was useful for drinks after a show, and it was there one evening that Zachary brought our star to grace us with her presence. Those of us who were there were surprised and delighted. At last we could have a chat with them rather than brief conversations about matters to do with the play. Sadly, it was not long before they had to leave, so she charmingly shook hands with each of us before heading for the door that Zachary held open for her. As she reached it, she turned, suddenly and dramatically, extended one arm in a wide and gentle sweeping motion, and, as soon as a dead silence fell on the room, with the arm now at full stretch, she breathed, "I leave my love [pause] with you all." Great stuff. We quite missed her when the play reached the end of its thirty performance run that had produced a figure of 86 percent at the box office.

I met them again about six months later when Zachary, of course, not only remembered my name but even remembered to enquire after our first real car: it was a brand-new turquoise Morris Minor. It chanced that he had been looking out of the bow-fronted dressing-room window at the time when I drove in from Sloane Square the first evening after I had bought it. It replaced the faithful taxi that I sold (for £5 more than I had paid for it) during the run of *Requiem for a Nun*. I didn't see Zachary again after that chance meeting, but memories of those days came rushing back nearly forty years later when I was enjoying a two-week residency in the drama department of the University of Texas at Austin. My early morning walks — before it got too hot for walking — always took me along the marvellous footpaths that had been organised by Lady Bird Johnson on the banks of the lower Colorado River, which flowed past my hotel. One of my journeys took me further along the northern side than I had ventured before. So for the first time, I saw a signpost that pointed towards the Zachary Scott Theatre. And soon there it was, a small neat building, certainly not at the hub of Austin, nor anywhere near the hub, but it was a theatre, named after a good actor and a charming man, and that doesn't happen to many.

We hadn't seen Percy Harris since her sensational black-and-white designs for *The Country Wife,* so it was good to see her back for *Requiem for a Nun* with four cool, clean-lined, elegant sets, and it was also good to meet the large, warm, cheerful Bertice Reading, who was stepping off the nightclub circuit to play the role of Nancy Mannigoe. She pronounced her surname as Redding. I so often thought of Ralph at the Lyceum whenever Bertice was around.

## Scene 33 ❧ *Lysistrata*, December 1957

It was an unusual Boxing Day for us in 1957, for, on December 26, we opened Aristophanes' *Lysistrata.* It was directed by a young, assured Greek, Minos Volanakis. We had heard of him, for he had founded the first Theatre-in-the-Round in Athens, and when later Stephen Joseph introduced Theatre-in-the-Round to England, Minos directed its first two productions. To us, the setting was huge, with acting areas on three levels. It was designed, appropriately, by another Greek, Nicholas Georgiadis. Along with its dizzying height, there was also a dizzying number in the cast. In addition to Joan Greenwood, whom I was delighted to welcome back, there were twenty-four others. Not even by squeezing could they all be housed in the four dressing rooms, so I had to woo Picky to allow us to spread up into her territory. I could see she was about to protest, but she relented, and I put a crowd of the young men up there. Perhaps it was the crowded conditions, but all was not sweetness and light in the wardrobe/dressing room. At one performance I was sent to part two young actors, who were having a real battle of fisticuffs. I had never before dealt with a fight such as this, so I was more than glad when peace was restored.

The show was a huge success at the Court where it played fifty-three performances, clocking up the same figure — 98 percent of seats sold — as *The Entertainer* had achieved earlier in the year; however, *The Entertainer* had only played thirty-six performances. By the middle of February 1958, *Lysistrata* had transferred to the Duke of York's Theatre in St. Martin's Lane. I could only hope for everyone's sake that there were more dressing rooms to house the actors comfortably.

## Scene 34 ✎ Spring and summer at the Royal Court Theatre, 1958

After the songs, dances, and general fun of Minos's production, to say nothing of the packed houses, we were brought sharply down to earth on February 11 with the arrival of John Osborne's third play, although this time Anthony Creighton's name followed John's since it was joint authorship. This excellent play, *Epitaph for George Dillon*, well directed by William Gaskill, saw Stephen Doncaster leaving his post as head of wardrobe and, for the first time since his set design for *The Crucible* almost two years earlier, being appointed the designer for John and Tony's play. Once again he came up with a cunning design that managed to show almost the whole of the ground floor of a typical family home at that time. He achieved this by setting a corner of the main acting area, the living room, downstage centre, which presented the audience with a diamond-shaped as opposed to a square room. The two downstage walls were only indicated and not built, as were the two upstage ones. *Epitaph for George Dillon* played thirty-eight performances at the Court, with a box office of 46 percent, but even so it became yet another production that moved to the West End. Here, at the Comedy Theatre, it ran for only six weeks from the end of May to the middle of July 1958. A short run under a shortened title in the hope that *George Dillon* might be more palatable to West End audiences.

Back at the Court, once *George Dillon* had moved out, we presented Barry Reckord's *Flesh to a Tiger*. The cast were black, mainly of West Indian origin, except for Edgar Wreford and the very white kid goat, whom I named Mr. Trench. The black actors seemed to know each other and were very enthusiastic, greatly encouraged by the indefatigable Tony Richardson, who was directing the play. But understanding many of them was another matter. Although the actors in this group were speaking English, it was a dialect that English audiences found nearly incomprehensible. An unusual stress on certain words in a sentence, their speech rhythms, and the West Indian accent were alien to theatregoers. Although the individual performances were very good, and although there was a brief glossary in the programme of some of the more unusual terms used in the production, nothing could make the dialogue come across with clarity.

The play went out on a short tour: I caught up with it in Cardiff where the cast reported that several of them had had great difficulty in finding lodgings. All had booked in advance into theatrical digs or small hotels around town, but when the front doors were opened, it wasn't unusual to be told that, unexpectedly, the room was no longer available, and with mumbled apologies, the door was firmly shut.

A project George had favoured from the start was inviting regional repertory companies to play at the Court for a week. The first such season occupied the theatre during July 1958, when the Glasgow Citizens', Belgrade Coventry, Salisbury Playhouse, and Leatherhead Repertory (where *Look Back in Anger,* as reported by John Osborne, had been so successful the previous year) each played a week. The production from the Belgrade collected the most and well-deserved praise: This was Arnold Wesker's *Chicken Soup with Barley,* directed by John Dexter.

## Scene 35 ❧ *End-Game* and *Krapp's Last Tape,* October 1958

At the end of October 1958, the close links George had with Samuel Beckett resulted in yet another of the double bills that still seemed to dog our footsteps. Since we had presented the French version of *End-Game* eighteen months earlier, Beckett had been working on an

English translation, with a hyphenated title now often dropped. George Devine was determined that we should be the first to present this version and that when we did, he would direct and also play the role of Hamm. This time, the double bill would not be the same as before; *Acte sans Paroles* being dropped in favour of a new play by Beckett, *Krapp's Last Tape*. He had written it in English especially for the rasping-voiced Patrick Magee. It would be directed by Donald McWhinnie.

I suppose of all the productions at the Court at which the public showed its displeasure, the laurel must be divided between Samuel Beckett's *End-Game* and *Krapp's Last Tape*. The very noisy exits from both plays by many of the small audiences (thirty-eight performances produced a box office figure of 28 percent) could not be ignored, for the old tip-up seats made a very loud clonk as they righted themselves, which must have been very satisfactory to those grumpily leaving. If the seats didn't tip-up of their own accord, then kicking them out of the way was obviously even more satisfying to the dissatisfied public. I think it must have been the visible and audible reactions of the public that made George change the order of the productions. Anyway, a short while into the run, *Krapp's Last Tape* preceded *End-Game* rather than following it.

But wherever *End-Game* was placed, and in spite of excellent performances — George correctly always knew that he had found the perfect Clov in Jack MacGowran — the choice of play did not find favour with the public. Perhaps it might just have tolerated a tale in which an autocratic blind man sits in a wheelchair centre stage while his servant runs many errands, which includes climbing a ladder a number of times to look out of a tiny window high up in the unadorned wall — only to report that he could see nothing. But what about Nagg and Nell? What on earth were they, parents to Hamm, doing at the side of the stage, each encased in a dustbin?

## Scene 36 ⋐ The Burt Lancaster affair

A bizarre letter from British Actors Equity was sent to Burt Lancaster, one of our hardworking assistant stage managers at the Court. It was an order to change his name because Equity did not want misunderstandings with the other Burt Lancaster, the extremely well known and very popular American film star. I suggested to Burt that he write back to say surely no one is going to think that this famous actor had come over to England and was working as an assistant stage manager at the Court. Equity remained adamant, so all I could then suggest was an extension to his first name and make it Burton. Burt, who told me that Burt really was his first name and really was spelt that way, most unwillingly agreed, but I hope that he wasn't made to keep it too long.

## Scene 37 ✥ The Long and the Short and the Tall, December 1958

December found the theatre busy by day for a week when Lindsay Anderson arrived to direct the Willis Hall play *The Long and the Short and the Tall*. Albert Finney was to play a soldier in the British army, with the lowly rank of private, named in the programme as "Pte. Bamforth, C." Also in Lindsay's strong cast were Robert Shaw, Edward Judd, Ronald Fraser, David Andrews, Alfred Lynch, Bryan Pringle, and Kenji Takaki. But Lindsay did not have a good start: He seemed curiously unsure regarding any aspect of the production and especially in his attitude towards the actors and their roles. The cast worked as well as was possible, and so the first week dragged by. At the weekend, Albert, who had not been feeling well, was diagnosed as needing an immediate appendix operation, and therefore he had to withdraw from the production. At once, the brakes were applied to the show, and for a while it seemed that it would be shelved indefinitely. Then the name of Peter O'Toole was mentioned. Peter had recently had great success at the Garrick Theatre in *O My Papa* that had transferred from the Bristol Old Vic Theatre where he had been enjoying an excellent season in a variety of roles. It wasn't long before *The Long and the Short and the Tall* was back in the schedule with the cast as before, except for the replacement of Albert by Peter.

The short break did wonders for Lindsay. He arrived for the first of the resumed rehearsals with utter confidence and great good humour and although the latter did not always last throughout a rehearsal, that was Lindsay. It was lucky for me that, from his production of Kathleen

Sully's *The Waiting of Lester Abbs* in June 1957, which was his first for the English Stage Company at the Court, he and I had got along very well. I sometimes wondered if our good relationship was due to our original meeting, when I was able to voice a comment I had been wanting to make to him ever since I saw his excellent movie, *This Sporting Life*. I had said, "I did so admire the way sounds from the next scene could be heard while one was watching the last few moments of the previous one. It was like a seamless handover in a relay race, and as I say this to you, I realise that this metaphor is more apt than I realised it would be, for your changeovers between scenes made the whole film race along with tremendous speed and skill." "Oh, thank you," he had said, but he glanced up at me to make sure I wasn't making fun of his film. It must have been obvious that I wasn't, for he very quickly smiled with pleasure.

Unlike *The Waiting of Lester Abbs*, which arrived under the banner of a Sunday night "production without décor," Alan Tagg's jungle took over the stage for *The Long and the Short and the Tall*, leaving just enough space for the hut, in which the action of the play would take place, to be constructed. The play was an instant success with the main focus centred on Peter's performance, but as a piece of ensemble acting, it was a gem. Each of the British soldiers had a role that was strongly written, and Lindsay made sure that each actor's character, especially that of the nonspeaking Japanese soldier, came over equally strongly. It was interesting that the public could welcome a play that was set in the Malayan jungle at the beginning of January 1942, thus making it happen about halfway through the Second World War, and without a woman in sight.

Very early on in the rehearsal period, Peter had asked me if he could have permission on a Friday in January to go to Birmingham where his sister was getting married. Because he had not known he would be playing at the Court on the date in question, arrangements had been made for him to be actively involved in the wedding. Knowing that Birmingham was only about one hundred or so miles up the M1 motorway, this seemed not unreasonable, so with Peter promising to be back by seven for an eight o'clock curtain, I said that would be fine and thought no more about it, until he reminded me on the evening before the event.

The next day, seven o'clock came and went, but no Peter. It was raining hard but that didn't give me cause for alarm, although I must confess I did get slightly concerned when seven-fifteen brought no sign nor any word from him. At the half hour call, that is at 7:25 PM, Burt Lancaster, who was the assistant stage manager on this show, reported that Peter was missing. "That's all right," I said with total calm. "I knew he would be a little late this evening, but I will keep a lookout for him and let you know when he arrives."

Five minutes later, still with no sign, I asked Burt to alert the understudies, and I went to the stage door hoping that I could somehow conjure up my missing actor. Very shortly afterwards, I found Oscar Lewenstein, who, in association with the English Stage Company and Wolf Mankowitz, was presenting the play, standing beside me. "What's this I hear about O'Toole?" he asked. "He's on his way back from Birmingham where he has been to his sister's wedding," I replied in my everything-is-perfectly-all-right-I-can't-think-why-you're-asking-me voice. Before Oscar could say anything, I ploughed on, "He is a little late, but I am expecting him at any minute." I had an inkling that I wasn't fooling Oscar, which proved to be an accurate assessment, for he spluttered out, "What do you mean by giving him permission? Did you consult anyone else about this? It is disgraceful. What are you going to do about it?"

Indeed, what was I going to do about it? Feeling a mite guilty and a trifle let down, I could have done with Oscar being in Birmingham and Peter standing by my side. But I was not going to give in just yet. "The understudies are getting ready," I said, as if that was the answer Oscar wanted, although I knew the only one he wished to hear was my telling him that Peter, his star, would be playing that evening. I could see the chances of that happening receding rapidly.

Time raced by, and I knew that I would soon hear over the Tannoy sound system the stage manager calling down the actors who had to be onstage when the curtain rose on the first scene. For this play, that call would affect the entire cast, except for Kenji Takaki, playing the Japanese soldier, and tonight, it seemed it would also be without Peter O'Toole playing Private Bamforth. Sure enough, the dreaded call, the beginners call, came over the Tannoy at 7:55 PM.

At exactly the same moment, I saw the most wonderful sight. There was Peter, in full wedding gear, running down the lane leading from Sloane Square to the stage door. "Sorry I'm late," he threw at Oscar and myself as he raced past and up to the dressing room. I happily left Oscar and hared down to the prompt corner, where I told Paul Stone, my wonderful stage manager, that he must expect the curtain to go up a little late, while Burt went scurrying off to make sure the understudies knew that they could now relax since everything was back to normal. At 8:04 PM the curtain rose.

Briefly, Peter's story was that all had gone well until, during the morning, it started snowing. It didn't stop the church ceremony, but when they reached the reception and it was still snowing, heavily by this time, they phoned the station to ask if the trains were running on time. No, the trains had stopped. Then to the Automobile Association to check on the roads, but the report was that any road travel beyond Birmingham's outskirts was extremely unwise. And so to the airport. No, there was no scheduled flight to Heathrow that afternoon, but a plane could be chartered.

At once the bride's brand-new father-in-law said that he would settle any cost incurred and that Peter must order the plane at once. This was done and soon Peter and the best man were winging their way south with Peter confident that he would be in plenty of time for the show. He hadn't counted on a written report from the captain of the plane to say they had not been given permission to land at Heathrow, and so they must fly onto a landing strip at Hartley Whitney in Hampshire. They touched down in a snowstorm about six-thirty, whereupon Peter and the best man raced to a hired car. Peter said, "We've got to get to Sloane Square by seven-thirty. Can you do it?" The driver replied, "I'll try, but it's a good thirty-five miles." They were in the car and away. There was no M3 motorway then or even a dual-carriage road to help the driver, and although it was fortunate that the majority of cars were coming towards them, leaving a reasonably car-free road ahead most of the time, the disadvantage was the reflection on the wet road of the endless headlights facing them.

My relations with Oscar had never been warm. They were now ice-cold.

## Scene 38 ✪ Last Days at the Court

After I had spent three years at the Court, Martin Case, who was manager at the Comedy Theatre in Panton Street, very much in the heart of London since it is within a few hundred yards of Piccadilly Circus, got in touch to say that he was moving to Rediffusion, a television company, and he would like to suggest to Mr. H. H. Wingate, the owner of the Comedy, that I take over. He said that he was certain that Mr. Wingate would accept anyone that he nominated, so all I had to do was to say yes, and the job would be mine. He was leaving on February 7, so could I start, if I wanted to go there, on Monday, February 9?

After some years with Tennent Productions and other West End managements as a stage manager or company manager, I had a good knowledge of what being a West End theatre manager entailed, and as I had several friends already in that position, I was sure I could call on them if I struck a problem I couldn't immediately solve. On the other hand, it would mean leaving the Court where I had been so wonderfully happy and so fully employed at all times, but there were two points about staying that tilted me towards the job at the Comedy. Firstly, I was very tired — often working seven days a week and often through the night in a job that demanded both hard physical and mental work. When I looked at myself, I wondered whether I would be able to continue to give the Court all that I had been giving if I stayed on, say, another three years.

Secondly, the Court had become very political. Perhaps I was too blinkered in that all I could think about was the theatre, the smooth running of the productions, and trying to ensure that everyone who worked at the Court were well looked after and as happy within the atmosphere of that wonderful little theatre as possible. Perhaps I was wrong to ignore life outside, but there were many around me who did not ignore events in the country. Many conversations were heated arguments about Aldermarston, the House of Commons, nuclear warheads, the prime minister, and the Cabinet. For my taste, far too many theatre members were expending their energies on marches in the country and in London, and thus not giving as much time and thought to the Court as I felt they should.

Of course, Elizabeth and I talked over the offer, and when she said that she didn't think I would be alive much longer if I continued at the Court, I knew that I should say yes to Martin and immediately give in my notice. From the financial angle, I couldn't afford to take a break between jobs. So when I noticed that there was a Sunday night "Production without Decor" (capital letters had crept in to the title) on Sunday, February 8, I said I would see that that play was all right and finish at the end of its performance. I would start at the Comedy the following day.

I phoned up to George's office the next morning, and yes, it was a good time if I wanted to go up to see him. His room was reached through a door on the upper circle foyer level that opened directly onto a short flight of stairs that curved to the right at the top. There one found oneself facing a small, narrow room, which had just enough space at the further end for a desk. Behind it was a chair for George, and in front of it a chair for visitors. Between the top of the stairs and the desk was a small table with banquette seating on two sides, plus a chair or two. In the days when I was allocated this room for a while, I found that, unless visitors announced themselves as they opened the door at the foot of the stairs, I never knew who was going to appear until they reached the top and swung round into the room. The placing of the desk had the great advantage that it looked out onto Sloane Square. It was good, while taking a telephone call, to watch the traffic easing itself around the Square.

I reported as briefly as I could my decision to leave. I did not mention my feelings regarding the political leaning within the company. I gave my reasons for wishing to go as firstly, a good opportunity for me to experience another side of theatre and secondly, Elizabeth's real concern about my ability to stay the course much longer. George looked at me through his horn-rimmed spectacles without speaking, and even when I stopped, he puffed at his pipe for a moment or two before he said how very sorry he was to hear the news. He quite understood, he said, and he wouldn't try to dissuade me for he knew me well enough to know that I was not rushing into anything without giving it deep thought.

We then spoke of the actual date for my going and who might be considered as a replacement. I got up and he turned to the desk. "I shall miss you," he said.

The Sunday night production, my swan song, was *Progress to the Park* by Alun Owen, an old friend and someone who had been around the Court a lot. The setting needed for this play was a practical window, but this was only to be a flat, in which was set the window and a small rostrum. The real snag was that it meant a complete strike of Alan Tagg's *The Long and the Short and the Tall* jungle, but this was eventually stored away, leaving a bare stage. Sunday held little more than setting the window with the director, Lindsay Anderson, and lighting the play. Peter Theobald, the lighting consultant and board operator, who had been not very cooperative for some time, became more and more difficult during the day, until he finally announced that if I didn't agree to one of the terms he had demanded as a condition to his staying, he would leave.

"I think you had better leave then," I said, and he did. This meant that there was no one to operate the lighting board that evening, although the lighting had been set. To save any worries, I didn't tell anyone that Peter had gone, so when rehearsals were over, I squeezed into the very small space in a corner of the balcony, where the compact lighting board had been placed, and experimented with the dimmers that controlled the lights. There were luckily no cues that would dramatically change the lighting, but only gentle ones that moved the focus of attention. During the actual performance, I worked on the principle of looking down to see whether the actors were sufficiently lit and if not, I would very slowly slide up a dimmer until the effect was better. If I chanced to be bringing up a lamp that I could see was way off the mark and about to light an area that was meant to be shadowy, then, as slowly, that dimmer went down and a new one would be brought up. After the show, no one complained or commented.

Two days before that eventful last day, I was clearing up in my office when a phone call asked me to go up to George Devine's room. On my way, I imagined George had sent for me to say farewell, but when I got to the top of the stairs, having announced myself from the door, I found Neville Blond, the chairman of the council, and Greville Poke with George. How extremely kind of them, I thought, they must have come to say good-bye. In a moment, I realised this was exactly why they were there. Mr. Blond was excessively complimentary about my contribution to the success of the English Stage Company, and then, and this did surprise me, I was presented with three beautiful silver Armada plates, one inscribed, "With best wishes and appreciation from the English Stage Company 1959." But if this was a surprise, another one awaited me, for when Neville Blond suggested we go down for a drink at the bar, it was indicated that I should go first. When I opened the door at the foot of the stairs, I saw why. The bar was absolutely packed with members of the company and staff, and in the centre was Elizabeth standing by the general manager, Pieter Rogers. I was embarrassed by having to listen to another very kind speech, this time given by Pieter, and then I was loaded with gifts, not only for myself but also for Elizabeth and for our two boys. I am sure it was Pieter who had organised it all so splendidly, for I think he would have enjoyed somehow keeping the crowds out of my sight on my way up to the office and then getting them assembled silently in the bar before I came down. It was a great occasion, and I was so grateful to everyone and especially to George Devine.

## Scene 39 ❧ George Devine

I don't think any of us who worked at the Court during the first three years of the English Stage Company could have had a better artistic director than George. Certainly for myself, I know I couldn't possibly have achieved all that I was able to achieve without being aware that George was somewhere around and that his knowledge of the theatre, his wisdom, his attitude to those who worked for him, his calm approach to life, and his availability would help me solve any unexpected problem. Naturally, my pride and the thought that he was busy held me back from going to him unless it was absolutely vital. When I did, the problem was always resolved easily and quickly.

During all the years George and I were treading the same theatrical path, we never had a social conversation: We only talked and discussed items that sprang from whatever productions we were involved with at the time or, when we got to the Court, were coming along in the future. For years I always thought of him and addressed him as

Mr. Devine, and I found it almost impossible to make the change to George when he insisted I call him by that name.

We only once had a disagreement. It was during a technical rehearsal with George and Tony Richardson sitting in their favourite seats in the dress circle from where they called comments on what we were showing them. All of us on the stage side of the house curtain had been in the theatre since early on Sunday morning, and now it was about 3:30 AM on Monday. Ted Bolton tracked me down and said that the day jobs of himself and his brother, Alf, meant they had to be on duty reading electricity meters at 7:30 AM, and although they would like to stay, they really had to go and get a little rest. They assured me, as if I didn't know already, that they would be back in the theatre as soon as they finished the meter work for the day. Bob Davies then appeared and said that he too felt he had to get a little sleep before his daytime job began, and so I went to the circle and said to George, "I am very sorry, but the boys simply have to go home now, and as I know you realise, we cannot go on without them. So may we please stop now and start again a little later this morning?"

To my surprise, the understanding George was not understanding at all. "They can't go," he said very pleasantly, as if that would seal their staying. "We shall be another hour or two, and then they can go." "Once again," I said, "I am very sorry, but I'm afraid that they have to. We are lucky that they have stayed as long as they have."

"This is quite ridiculous," said George, with a marked change of tone. He continued in this vein, until at last unwillingly, I chipped in with, "It's no good, Mr. Devine. I am going back to thank them and to tell them to get off and be back as soon as they can." I left George, and shortly afterwards, all the staff and stage management had gone. Seeing that George and Tony had left the circle, I switched out the working lights and also went home. This little incident, witnessed only by Tony, was never mentioned again nor did it make any difference to the excellent relationship between George and myself. He was far too good a manager not to know when he had to accept a situation such as this — even if it had taken a moment or two longer than I had anticipated.

Once I had left the Court in February 1959, I never saw George again. At first, when I was at the Comedy Theatre, I knew that he would be as busy as ever at the Court, after which I was over ninety miles away at the Shakespeare Memorial Theatre in Stratford, only coming back to London for brief visits to the Aldwych. When I heard he was ill, I would have liked to have been able to see him, but I was not only totally occupied at the Aldwych, I also thought he might have forgotten me after several hectic years. I felt the news of his death very deeply: It seemed plain, looking at the situation from the outside, that he had worked and worried himself to death. Laudable though it was to work with such intensity in order, as he must have thought and doubtless he was right, to keep the English Stage Company operating as he wanted it to operate, it seemed that he was one of those whose loss to the theatre was incalculable. A great man — and I was so fortunate to have been able to work with him and for him.

# Act Two

## The Comedy Theatre, Panton Street, 1959 to 1960

Appointed manager of the Comedy Theatre, a few hundred yards from Piccadilly Circus. Stage management is left behind, and attention is moved from the actors and plays to patrons, staff, catering, and the fabric of the building. On the stage, productions such as *Five Finger Exercise, A Passage to India,* and *Rosmersholm.*

### Scene 1 ✎ Starting at the Comedy Theatre, February 1959

Moving from the Royal Court to the Comedy Theatre made me think of Mrs. Patrick Campbell's delicious remark, "Oh, the deep, deep peace of the double bed after the hurly-burly of the chaise longue." After three years of hurly-burly, the peace at the Comedy Theatre was extraordinary. The building only really woke up when the ushers, usherettes, and bar staff came in of an evening to the front-of-house, while the cast, stage management, and show staff came in backstage. There was one other member of the evening staff, but he was mainly an outsider. He was the linkman, and his job was to find a parking space for the patron arriving by car, to hold taxi doors open for the patrons on arrival, and to hail taxis at the end of the performance. Generally, he was there to assist the arrival and departure of patrons and, as a sideline, to answer endless questions from passersby. The curious title of this job goes back many years to the days when such an employee would, as now, assist patrons. He would do this by lighting their way as they approached the theatre by carriage, sedan chair, or other means of transport. There being no street lighting, he would create light by holding aloft a link. This was a flaming torch made of pitch (a semiliquid form of black tar — hence the expression "pitch-black" when referring to a dark night) and tow (a form of hemp). The combination, when lit, gave a good and lasting light.

The cleaners' times were early morning, so they were reaching the end of their work by the time I arrived at 10:00 AM. Then silence took over the auditorium. The two ladies in the box office kept up the constant sound of cheerful chatter, but it barely reached the foyer, while backstage, the very few full-time staff went silently about their maintenance work and preparing for the next performance.

The Comedy Theatre fronts on to Panton Street, and it was only a few yards along that street towards Haymarket that I had to walk for my first job of the day. On five mornings a week, I had to pay in the previous night's box office and catering takings, plus, once a week, the cash from the telephone call box. There was only one public telephone in the theatre, which was well placed in the quiet corridor on the way to the boxes on the right-hand side of the auditorium. On Saturdays, except during term time, our elder son, Guy, used to come up to the theatre with me and amongst the many jobs I could find for him that helped me was emptying the phone box's cash container. The cash then had to be sorted into its various denominations and counted before the final task of adding these sums up to produce the amount taken during the week. It was often surprising how many calls had been made.

I enjoyed my time at the Comedy. Again a good staff, although the "casuals" (that is, those who were engaged for duties during performances only) came and went with varying degrees of notice. I soon learned to say to myself, "Well, that was a thoroughly good evening with the front-of-house staff in top form, but how many of tonight's excellent team will be here tomorrow?"

It gave me great pleasure working for Mr. H. H. Wingate. He was a short, dapper businessman and a successful one at that. I didn't realise how fortunate I was to be totally in control of his theatre, whereas friends who managed theatres that were part of a chain had to obey orders coming down from head office whether or not they were suitable for every theatre in the group. Not only did Mr. Wingate own the Comedy, but he really loved the theatre — when it was empty. He never came to a performance, for the public were, in his eyes, defiling the place. Once a month, he came to view his property, and it was then, as we walked around the whole building, that I was able to point out how this room or this corridor or this length of wall now needed attention — whether repair, replacement, or general refurbishment. If the work would enhance the appearance of the area concerned, then he never demurred. As soon as possible after the visit, I would talk to the readily cooperative and excellent craftsman, Mr. Cooper, and soon the work would start. Mr. Cooper (he was always Mr. Cooper, I never knew his first name) was Mr. Wingate's right-hand man on the maintenance side within the Wingate empire — which consisted, among other properties, of the extremely comfortable Curzon Cinema, which was situated close by his offices in Chesterfield Street, Mayfair.

I was sorry at times that I was now working in a West End theatre where there was no loyal audience who came to as many productions as possible and who therefore noticed alterations and improvements to the front-of-house, as happened at the Court. After Alan Tagg designed a new colour scheme for the auditorium there, the change was noticed at once and commented upon favourably by many. This is perhaps not a good example, for the difference was so very marked and the result so good. But at the Comedy, I felt that everyone who came to a performance was coming to this theatre for the first and possibly the last time. Therefore I made sure that the whole theatre was kept spick and span at all times. This was done with the hard work of a splendid team of cleaners, which included Danny Buckley, amongst whose jobs was brass cleaning. I added to the amount of brass he had to clean by getting him to attack the large brass plates, set into the green carpeting, that covered the opening and closing mechanism of the doors leading into the auditorium. When Danny had finished polishing them, he and I agreed that they looked wonderful, and we didn't care how many members of the audience noticed them. We enjoyed looking at them, and so did Mr. Wingate on his next visit.

Mr. Wingate also noticed that I had had the stable door of the foyer cloakroom repositioned. The lower half supported a shelf on which patrons would rest their coats when handing them in on arrival. However, the upper half of the door had been hinged so that the attendant had to move round it to get to the coat hooks. After I gave it a brief time-and-motion study, Mr. Cooper swung into action and changed the hinges to the other side of the half door, and soon a delighted attendant was commenting how less tired she was now that the coat hooks were so close.

When Mr. Wingate had had a good look around the theatre, we then went out to lunch, which meant going to the Grill & Griddle on the first floor of the Lyons Corner House in Coventry Street. One could get a very good meal there at the usual Lyons reasonable price, though not quite as reasonable as meals being eaten by those who were seated in the large room on the ground floor. By chance, the day of one of his visits coincided with an announcement in the press that he had joined the ranks of millionaires. We were far too busy to think of this state of his affairs during our theatre tour, and I didn't find an opportunity over lunch somehow to congratulate him. Anyway, it couldn't have happened overnight, with Mr. Wingate saying to Mrs. Wingate, "If you can hold off payment to Fortnum and Mason for a few days, we will go over the million mark." However, when I asked the waitress for the bill and she placed it in front of me, he leaned over, took the bill, and said, for the first and only time, "After what they say about me in the papers, I suppose *I* had better settle this."

I felt very fortunate now to have an office of my own and of a fair size so that I could entertain there when necessary. It also had the advantage of being a short distance from one of the many boxes, which, if unsold, was useful, since I could make a quick auditorium check to see whether the majority of the audience was seated, especially at the end of an interval. Better still was the short distance from my office to the foyer and box office: These were the areas I visited the most, so their proximity was enormously helpful. I could also always check on the weather for the office had a good-sized window — a change from the early days at the Court.

What I missed very much at the Comedy was the contact with actors, so I started calling in on the occupants of the dressing rooms once or twice a week. During these visits, I could see that all was well, tell them any reactions I had heard from patrons leaving the theatre, and let them know in broad terms what the houses had been like and how the box office was doing in advance sales. The backstage part of the theatre had been damaged in the Second World War, but eventually it had been pulled down and a new dressing-room block was built with offices, independent of the theatre, above. Whenever I was walking around the two floors of dressing rooms, I remembered the dark and depressing room on this site that Larry Skikne (the change to Laurence Harvey was still a few years away) and I had to share for a Services Sunday Society/Reunion Theatre Guild performance in 1946 in which he was acting and I was appearing. I also remembered how, if we wanted to wash, we had to go to the landing where there was a cold water tap over a basin or, to be exact, a cleaner's shallow sink. This was inconveniently placed under a flight of stairs, so that one had to be careful, after bending over the sink, not to straighten up too sharply or one got a hearty crack on the back of the head.

In the Comedy Theatre's post-war rebuilding programme, the stage door was moved from the back of the building to the side on Oxenden Street — up a few steps and there was a good-sized room for the stage-door-keeper. The firemen had not been forgotten, for across the hall, they had been allocated a small room that was well furnished, including a bed and a little electric oven. There were two firemen working alternate days on a twenty-four-hour shift basis, but they never met for they didn't like each other. The system they had worked out was that, at the daily changeover time, the outgoing one would go into the stage-door-keeper's room, while the incoming one went straight to the fireman's room. As soon as that door shut, the one at the stage door went quickly down the steps into Oxendon Street and away at speed.

The constant complaint from the tidy one was the terrible state in which their room was left by the untidy one. This reached a climax one day when the tidy one, meeting me backstage, poured forth the usual stories as to what sins the untidy one had committed, which ended when I was told, "Oh, 'e's very laxative about 'is job, Mr. 'allifax."

When I started at the Comedy, the day's work for the very elderly stage-door-keeper was split into a morning shift, time off in the afternoon, then back for the evening shift. He lived in Richmond, reasonably close to the station, but the time he spent travelling cut deeply into his afternoon break, which he spent at home. I therefore suggested that he take his break during the morning, instead of the afternoon.

This would mean that he would not have to leave his home until lunchtime and once at the theatre, he could stay for the remainder of the day. This arrangement affected the firemen because they manned the stage door when the stage doorkeeper was not on duty, so they had to be consulted. I had to approach them separately, of course, but they both agreed at once, each saying that they were on duty in the theatre anyway, so whether they acted as stage-door-keeper in the morning or the afternoon made no difference. It was such a pleasure and a relief to get their separate agreements. The system was put into operation immediately, and I'm glad to say worked well.

I wished I could help the elder of the two firemen, for he too was getting on in years. I often worried what would happen if there were a fire, say, in the balcony (the second floor above street level). The worry wasn't whether he could deal with the fire — for he, like his mate, had been a professional fireman — but whether he could climb up there. The second worry was, if he did eventually manage the climb, whether he would have any breath left to deal with the incident.

They both had a habit I couldn't get them to shake off. After every evening performance, they had to chain and padlock every exterior door in the building. The fireman on duty would collect all the chains and padlocks long before the end of a show, thread his way through to the front-of-house, finally to stand by an exit door, ready to chain and pad-lock once the audience had been hustled out into the street. All this was fine, but on the stroll through to the front, both firemen managed to jangle the chains in such a way that the irritating sound could be heard in the auditorium. If a play's final scene was a quiet one, this noise was the last sound an audience wanted to hear. When asked repeatedly not to do this, they both obliged for a day or two, then it was clink-clank-clink again.

## Scene 2 ⊗ Learning a new side to the profession at the Comedy Theatre

At the Comedy Theatre I learned much about another side of the theatre that I had only witnessed from the outside: how intensely irritating the public could be when booking a seat at the box office. After dithering indecisively for several minutes, the person peering through the shiny brass bars at a remarkably patient clerk would finally and firmly decide that it was, after all, the evening performance on the following Wednesday for which she wanted two tickets. With relief, the clerk would pull the book of tickets for that performance from its pigeonhole and tear out two tickets. Far too often the sound of those tickets being parted from their stubs would immediately prompt a little cry from the other side of the grill. "Did I say Wednesday? I am so sorry but of course that is the day when Dora goes home, so would you remind me what seats were available on the Tuesday." One awkward person could so upset the clerk that his annoyance would be passed on to the next several people in the queue.

I also learned how it was possible for an usherette to make a bit on the side by accepting a £1 note (a not inconsiderable sum) and sometimes even a £5 note (a very considerable sum) in payment for a handful of programmes. This would be proffered by the host of a party of four or six, to whom the usherette would say to his departing back as he organised his party into their seats, "I'm sorry, sir, I haven't the change at the moment, but I will give it to you in the interval." As often as not, I'd be telephoned the next morning by a patron saying that the promised change had not been handed over during the interval and would I please send the money at once. I would apologise and then ask where the patron had been sitting. That evening I would mention this phone call to the usherette in charge of that row, and immediately the money would be forthcoming. "Oh, that's right. I looked for him during the interval, but I couldn't find him. I've got his change here in this other pocket." And out would come the correct sum, which I am sure, if I had not been contacted, would have stayed in that other pocket for several days before it was absorbed into her purse.

Then there was the bar staff. The speed with which drinks were dispensed was amazing, but even more amazing was the memory of the bartender. If I asked whether an interval had been busy, the answer would always be on the lines of, "Here, there were two whiskies and an orange juice; here, two gin and tonics and two sherries." And so it would go, with the exact spot at which the various drinks had been ordered pointed out. When I first went into one of the four bars, I noticed that they used an old-fashioned method for measuring spirits, such as whisky, gin, and so on. The modern method was to equip bars with optics whereby the customer can see the liquid dropping from an inverted bottle into a glass container. Once the container is full, it is released into a glass. At the Comedy, spirits were measured by pouring the drink out of its bottle into a little pewter measuring jug and from there into a glass. That appeared quite straightforward, until I learnt that it was possible to press a silver sixpenny piece into the base of the pewter jug (pewter being a soft metal) where it would be held secure. Thus, each time the jug was used, not quite the full amount of spirits went into the glass and soon the amount displaced by the sixpence was equal to a full bottle. This bottle would be spirited away under cover of a raincoat and darkness, and — surprise, surprise — there would be no discrepancy at the next stock-taking.

The Comedy Theatre ran its own catering, instead of engaging an outside catering firm. After I had been at the Comedy a short while, the catering manager or manageress, as she was called in those days, gave her notice, and I was allowed to appoint her replacement. I chose Joy Fairgrieve. Joy's name was well chosen for she was a joy to work with, and soon the catering side of the theatre was spinning along extremely well. She oversaw the staff in the bars and the cloakrooms, both engaged and was in charge of the usherettes (few, if any, ushers then), kept the accounts, and ordered stocks of confectionery, drinks, and programmes.

The usherettes sold the programmes and when a show was due to close, the game was to see how few programmes were left after the last performance without any patron having to be told, "I'm sorry, but we've sold out." I would advise Joy, as a last night hove into view, how the booking was going for the final few performances, while on the very last night, I would keep a beady eye on whether my predictions were going to be correct. It wasn't unusual for me to be told by the usherettes on one level that their stock of programmes was running dangerously low, which would mean my racing up a floor or two to check with the girls up there. If they said it looked as if they would have plenty left over, I would take a dozen and hurtle back to the original floor. For one production, only two programmes were left unsold, but we weren't always as fortunate as this.

# Scene 3 ❧ Productions at the Comedy Theatre, 1959 to 1960

There were many good productions at the Comedy during my short time there. The only unsuccessful play was *Look on Tempests*, which starred Gladys Cooper. She caused a stir in the neighbourhood each time she came to the theatre because she arrived in a vast pink Cadillac, and somehow there was always a space for this beautiful machine driven by this beautiful lady. I count myself lucky that she played at the Comedy even for three weeks.

Another production — this came in from the Oxford Playhouse — was E. M. Forster's *A Passage to India*. One night, the president of India, General Ayub Khan, came to a performance, and when I went to his box to ask if he wished to be entertained during the interval, he declined the invitation but asked if he might meet the actors after the show. Such a meeting was arranged, and the large company lined up on the stage so that when I led His Excellency through the pass door, he immediately faced the first actor at the end of the long line. Since the actor was dressed as, and looked like, an Indian, the president asked him, "In what part of India were you born?" To which the young man replied, "I was born in Hoxton, sir, in the East End of London."

E. M. Forster also came to the production, but he didn't connect with the company, so he didn't experience the same surprising response as did the president. He had a gentle charm and charisma, and he declared he was pleased with the production.

The most frequent visitor was Hayley Mills. When I started at the Comedy, Peter Shaffer's first play, the excellent *Five Finger Exercise*, was in residence and had been for some time. Hayley's elder sister, Juliet, was playing the stage daughter to Adrianne Allen and Roland Culver, and it obviously gave huge pleasure to the young Hayley to be able to slip into the auditorium to watch Juliet's scenes. I would hear someone racing round the corridors and there would be Hayley making sure she was going to be in time for Juliet's next appearance.

The theatre is one of those professions where one can establish a friendship during the run of a play, not see that person for months or even years, but when fate puts one together in another show, the friendship continues as if there had been no break. This happened with *Five*

*Finger Exercise.* I first met Adrianne Allen when I was the stage manager for Noel Coward's *The Vortex* during the run of which Elizabeth and I became good friends with her. The renewal of this friendship made it easy for me to get to know the cast of the Shaffer play, for she took me round and introduced me.

*Five Finger Exercise* was a very good play for a theatre manager to have in his theatre. Theatregoers enjoyed it very much, and it was a pleasure to see the looks on the faces of patrons as they happily left after the show. After I had been at the theatre for a few nights, observing the contented patrons, it dawned on me that I was missing an opportunity.

The catering manageress had hardback copies of the text of the play on sale, but by the end of performances, these had been checked in and locked away in her office. These books sold well during the evening, so I was sure we could sell several more as the audience left. I therefore arranged that I should be left with several copies each night. I never changed out of my dinner jacket until the last of our patrons had left the theatre, and this habit stood me in good stead now: It gave me the appearance of someone in authority, and standing at the end of the foyer bar on which the books were prominently displayed, I made several sales each evening. Wonderfully satisfying.

It was also wonderfully satisfying to me when the New Year, 1960, saw a production, *Rosmersholm*, come in from the Royal Court. At once, the theatre was filled with friends from the English Stage Company, among whom were Sophie and Percy Harris (under the mantle of Motley), Stephen Doncaster, and Paul Stone as stage manager. In the dressing rooms also were friends of long standing — Dame Peggy and Alan Dobie among an excellent cast.

## Scene 4 ✆ Enticements from the Shakespeare Memorial Theatre

During the summer of 1959, Patrick (Paddy) Donnell, the general manager of the Shakespeare Memorial Theatre, Stratford-upon-Avon, reappeared. It was he, assisted by his wife, Floy, who had brilliantly managed the 1955 Continental/Scandinavian/United Kingdom tour of *The Tragedy of King Lear* and *Much Ado About Nothing*, which ended at the Memorial Theatre in Stratford. And it was Paddy who was kind enough to ask me to stay on at Stratford after the tour, but by that time I was preparing to go to the Royal Court, so I had to refuse. Still, he didn't give up, and he would appear every now and then saying he thought it time I left London and moved to Warwickshire. A year later, his most serious call came when his manager/licensee was leaving, and the offer as a replacement was very firm.

It would mean leaving the Comedy after only twenty months, but from the family point of view, Elizabeth and I decided that the autumn of 1960 was a good time to make a move, and so I accepted.

Between the matinee and the evening performance on my last day at the Comedy, one of the usherettes came to my office and asked if I would go down to the stalls bar. Rather surprised, I obediently followed her. She opened the bar door, and there was the whole front-of-house staff, and I was presented with a very handsome desk set, comprising a large desk blotter, a hand blotter, and a pen tray. "For your new office at Stratford," they said. I was enormously touched and found it very hard to thank them. I was very sorry to have to say good-bye to them all, though, during my first summer at Stratford, I had the pleasure of two visitors from my Comedy days. One was a member of the front-of-house staff, and the other was one of the tellers from the Haymarket branch of the National Provincial Bank.

As with my move from the Royal Court Theatre to the Comedy— off with the old one day and on with the new the next — so it was with the move from the Comedy to Stratford. My last day at the Comedy was a Saturday, much like any other Saturday: up to the theatre for the morning, when I was able to say good-bye to the wonderful group of cleaners, then home for lunch and the afternoon before returning to the Comedy in time for the first house. When the curtain fell on the evening performance and I had seen the last of the audience leave the theatre, I changed back into street clothes, packed up the remainder of my belongings still at the theatre, bade final farewells to those I passed on my way to the stage door, then down the steps into Oxendon Street and good-bye, Comedy Theatre.

# Act Three

## The Shakespeare Memorial Theatre 1960 to 1961
## The Royal Shakespeare Theatre 1961 to 1963

A move to the large, red-brick Shakespeare Memorial Theatre in the compact market town of Stratford-upon-Avon. The range of responsibility increases. Only plays by Shakespeare are presented during the seasons (April to November). Many memorable productions including Peter Hall and John Barton's *The Wars of the Roses* and Peter Brook's *King Lear* with Paul Scofield. The company takes over the Aldwych Theatre in London, where modern plays and classics are to be presented.

### Scene 1 ✆ Stratford-upon-Avon 1960

I arrived in Stratford-upon-Avon in October 1960 to become the Shakespeare Memorial Theatre's manager and licensee. Becoming the theatre manager was straightforward after the Comedy, except that in the theatre in the middle of London I was totally in command, responsible only to the seldom-seen Mr. H. H. Wingate. (I never learned what those mysterious initials stood for.) Now I was responsible to Patrick Donnell while being totally in charge of many departments, although some, such as catering and the picture gallery, had managers.

Attached to my title was the word *licensee*, and this was another matter. About all I knew of this post was that every publican, who held a licence for his or her premises, was responsible for them and for the orderly behaviour of customers within those premises. The publican's duties and responsibilities seemed to apply to me, except that I was the nominal head unlike a publican who actually worked in the bar. It certainly was not a part of my new job that caused me any sleepless nights, in fact, I seldom remembered that I was the licensee of the theatre.

Strangely it didn't faze me, but I was certainly very aware of the size of the building. My immediate reaction on going into the foyer was that surely the whole Royal Court Theatre could be fitted in that space. With its large bars, a big riverside café, a capacious restaurant, to say nothing of the vast area backstage, the floors of offices and the numbers employed to staff it all — without doubt, I had come to a very, very big enterprise.

I found the theatre buzzing with the success of the current season, which had been Peter Hall's first as the managing director, and also with his future plans that included a company playing in London as well as in Stratford. Peter had had the brilliant idea that he would be able to attract actors to join the company and to stay with it for a much longer time if they could be offered a season of Shakespeare at Stratford followed by a season of new and classic plays, with perhaps a sprinkling of transfers from Stratford, in the West End of London. The theatre that had been acquired in London was the Aldwych, an attractive Edwardian building and a twin of the Strand Theatre. They were both built on the same block, with the Waldorf Hotel sandwiched between. Neither theatre can claim to be in the heart of the West End; in fact they are very much on the periphery of that area, only the Royalty being farther east.

Most of what I learned at the Comedy was invaluable for my job at the Shakespeare Memorial Theatre. I had run the Comedy on my own, which had meant being in the theatre every day from Monday to Saturday, with afternoons off except for the two matinee days. At Stratford, I had an assistant manager who was on duty for matinees and for five evenings a week. However, at the sixth evening performance, I stood in for him, and I found this once-a-week spell of duty very useful and instructive. It was a good way of getting to know the staff — many of whom had been at the theatre for a very long time — and I was also able to study the audiences to check on the way they used the front-of-house and where bottlenecks occurred.

As soon as I started, I was told that, unfortunately, my assistant had been sure that he would be offered the job that came to me, and he showed his displeasure in many ways. I would have understood his annoyance if I had gone to Stratford knowing nothing about the job, but with the training at the Comedy and with the length of time I had been in the profession, I felt confident that I was well qualified for what was ahead. I had to be very careful when suggesting alterations in areas that lay within his province.

After the comparative loneliness of my job at the Comedy, now I was right back in the centre. My office was on the ground floor of the main building, halfway along a corridor that led from the stage-left pass door to the foyer, and it was conveniently next to the general office. It was a narrow office with one window at the farther end from where, apart from the frosted lower panes, I could look over to the cottages along Waterside. This window was one of several along the side of the building outside which the box office queue of mainly students reached and went beyond. Young people would sleep overnight on the large paving stones, so that when I reached my office in the mornings, I could hear their chatter as they got to their feet in readiness for the box office opening at ten o'clock.

## Scene 2 ☙ Finding a new box office manager

My office at the Comedy had a friendly feeling whereas my new one had nothing about it that was friendly, so I instituted a rule that my door would always be open. This meant that people passing on their way to or from the foyer would either call out a greeting or drop in for a chat. Next office along the corridor housed the assistant manager and beyond him was Paddy's office or rather offices, for there was a communicating door between his office and the one that housed his secretary. These offices had originally been dressing rooms, presumably for the leading actors, for if I turned right out of my office, it was only a few steps before I was in the stage-left assembly. Every time I walked past, I automatically thought of the Royal Court. The first time I crept by during a matinee and saw what seemed like at least twenty soldiers lining up for their entrances, I nearly laughed out loud. A crowd in the assembly at the Court usually numbered three, if we were lucky.

Peter Hall's offices, for he too had a secretary's office next to his, was one floor up in the corner of the 1932 building. Like myself, he too could look at the cottages along Waterside though he had the added pleasure of a wonderful view across the lawns of the Bancroft Gardens. Come to think of it, with his workload I doubt if there was much time for gazing.

When I went to Paddy's office to check in, he told me that the box office manager was leaving at the end of the week, so my first task was to replace him. "There's no particular hurry for we have a very good staff, but the sooner the better. It is a very responsible position, so we need someone of great and varied experience," said Paddy. "I wondered if you knew of any West End box office manager who would like to come and live in the country." I said I would give it some thought, although I could see that getting someone from London would be a long process. As soon as Paddy told me about the impending vacancy, I thought of Leslie Mitchell, although I didn't mention his name to Paddy. I had met Leslie when *The Country Wife* transferred from the Royal Court to the Adelphi Theatre halfway along the Strand. He was always calm and unhurried, and he had a twinkle in his eyes as if he enjoyed dealing with the public. We had got along very well, and I was sure that that relationship would immediately re-establish itself if he came to Stratford.

I started by telephoning him to get some idea of his immediate reaction. This, to my enormous surprise, was not unfavourable, but there was a big problem. He looked after his elderly mother, and he didn't think she would like the idea of leaving the house in which she had lived for very many years. I tried to be honest with him regarding the job, for along with all the domestic problems he would have, such as finding a place to live, I was sure he would have a frosty reception at the box office. The staff were naturally not pleased that they were being asked to carry on without a manager, yet there was not enough faith in their work to let the situation continue that way. Instead, they were being asked to keep things going until a complete outsider came down from London. At the same time, I was certain that if Leslie accepted, his personality and expertise would win them round very quickly.

## Scene 3 ⚭ Living in Stratford-upon-Avon

Filling such an important post was not the type of problem I would have chosen at a time when I was trying to sort out what my new job entailed, in addition to finding a new home. I learned that I would be responsible not only for that great building on the banks of the river but also the Picture Gallery and the properties.

In 1960, the theatre at Stratford was an affluent place. During the fifties, it had joint artistic directors, Anthony Quayle and Glen Byam Shaw, who had presented seasons in Stratford from spring to autumn. When the seasons came to an end, they sent tours abroad and arranged transfers to London, all of which had proved very lucrative. Sir Fordham Flower, who lived in Stratford and whose great uncle had founded the original theatre in 1879, was the very able chairman of the Governors of the Theatre, and he kept a close but supportive eye on the company's activities.

Over the years, the theatre had invested in local properties, or buildings. Most of these houses, flats, or cottages were occupied by serving or past employees at the theatre. However, some were made available to members of the company who would be coming down for a season. Ensuring that these buildings were well maintained came my way, though I was extremely fortunate in that, in addition to the job, I inherited a very talented small group of craftsmen, my workforce, who knew all the properties owned by the theatre extremely well, and they cared for them in every sense. Many of the cottages along Waterside belonged to the theatre, and so did the Arden Hotel across the road from the Picture Gallery.

Two or three miles away in Tiddington was a very splendid house called Avoncliffe: This also belonged to the theatre and was at the managing director's disposal if he wished to live there. It was built on the banks of the Avon, and although this sounds very grand and romantic, it was not as broad a river as it becomes when flowing past the Bancroft Gardens, on past the theatre and so to the weir beside another large, theatre-owned property, Avonside. Peter Hall, his actress wife, Leslie Caron, his two children, and Simpkin, their old English sheepdog, lived in Avoncliffe. There was plenty of space in that large handsome house, built on two levels, to house Peter's family with ease, while at the same time allowing the remainder to be turned into further living quarters. In what had been the kitchen area, there were two flats and a bed-sitting room, while the old stable block had been converted into a very pleasant apartment.

Leslie Caron must have been very lonely at Avoncliffe once *Ondine* — in which she played her only role for the company — was withdrawn from the repertory at the Aldwych Theatre. After a busy and a successful career as a dancer in Paris and a film star in Hollywood, she was then left mainly on her own in a big house in a village in the heart of England. Peter was always in his office by eight-thirty each morning — so I was told — and left late in the evening, especially if he wished or had to meet visitors from London in the interval of a performance. I was aware of Leslie's situation since I heard from the locals that they would never dream of inviting her to their homes, either with or without Peter, since it would seem to their neighbours and friends that they were only asking her because of her stage and screen fame. Later, I became even more aware, because she was so often telephoning me asking for various maintenance work, major and minor, to be carried out at Avoncliffe. All too often I seemed to be going out there to get my instructions as to what was needed and by when the work must be completed.

Some of the work was certainly necessary, such as when the roof leaked, which it did with unfailing regularity, but there were other tasks that could really have waited until the necessary section of the workforce, made up of carpenter, plumber, two painters/decorators, and two gardeners, completed whatever was currently being worked on. But I would never mention this concern to Leslie for, of course, other work was, quite understandably, of no interest to her. She loved Avoncliffe, and her enthusiasm, her charm, and her French accent could only too easily overwhelm any thoughts I might have, such as, "I wish Tom could be allowed to finish replacing rotten windowsills at the Arden Hotel before going over to Avoncliffe." Pointless to think such a thought. The sills would have to wait.

By the time I had arrived in Stratford, her interior decorative schemes were finished, so I never saw the long first-floor corridor in its original state. Now it was completely wallpapered, up one wall, over the ceiling and down the other side, while curtains, of the same paisley pattern as the wallpaper, were hung and tied back at the two or three places where the line of the corridor was broken by arches. The effect was lovely and it was always a pleasure to look down this vista.

I came in for the next tasks that Leslie was planning for Avoncliffe. Some of the large sweep of lawn would have to be sacrificed (my word, not Leslie's) so that a formal garden could be laid out there. There were to be wide walks between lines of white standard roses. These would provide a gracious view from any of the three French windows of the splendidly proportioned drawing room that lay across one end of the house. There also had to be a cleaning-up job on the riverbank.

As the amount of traffic using the narrow, medieval Clopton Bridge increased, Peter, who had to drive over this bridge each morning to reach the theatre, called me in and announced that he had decided his method of travel should be by river. He said that he would like the landing stage at Avoncliffe to be made safe, and he would need a landing stage near the theatre where he would moor his boat. The Avoncliffe landing stage proved to be attractive, rickety and, like the remainder of the riverbank, overgrown. While the workforce made an excellent job of reinstating the landing stage, Leslie arranged for the purchase and delivery of many truly enormous white rocks. She then instructed the firm who brought them to place them at intervals and at different heights along the steep riverbank. They looked magnificent.

For a landing stage at the theatre end, the obvious place to choose was one beside a boathouse. This stood very close to the ferry that crossed from the theatre side of the river to the recreation ground. Luckily, I knew the owner of the boathouse and landing stage, for he was the ex-general manager of the theatre, George Hume. Although the boathouse was used as the office where bookings could be made to hire boats, I was immediately able to make arrangements for Peter to moor there. Since the boathouse was at the farther end of the beautiful theatre gardens, Peter, having navigated his way from Tiddington (passing under Clopton Bridge), would have only a short walk through the gardens — with the river on his right and the convenient pub, known to one and all as the Dirty Duck (although its real name was the Black Swan), on his left — to the stage door. I never actually witnessed his arrival at or departure from the Hume landing stage, and although I am sure he did travel a few times by boat, I always had a feeling that river journeys soon fell by the waterside.

Early on, I noticed an immediate difference in the distances from the theatre to their homes of those who worked at Stratford and those at the Royal Court. Staff at the Court would simply turn up for work, and if asked where they lived, the answer could be anywhere in that vast metropolis, and the journey could have taken them at least the best part of an hour. In Stratford, most of the staff were locals born and bred, and because of that, the general office closed at one o'clock each day and did not reopen until 2:30 PM. This hour-and-a-half break allowed a large number to walk or cycle home for lunch. Of course, there were many, such as myself, who had been brought to Stratford for a specific purpose and by 1960 were living in the town or in nearby villages. The members of this group, having completely settled in and accepted the rural lifestyle, would also be grateful for the thoughtful management that allowed them to get away from the theatre at lunchtime.

Settling in sounded easy, but would it turn out that way? This is what Elizabeth and I were going to have to face, and so would Leslie Mitchell, if he could persuade his mother to come with him to Stratford. Would we, like so many who had agreed to move to Stratford, remain in the area for the rest of our lives?

## Scene 4 ℘ Handel on the river, fireworks on the land

Another little job that Peter gave me in 1961 grew out of an idea put forward by Brian Priestman, the music director: The theatre band would play Handel's *Musick for the Royal Fireworks* on a boat in the river opposite the theatre, and in between each piece of music, there would be fireworks as Handel had planned. I was asked to organise this, and a date towards the end of August was chosen. On this night, the performance in the theatre would be *As You Like It*, in which the band not only played but would be in the orchestra pit for the final dance. As we discussed the various strands on which the success of the evening depended, we realised that they all interlocked neatly. *As You* came down at 10:45 PM, at which time the band could make its way to the embarkation point. At the same time, some of those who had been at the performance might enjoy watching the event. Finally, we could be sure that it would be completely dark. Eduardo Milano, the restaurant manager, was then engaged in the planning. Although the majority would hear and see the performance for free, tables for supper could be booked in the restaurant to help finance the event. They would provide a good view and almost certainly good acoustics, to say nothing of an excellent meal, which would ensure a wonderful end to the day.

The fireworks themselves would have to be set up on the riverbank opposite the theatre. Since that bank was owned by the town council and was part of the town's recreation ground — locally known as the Rec — I would need to get the council's permission before anything else. However, there was also the little matter of a boat that could seat the necessary number of musicians with a commanding place for Brian as conductor. The only such craft that I could think of was a barge. And where were there barges in the locality, but with the army. And where was the army, but at an ordnance depot at Long Marston, about ten or fifteen miles away.

I approached the town clerk whose immediate reaction was favourable. So next it was a visit to Brigadier France at Long Marston. He was enormously enthusiastic. Yes, he could provide a barge of the appropriate size. Yes, he would get it to Stratford on the morning of the concert. Yes, he would arrange for four of his men to be given the necessary length of rope each so that the barge could be moored close to the theatre while the band boarded. At that point, the two on the opposite bank would pull the barge to the centre of the river where all four would tie it off.

I contacted several firework-making firms before I found one whose representative became very keen on the idea. We worked out a programme that would suit the music and, importantly, was affordable. By the time this side had been tied up and the council had formally given its approval for use of the Rec, the bookings were coming in very well for the salmon-and-champagne supper that Eduardo would serve in the restaurant. Reports from Brigadier France let me know that all his plans were also going well and the barge would be moored off the theatre on the morning of the concert, ready to undertake what he quaintly termed "a dry run." During this, the soldiers could see the position in the middle of the river where the barge should be tied off for the actual concert. All we needed now was for it to be calm and dry.

The weather during the week leading up to the appointed evening was rotten and the actual day dawned no better — rain and high winds. But the clouds were racing along, and at times there were breaks when I could see welcome patches of bright blue sky. Brian called in to say that he had bought plenty of clothes pegs so that the music could be held securely to the music stands. I then showed him the route I had worked out that would get his musicians in the quickest possible time from the orchestra pit to the front-of-house without getting too caught up with the audience, since all would be going in the same direction. The embarkation point was down a few steps from the forecourt of the theatre so, with luck, it would not be long, following curtain down, before the band could be on the barge and sailing towards their destination. I then took Brian to a get-together with the supervisor of the fireworks to ensure he would understand the torch, or flashlight, signals that Brian would be sending from the barge. These would indicate when the next batch of fireworks should be let off.

By lunchtime on the day, all appeared to be ready, and even the weather decided to cooperate, for as the hours passed, the skies cleared completely and even the wind dropped to a steady breeze. All those concerned assured me they knew exactly when they should be doing what, so, since Elizabeth and I had been invited to join a group in the restaurant, we made our way there with everyone knowing where I would be in case of a hitch. And some kind of hitch there appeared to be, for there was an excessively long time before the barge could be seen as it was expertly pulled to its midriver position and neatly and firmly tied off. Brian could easily be seen standing high at one end of the barge, while the musicians seemed to have plenty of room, fitting neatly into their quarters. Those in the restaurant were not bothered by this delay, but I couldn't dismiss the nonarrival of the barge at its appointed place at the appointed time with the same lack of concern.

Without further ado, Brian raised his arms and the concert began. It was a huge success. The music came across the water clearly, the breeze by this time being very light. The burst of fireworks after each section of music — some of which were extremely short — were brilliant, and the finale was spectacular. A wire, about eight feet off the ground, had been set up along a considerable stretch of the riverbank, and along this wire whizzed a series of fireworks. They flashed and spluttered and exploded in showers of sparks. The effect was wonderful. The return of the band to the landing stage seemed to be flawless, thanks to the soldiers who did Trojan work, and Brian professed himself delighted with the evening.

The next day I was told why the band had taken so long to get to the barge. What I had not reckoned on was the enormous public interest in a free firework display. It seems that literally hundreds lined the riverbank, and they were packed tight in the area between the forecourt and the landing stage. Having found what they hoped would be good viewing places, they were not keen to move — in fact many were totally unable to move — so that the musicians, with instruments, could only squeeze past them very slowly indeed.

Peter, Paddy Donnell, Brian, and I had a meeting to discuss the event, following which I had to make a series of telephone calls. These were to check the availability of all suppliers of goods or personnel for an encore of the whole event in exactly four weeks time. Peter slipped in that little bombshell after saying he thought the event had gone well. All were amazed and delighted at the number of the local populace who crowded around the theatre to watch and to listen.

The town clerk was sure he could get permission for the use of the Rec again, Brigadier Bob France and the firework firm were delighted to be invited back, and Paddy gave me permission to examine a new embarkation point for the band. I had to find an area where there would be no public, so I started at the green room, which was really a canteen for staff and company and was on the ground floor at the back of the building overlooking the river. Immediately outside its French windows was a terrace edged with a wall that did not obstruct a view of the river from the green room. Several feet below this wall was a short path that connected the theatre gardens with the Theatre River Room, a snack bar facing the river: When visitors came this way, they were not able to gawp into the green room, thanks to the low path and the brick wall. Between this path and the river was a gentle slope covered with shrubs, and it was through these shrubs that I wanted a path made. The gardening side of the workforce could see no problem in laying a short, firm pathway and removing some shrubs, which could be reinstated once the path was no longer needed. The final items were signs to be painted that would politely indicate that the lower path was temporarily out of bounds to the public.

The weather for the second concert was even better than for the first. It was a balmy autumn evening, the crowds were even greater, and the band, not having come into contact with the public, reached the barge remarkably speedily. The four sappers pulled expertly on their ropes, and the barge sailed out into the centre of the river and was tied off in record time. The only uninvited event was the appearance of a harvest moon. Shortly after the performance began, this huge pink and gold disc rose majestically on the further side of the Rec. It continued to climb at speed, casting more and more light on the scene so that the operators on the opposite bank, hitherto unseen, could now be spied dashing to and fro, and the surprise finale of the exploding fireworks racing along their eight-foot high track was lost.

Never mind, for once again it was counted a triumph. Once again the band played wonderfully with Brian not only conducting brilliantly but managing to flash his torch signals neatly to the firework operators. The sound values, aided by the water, was glorious. Once again the restaurant was packed, and another delicious meal was served, and once again the whole evening helped the rapport between town and theatre. To my surprise, some who had been to both events declared that they really enjoyed seeing the firework operators operating, so perhaps it was only myself who was disappointed. But it certainly was a spectacular moon.

## Scene 5 ⚭ Ernie

Another strange event that I had to organise began with Paddy telling me that the announcement of the National Savings Premium Bond winner would take place in four weeks time on the lawns at the theatre end of the Bancroft Gardens. Would I arrange whatever was necessary? The Department of National Savings, having encouraged the public to buy these numbered bonds, had then developed a machine, known as Ernie, which was permanently housed in the Lancashire town of Lytham St. Anne's where it somehow produced the winning number out of all the bonds each month. The individual who had bought the winning number was rewarded with a financial prize of considerable worth, so the day on which the monthly draw would take place was awaited eagerly. A further encouragement to the public was the decision to site the venue for the announcement of the winner in a different town around the country each month, and it was looked upon as a great honour for a town to be chosen. I learnt that a rostrum would be needed on which would sit representatives from National Savings and from the theatre in addition to the mayor and several local councillors. These worthies would be joined by an actress from the theatre company, who would call out the winning number as, digit by digit, it came through on the telephone.

It was up to me to choose the actress, and at once Judi Dench came up in my mind. To my pleasure, she immediately said yes, she would be happy to undertake this task. I then asked Eddie Golding, the master carpenter, to join me in the Bancroft Gardens to find a suitable place for the large rostrum he said could be made available for the chosen day. However, when I thought of just plonking down a rostrum with a table and chairs, it seemed a very unattractive scene, so I cajoled Eddie into allowing me to borrow some pillars from the *Othello* set, with some drapes to loop between the pillars. When it was all set up, with handsome chairs and a good cover on the table, the total effect was very elegant.

Judi, beautifully dressed and looking enchanting, arrived precisely on time, as I knew she would, and joined those already sitting at the table. As with the fireworks evenings, here was another occasion when I prayed for fair weather. Again I was lucky, for the day dawned calm and dry with occasional sun. There was a goodly crowd of locals and visitors, whom Elizabeth and I joined as we waited for the great moment. First there were speeches, including a delightful one from Judi who confessed that she had always thought that Ernie was a benevolent uncle, since, she went on, she had no idea that Ernie was in fact an acronym for "electronic random number indicator equipment." She read this extraordinary title out with a straight face, but there was mischief in her eyes. She got her laugh, and then she moved from the rostrum to stand beside the girl who held the telephone from which the figures would be given. As Judi was quietly told a number that was coming over the phone, she called this number out with her usual excellent projection and clarity of speech. At once, one of the National Savings staff placed a huge version of this number onto a specially prepared row of hooks, which everyone could easily see. Soon, Judi had called out the complete seven-number figure. At this point we were all primed to await the answer to the next heart-stopping event. Was this number held by someone who lived in the neighbourhood? Deathly silence while we waited for the answer to come through. Finally, it came down the wire. But no, that was too much to hope for. It was quickly announced that the winner lived in the southeast, whereupon Judi was thanked for having graced the occasion and carried out her duties so delightfully; after which, all the locals wandered off, disappointed at their lack of success, all the dignitaries melted away, and Eddie and his excellent stage staff struck the drapes and the pillars, dismantled the little stage, and the gardens returned to normal.

## Scene 6 ❧ Applying to the magistrates for the renewal of the theatre's licence

Because I was the licensee of the theatre, once a year I was summoned, along with all the publicans of Stratford and the surrounding villages, to a meeting when our various applications for renewal of our licences to allow us to sell wines and spirits on our premises were granted or withheld. We had to appear before a magistrate at whose side sat the chief constable, and it was he who was called upon first to tell the magistrate whether we had behaved ourselves during the past twelve months and whether our houses had been well managed. I only had to attend two of these affairs, and I am glad to say that in spite of the chief constable announcing how many drunks, disturbances outside hostelries, drinking after hours, and suchlike heinous crimes on his patch had been committed during the past twelve months, in the main we got very good notices from him. All our licences were renewed and we all moved out into the clean fresh Warwickshire air, pleased with ourselves and glad that the excellent way we had conducted our houses had been recognised.

The chief constable used to call in on me on various items of business, but it certainly made me realise what a very small town I was living in. He arrived one day and, after the usual pleasantries, said, "You were going home very late last night along the Tiddington Road." "Yes," I said. "We had been out to dinner in Hampton Lucy." Even while I was telling him this, I wondered how this unimportant piece of information had reached him, and if one was planning to be up to no good in the area, how careful one would have to be.

## Scene 7 ◑ Visitors

It was hardly surprising that much time was taken up with looking after visitors. There were those who came down from London to a matinee or evening performance, driving back afterwards, and those who were in the town by day and who came along for an arranged meeting. Of the former, this often meant meeting them before the show and giving them refreshment in the interval. This was easy during an afternoon performance, for I could offer tea in the office. Perhaps one of the most distinguished visitors to a matinee was Lord Montgomery of Alamein, who, as General Montgomery, turned around the fortunes of the Second World War for the Allies. He was the commander of the British 8th Army in the Middle East, and with these troops he won the Battle of Alamein, which led to surrender of the German and Italian forces. It happened that both my sons, Guy and Clive, were at the theatre that day, and Lord Montgomery indicated he would like to meet them. As he, unasked, gave them his signature, he also gave them a piece of advice: "You must decide on your future career by the time you are sixteen."

When visitors came to an evening performance, it meant that I stayed around to meet them at about seven o'clock, chatted over a drink before guiding them to their seats at about seven-twenty, after which I would drive home — a five-minute journey — to join Elizabeth for our evening meal. I could sit over that for about an hour before returning to the theatre in time to meet my guests as they came out for the interval.

A treasured visitor, brought to the theatre by Floy Donnell, Paddy's wife, was B. Iden Payne. He was over eighty, but he was determined to be shown round the whole theatre, for this was the building — then only two years old — that he would have come to when he was appointed director of productions in 1934. During his eight years at Stratford, his productions are reported to have very much echoed the style of those of William Poel, who, forty years earlier, had concentrated in his productions of Shakespeare on the scenes flowing from one to the next and played at a reasonable speed. Iden Payne left the theatre in 1942, and as Floy and I ambled round with him, he said there was very little difference in what we were showing him and how he remembered the theatre twenty years previously.

Another group whom I promised to show over the entire theatre was a group of two hundred. The request for such a visit came from a clergyman who wrote to say that Stratford was the last town they would visit on a day's outing, and it would be wonderful for his group if they could see the backstage of this great theatre. He then told me of the terrible afflictions suffered by the members of his group. The thought of them not being able to hear or to speak — for they were either deaf or dumb or, terrible to consider, both — made me reply at once that of course I would be delighted. The chosen day was a Sunday, and as usual, the theatre would be shut, so there was no problem there.

I never went into town on a Sunday in midsummer, and although I knew there would be many tourists wandering aimlessly around, I was not prepared for the crowds mooching along, swarming over the gardens, boating on the river, and completely filling all the central streets so that almost as many were walking in the road as there were on the pavements. I managed to reach the theatre, driving slowly and trying not to have to nudge too many road walkers out of the way with a wing of the car, in plenty of time before the coach-loads of my visitors disgorged at the edge of the small car park behind the Picture Gallery and then surged towards the stage door.

To my horror, suddenly the gloomy day-trippers, who had been peering in through any of the theatre windows that they could find, saw a way of getting into the building. I had to halt the hordes at the stage door, whilst the rector forced his way to the front. There I was able to ask him to vet all those entering, while I went ahead leading them into the conference hall.

After some time, I was faced by what seemed more like two thousand than two hundred, but the rector said they were all there and would I give them a talk on the theatre. One of the party would let the group know what I was saying by means of sign language. After my introduction, which included the fact that we were standing in the shell of the old theatre that was burned down in 1926, I told them that we would next go into the auditorium, where I would talk about that area. After that, I would take them round the whole building. But would they please follow each other closely, for I would be at the front, and it was up to them to keep in touch with what would be an extremely long line. Two hundred heads nodded and smiled, and I was assured that they all understood and were very grateful.

Off we went, and I wandered along, allowing plenty of time, especially in the dressing-room corridors, for these had rows of wardrobe rails heavy with costumes. I knew from experience how visitors loved to feel the material, especially that used for the members of the Senate in *Othello*: these were a glorious shade of red and incredibly heavy. We passed through to the dress circle foyer, crossed that, and went down the curving staircase past the door to the restaurant and so to the little fountain at the foot of the stairs on the main foyer level. From there, we went through the café that faced the river and back to the conference hall. In they came, smiling and happy, ten, then twenty, and so to twenty-five, but then there was a gap — a gap that was not filled. We all gazed in silence at the door, but we couldn't will any more to appear. "Oh my God," I thought. "How do I find the rest?"

"Stay here," I instructed those around me, and I dashed off. As I left, I instinctively turned towards the way I had just come, but I realised at once that it would be much more satisfactory to start from the beginning and take my same route, picking up the strays on the way. Up the dressing-room stairs I went: no sign along the first corridor then, as I turned the corner into a much longer corridor, I caught myself on the point of shouting, "Is anybody here?" but stopped in time. It hit me that if they could hear, they couldn't respond, and if they could respond, they wouldn't have heard. Racing on, I was relieved to find a large number in the circle foyer and others gazing out windows on the staircase or in the café. They were quite glad to be rounded up and shepherded back to the conference hall.

Some months later, a group of unwanted visitors turned up at the theatre. I was getting ready to leave home one morning when I heard the town sirens wailing. All who heard this creepy sound would know that there was a fire, and the voluntary firemen were being called to the fire station at once. The majority of these men worked at their normal jobs, which they were permitted to leave as soon as the siren was heard. "Perhaps the theatre's on fire," said Elizabeth. "That's a nasty thought," I said. "I'd better get down there fast just in case you are right." And, of course, she was.

It turned out that an off-duty chef had been sitting in the one and only easy chair in the chefs' changing room. He fell asleep while smoking a cigarette. This managed to set fire to the armchair that was in the middle of the room and under one of the sprinkler systems. This immediately reacted as it should by dousing the room — and the chef. At the same time, an alarm went through to the fire station, and so the whole organization sprang into action. I went quickly up the main dressing-room stairs to find the top corridor awash with all the water from various sprinklers that had obviously felt their support was necessary. Seeing a fireman, I asked about the fire. "It's out," he replied. "That's great," I said. "But water is getting into all the dressing rooms on this floor, and it looks as if it may get into the wardrobe, so can you now turn off the sprinklers?" "Can't do that," he said. "The officer is the only one permitted to give those instructions." There was a pause as I watched some of the water very attractively cascading down the staircase before he added, "He's on his way." Another pause. "I think."

By the time he got there, some of the firemen had fitted a tarpaulin across the dressing room staircase at one end and draped it over the sill of a half-landing window at the other. Certainly much of the water was taken out of the building before splashing down onto the terrace outside the green room. But, as I am sure with many fires, much more damage was done by the water than would have been done by the burning armchair.

One of the theatre cottages in Chapel Lane also caught fire some time later, but in spite of, thank goodness, not having a sprinkler system, it was soon put out. It had apparently started in the huge wooden beam laid across an inglenook fireplace. The firemen thought that within the beam the fire had probably been preparing itself for a blaze for some time because of the heat and sparks from the logs in the big open hearth.

## Scene 8 ❦ Waterside cottages

As time went by, some of the cottages along Waterside were vacated by the families who had lived in them for generations. Most of them were in their original state of two rooms upstairs, two down, and no bathroom, but at least most had a simple kitchen extension at the back. As soon as a cottage was vacated and thus came back into the charge of the theatre, I got in touch with Mr. Harvey, a local architect, and together we worked out how we should update and improve the space. This usually meant turning the two downstairs rooms into one very good-sized room and repositioning the staircase. This we swung round so that it hugged one wall of what had become a much larger space, instead of acting as a divider between the two rooms. At the back of the house, the kitchen extension had to be taken down and rebuilt in such a way that a reasonably spacious kitchen and a bathroom could take its place.

In the Shrieve's House in Sheep Street lived a splendid lady, Mrs. Waldron She was very sweet and kind, and she did much good work in the town, including visiting the old and ensuring that the authorities were taking good care of them and that they took good care of themselves. One old lady, who lived in a theatre-owned cottage along Waterside, came under Mrs. Waldron's wing, and at her first call, she asked the old lady if she was getting plenty of milk. "Oh, no," was the reply. "I can't afford milk." "Then I shall see to it that a free pint of milk is delivered to you every day," declared the good Mrs. Waldron, and sure enough, as the old lady reported a week later, the milk started arriving daily. "And are you drinking it?" asked Mrs. W. on her next visit. "Oh, yes," replied the old lady. "And thank you, ma'am, very much. It's very kind of you."

Two months or so after this, carpenter Tom Sales let me know that another cottage would soon be vacated, and this proved to be the old lady's. "She's been taken to hospital, I hear," he reported. The best place for her, but sadly she didn't live long. Since she had no close relative to whom the cottage could be passed, it came back to the theatre. As soon as they had the time, Tom and plumber Ralph went to check on the state of the place and were soon back in my office. "Oh, the smell!" was about all they could say for a while. They thought at first that it was the smell of the cottage not having had doors or windows open for years. But then they found the culprits. Neatly ranged round the walls were sixty-three unopened bottles of sour milk.

It wasn't long before Leslie Mitchell phoned to say that his mother had agreed to come to Stratford, and therefore he was able, gladly, to accept the offer to become the box office manager. None of the theatre properties suited him, so that meant we had to find two or three houses from which he could choose. He very much liked one at the farther end of the Loxley Road, and he was soon happily installed there. And there he stayed for the whole of his long and successful engagement at the theatre.

I had realised from the start that the theatre and the town were very closely linked, although the town would not admit this. It would be possible to think that the townsfolk resented the theatre and certainly that they did not like the annual influx of actors. But as I got to know some of those who lived in or near the town, I learned they never wanted to get too friendly with a member of the company for they knew only too well that after a few months most of them would be gone. What I hadn't reckoned on were the ties my predecessor had with some of the locals until I was telephoned several times by private individuals as well as hoteliers who all said more or less the same thing, "Welcome to Stratford. Now, for some time we have been given the chance to buy up blocks of seats in advance of the opening of the main booking and may we take it that this procedure will continue?" This didn't seem a fair distribution of what were often regarded as gold dust to the normal theatregoer, so I said that I was sorry, but no, I wouldn't able to continue this system. I had a feeling that the hoteliers would be able to get tickets by other means, and sure enough, they used to send members of their staff to join the queue for the first day of over-the-counter sales with orders to buy as many tickets as possible.

## Scene 9 ✑ The mayor of Stratford-upon-Avon's reception

When John Shakespeare (William's father) was mayor of Stratford-upon-Avon, he welcomed the actors who came to play in the town by inviting them to a council reception and this became an annual event. So it wasn't long after the new company assembled at the start of the 1961 season that Elizabeth and I, at our first local social occasion, joined the queue up the stairs at the town hall waiting for the fat little beadle, in his role as attendant on the mayor and in his medieval-style costume, to announce us. We were behind a young actor, Sebastian Breaks, while in front of him was Sir John Gielgud. The beadle asked Sir John his name, which was immediately given to him, whereupon the beadle turned to the reception line and clearly announced "Sir John Gielgud." He emphasised the "Sir," then paused slightly before he called the other two names, which he ran together as if they were one. Sir John went forward on his way to being greeted by the mayor, while the beadle looked enquiringly at the next guest. He listened intently as Sebastian gave his name and then called out, "Sir [pause] Bastian Breaks."

## Scene 10 ✑ Shakespeare's birthday, April 23, 1961

The other annual grand occasion was on April 23, Shakespeare's birthday, and on this particular day, his 397th. This event was organised by Dr. Levi Fox, the excellent and tireless director of the Shakespeare Institute. Traditionally, there was a reception at the theatre, followed by a luncheon, which was held in the conference hall (many years later transformed into the beautiful Swan Theatre) at which there were a number of important speeches.

After the luncheon came the ceremony of unfurling the Flags of All Nations. There seemed to be more nations each year, which meant that the number of ambassadors from these countries also increased, and so did the number of flagpoles. These were set up along Waterside, in a double row up the centre of Bridge Street and along High and Chapel Streets. The ambassadors (or, occasionally, their understudies) were the VIPs on these occasions, and they set off from the theatre having been marshalled so that those whose flag was farthest from the theatre led the procession. This arrangement meant that the ambassadors were soon neatly placed in front of their appropriate national flags, which, on a sign, were unfurled simultaneously. The walk then started again, the destination being Holy Trinity Church where Shakespeare is buried. There was a short ceremony in the church before those who had taken part in the walk repaired to Hall's Croft where refreshment was available in the beautiful gardens. This concluded the day's events.

The year 1961 was not a good one for Shakespeare's birthday. It pelted rain and the wind joined in the fun. Some of those in the walk decided to brave it out in whatever clothes they had worn for the journey to Stratford, but others were prepared for this vile weather, especially a distinguished member of the 1961 company, Dame Edith Evans. When the time came to leave the shelter of the conference hall and go out into the storm, she set off in fine style. She didn't give a jot for the weather since she was completely enveloped in transparent plastic, starting with a hood covering her head and shoulders, down to her sensible walking shoes, which were also wrapped in plastic. If there were the usual crowds of spectators lining the streets to check out what the ladies in the procession were wearing, they were welcome to look, and if they saw and smiled at the sight of one rainproofed elderly lady, she didn't care. She was not going to let a little rain stop her from going to the church.

## Scene 11 ❧ Glen Byam Shaw and Peter Hall

Beyond Trinity Church, in the Old Town part of Stratford, were the workshops where scenery was constructed and properties were made. I think it was probably in this part of the company that the changeover in the directors of the theatre, Glen Byam Shaw handing over to Peter Hall, was most sharply felt. Glen was a director who arrived for the first rehearsal of a new season knowing the names of every member of his company. There were usually many weeks between a series of auditions and the first rehearsal, and many of the younger members would only have been seen by Glen at an audition but not again until they turned up in the conference hall. Because of this, he would ask for photographs of all the actors he didn't know, so that he would be able instantly to put a name to a face when it first appeared at Stratford. It was strange how very similar ten young men could look when a group was standing in an uneasy huddle at the first read-through of the first Shakespeare production at the start of a new season.

Glen also paid especial attention to the workshop staff. He would ask the production manager if a certain piece that was being constructed in the workshops could have some alterations made to it. The next time Glen paid one of his frequent visits to the workshops, he would speak to as many of the staff as possible, not only addressing each by name but enquiring after a wife or a child about whom, perhaps, he had heard worrying reports when he was last in the shops. He would also examine the piece being altered, check its progress, and ask if the alterations had caused any problems.

Peter Hall's regime was totally different. He had a mammoth agenda, and so there was no time for him to behave like a benevolent squire. If he wanted a piece of scenery altered, he would ask the stage management to inform Desmond Hall, the totally dependable production manager, what was required and when it would be wanted for use in a rehearsal. It would not occur to Peter to go to the workshops to inspect progress: that was the job of his production manager and the staff at the workshops. The shock waves from the change of style reverberated round the workshops for a considerable time.

## Scene 12 ❧ Peter O'Toole and Christopher Plummer

Among the many members of the company I met on my first day at Stratford were several whom I had got to know at the Comedy Theatre, such as Eric Porter (*Rosmersholm*), and at the Royal Court, Frances Cuka and Jackie MacGowran (*End-Game*), and Peter O'Toole (*The Long and the Short and the Tall*). It was the latter who said, "Come and have a drink in the Dirty Duck this evening. I have something I must tell you." We duly met up, and I was introduced to the famous pub, conveniently placed along Waterside and facing the theatre gardens, so that one could get away from the theatre atmosphere and yet be only two minutes from the stage door. I remember making the same comment about The Chelsea Bun, but that's all they had in common.

"Peter Hall asked me to be one of the leaders of the new company he is setting up for the move into the Aldwych Theatre," said Peter. "I think playing in Stratford and London is a brilliant idea, and I agreed, but I have just heard that David Lean, after a period of not being sure, now really wants me to play T. E. Lawrence in a film called *Lawrence of Arabia*." Peter paused for a moment and then dropped his bombshell. "So I've had to tell Peter I am pulling out of the Aldwych contract."

Peter O'Toole was having a tremendously successful season at the Shakespeare Memorial Theatre. He was Petruchio, with Dame Peggy Ashcroft as a wondrous Katharina, in *The Taming of the Shrew*, Shylock in *The Merchant of Venice,* and Thersites in the famous Peter Hall/John Barton production of *Troilus and Cressida,* which was played in Leslie Hurry's sandpit. For London audiences to be able to see him, so soon after they had read of his triumphs at Stratford, would give the first full season at the Aldwych the most enormous boost.

"Good God, Peter," I said. "You can't do that. I know how much P. Hall is relying on you and the parts he has offered you are tremendous." Peter said he understood, but he had to make the movie; it was far too important to his career. He was very sorry to have to do this, but there was no other way.

Much later that evening, I returned to the theatre, and as I wandered through the theatre gardens, I thought back to what Peter had told me, and I knew, much against my will, that his decision not to go to the Aldwych was right, as far as his career was concerned. At the same time, there had been many a major film in which an actor had the major leading role but which, in spite of huge publicity, had not found favour with the public. Such a reversal could badly affect an actor's career. Peter Hall was understandably furious, and he called a meeting to see if anyone could come up with a solution. We all knew that there is no way one can take an actor to the side of a stage and say to him, "Now go on out there and act." Similarly, even if the theatre won a court case, it would be a hollow victory.

Christopher Plummer was chosen by Peter to replace O'Toole in the first Aldwych season, and because of this additional casting, Christopher became the first actor to commute between Stratford and London. He had been contracted to come to Stratford to play Richard III, and this play was still in the repertoire in Stratford when, two months later, he suddenly became a member of the first Aldwych company.

Thus, in order to play in Lucienne Hill's translation of Jean Anouilh's *Becket* in London and still play Richard in Stratford, he had to commute the ninety-five miles. He and I discussed how and when he should travel to London on the occasions when he had two consecutive performances, one in each theatre. I suggested that, rather than drive down early on the morning of the performance at the Aldwych, I thought he would get more rest if I had a chauffeur-driven hire car waiting at the stage door at Stratford in which, as soon as possible after curtain down on *Richard III*, he would be driven to London.

At that time of night, the journey shouldn't take more than two and a half hours, so with any luck he could be in his London flat by 1:30 AM at the latest. I said it would be a large car, and I could guarantee a good driver, so really all he had to do was to get quickly to the stage door. Christopher thought this sounded fine, so I said I would put it in hand. Of course, after the first commute I would check with him as to how he had got on and find out if anything in the plan needed changing. Luckily it didn't.

Christopher Plummer was not my favourite actor at Stratford. On arrival, he let everyone know that although Sir Laurence had done a fair job when undertaking Richard III in one of the Old Vic's mid-1940s seasons at the New Theatre in St. Martin's Lane, he, Christopher, would now be able to show everyone how the part should be played. Not the most diplomatic way to start in a new company. But it wasn't so much this attitude that annoyed me as his complete lack of consideration for the audiences, especially those who would, for financial reasons, be buying a relatively cheap ticket for a standing place. These theatre enthusiasts, mainly young people and students, were the ones who started to queue during the evening before their chosen performance and who eventually settled down to sleep on the flagstones outside the ground floor office windows.

The next morning, if they were lucky enough to get standing tickets for the 7:30 PM performance, they then had the day to while away before getting back in plenty of time to queue again to get a good standing place at the back of the stalls. The ideal was to be among the first to get into the auditorium when the House opened at seven o'clock, since they would then have the advantage of being in the front row of fellow standers, as well as having the metal bar, that was fixed just behind the back row of the stalls, to lean against.

When I walked amongst the audience as they arrived for a performance, I would see these young people sitting on the floor at the back of the stalls. There they would stay until the pressure of the incoming audience forced them to stand up and to ease forward to take up their chosen places. As the time moved to 7:30, they would brace themselves for the performance, knowing that the effort it had taken to get to this position at this time was at last going to pay off. But they weren't reckoning that this particular play cannot start until the leading actor is on stage ready with the opening speech.

This fact appeared not to have occurred to the leading actor either, for one morning, early in the run, the house manager told me that Christopher had been very late down for the opening of the play the previous night. At the next performance, I went to the prompt corner just before curtain up. There was no sign of Christopher. I went straight up to his dressing room and pointed out that on the previous evening the curtain was very late going up. I went on to explain to him that even ten minutes could mean a lot to many in the audience especially those who were standing. "I'll come down when I feel like it," was the response. "We'd all appreciate it if you could feel like it now," I said and left him. He gave it a few minutes and then took his time making the journey to the stage. But from then on, although never actually leaving the dressing room when he got his call, he was never more than two or three minutes late.

## Scene 13   Actors' accommodation in and around Stratford-upon-Avon

When it came to finding accommodation for London-based actors, I had great help from Floy, who became my assistant in this part of my work. Her local knowledge was of enormous help, and I really enjoyed checking over possible places with her. It would start with a letter asking us if we knew anywhere that an actor and family could rent. From the information given, we could check which of the theatre properties were still available. Should there be one or two, we then had to match up the actor's wishes with what the properties offered. If the two sides were obviously incompatible, then Floy and I had to move into the commercial market, and we became the middlemen between local estate agents and the actor. None wanted to be too far from the theatre, and there would also be a request for news about schools, local transport, shopping, where to walk a dog, and so on. At the same time, we would be told exactly the sort of house the actor and his wife had in mind and exactly the amount of rent they could afford.

It was Floy who finally tracked down a little cottage for Dame Edith Evans. We had drawn blanks everywhere, but at last someone known to Floy agreed that a cottage she owned in Scholars Lane could be rented, furnished. I was appalled when I went to see it: it was a one-up, one-down little place with a narrow galley-type kitchen at the back of the downstairs room. The real problem was the bathroom, which was reached via the "garden" door, across a small yard, and so to a detached brick hut. There was no shelter from the elements between cottage and bathhouse, so I put my artisan workforce onto this area, and soon carpenter Tom Sales, the ever-dependable and quite superb craftsman, had built a covered walkway, and the equally dependable and most wonderful plumber, Ralph, had the plumbing under control so the place didn't seem quite so dire.

The great day came when Dame Edith arrived, and we invited her to have a look at her lodgings. She had been quite in favour of it because we were able to tell her it was very close to a Christian Science Chapel, but her look-around was carried out in almost complete silence, with just the occasional "hmm" — or was it "humph"? The inspection didn't take long, needless to say, and soon the three of us were back in the living room, which she surveyed once more and then, in that unmistakable voice, she said, "But it's just a workingman's cottage," with the words working and cottage split with small pauses between each half of each word. Her only request was for a fan heater, which we delivered almost on the instant: I switched it on, whereupon she sat in one of the comfortable armchairs, gazed about her in her haughtiest manner, and at last declared that the cottage would be quite satisfactory. Floy and I breathed again. Thanks to Floy, the workforce, and the fan heater, we had another satisfied customer.

It took a long time before I was sure Sir John Gielgud would also become a satisfied customer. There was nothing in the area close to the theatre, so it meant fanning out into neighbouring villages. Not that this would completely solve the problem, for it would mean he must hire a car to get him to and from the theatre. Elizabeth and I took to looking over properties of all kinds during evenings or at weekends, but although we nearly decided on one near Evesham — a beautiful house with a spectacular view — the distance of about fifteen miles was just too great.

The time for Sir John's arrival was getting dangerously near when one of those minor miracles happened. A detached house, on the opposite bank of the river to the theatre and only a short way along the Tiddington Road, was available for letting. The house proved to be perfectly acceptable, and the river was at the end of the garden, so I was able to imagine misty Warwickshire mornings with Sir John at the end of his garden waving to Peter Hall as he chugged past in his motor launch on his way to the theatre. For Sir John to reach the theatre, he either had to cadge a lift from Peter, or he had a short and pleasant walk over Clopton Bridge and across the Bancroft Gardens

To maintain the flow of rent from the properties during the winter season, as many as possible were let to actors and staff from the visiting companies. This meant that there were several spasms of exceptional busyness, such as when the actors, who had been in occupation for many months, moved out (many to start at the Aldwych) and the first of the actors, or staff, of one of the winter season companies moved in. Inventories had to be checked with the outgoing tenants, followed by each property being given a thorough spring-cleaning. Discrepancies discovered during the inventory check had to be replaced, and a fresh inventory prepared.

For houses and cottages we rented for leading actors, we agreed upon the inventory with the owner or estate agent before the actor moved in. It was essential at that time that any extra item we put into a house for the added comfort of its future occupant be clearly noted on the inventory, so that we could remove the same at the end of the occupancy without the owner of the property claiming that it was there when we took over.

It was extraordinary what outgoing tenants left behind. If the piece seemed to have a useful future or might be of some small value, we would get in touch with the actor, who invariably said, "Oh, no! I didn't know I had left it. Thanks, but I don't want it now." We would then sell it. Christopher Plummer left an Algonquin Hotel hand towel. I decided it had no value.

## Scene 14 ❦ The final 1961 productions at Stratford-upon-Avon

Dame Edith had come to play once more and, as it turned out, for the last time, the Nurse in Romeo and Juliet. This was the fifth in a six-play season — a season that proved for me to be one that when, as I watched the productions steadily following one another onto the stage, I hoped that the next one would be the one to catch fire and make one proud to be associated with it. At last *As You Like It* arrived, and the atmosphere lifted at once. It was very well directed by Michael Elliott with a wonderful set by Richard Negri and a shining, beautiful Rosalind from Vanessa Redgrave. It was one of those productions where everything seemed to be touched with theatrical magic and even the occasional imperfection could not spoil the whole. Vanessa was superb, and of all the scenes in which she excelled, the one that comes to mind is the epilogue. After the pairing off of the couples and the final dance, she turned, walked a few steps downstage and put out her arms towards the audience as she started to speak. At that moment, I felt everyone wanted to rush up onstage to hug and be hugged by her.

I called in on Vanessa before a performance once and found her making up, but because she was short-sighted, her face was practically pressed up against the glass. "Isn't it awful how close I have to get to the mirror," she said. "But I'm not the only one. Max Adrian is next door and his mirror is back-to-back with mine and if you were able to whisk away the dividing wall, our noses would touch."

The final play was Sir John Gielgud's *Othello* directed and designed by Franco Zeffirelli. Word seeped along the corridor that Franco was designing the settings as if he were directing an opera and that if we were used to seeing sumptuous sets and costumes, "we ain't seen nuffink yet." The final straw that must have broken the backs of several camels was the house curtain. Franco was determined that the one that had been there for years should be replaced for his production by another, since, after all, the house curtain would set the tone of the production from the moment the audience came into the auditorium, it could not be made of flimsy material but must be, like the sets, sumptuous. Sumptuous. What a pleasure to be able to use a word the sound of which exactly matches the look of the object. By the time this curtain entered the fray, Franco had already gone over budget, but he was eventually allowed to have his way. In time for his production, beautiful cherry red house curtains replaced the homegrown set. Sumptuous was indeed the word.

The settings were gorgeous, but there was a penalty attached. The scene changes often seemed to take as long as the scene that followed, and although one gasped as setting after setting was revealed, the gasp was apt to turn into a yawn. Any momentum the actors gained was soon lost as we waited for the next scene to appear, and when it did, as in the armoury scene, one could only wish that it hadn't. I do not want to make a list of great theatrical disasters, so I will only mention two, both of which happened in this scene. Firstly, one-half of Sir John's moustache unglued itself, which meant that for much of the scene, half of this accurs'd object swung round so that it became almost an extension of that noble nose. Maybe Sir John was unaware of what was happening literally under his nose, for he never tried to reinstate the errant half of his moustache. And secondly, as if that were not embarrassing enough, he walked towards a wond'rous solid pillar in the armoury scene and gently leaned against it, whereupon the pillar failed to support him and gently leaned with him.

## Scene 15 ✑ Sir John Gielgud

It was good to be working with Sir John Gielgud again. He and Dame Peggy Ashcroft were such great leaders in the 1955 Shakespeare Memorial Theatre tour of *The Tragedy of King Lear*—the full title was used— and *Much Ado About Nothing*. During the tour, as was the custom at the end of each performance, a leading member of the company would step forward from the curtain call line and say a few words. These would be short but complimentary. "Ladies and gentlemen, thank you so much for your very warm reception this evening. It has given us enormous pleasure to come to your handsome city and to play in this beautiful theatre to which we hope to return one day. In the meantime, thank you again and good night." In 1955, it was Sir John who made the curtain call speeches in the many cities of the many countries that we visited, and these speeches were always from the heart and often very emotional. The only difficulty he had was extricating himself from a subordinate clause. Once he embarked on one, I knew we were lost, for he seldom could remember how he got into it, and to solve this problem, he bravely dived into another — only to realise, as he ploughed charmingly on, that it was making matters worse. His original subject was now so far away, it would never be recalled, so how about another subordinate clause, he must have thought, as the words came pouring out? By the end of the speech, I had a fantasy that the stage floor around him must be littered with subordinate clauses that had never got back to their roots.

I had heard that he often made comments that came out in a way he never intended. He acknowledged his habit of dropping bricks once at the Hebbel Theatre in Berlin. Sir John wandered onto the stage when we were setting up *King Lear*, and our chat turned to the amount of rebuilding in progress in the locality. At that moment, a neighbouring wall or building must have been knocked down, for there was the most colossal extended roar, whereupon Sir John exclaimed, "Oh, my goodness! All those dropping bricks. They sound just like me."

Sir John had used that same "oh, my goodness" exclamation two weeks earlier when we were in Vienna. We opened the continental tour in that truly splendid city, and Sir John happened to call in at the theatre when we were checking out the "moon" cloth. This was a huge piece of black material that had a half moon attached to it. When we had first hung this during an all-nighter, the fireproofing had, like the gentle rain from heaven, fluttered down in a vast cloud, filling the air. It gave me the most horrendous attack of hay fever, so when, several hours later, I saw the cloth being lowered slowly from the flies and, at the same time, noticed Sir John tentatively stepping onto the stage, I called out, "Don't come on for the moment, Sir John," which request was greeted with the delicious "oh, my goodness!" as he turned and fled with speed.

This theatre, the Wiener Burgtheater, was a large theatre that suited our Noguchi-designed setting of a huge square box in which as few pieces of scenery as possible were used, and most of those that did appear were moveable. They were on castors, about seven foot high, and many were two-sided, each side being painted differently to indicate a different location. The younger actors pushed them on cue to various marks painted on the stage cloth. These poor young people had to stand, unseen by the audience and sometimes for very long periods, in the narrow space between the two sides of their triangular pieces. The intention was to create in a scene change the effect from the front of these various bits of scenery moving by themselves. At least I hoped and thought that was the effect, yet many years later, I was told that from a certain row in a certain theatre it was possible to see under the moving pieces, and the audience could watch little feet shuffling along. Another illusion shattered.

The heath was indicated solely by a huge rock that, at the end of one scene, had to roll over exposing another side and thus denote another part of the heath. Whether any member of an audience ever looked at the rock after it had moved and realised at once that now we must be on another part of the heath is questionable. The rolling over was done by a stagehand offstage pulling on a couple of wires. This little task presented no problems until we got to Hamburg. I asked the resident stage manager if he would please provide me with a stagehand who would be responsible for this rock move and a pleasant, smiley man was duly presented. Speaking slowly and not too loudly, I hope, I explained what he had to do and I showed him the cue lights, letting him know that when the red light went out and the green one came on, that would be his cue to pull the wires. "The cue will come after about seventeen minutes," I said and I held up my fingers until I had reached the required number. He nodded, smiled, and repeated, "Seventeen minutes." So I said, "Yes, good, thank you," and left him. There was plenty to do.

It was easy to see most of the stage from the prompt corner in this theatre and this is where I was standing during the first performance when I noticed the rock begin to shudder slightly and then roll into the position it was due to be in at the end of the first cue. But the assistant stage manager on the book had given no cue as yet. There was nothing to be done because the stagehand had done it, so I wandered up the side of the stage to be met by a broadly smiling stagehand, the rock mover, coming towards me. I smiled back. He came very close and in a whisper, said, "Seventeen minutes," and pointed to his wristwatch. "Very good," I whispered back. "Thank you very much." None of the actors complained about the wayward rock, so I said nothing either, but from then on, I never tried to be helpful by indicating approximately how long the appointed rock mover would have to wait for the cue.

As with all touring abroad, to the actors it seems like a holiday except that their presence is required in a theatre most evenings, although certainly not every evening. But when two plays are being toured, often the actors have a free day while the stage management and staff will be changing over from one play to the other, hindered the while by the language problem. Interpreters in all the countries we went to did a wonderful job, but seldom did the requested number of these invaluable and vital people turn up. If they did, they were, understandably, not always fluent with theatrical terms.

In Zurich, I was allocated a young man, Hans, who blessedly spoke good English, as the call boy. I gave him the call book, showed him that each page gave details of which actors were next to be called and that against each name was their dressing-room number. I added that I would signal to him when it was time to make the next call. "Yes, yes," he said with a winning smile, so, feeling I could trust him, I went on preparing for the first act. He did a wonderful job as call boy during that act in spite of the fact that it was a curiously planned theatre backstage: All the dressing rooms and the canteen were on the opposite side to the prompt corner, so with our boxlike set opened out to its fullest, Hans had a lot of ground to cover once he was given the go-ahead to call the next actor, and often he was only just back from one call before he had to set out on the next.

At the end of the interval, Hans and I arrived back at the prompt corner at the same time: he had been calling the beginners (Sir John and David O'Brien as the Fool) for Act II, and I had been giving instructions to various stage hands as to their duties for the next act. Hans reported that all was well, so I gave a signal to the stage manager for curtain up.

With the prompt corner down left and Sir John and David due to appear up right, the distance between us was quite considerable. The storm got under way with thunder and lightning, but no sign of Sir John who should have entered first with David following him. There was obviously something wrong, but just before I left the corner to investigate, I saw David enter, with his left arm holding his cloak as if to shield his face from the storm, while extemporising some Shakespearean-like invective against the weather as he slowly crossed the stage. Not a sign of Lear though.

I ran upstage left, behind the forty-foot backcloth and over the seeming acres of stage right to the dressing-room staircase. As I raced up the first flight, I cursed the theatre once more, this time for having none of its dressing rooms on stage level. I burst into Sir John's room only to find it empty except for a rather scared-looking dresser. There could be only one other place, I thought, as I hurtled down the stairs and along a corridor at the end of which was the canteen.

Just before I reached the door, I came to a complete stop in the manner of most of Disney's animals who, in order to stop, dig their heels into the ground accompanied by a squeal of brakes. I opened the door in a relaxed manner, and yes, there was Sir John, sitting on a bar stool at the counter, drinking coffee. "Sir John," I said, with a calm I did not feel, "I'm afraid you're off."

I might have guessed his reaction. "Oh, my goodness!" he said, immediately swinging himself off the seat and following me at speed down the corridor, across the wide stage-right wing, area and so to the up-right opening. By chance, David, still onstage and still endlessly, as it must have seemed to him, battling back and forth against the storm, had just reached that same place. Sir John passed me and dashed onstage until he met David who swung round to follow him, and as they set forth across the stage, I heard, with grateful relief, "Blow, winds, and crack your cheeks!"

Two impresarios masterminded the tour, one was Dutch and the other German. Each in his own way had a slight physical defect. As we went from one country to another, we switched impresarios. On one of these journeys, I was sitting on a coach across the aisle from Sir John. In an effort to close a rather strained conversation about the ability of German stagehands, I mentioned that this would be one of those days when we would change from one impresario to the other. "Oh, yes," said Sir John . A pause as he considered the information, and then he added, "Better a wall-eye than a barracuda mouth." It was fortunate neither was on the coach.

It was very easy to be deceived by the young-looking, fifty-one-year-old Sir John when made up and in costume as King Lear. The stance, the long white beard, and the cloak — or, rather, cloaks, for Noguchi designed a series of cloaks, the first punctured with small holes and subsequent ones punctured with increasingly larger holes as the play progressed — could easily cause one to think that he really was an old man. Therefore I often found myself being sorry for him when he had to take many curtain calls, for he looked so absolutely exhausted.

On one of our days in Hannover, an opera was scheduled for the evening, so we had to give a matinee. The theatre was packed, and the performance on the huge stage went very well. Sir John seemed drained as he bowed to the tremendous applause that greeted the first of the curtain calls, which was taken with the twenty-eight-strong company in one long line some way upstage. The vast house curtain came in, and as arranged, the company started to move down to the front of the stage for the second call, whereupon Sir John suddenly leapt ahead of the line and did a jitterbug step right down to the curtain line. I was sorry the audience couldn't see him. The company took two more calls, and then I indicated to the local stage manager that this was the end, so he called for the houselights, and the company broke up and went to their dressing rooms. But the applause did not stop, in fact the noise became even more vociferous, so the stage manager pressed a button for the enormous iron curtain to start on its journey to cover the house tabs, which were then flown out.

The audience was unstoppable and as soon as the two parts of the iron curtain, that came rumbling round from left and right, met in the middle, some jumped up on the apron stage and started hammering on the iron, making an extraordinary, frightening noise. At this, I told the stage manager to stay there, and, as in Zurich, I dashed off to Sir

John's dressing room — close to the stage this time, although, with the size of the stage, that isn't saying much — and asked him if he would take a solo call. At once, he was out of the room and hurrying across another massive side stage towards the stage manager, who was standing by a door set in the iron curtain. When Sir John was ready, the door opened, and he stepped out to be greeted with the most tremendous roar I had ever heard. Flowers were thrown onto the stage, and the applause remained thunderous (the noise quite put our storm effects to shame), as he accepted several bouquets before, at last, he gave a final wave and turned back to the door, which the local stage manager closed quickly behind him.

It should have been a tiring tour for both Sir John and Dame Peggy, for in addition to their respective roles of Lear and Cordelia, they also played Benedict and Beatrice in *Much Ado About Nothing*. But they never showed it. After an evening performance in Berlin, I heard Dame Peggy call out at the stage door, "John and I are going to a nightclub. Anyone coming?" I gathered this was not unusual.

For several weeks in the middle of the continental part of our tour, Dame Peggy was not with us. She apparently had a clause in her various contracts that she would always be allowed to be absent from a production for four weeks each summer in order for her to visit her family. The part of Cordelia, we were told, would be played by Claire Bloom.

This young actress must have been well known all over the world at that time, because she had recently played opposite Charlie Chaplin in his film *Limelight*. This had brought tremendous publicity for both of them and for the film, so we looked forward to her joining us. Rehearsals had to be fitted in to the touring schedule and from that point of view, it was fortunate that although Cordelia appears twice in the play's final scene — once briefly in the early part and then, when she is dead, towards the end — George Devine, as director, declared that, to save time, once Cordelia and Lear are led off "guarded," there would be no need to rehearse any more of that final scene, and thus Claire had to wait until her first public performance before Lear carried her "dead in his arms" onstage.

When we were first rehearsing the play in London back in April, Sir John had asked if I would lift up Dame Peggy at this point in the play and hand her to him just before he had to enter for the "howl, howl, howl, howl" speech. When I first lifted Dame Peg, I found she weighed a sugarplum, even though she no longer had quite the slim figure of her youth, so this bit of offstage business had raised no problems either for Sir John or myself. I didn't anticipate any with Claire to whom I explained the system that Sir John had requested. She said it sounded very sensible, and I thought no more about it.

We had reached Hamburg by the time Claire had to play before the public for the first time. Another vast theatre that was packed. The whole show went completely smoothly in all departments and Claire proved a lovely and confident replacement for Dame Peggy. Even so, it was a relief to realise that Lear's "Howl, howl . . ." was drawing near since it heralded the end of the play. Claire joined me, and at a comfortable time before Sir John would arrive to take his burden, I started to lift up this slip of a girl. To my amazement, she seemed the proverbial ton weight, and I had only just got her correctly in my arms ready for the handover when Sir John appeared. How was I to tell him that he must be prepared for a body that was considerably heavier than his previous Cordelia? I couldn't think of any other way but to stare down in horrified fashion at my charge, and then slowly shake my head from side to side. I thought at first I would have to risk that Claire was not looking, but decided to glance in her direction. As I sincerely hoped, I saw she was already acting dead.

Sir John seemed to get the message, yet even then he didn't appear totally prepared for what was to come. I handed Claire over and his knees buckled slightly, but in true trooper fashion, he immediately started with his four howls as he made his entrance. It might have been my imagination but these cries sounded even more torn from his very soul than they did at any of his other performances.

## Scene 16 ❦ The 1962 season, including the unexpected *The Comedy of Errors*

The year 1962 was a good solid season at Stratford. Perhaps because I had never had the chance to see it before, my favourite production was *Cymbeline*, wonderfully directed by William Gaskill, which was to be followed by the final production of the season, *King Lear*. With Peter

Brook as director and King Lear to be played by the great Paul Scofield, the advance interest in this production was enormous and booking was exceptionally heavy. However, at the end of July, Peter Hall called a company meeting at which he announced that he had had a cable from Paul Scofield, who was then in a production in New York, to say that he was heading for a nervous breakdown and no way could he start rehearsals in a week's time. He was not even sure if he would be able to join the production at any time, but that depended on how he progressed.

Peter explained to the company about the heavy booking for the play and said that he didn't want to lose a lot of goodwill by replacing performances of *King Lear* with performances from the current five plays in the repertoire. He was sure many of those who had booked for *King Lear* would have seen the other productions already, so he offered the company the chance to come up with suggestions as to what should be done. Within an incredibly short time, a group went to Peter and said that they wished to do *The Comedy of Errors*. Clifford Williams, who was lighting *Cymbeline*, would direct, and he and John Wyckham (technical administrator) would design the set. Ian Richardson and Alec McCowen would play the Antipholus twins, Ian Hewitson and Barry MacGregor the Dromio pair, while Diana Rigg would be Adriana.

Five weeks later the production was on the stage and was a sensation. It was a joyous production of a play that had not been seen for many years. It made those who had scorned it, and reckoned it to be one of those Shakespeare plays one just did not offer the public, to view it anew.

It was also in 1962 that Irene Worth came over from America, first to play Lady Macbeth to Eric Porter's Macbeth, to be followed by Goneril in Peter Brook's *King Lear*. She had asked if Floy and I could find her a small house, close to the theatre and soon we found a "possible" at the theatre end of Chestnut Walk. It was rather shut in and gloomy, but she kindly professed herself delighted with it.

One evening we arranged a small dinner party to which Irene and a very dear friend, Katherine Quinney, wife of a local dairy farmer, were invited. The main purpose of the evening was to reunite Katherine and Irene, for we knew Katherine's story of how, when evacuated to America during the Second World War, she was desperately homesick. One day she was taken to a theatre to see a play in which Irene Worth was starring and was so overcome at watching an actress she thought was English, that at the end she went round to see Irene in her dressing room. Now we could put these two together once more.

During the evening, Katherine told Irene this story, whereupon Irene immediately said, "Oh, yes. I remember a little girl, in floods of tears, standing at the door of my dressing room and then rushing to me and hugging me." They talked about this moving moment for some time before Irene said, "I also remember that you asked me for a signed photograph. I wonder if you have still got it?" Katherine thought for a second and then ingenuously replied, "Oh, yes, I think it's up in the attic with all the other rubbish." It was only when Irene gave one of her deep, rich laughs did Katherine realise what she had said.

## Scene 17 ☞ *King Lear*, 1962

Slotting *The Comedy of Errors* into the 1962 repertoire at Stratford gave Paul Scofield time to recover completely, and he arrived in fine form for the start of rehearsals of *King Lear*. Peter Brook, as director and designer, gave several days — and nights — of worry to many of the production departments, especially in the wardrobe. This seemed to be acknowledged in the programme for the costumes were singled out to have been designed by Peter Brook "in collaboration with Kegan-Smith." Like so many in all walks of life, Cyril Kegan-Smith, wardrobe manager, was not averse to having a moan, and he certainly spread his moans around liberally while the costumes for the daughters of Lear were being designed. Peter Brook had a clear idea as to how they would look—Goneril, Regan, and Cordelia would all wear the same style— but it was the choice of material that caused most of Cyril's worries. Peter had asked him to make up one of the costumes, but when Cyril asked what material he should use, he was told that he must choose a material that he thought would be suitable, and the dress must then be shown to Peter before the next morning's rehearsal.

The simple dress was ready in the morning and was proudly shown to Peter, who said he didn't like the material Cyril had used, so would he make another using a different material and have it ready for show-ing at the end of the day's rehearsal. "But will you tell me what you don't like about this material?" requested Cyril, which got him nowhere. The material was not right and that was the end of the matter. That evening the same scene was enacted. Again, Peter would not say why he objected to the material, only that Cyril must have another dress in another material ready for inspection before the next morning's rehearsal. "Every night we are working until all hours and we are all exhausted," Cyril let everyone know. He wasn't going to suffer in silence. At last, after several materials were tried and rejected, he came up with leather, and this satisfied Peter. And no wonder. They were significantly right — unadorned, with skirts to the floor, giving each character the look of being covered in malleable steel.

The production was superb, acknowledged by press and public. There were very few performances in Stratford, but a month after it had opened, it transferred to the Aldwych. The scene that has stayed with me, and the one that I used to say I would like to see wrapped in cellophane, tied with a huge bow, and marked "absolute perfection" was the scene when Lear, Paul Scofield at the very top of his considerable form, and his Fool, most marvellously played by Alec McCowen, try to cheer up the other by telling terrible jokes. The interaction between those two great actors was intensely moving.

There had been much shaking of heads during the rehearsal period when Peter Brook announced that there would be only one interval, which would come after two hours and ten minutes. "Unheard of" was the instant response, followed by, "the public will not stand for it — or rather, sit — for such a long time" and "no other theatre would make their public suffer for so long before being released. " But with this immensely strong production in which one brilliant scene flowed with-out pause into the next, no one seemed to notice the passage of time. Listening to comments as an audience made its way into the foyer at the interval, I often heard a voice, in total disbelief, say, "Do you realise it is nearly a quarter to ten?" but never, "Do you realise that that act was two and a quarter hours long?"

On Boxing Day, it began to snow and it went on and on snowing and then the great freeze joined in. It was a really tough winter with paths and gardens disappearing beneath several layers of snow and ice and not being seen until well into April. It was not long before it was officially declared that the Avon was completely frozen beside the theatre. At once there were skaters and walkers out on the ice who were able to view the theatre from an angle that previously one had to be in a boat to see.

## Scene 18 ⚬ Winter seasons at Stratford-upon-Avon

Each year I had to fill the theatre with touring productions for the weeks between the end of one season, which could vary between mid-November to early in December, until around the middle of the following March, when the theatre would be dark while the productions for the next season were prepared. Sadler's Wells Opera could be relied upon to spend four weeks with us, which would cover Christmas and the New Year, but there always seemed a formidable number of weeks either side of this period for which I must find productions that would draw the populace away from their firesides. There was no question of my going round the country in the late summer checking out plays that would still be on tour during the winter. I had to rely on what management could offer me, which I would then have to evaluate by considering author, director, designer, and cast.

Thinking back to my H. M. Tennent days, I was only too used to being contracted as stage manager to a production that appeared, from every angle, as if it were going to give me solid employment for a very long time, only to have it slide away into oblivion after a desperately short run. Those of us in such a production knew that its life could not be prolonged even if there were a very starry name on the bills. It was also well nigh certain that no matter who tried to tinker with the play — a new scene here, dialogue cuts there – seldom did any of the first aid make any appreciable difference. Unhappily, several of the productions I booked for a week's run during a winter season were so patently of the "sliding to oblivion" type. Although I was so very sorry for all those concerned, I was also sorry for the locals who bravely came to see these shows. At the same time, I was embarrassed for myself for having invited them.

Although the locals complained during the summer that they could never get a seat in the theatre (Me, "Have you tried the box office?"

Complaining Local: "No." Then adding hurriedly, "You see I know it will be no good. You're always full!"), they didn't come along in great numbers during the winter either. Because we had such wonderful houses for most weeks during the summer, they made the not-so-wonderful houses during the winter feel more empty than they actually were. Our winter patrons did not only come from the vicinity of the theatre but from the villages around, and I was always only too aware that if nature wished to put down a cloak of mist or fog, with icy roads thrown in for good measure, Stratford was invariably chosen as the centre for such hazards.

## Scene 19 ❧ Alterations in the theatre

During my first summer, it was possible to see that we could have sold out each house at least twice, such was the pressure on the box office, and it seemed awful that we were having to turn away so much money. This made me look around for places where it might be possible to get in a few more seats. The first area I studied was the stalls, and to my surprise, I found one of the rows towards the back had one more seat on one side than the other. There seemed no reason for this, and there also seemed to be enough space, with some adjustments to the whole row, for one more seat to be put in, and soon, Tom Sales had installed the extra seat. One more seat was good, but I would have liked more, so I moved to the dress circle and there I found, behind the back row, two large spaces that were unused. If the small openings to the circle were enlarged and steps up to the areas were constructed, then it would be possible to form two new boxes. I was sure they would sell, even though they would be the furthest circle seats from the stage. These alterations took longer than the single seat, but at last the new boxes were finished, and the public flocked in.

The system for selling programmes was also not as efficient as it should have been. A trestle table was placed just outside one of the doors leading into the stalls, but there was no indication that it was there. When the public filled the foyer, it was often impossible to see that programmes were for sale at this place. It seemed essential that a new selling point should be built in a position that would be readily visible by all. The counter also needed to be at a much higher level than the trestle table, which caused vendor and purchaser to bend down at some point in the transaction.

The only possible place for such a structure was between two of the main entrance doors. It would mean losing a wall on which photographs of current productions were hung, but I was sure we would do more business from this higher counter than from the trestle table. Once again, Paddy Donnell was very supportive, and at last permission was given for the counter to be built. When it was finished — another example of Tom Sales's beautiful craftsmanship — it looked wonderful, while at the same time programmes of all the season's plays could be stocked and displayed and the foyer lost the look of a village hall.

I always thought it a pity that a sizeable slice of the foyer was taken up with the box office, to say nothing of my worrying that the box office staff had to work in a windowless area. This goes back to 1932 when the new theatre — the old having burned down in 1926, which event prompted George Bernard Shaw to send a one-word telegram to the management, "Congratulations" — was nearly ready for opening. At that time, Auntie Norah (as she was universally called), who had been the box office manager in the old theatre and who would fill that post again in the new, was invited to the building to be shown around before the time came for her to move in. Since she lived in one of the pair of two-storey houses that face directly up the side road that leads to the main entrance of the theatre, she hadn't far to go.

She was shown everything, and she professed herself very impressed, but as she was taken to a foyer door at the end of the tour, she dared to ask, "And where is the box office?" to which the only answer, her hosts shamefacedly realised, was "There isn't one." At that late date, it would be impossible to alter the facade of the building to incorporate a box office that would enjoy natural light and air. So a space had to be found within the foyer, and there it still stands — jutting out into an often overcrowded public area. As I write this, I thought back to 1932, and it struck me that the size of the foyer must have been remarked on with appreciation, for it surely would have seemed palatial compared to the theatres that local audiences would have experienced in Birmingham and Coventry.

At about the time of Auntie Norah's visit, it was discovered that, although the lady architect had provided a well-appointed room for ladies on each level, there was no such room for gentlemen, either for the stalls or the dress circle. It was obvious that finding space for a room on each level was out of the question, so it would be necessary to construct a single room, equidistant from both. It was solved by creating a mezzanine floor at the river end of the foyer, with stairs down from the circle and up from the stalls. This solved the problem, but it spoiled what would have been an uninterrupted view of the charming brick staircase as it curves round the little fountain outside the Stalls Café. Still, the foyer was given a splendid example of 1932 art in the shape of a large clock that was set on the mezzanine wall once that was in place.

## Scene 20 ℚ Local events in Warwickshire, 1961 and 1962

We were lucky to be at Stratford in the early 1960s, for in 1962 the new Coventry Cathedral was to be consecrated, and as part of this important occasion, the City of Coventry arranged for a 1962 Coventry Cathedral Festival. There were many events organised to raise funds for the festival. One of these, on Friday, November, 10, 1961, was a Midnight Matinee at the Coventry Theatre. David Nixon, the TV magician was master of ceremonies. Sir John Gielgud had a solo spot as well as closing the show; Dame Peggy Ashcroft gave the charming description by the nineteen-year-old Victoria of her 1837 Coronation, taken from John Barton's *The Hollow Crown*; ballet dancers Anton Dolin and Alicia Markova each danced a solo; Vanessa Redgrave and Tommy Steele teamed up in a turn entitled *Speed Maniacz*; and Teddy Johnson and Pearl Carr sang. The Belgrade Theatre Company presented Harold Pinter's *Trouble in the Works* with a cast that included Derek Newark, Sheila Keith, Bridget Turner, Ian McKellen, and Ronald Magill.

On Friday, June 8, 1962, there was A Service of the Arts at Coventry Cathedral to which Elizabeth and I were invited. Although we planned a leisurely drive on a beautiful summer evening, we didn't leave Stratford at the time we had intended so we arrived in Coventry dangerously near the 7:30 PM start. By the time we had parked, it was a minute or two before the half hour. As we hurried up the walk towards the west door, to our horror we saw the bishop of Coventry come round a corner of the building towards us. A second later, we realised that the bishop was heading a very impressive procession, which was fast approaching the west door from one side, as we were hurrying at great speed from the opposite direction. "Who's going to get there first?" I panted. It looked for a moment as if the bishop would win, but noticing us — how could he fail? — he kindly signalled to us to keep going thus allowing us to pass through the door a fraction ahead of him.

Those inside the cathedral, who had all been waiting there for some considerable time, heard the cathedral clock chiming the half hour, which they knew was the cue for the procession to enter. At that moment, movement was heard at the west door, so the large congregation rose to its feet. Those who turned round to see the procession enter did not immediately see the expected Great Cross but two extremely hot, flustered and very late fellow members of the congregation, who were wishing that they too had been sitting waiting patiently in the cool of the beautiful new cathedral for a very long time.

## Scene 21 ⚘ The return to London and the hotel in the Victoria area

I didn't see out the 1962/1963 winter season for Peter Hall had asked if I would go back to London and take over a new post at the Aldwych Theatre, to be curiously titled London manager, and I had said that I would like that very much. I was terribly sorry to leave all that Stratford offered, but working at the Aldwych was very attractive. We decided that until we bought a house in London, Elizabeth and the boys would remain in Stratford and I would stay in a London hotel for five nights a week, joining the family at weekends. I booked into a small hotel in the Victoria area where I had the most unnerving experience. The hotel provided rooms only, no meals of any kind. This suited me, since there was so much to read about and check over at the Aldwych that I was happy to leave the hotel very early in the morning. At the other end of the day, I remained at the theatre until very late, when I walked back to Victoria in time to have a bath and get to bed.

I had been there for several days following this routine but one night, about 11:30, I reached the hotel, unlocked the front door, and went up to my room. I unlocked that door and went in and at once I felt that something was different. Then it dawned on me: The room was totally bereft of my possessions. There weren't many places in the room where my things could have been stashed away, so I checked the number on the door and checked the number on the key. Both were as they should be, except there was no sign that I had ever been there. I at once thought of that creepy story "So Long at the Fair," not that it solved my present predicament.

I went downstairs looking for some room marked office, even though I did not expect anyone to be on duty, for it certainly wasn't the type of place that had a night porter. All was in darkness or if there was any light, it must have been a bulb of the least wattage possible. I was just about to leave the house and check in elsewhere for the night, when I heard a noise and turning round in the gloaming, there was mine hostess, suitably clad in dressing gown and not looking her best. "Where are all my belongings?" I immediately demanded. "I've put them in the office," she replied grimly. "But you have no right to do that," I said, trying to keep rational and calm. "Oh, yes I have. You have not paid for your room." "But no one has asked me for any money, and I imagined, like other establishments [I was quite proud of finding that word at that time of night] that you would submit an account at the end of the week." Luckily I had put a week's rent in an envelope in my briefcase in readiness, so I produced this, and I suppose it was this show of good faith — I had the exact amount and the envelope was addressed to the hotel — that made her unbend a very very small amount.

However she wasn't going to let me win. She led the way down to the office — no such word marking this door from any other — pointed to my suitcase which was on the floor beside the desk, and said, icily, "Give me that envelope, then take your case and go to the room you have been using. But I want you to leave by eight o'clock in the morning, hand in your key as you go, and don't come back."

Later that morning, quite by chance, a good friend, Ann Robinson (who had been my greatly cherished and invaluable co-stage manager for two of the productions for which I was a stage manager during my H. M. Tennent days), telephoned to ask how I was getting on, so of course I told her what had so recently happened. "That's all right," said Ann. "There's a room at the top of my house, and you are welcome to use it as your base until you and Elizabeth have found a new home." Gratefully I accepted this kind offer and happily joined fellow itinerants, actors Peter Sallis and Jeremy Kemp, while Elizabeth, making day dashes from Stratford, and I scoured London for that new home. Although we looked round houses in parts of London known and unknown to ourselves, we found that we were drawn back to the Southwest, and finally we bought a house in Putney within a quarter of a mile from where we had previously lived in Barnes.

# Act Four

## The Aldwych Theatre
## London, 1963 to 1966

Appointed London manager of the Royal Shakespeare Company at the Aldwych Theatre. A State Gala at the theatre. Three World Theatre Seasons. The use of simultaneous translation. The Lord Chamberlain and censorship. Celebrating Shakespeare's 400th birthday with many productions including *The Beggar's Opera, The Birthday Party,* and *The Marat/Sade.*

### Scene 1 ᘓ The Royal Shakespeare Company, Aldwych Theatre, London, 1963

The great joy of the move was that I would be working for the same organisation but in a different theatre — and how different. For the past two years, we had been driving up to London to see the latest productions at the Aldwych, so I was familiar with the layout, but whereas at Stratford there were often people dropping in to my office for a chat because of my open-door policy, at the Aldwych that did not happen. My office door was just as open, but no one was going to climb seventy-two stairs from the foyer for a fleeting passing-the-time-of-day chat, and the only people who actually passed the door were office staff on their way to the washroom next door.

The Aldwych also seemed so small after the Memorial Theatre, which in 1961 had been renamed the Royal Shakespeare Theatre. Although everyone who worked at the Aldwych was employed by the Royal Shakespeare Company, or the RSC as it had quickly become under the expert guidance of John Goodwin, head of the publicity department, the theatre was not owned by the company. The owner was Prince Littler, who licensed it to Mr. D. A. Abrahams, who rented it to the Royal Shakespeare Company. By the end of the year, however,

Mr. Abrahams bought the theatre, which pleased me since I much preferred dealing with his director of administration, John Hallett, rather than Mr Littler's Frederick Carter. As with Mr. Wingate, although not so regularly, I used to have visits from Mr. Abrahams, which were followed by lunch at the Savoy Grill (several notches up from Mr. Wingate's Lyons Corner House). There was no question here as to who was paying; in fact my host must have been very well known there, for no money of any type changed hands while I was around — a very civilised way to live, I thought. Before we went into the Grill Room, we sat outside, where we were each immediately presented with an enormous glass of sherry (no sign of an enquiry as to what I would like to drink, I noted). These were followed by another glass, which I could certainly have done without, but Mr. Abrahams didn't permit such heel-tapping. I was there to give him an up-to-date picture of what was going on at the Aldwych, as well as all the theatrical news from the world of subsidised theatre. On his side, Mr. Abrahams would chat about his world of commercial theatre. These were extremely pleasant occasions for he was very good company, and I naturally warmed to him because of his real interest in the theatre, not only the Aldwych but worldwide.

When I arrived in February 1963, John Roberts was the general manager, and I enjoyed working with him a lot so I was sorry when a few months later he left the company. Among his many talents was the ability to talk on the telephone so excessively quietly that even when I was sitting across his desk from him, I could not hear a word he was saying. At the Aldwych, there was a finance department and a publicity department, and it was to this latter department that John Goodwin came from Stratford for two or three days each week. He used to arrive full of country bounce and energy. Those of us jaded with London air and local pressures of traffic and general street noises, would comment amongst ourselves that we would all have John's drive and enthusiasm if we could also enjoy his work pattern of split weeks — half at Stratford and half in London.

At the other end of the building was David Brierley. He was titled repertory stage manager and was directly in charge of the acting company, stage management, and stage staff, which duties he carried out quietly and with great efficiency. Placed behind the stage door was a small canteen, brilliantly run by Maggie Roy, who managed to produce excellent light meals as well as the necessary teas, coffees, and snacks from the smallest of kitchens.

With the exit of John Roberts, the whole theatre came under my control, with responsibility, as at Stratford, to Paddy Donnell, although he seldom came up to London. I had "inherited" a very good house manager, but he very soon left to become an impresario, and I engaged Peter Sibley, who proved an excellent choice.

It was a huge pleasure to start at the Aldwych: *King Lear* was playing in rep with Durrenmatt's play, *The Physicists,* which had opened in January 1963. Both plays were directed by Peter Brook, who had instituted an innovative start to a performance. The house curtain was to be up when the audience came in. Very sensibly, Peter said he wanted the audience to study the set while waiting for the play to begin, rather than during the first few minutes of a performance. Peter put forward the theory that once the house curtain rose to reveal the set, no one took in a word that any actor spoke, for they were far too occupied with eyes roaming around the setting. So often, during these initial minutes, Peter contended, the roots of the story were exposed.

To add to the audience's surprise at being able to see the set of *The Physicists,* there on the stage, lying on the floor down left, was a young woman. She lay quite still so that after a while the audience guessed that she was an actress acting dead, but many more went further than mere speculation by going right up to the edge of the stage (as at the Royal Court, the orchestra pit had been filled in, although the boxes had not been converted into assemblies, with one now housing the lighting board, and the other the sound equipment) and discussing this unusual sight at close quarters. The main question they asked each other was "Is she real?" This was nearly always followed by a request to one of the party, such as, "Go on, Hugh, you're tall. You should be able to reach one of her legs." But they never could, for she was just out of range. When they read their programmes, they would see that Patricia Conolly was playing "A Dead Nurse."

It was very good that so many friends from Stratford were in this excellent production, for it made the routine I had started at the Comedy and continued at Stratford of visiting dressing rooms during the half (thirty-five minutes before curtain up) easy and a real pleasure for me.

## Scene 2 &copy; Peter Daubeny

By the time I met Peter Daubeny, he was a well-known figure in the theatre world for, as an independent impresario, he had been bringing foreign artists and foreign companies to England for many years with great success. I liked him at once, and although he could get extremely irritable when things did not go his way, we always got on very well. He was more than ably helped by his wife Molly, who was always totally calm and sensible, and there is no doubt in my mind that the pair made a wonderful team. They deserved our thanks for all their hard work and perseverance. These attributes were necessary when they were collecting companies from overseas and presenting them independently at first and for many years in a West End theatre, and then at the Aldwych, under the Royal Shakespeare Company's wing with Peter Hall's guidance and encouragement.

Peter Daubeny had lost most of his left arm at Salerno during the Italian campaign of the Second World War. When Molly and Peter accepted our invitation to come out to Putney to dinner, Elizabeth mentioned to Guy and Clive, then in their early teens, of Peter's loss and suggested that perhaps it should not be remarked on in case it might be a subject he wouldn't want to talk about.

During the evening, Peter behaved as he always did, which was never to sit still for very long. Whether at a formal meeting or just the two of us working out plans in my office, he would unexpectedly leap up and start prowling round the room with his right hand clutching the left shoulder, which emphasised the fact that there was nothing in that left sleeve below his clasping hand. It was probably these actions that caused Clive, suddenly and seriously, to ask, "How did you lose your arm?" At once, Peter answered him at length and in a quite calm and matter-of-fact manner that made a deep impression on all of us. He was an unexpected man.

## Scene 3 &copy; The Peter Daubeny season, Aldwych Theatre, 1963

Peter Daubeny had come on the scene very soon after I arrived at the Aldwych. He was to present a special season in that theatre under the title "The Peter Daubeny Season." During the four-week run, London would be able to see the great Irish actor, Micheal MacLiammoir, in two "entertainments," directed by Hilton Edwards. *The Importance of Being Oscar* and *I Must Be Talking to My Friends* for the first three weeks, while in the fourth week Peter would present Vittorio Gassman and his Theatro Popolare Italiano in *The Heroes*. The Italian actors would be speaking in their native tongue.

I had the enormous pleasure of working with Micheal (I always had to be careful to spell our shared first name the Irish way) when I was the stage manager for Tennent Productions, Ltd., of *Hedda Gabler*, in which he played Judge Brack. It was Micheal, soon after we opened this production at the original Lyric Theatre in Hammersmith, who pointed out that when I was calling the quarter hour over the Tannoy, I pronounced the word *quarter* as "korter." "Dear boy," he said, in his wonderful, rich, old-actorish-type voice. "Don't forget that there is a *u* in the word *quarter*." Since that lesson I have never forgotten the *u,* and now every time I hear someone on the radio use the word, when it is almost invariably "korter," I think of that endearing man.

It was George Devine, playing Tesman in that production of *Hedda Gabler*, who told me that at every performance he was amazed by the way Micheal, as Judge Brack, could sit with him at a table in the inner room of Percy Harris's perfect set and regale him with endless, brilliant stories — different every day — while at the same time he was able to listen for several cues that Dame Peggy Ashcroft, as Hedda, would be giving him. These cues were of the "speak more quietly, Thea dear, I think Judge Brack can hear us" type. All that was needed then was for Micheal to make no more than an almost imperceptible move in his chair or perhaps the slightest turning of his head towards Tesman, and without fail, they were given — even though the low-toned conversation between the two men in the inner room continued unbroken.

Micheal's two solo shows at the Aldwych during April and May 1963 went so well that, following the Gassman company's visit, he returned for a two-week extension. The majority of these extra performances were those of the Oscar Wilde, which had been much the more popular of his pair. Gassman's shows had been done well, but I found the one performance I watched to be one of the most irritating and the most boring I had been subjected to in many years of theatre-going. This had nothing to do with the actors, and I was delighted when those around me were laughing and chuckling with evident, almost too evident, delight. It was as though my neighbours' reactions were underlining the fact that I couldn't understand Italian, whereas they could, and — ho, ho, ho — what a lot of good lines I was missing because of my lack of linguistic skills.

## Scene 4 ᘓ Setting up simultaneous translation for a World Theatre Season, 1964

It was because of this visit by the Italian company that, when Peter Hall told me later in the year there would be input from Peter Daubeny as part of the Royal Shakespeare Company's celebration of the quarter-centenary of Shakespeare's birth, I reacted as I did. He would be presenting a season at the Aldwych to be called World Theatre Season, which would consist of visits, of one to three weeks each, by companies from around the world. The Royal Shakespeare Company actors would not be involved. It sounded very exciting, but I felt I had to point out to Peter that no way was I going to sit through week after week of not understanding, such as I had had with the Gassman Company. I then asked if he would mind if I investigated a system of instant translation. I had never experienced such a system in a theatre, but I knew it was used at the United Nations and similar multilingual diplomatic meetings. Peter said I could go ahead with this idea, but it must be self-financing.

It was not long before I found a company who specialised in such systems and a representative, Mr. Montague, came to see me. He seemed very excited at the plan, and we examined the way we could wire up every seat with a jack plug into which the lead from a pair of headphones could be slotted. He also looked for a place where a soundproof booth could be placed in the auditorium in which the translators — I told him there would never be more than two — could sit and get a clear, straight-ahead view of the stage. Placing the booth like this would help the translator's to match up, as far as possible, the English they would be speaking into their microphones with the foreign-language speech from the stage. We could find only one possible place for a booth, and this was at the back of the stalls. Certainly, this position would mean that we would have to take out some seats, but the idea had such strong support that it was reckoned to be worth the loss of income. At least the place was in one of the cheaper areas of the theatre.

The London County Council (LCC) would need to grant the theatre a licence for the system, so I made contact with the necessary department whose representatives at once showed us a snag in our plans. The idea was approved in principle, but it had to be set up in such a way that there were no wires in the auditorium. As it was pointed out to me, in the event of a fire, all those with headphones would rip them off and the wires plus headphones would without doubt cause horrendous hazards to those rushing along the rows of seats on the way to the exits.

From the LCC, I learned that such a system was already installed at the Westminster Theatre, which, permanently it seemed, was occupied by an organisation called Moral Re-Armament (MRA). I made an appointment with the theatre manager, Mr. Pither, and went to the Westminster to meet him. He explained briefly about the incumbents in his theatre. He said that MRA was a worldwide organisation and that its followers came in groups from many countries to the Westminster to see the special productions, which were played in English. Translators, housed in booths built into the back of the circle, provided instant translations so that every overseas patron could understand what the actors were saying. Each group told Mr. Pither the date of its visit and what language would be needed. At once, the efficient Mr. Pither called in the appropriate translator.

Even while I was thanking him for his help and for showing me the booths, I knew that this was the very opposite of what I required. So I pressed ahead with a system that would suit our patrons, all of whom, if they wanted a translation from a variety of languages during a season, would be hearing it in English. By this time, Mr. Montague had shown me a baton-type receiver that would be easy to hand out and to handle. When hired, the baton would become the patron's property until the end of the performance, when it would be returned. These plastic batons were a little over a foot long with a small circular piece at the top that held the tiny speaker. At the other end, the narrow central column bulged out slightly to form a convenient handhold, as well as housing a battery. The licensing authority was pleased with these, and they also approved of the site at the back of the stalls where the booth would be placed.

Kitty Black was engaged as producer and editor of the simultaneous translation (as the system was now termed) side of the season. This meant that she was responsible for arranging for a visiting company's script to be translated and then to engage the one or two translators we decided would be necessary for each particular play. We also thought that the public would appreciate a woman reading the lines when an actress on stage was speaking, with a man reading those for actors, but we didn't make it a hard and fast rule: The composition of the play was really the final arbiter. All this Kitty accomplished with great perseverance, flair, and success.

As far ahead as possible before the arrival of each company, I had to send a copy of the scripts to the Lord Chamberlain, in his role as censor, in both its original form and in the translated version that Kitty Black had arranged for her translators.

## Scene 5 ❧ Preparations for a State Gala at the Aldwych Theatre

However, long before all these plans, for what proved to be the first of a series of annual World Theatre Seasons, were put into action, another unusual event turned up. Peter Hall came to the Aldwych from a meeting at Buckingham Palace with Prince Philip who had explained that in July there was to be a state visit by the King and Queen of the Hellenes (up until now, I would have referred to their Majesties as being the King and Queen of Greece). Prince Philip explained that during such visits by foreign royalty, an evening at Covent Garden for a performance of opera or ballet would be arranged. This year, the royal guests' visit to London coincided with a season at the Royal Opera House of the Bolshoi Ballet, and it was thought that Her Majesty should not take her guests to see a foreign company. Would the Royal Shakespeare Company be able to offer, instead, a performance of *A Midsummer Night's Dream*, which would, of course, be entirely appropriate since the scene is set in and near Athens?

Peter was able to say that by great good luck, this play would be part of the summer repertoire at the Aldwych, and since booking for it had not yet opened, it would be perfectly possible to schedule that play for whatever night suited His Royal Highness. "You have to get in touch with a department called Government Hospitality, and they will fill you in with whatever special arrangements you will have to make for that performance," Peter was told. This information was immediately passed on to me, and I was asked to go ahead.

Whichever casting department arranged that Sir Geoffrey Macnab should be my State Gala contact with Government Hospitality couldn't have cast anyone more perfectly suited to his role: He was very efficient, very relaxed, and had a glorious sense of humour. It was a real joy working with him. He came to the theatre as soon as the preliminaries were out of the way, and I introduced him to Paul Anstee, who had been engaged as designer of the front-of-house for the occasion. Again, I was blessed with another really delightful and talented person with whom to go through the problems and worries of preparing for the gala. Paul was as amazed as I when Sir Geoffrey said that every area into which or along which their Majesties would pass must be lined with material. So first we had to work out their route and, even more importantly, decide the position of the royal box. The ideal place must: provide easy access with the fewest number of stairs; accommodate the sixteen-strong royal party, of which eight would be top royals; position all the royal party so that they could see and hear the performance clearly; and position the royal party so that the audience could easily see the top eight royals and, if possible, the remaining eight as well. In addition, we would need a royal retiring room for the interval.

To reach the stalls or the back of the dress circle meant stairs, but the front of the dress circle and the circle boxes were on a level with the foyer. So it was, of course, to this area that we went immediately. The first places to investigate were the two boxes, for although Paul and I knew that they could only accommodate three on each side, Sir Geoffrey had to see for himself. The three of us agreed that they would have been fine but for their size, so they were dismissed. The next possible place was the front row of the dress circle with eight each side of the central gangway, but although Sir Geoffrey was tempted, he also had to turn this possibility down, since so few of the audience would be able to see the royal party. I didn't bother to suggest the front stalls because of the stairs, so all I was left with were the sites that I had reckoned from the start would certainly be possible.

On each side of the auditorium and forming a link between the front rows of the dress circle and the boxes were two unconnected levels, each containing a few seats. The upper level was, in box office parlance, a box, although it was quite open with no enclosing walls. Its advantage was that the only means of access was by its own door, which led directly from the circle's outer corridor. The lower level was an extension of the front row of the dress circle, making them slip seats. They were reached via another door off the outer corridor, which led to the front rows of the dress circle.

My plan was to close off the lower levels from the dress circle and then, hard against the wall of the dress circle boxes (the ones we had had to reject), build new short staircases. These would link the upper to the lower levels, and since each level could seat four persons, the whole royal party would be sitting in identical positions on either side of the auditorium. The four top royals would occupy the lower level seats, while the remainder, equally divided into two groups of four, would sit in the upper levels. Both areas would need special chairs that would come from Buckingham Palace, and we could only hope that these would fit in the confined space on the lower levels.

Sir Geoffrey agreed to this plan and he also agreed that the top royals should sit on the lower level, in spite of the lack of space, since more of the audience would see them there. Very quickly he decided he would suggest to the foreign secretary that Her Majesty, Prince Philip, and the King and Queen of the Hellenes should sit on the lower level on the audience left of the auditorium, while the remaining four of the top royals, including the Queen Mother, would sit on the lower level on the audience right.

Arrangements were made at once as to how and when the work should begin on the necessary alterations to the new boxes. When this work was about half completed, Lord Hume, then foreign secretary, came to inspect the theatre so that he could act as guide on the gala night. This was now confirmed as Wednesday, July 10. He arrived exactly on time, and his tall, spare figure was soon exploring the front-of-house. We climbed the stairs that led out of the foyer to what would become the royal retiring room, back to foyer level into the gently sloping outer corridor, and round to the door of the audience left royal boxes. There was little light in the auditorium since the electrics were lighting the production that had just been set up on the stage, and coming in from the brightness in the outer corridor meant that the auditorium seemed darker than it actually was. This did not deter Lord Hume; as we stood in the upper box, I pointed to the lower level and said that Her Majesty would be seated there, and he immediately dived towards it. There was as yet no carpet on the new staircase nor was there a brass handrail in place, so the foreign secretary nearly reached the lower level quicker than even he had planned, for he misplaced a step and appeared to topple forward. Luckily I was close behind him and was able to clutch his arm, and as if nothing had happened, he continued on his downward path at, I was glad to note, a slower pace.

The Hellenic royal family was not the most popular of royal families as far as many Britons were concerned. Thus, security became a very big part of this whole exercise, since it was felt certain that demonstrations were bound to occur during their London visit.

I was soon invited to go to the headquarters of the Metropolitan Police, which was still housed in the New Scotland Yard building with the distinctive horizontal white stone stripes. It faced the river and was on the opposite side of the road to Big Ben. I had to go through all the plans for the evening, and I left with a request that I take back, as soon as possible, the names and addresses of everyone, absolutely everyone, who would be in the building during the day and during the evening of the State Gala. I duly took this list, and it was carefully looked through with the occasional question. When that was completed, I was told to return in ten days time when the results of closer inspections would be available.

I went back as bidden, but this time the atmosphere was not quite so cordial. "We are concerned about the inclusion of two of the cast. They have each, at various times and at various locations, made political speeches that indicate that they may use the stage as a platform for more political haranguing, and this must not happen. We have to ask you to recast these parts, although, of course, we will want to have full details of the actors who are the replacements to ensure they are accept-able." I was appalled and said that this was well-nigh impossible. The two actors were playing leading roles, and quite apart from the fact that the director of the production, Peter Hall, was not too well and was busy at Stratford, it was extremely important that the company present the production that had been so very highly praised. I went on to say that, however good the replacements might be, the high quality of ensemble playing could not be maintained if there were two new actors. I added that I would also be worried at reactions from the remainder of the cast, to say nothing of those working in other departments of the company, if these two were not permitted to play on the night of the gala.

There was much discussion at the other side of the desk, and then I was told that they appreciated what I had said so I would be allowed to present the full cast as I had requested, but the total responsibility for an incident-free performance lay with me. If I would accept that responsibility, then the production could go ahead. With the thought of possibly having to be carried off to the Tower, I said that of course I would accept the responsibility, since I was absolutely certain that no one on that stage would misbehave in any way during the perform-ance. Superstitiously, I was touching the wooden frame of the chair as I said this. I told no one about the outcome of my Scotland Yard vis-its. I was certainly concerned as to how much those at the Yard knew about persons they considered held subversive views, for not only were the two actors named, but the police were able to quote briefly what these two had said at public rallies many years previously.

## Scene 6 ✆ A State Gala at the Royal Opera House, Covent Garden May 1963

Two months before the State Gala at the Aldwych, there was a gala at the Royal Opera House, Covent Garden. Sir Geoffrey thought it would be a good idea if I attended this function, for I would then see how the staff at Covent Garden, which had often housed such events, dealt with State Galas. Elizabeth and I duly presented ourselves at the mag-nificent building into which we seldom ventured. It was a comfortable feeling that we were not responsible for anything that happened that evening. Our seats were on the same level as the royal box into which, across the great divide of that splendid auditorium, we could see with ease, for all the box partitions between our seats and the royal box had been removed. In fact, our view of the royal box was much better than our view of the stage, which, to put it mildly, was nil. We were placed not only almost next to the proscenium arch, we were also in the second row. Still, that had its compensations, for in front of us were Lord and Lady Hume's daughters, and when what was happening — or not happening — on the stage permitted a quiet conversation, we were able to exchange news and views. The music sounded lovely and if a dancer jumped high enough, I was often able to see an outstretched hand, so that was exciting.

Came the interval and we had been told to go and mingle in the royal retiring room, which we dutifully did, although this mêlée didn't seem so different from any other of similar, but perhaps less exalted, versions we had ourselves come across. The only uncommon event was when the crush caused Elizabeth to step back, neatly treading on Prince Philip's foot, but this was only a momentary hiccup during a smooth interval. We were very honoured to have been invited, and the whole evening had a very warm, opulent feel to it, but I cannot say that I learned anything from it.

## Scene 7 ⬤ Paul Anstee transforms the Aldwych Theatre

All this time Paul Anstee was well ahead with his designs and seamstresses all over London must have been busy making curtains and swags and tiebacks and coverings for walls. The one space that he and I decided from the start must be filled in was the large circular hole between the foyer and the royal retiring room, as the dress circle bar would become, otherwise Paul was free to let his excellent taste take over. He told me that he intended to continue the theme and the autumnal colours of Lila de Nobili's beautiful stage designs for *A Midsummer Night's Dream,* so that they would be carried into the auditorium, on into the corridors, round to the foyer, and up to the dress circle bar. Thus, when the transformation of the theatre would begin, brocade and velour in various shades of soft browns, greens, and yellows would appear. I was soon airily mentioning baldachins and palanquins as if I had always known of the words and in what context they could be used. The architraves of all doors and openings would be covered with canvas, painted as swags, over the openings and down the sides. The royal boxes on the upper levels were to have high backings of heavy dark-green curtains, lined with yellow brocade, and swept back deeply on each side, while the original corridor wallpaper and the foyer walls would disappear under yards of luscious medium-brown velour. The foyer's circular opening in its ceiling having been boarded over would be covered with material, pleated on the top with swags round the outer rim.

## Scene 8 ꩜ During the Day of the State Gala

Checking my desk diary for Wednesday, July 10, 1963, I found these entries:

| | |
|---|---|
| 7 AM | Start |
| | District Surveyor to visit to check steel scaffolding |
| 11–12 | Statuary |
| 2 PM | Collect Buckingham Palace chairs — |
| | Trade Gate B. Pal Rd. |
| | Arrange collection |
| 3:45 PM | Company to look at Decorations |
| | + John Collins — Cov Garden |

Then, after several blank lines, there are a couple of words, which were entered in the days when the event was to be kept as secret as possible:

Special Perf.

We certainly needed that seven o'clock start. By that time, special carpeting had been laid overnight and most of the hanging had been hung, while acres of flowers were arriving to be placed everywhere — in the foyer, along the circle front, in, around, and above the royal boxes, and up the staircases to the royal retiring room. Here, the first thing to catch one's eye was the new vast central circular table covered in deep blue velvet, in the centre of which was placed the most enormous and most beautiful floral display, which exploded out of a cornucopia.

There also appeared a large number of real trees. Some were tied to the newel posts of the stairs leading from the foyer to the dress circle bar, but the majority were larch (or were they silver birch?), which were placed around the walls of the bar and in front of, and completely hiding, the bar itself. All of them had lamps placed under them, so that the light filtered up through the leaves. The effect was magical, and that normally staid, formal, bland, dull, dingy room, with the hole in the middle, was indeed, like Bottom the weaver, translated.

It was the usual nonstop day with all seeming to be happening as and when it should until I was called to the phone. Peter Hall was not well enough to travel to London, so would I please take his place. I hadn't been prepared for this, but at least I had plenty of time — or so I thought — to consider what difference it might make to what I had vaguely planned for myself that evening. However, so much was going on that my new role was pushed to the bottom of the heap and forgotten.

At three o'clock, all the theatre's doors were shut, and from then on security was in charge of the building, and the big search began. They literally went from roof to basement examining everywhere, I was told. The loyal band of cleaners had been lovingly giving everything a special extra clean and polish, but they were able to get away in time to prepare themselves for the evening. I had felt it was not fair, considering how much extra work they had had to put in, for them to leave the place spick and span and then go home. So I had told them to come back at a suitable time when they were to tuck themselves into the tiny foyer cloakroom, which would not be used that night, from where they could peep out and watch the arrival of the guests.

The Royal Artillery Band, who were to play a fanfare and the national anthems, arrived in force, and so did a selection of yeoman warders looking as splendid as ever in their Tudor uniforms. The chairs from the palace were duly delivered, and thank goodness, they just fitted into the lower boxes, although there was not a lot of room for passing along in front of them. However, I knew from past experience that the royal family are the most wonderful guests. So long as clear indications are given, they will place themselves wherever they realise they have to be, with absolutely no fuss. Although Lord Hume, with Lady Hume this time, had come for another walk over the route two days previously, they wouldn't be able to help the top royals into their boxes, for there was room only for those who would be sitting on the Buckingham Palace chairs.

Suddenly, at about six o'clock, the theatre stopped dead in its tracks. How word got around I don't know, but there was a definite sense of controlled alarm in the front-of-house. It was quite uncanny. Then the feeling turned into words: a coat was seen on the chair on which Her Majesty would be sitting. It hadn't been there when a security man had checked the chairs only a short while previously. The theatre held its breath, while security very slowly approached the offending article and gingerly picked it up. Relax, relax. All is well: it was a raincoat left by another security man. Panic over. Fine. So the panic was over, but how on earth did it happen to get there? Would the owner really have walked into that bower of flowers and put his raincoat down in such a special area on such a special chair and forget it? Oh, well, not worth thinking about further. We had the all clear, and all was well again except that I looked at my watch and Paul and I had far less time than we had reckoned in which to change into full evening dress. Up the seventy-two stairs to my office at a run, where we managed the change — no top hats but certainly white tie and tails — in record time, followed by a dash down the stone stairs with my little medals clinking together on each step (I had been amazed when I went to Moss Bros to hire full evening dress and was advised how many medals I was entitled to wear as a result of being involved in the Second World War), and into the foyer just in time to greet the chairman of the Board of Governors of the Royal Shakespeare Theatre, Sir Fordham Flower, and Lady Flower. We lined up in front of the box office to become the reception committee, and shortly afterwards we were greeting the first guests.

## Scene 9 ✎ The State Gala, Wednesday, July 10, 1963

The police were more than ready for demonstrators, who sure enough turned up. Many held banners on which were words, such as "Release the political prisoners," "Restore human rights in Greece," and "Stop political persecution in Greece." Barricades had been set up along the edge of the pavement opposite the theatre, and mounted police clopped backwards and forwards close to the barrier. Little sound, other than usual crowd noises, came from those opposite, until the first guest, the Labour prime minister, Mr. Clement Attlee, arrived. As his official car drew up, the shouts began and continued from then on with greater and lesser volume, depending, it seemed, on the occupants of the cars. That a Labour prime minister should be booed was strange, but when the Queen Mother was also given the same unpleasant treatment, I realised my first thought — that it was the occupants of the cars who were being jeered — was wrong. The demonstrators were shouting at any official car without actually knowing who was inside, for the cars were between those stepping out onto the pavement and them.

None of those verbally attacked showed the slightest sign of being affected by the reception, for they got out of the cars, which stopped exactly beside the red carpet, and walked smiling and apparently relaxed under the special awning that led them into the circular outer foyer and up the few steps to the inner foyer. There they were totally out of sight of the onlookers across the road. I had arranged for the awning because I hadn't liked to risk the weather — even in July. Although from that point of view, it was unnecessary, for the evening was dry and calm. However, in the end, the awning proved another shield for the guests.

The majority of the audience in the stalls and dress circle was the Diplomatic Corps, who, being used to such affairs, were already seated in the correct order of precedence by the time the royal party began to arrive. Soon the foyer was crowded with royals, all of whom greeted each other as if they hadn't met for several days. Doubtless they were discussing the demonstrators, who now somehow managed to increase their volume as car after car drew up. Just behind me, as I stood in front of the unused box office, a tiny Greek reporter was giving a running radio commentary on the arrivals, but it must have been difficult to understand what he was saying for the foyer was abuzz with conversation. Princess Alexandra, the daughter of Princess Marina, without doubt the Royal Shakespeare Company's most frequent royal visitor to the Aldwych, kindly came over to chat with me for a while, presumably because she saw that although everyone seemed to know each other, I was not part of that elite.

At last, there was a move towards the auditorium for the sixteen royal guests who would be seated in the royal boxes. As arranged, these sixteen skillfully split into two groups of eight, each passing down the curving corridors — which looked so beautiful and inviting — towards their respective boxes. The top royals had some fun entering the narrow passage caused by the large chairs, which meant they had to squeeze their way towards their seats. All went well, even though the poor Queen Mother had real difficulty with her crinoline as she moved past three chairs to reach her seat directly across the auditorium from that of her elder daughter, Her Majesty the Queen. I hadn't thought of catering for such a gown, but, come to think of it, even if I had, there was nothing I could have done about it except to warn her private secretary of the space problem.

We had the fanfare and the anthems, and then the performance began. I was at once horrified to find that, from within the auditorium, I could hear the barracking from without, and I am sure that this unpleasant sound must have affected the audience, for I cannot give them many marks towards being the best audience ever at a performance of *The Dream*. But I had another worry: What about the subversive pair? Each time either of them came onstage, I was prepared, but up to the interval, nothing untoward happened. Even so, I was only too aware that we were only halfway through the evening.

## Scene 10 ℚ The interval in the State Gala

The dress circle bar looked great. Pity the well-worn carpet couldn't have been replaced, but who would glance down at that when the whole space would be filled by the time those invited had arrived and soon they were there, again in perfect order of precedence. The actors chosen to be presented had somehow managed to beat the royal party in a race round the outer corridor and up the stairs to the bar and were duly lined up with their backs to the trees, facing the centre table with its monster flower arrangement.

I wasn't quite sure how I was going to present all the actors to the royal party, so I stayed with Her Majesty, and in her usual brilliant way, she passed down the line of actors, greeting each with a few words. Prince Philip followed the Queen, but he was much slower than usual. In fact, I don't think he got further than the stunning Diana Rigg during the whole interval. The Queen Mother seemed quite content to pass down the line, brightly chatting to anyone she came across. Soon the line of actors blessedly broke up, and it just became like any family party — in fact, so much so, it wasn't easy to get the actors to leave a conversation in order for them to rush back so that the play could continue.

At last the royals returned to their seats, and we were back into *The Dream*, although there were still the unwanted cries from the street, which by now had become a very ugly roar. For the remainder of the evening, the sound never let up, and somehow the roar became more and more menacing.

## Scene 11 ✆ Act II of *A Midsummer Night's Dream* and after the State Gala performance

Standing in the foyer during the second act was a most unpleasant place to be. Even though mounted police were still in evidence and there certainly were a large number of police in the street, the sound seemed to forecast the sudden breaking down of the barrier. By now I had forgotten about the two actors; all I could think of was whether the audience would get away safely.

At last the play was over — and I am sure I wasn't the only one who was relieved — and the most miraculous arrangement, impeccably planned by the police and Government Hospitality, came into play. As each VIP crossed the foyer towards the front doors, a call came up the stairs from the street announcing that his car was awaiting him. Unlike Lady Macbeth's urgent request to her guests, as she hustled them out into the night after that disastrous dinner party, that they stand not upon the order of their going, here the order of their going was very important, and in some magical way, all seemed to know that order.

When the steady but speedy flow of VIPs moved towards the front doors, they passed the sergeant in charge of the yeoman warders. He was standing in front of the box office, saluting each VIP. The speed with which they travelled towards the street seemed to demand that the sergeant's right arm be in almost constant motion, for scarcely had it dropped to his side after one VIP had been saluted, it had to shoot up again as the next VIP came into view. Each salute was impeccable, with the arm and hand making one perfect straight line.

At last the exodus tailed off, until, with the departure of the Duke of Edinburgh, who was leaving for the post-performance reception at Lancaster House, the only guests remaining were Her Majesty and the Queen Mother. Since they were not going to the reception, there was to be a slight gap between the stream of cars making for Lancaster House and their cars, which would be going to Buckingham Palace and Clarence House respectively. Thus they stood in the centre of the foyer chatting, while the sergeant, who had saluted as soon as they had appeared, could do nothing but hold his salute while they were in front of him. After a while, Her Majesty looked towards the street, and as she did so, she caught sight of the sergeant. At once she said, "Oh, please put your arm down, Sergeant."

Out in the street, no barriers were breached and nothing was hurled nor were any untoward remarks or gestures made from the stage, so the evening was counted a success. Inside the theatre, all that had to be done was remove all the flowers, hangings, and decorations so that the theatre could be back to normal by 7:30 PM the next evening when *A Midsummer Night's Dream* would be played to a paying public. And the chairs had to be returned to Buckingham Palace.

## Scene 12 ✎ *The Beggar's Opera*, Aldwych Theatre, July 1963

Playing in repertoire at the Aldwych during the summer of 1963 alongside *A Midsummer Night's Dream* was a production of *The Beggar's Opera,* directed by Peter Wood. The design was by Sean Kenny whose approach to theatre design was exciting and different. He didn't work at the Royal Court during my time there, although we only just missed each other, since his first design was for William Gaskill's production of Donald Howarth's play *Sugar in the Morning.* This was followed by designing for George Devine (Sean O'Casey's *Cock-a-Doodle Dandy*) and for Lindsay Anderson (*The Lily White Boys* by Harry Cookson and Christopher Logue), but it was Lionel Bart's *Oliver!* at the New Theatre that confirmed all the good things I had felt about him. During preparations for *The Beggar's Opera*, I had to go to White City on several occasions since Sean was designing for the BBC, and the pressure at which they worked him there meant that he wasn't able to come up to the Aldwych. He at once joined my private list of designers with whom I liked working, but then, without exception, all the designers with whom I worked I liked enormously.

Peter Wood's approach to John Gay's comedy was to make the majority of the cast be convicts waiting deportation in a ship that would take them to Australia. The setting was a yard below a quayside, whose granite blocks formed a solid backing to the set. Scarlet-coated soldiers paraded high up along the harbour wall, and beyond them, tied alongside, was a large sailing ship. The convicts, watched from above by the soldiers, acted out a play in the yard, using a series of empty crates to denote a change of location, until at last their guards came down into the yard and ordered the convicts to climb up the granite steps and board the ship.

There were two identical sets of steps, one up left and the other up right, and as the cast climbed these steps to the quayside, they sang one of Gay's haunting songs. When the last of them were aboard, the two ends of the huge granite wall, pivoting from a central point, swung slowly towards each other until they met downstage centre. As they came together, one could see that the two ends had become the stern of an old wooden walls ship, such as one knew from illustrations of Nelson's HMS *Victory*. This meant we were presented with a view of the stern of the ship, which held a series of small-paned windows with the name of the vessel painted below. Some of the actors looked through these windows, while, above them, others stood on deck at the very stern of the ship. All continued to sing as a sail was hoisted that at once caught the wind and bellied out. At the same time, dry ice floated in from either side of the stage, and the revolve began to move very slowly, to the right for a foot or two and then very slowly to the left for the same distance. This, to my amazement, gave the impression that the ship was on the move. The cast on board continued singing and the curtain fell. The whole scene, from the movement of the quayside to curtain down, could not have taken more than a few minutes, but the effect was stunning. Sadly, the critics did not approve of the production, their main complaint being that the singing was not up to the standard they expected. I could never agree with them since what was given by the cast, led by Dorothy Tutin, a delicious Polly, and Derek Godfrey, a virile Macheath, was a fine and varied presentation of the convicts. They sang as those characters would have sung and not as fully trained singers, so that one could believe totally in what one was seeing and hearing.

## Scene 13 ✆ *The Representative,* September 1963

That year, 1963, was a good one at the Aldwych with an extremely interesting and varied repertoire sandwiched between two excellent modern plays, with *The Physicists* at the start of the year and Hochhuth's strong play *The Representative* to end it. Clifford Williams directed the British premiere of the latter play in settings by Ralph Koltai, with both of them contributing enormously to the impact this play had on the public. In the leaflet that announced *The Representative*, it told of Hochhuth's claim that Pope Pius XII failed to take a strong stand against the Nazi extermination of the Jews during the Second World War. The penultimate of the six settings took place in a throne room in the Vatican in which Pope Pius XII, played by Alan Webb, appeared. The final scene, Act II, Scene 3, was set in Auschwitz, October 28, 1941, at dawn.

In the Aldwych's sixteen-page programme, eight dealt only with the Royal Shakespeare Company and the production. Of these eight, two were taken up with a short paragraph announcing that, due to the controversial nature of the play, the Royal Shakespeare Company had printed a special twelve-page supplement to the programme, which was on sale for two shillings and sixpence. The remainder of the two pages contained a brief paragraph stating that the Lord Chamberlain had requested the Royal Shakespeare Company to print in every Aldwych programme an authoritative Catholic opinion. This was a letter from G. B. Cardinal Montini, Archbishop of Milan, to *The Tablet.* The letter reached this Roman Catholic publication, the programme stated, an hour before the author was elected to the papacy. Then followed the letter, a full page and a half in length, justifying the conduct of Pope Pius during the war, in particular his not publicly condemning the massacre of the Jews by the Nazis nor expressing opposition to Hitler.

This play, and its presentation, has stayed firmly in my memory, but I have another memory of that time, although of a more domestic nature. The production was being given a dress rehearsal which came on a day when it was necessary for me to take our Welsh collie, Andrew, to the theatre each day, there being no one at home to look after him. He didn't mind this break in his normal routine, except that he refused to be left alone in the office, so if I had visits to make around the theatre, he came with me. This led to us both watching the dress rehearsal of *The Representative* from the back row of the upper circle, which was easily reached from the reception area of the offices. The scene was Act I, Scene 2, "The Jagerkeller at Falkensee." The only entrance into this scene was through a door upstage centre. At one point, Gordon Gostelow, as Kurt Gerstein Obersturmfuhrer SS, suddenly entered through this door. He was wearing a peaked cap and was dressed in a long dark-green greatcoat with two rows of shining buttons.

Andrew had been totally quiet up to that point, watching the play far below us, but the sight of someone in a uniform stirred his antagonism. He must have thought this walking greatcoat posed a risk to me, for when Gordon took a step forward, a low growl started beside me. I told him that it was a play and not to worry, but Andrew knew better. The growling increased slightly in volume each time Gordon moved, so I decided that before it went further, we had better exit. This move justified everything that Andrew had been suspecting. He pushed past me to reach the door first, and as I swung it open, he raced out onto the landing, barking furiously at the enemy that must be out there. He had a good bark, and it reverberated around the stone staircase for a little while before I was able to show him that all, truly, was well and I was safe. Much later, I went to Clifford Williams to apologise for the great outburst from the gods during the rehearsal, but unexpectedly he denied hearing anything untoward.

Little could either of us know that four years later, Andrew would himself be treading the boards. He appeared in *A View to the Common* by James Casey, which earned him a mention in the headline to Milton Shulman's notice in the *Evening Standard:* "At the Royal Court — applause for a barking dog!" There was also a mention in Eric Shorter's notice in the *Daily Telegraph:* ". . . and that despite the good acting of Victor Henry and Malcolm Tierney the witty barks of the dog (kindly loaned by Elizabeth Hallifax) should draw most instantaneous sympathy."

## Scene 14 ◎ *The Wars of the Roses,* January 11 to March 12, 1964

The 400th anniversary of Shakespeare's birth fell in 1964, and Peter Hall was determined that it would be celebrated in a way to do the Bard of Avon proud — both at Stratford itself and also in London. At the Aldwych, the year would start with the final three weeks of the hugely successful *The Comedy of Errors,* after which Shakespeare's three history plays, which made up *The Wars of the Roses,* would transfer to London from Stratford. The three plays would be presented in repertory, although *King Lear* would drop in for three performances in February before it went on a world tour, when it would be accompanied by *The Comedy of Errors.*

However, *The Wars of the Roses* nearly didn't make it to the Aldwych. At Stratford, a huge table, set across the stage downstage centre, played a vital role. Although there was plenty of room in that theatre for this table to be struck into the wings, the same could not be claimed at the Aldwych. There, wing space on stage right was a few feet, and while stage left could offer more, it still was not enough for this vast table to be stowed out of the way of other scene changes. Peter Hall and his designer, John Bury, tried every which way to crack this problem, such as checking whether it would be possible to use a table of greatly reduced proportions, but there seemed no answer. I suddenly thought of a possible way out. I suggested that maybe the top of the table could be part of the floor and that a mechanism could be produced that would raise the table to its correct height when it was needed, while letting it sink back to become level with the stage floor when the scene was over. Luckily, this did prove possible, and so, to my great relief and delight, this exciting trio of *Henry VI, Edward IV,* and *Richard III* came to London.

The first performance on Saturday, January 11, 1964, was to be the first of several Saturdays when the three plays would be performed on the same day. In spite of the fact that *Henry VI* started at 10.30 AM, the theatre was always packed. Many came for the three plays, and those who did, and who discovered during the day that their neighbours were also there for all three plays, soon developed friendships. Some patrons jokingly complained that the intervals between the plays never gave enough time to discuss what they had seen and wonder what fate would deliver to those characters who continued from one play to the next. There were also long discussions about the entire cast, noting who had been given a small part in one play but had turned up in a longer one in another. The theatre became exactly like repertory theatres of old, when actors were engaged for season after season and regular theatre-goers, although never meeting them, would consider these long-term company members as their friends whose performances would be compared and evaluated. This was part of the fun of being faithful patrons of a repertory theatre. It was during this period at the Aldwych that I passed two smart young men as they made their way to the stalls for an evening performance and I overheard one saying to his companion, "I come here so often I feel as if I live here."

When planning the all-day Saturdays, it was obvious that, for the public, the break between the plays must allow comfortable time to have a reasonable meal and a chance to wander around. But for the actors, there would not be time to take off costumes and makeup, find a meal locally — perhaps vying with some of the audience to get served — and get back to the theatre in time to prepare for the next play. I therefore canvassed local cafés and restaurants, of which there were precious few, to see if any would be willing to send round a hot lunch for the cast. One little Italian restaurant was situated in the Strand only a few doors towards Fleet Street from the foot of Aldwych; since this made it relatively close, it looked a distinct possibility. Yes, they would be very happy to provide a hot meal for the considerable numbers involved, and since the price was very reasonable, I clinched the deal. They proved to be an excellent choice, arriving exactly on time. The meal was hot, and there was plenty for everyone who wanted to take advantage of what was provided.

On Saturday, January 11, the first of the all-day performances, I left home very early since there was so much to check over before the first audience would arrive. As I was driving along the King's Road, I passed the World's End pub just beyond which was a bus stop.

Leaning against the post was the unmistakable thin, elongated figure of Henry VI in the person of David Warner, so I was able to deliver the first of the kings to the theatre in better shape for the long day ahead than if he had had to travel up by bus. There were only four all-on-one-day presentations (10:30 AM, 3:00 PM, and 7:30 PM), and all were received triumphantly by their audiences. They applauded the actors for their performances and for keeping up their energy over the long day, while at the same time the majority of the audiences were secretly applauding themselves for having arrived at the theatre at about 10:15 AM and not leaving finally until 10:45 PM. An important and delightful member of one of those audiences was Princess Marina, Duchess of Kent. She had accepted an offer of tea during the interval of *Edward IV*, the afternoon play. As she appeared in the dress circle bar on her way to the office of Peter Sibley, the house manager, she did a mock weak-at-the-knees collapse before coming forward and saying, in her delicious accent, "It's marvellous."

## Scene 15 ❧ *The Rebel*, February/March 1964

For nine performances in 1964, four in February and five in March, *The Rebel* was presented. It was devised and directed by Patrick Garland, who had collected rebellious work by, amongst many, Arnold Bennett, Camus, e. e. cummings, Billy Fury, Ned Kelly, and Wilde, which were enacted or read by Peter Bowles, William Marlowe, Bryan Pringle, Clive Swift, and David Warner, with songs sung by David Andrews, Maureen Kennedy Martin, and Ian McCulloch.

It was an interesting mélange but it wasn't the content that raised many hackles, but the Lord Chamberlain's reaction to a poem by e. e. cummings entitled "Song of Olaf." This poem as a whole was said to be very offensive, but there were several lines to which the Lord Chamberlain took grave exception, and these were strictly not permitted to be spoken from the Aldwych stage.

Peter Hall was outraged, as indeed was Patrick Garland and many more. All were totally perplexed that anyone of any age could walk into any bookshop and read the e. e. cummings poem without hindrance, to say nothing of the fact that it had been read in full on a BBC TV Monitor programme, and yet it could not be read from the stage.

This was at the time when a campaign to rid the theatre of the Lord Chamberlain and the outmoded censorship rules by which he and his officers worked had been started, but it would still be some years before it became successful, so the Lord Chamberlain's rule was law. Pleading did not soften his outlook, and we seemed to have reached a deadlock, when I suggested to Peter that the poem should be printed and a copy placed on every seat.

Before the poem was read, it would be announced from the stage that there were certain lines to which the Lord Chamberlain had taken exception, which had resulted in a ban on these lines being spoken by an actor during a performance. At that point, the houselights would be brought up, and the audience would be encouraged to follow the printed poem as it was being read by an actor. When he reached a forbidden line, he would stop speaking, allow time for audience members to read the line for themselves, after which he would continue. Peter accepted the idea; the poem was printed and the arrangement for its presentation worked. It was a pity that the town did not flock to the nine performances of *The Rebel,* but I think those who knew what was taking place during them got some satisfaction that, in a small way, the Lord Chamberlain's office had been foiled in its attempt to have the poem removed from the programme.

## Scene 16 ℚ The first World Theatre Season, March 16 to June 13, 1964

Twelve weeks. Fifteen productions. Seven companies. Seven sets of directions for getting to the Aldwych from whichever hotel was being used. Seven large signs of welcome in the various languages that would be placed above the stage door. Many more signs, again in the appropriate languages, to be placed backstage, which would guide our visitors to the dressing rooms, the stage, the green room, the makeup room, the wardrobe, and so on. Interpreters had to be engaged who would be able, for instance, to make a member of the Aldwych stage staff understand a member of the visiting company's technical staff very quickly.

Speed of translation was essential. It soon proved relatively simple to find interpreters who were faultless in translating normal conversation, but it was not so easy to find those who could appreciate what technical item was being referred to by either team of technicians and who could at once describe that item, again in technical terms, so that it was understood immediately by the other team. In other words, here was the same problem that many of us had had during the *Hedda Gabler* and the *King Lear/Much Ado* tours in the middle 1950s except, of course, now it was mainly English into a foreign tongue rather than the other way round. The amount of work required from our backstage staff was at times going to be very heavy. Waiting around for a sentence to be translated could hold up a certain part of the work, and this could easily lead to irritability. I was also allowed to engage a liaison officer, whose duty was to be backstage all the time with the various companies, ready to answer questions, solve problems, and know where to go and whom to contact.

Peter Daubeny was a great source of information about the various companies, letting me know of any particular difficulties he foresaw or of any special request they might make. He also let me know how he was getting on with his plan to invite a member of the royal family to the first performance of every company. This meant that I had to know how many would be in the various royal parties and decide where they would sit and where they would go for interval drinks. Once again, as for the State Gala, it was a case of the less clambering up and down stairs the better. In the main, the royals sat in the front row of the dress circle. Even though these seats were on the same level as the foyer, a number of stairs still had to be climbed to reach the dress circle bar, and so to the house manager's office for the interval. But this was better than bringing a party up from the stalls and then subjecting them to a second flight of stairs.

For one particular visit, it was important that our VIPs were seated in the stalls. To save them battling their way along a row filled with the public to reach their places in the centre, I had three seats taken out from the middle of four rows of stalls, the final row of which backed onto a cross aisle. This meant the party could walk with ease along this aisle, turn down the new break in the stalls seating, and then divide up, with some of the party on the left and some on the right. For the interval, I used a room that in reality was little more than a slightly larger than normal corridor linking the front stalls with a pass door.

This "room" was close to the party's seats, and there were no stairs to negotiate once the stalls had been reached.

The audiences were always very understanding about royal visitors in spite of being asked to get to their seats five minutes before curtain up so that the foyer would not be too crowded when the royals arrived, and it was possible for me to arrange the line-up of those who were to be presented. The members of the public in the area where the royals would be sitting were also asked to stay in their seats during the interval until the royals had passed and also at the end of the evening until the royals had left the auditorium.

Sometimes the foyer was anything but clear: This usually happened when it was raining or when there had been a traffic holdup in the neighbourhood. But the royals, as ever, appeared not to notice and behaved as if they had all the space in the world. I felt it better that the public did not sit in the seats directly behind them or the ambassador of the country concerned, so Elizabeth and I used to take those seats, and then beside us I placed members of the embassy staff. Since my seat would always be at the end of a row, it meant I could with ease slip in or out as occasion demanded.

Before the start of each company's first performance, and also when royalty was present on an evening that was not a first performance, we would play the visiting country's national anthem before our own. Then at the end of the first performance of each play, Peter Sibley would pass down the line of the visiting actors at the curtain call presenting each actress with a bouquet.

The box office was very cramped, and the staff had been operating in conditions that made their always difficult work even more so. Luckily, John Hallett and Mr. Abrahams were sympathetic, and at the start of the first World Theatre Season, alterations were made to extend the box office by incorporating what had been a broom cupboard. This gave the staff more room but did not destroy the original look of the foyer. Although the demand on the staff during the first two and a half months of 1964 had been tremendous, mainly due to *The Wars of the Roses, The Comedy of Errors,* and the sadly few performances of *King Lear,* it was soon obvious that the demand for seats for the World Theatre Season would be terrific, so a temporary postal room must somehow be found. It was not until I went to a floor high up in the front-of-house that I discovered a room that, although far from ideal, certainly would provide working space for two or three temporary staff who would open the mail and register postal bookings.

Allocating tickets became the usual balancing act of wanting to give everyone the best seats in the area requested, but knowing, as ever, that this was impossible. This was especially so in the front rows of the stalls and the dress circle since so many seats had to be put on one side in readiness for a call from an embassy, from a private secretary, or from the visiting company. There was a wonderful response from those who wanted to come to the theatre to hear a performance in their own language and those from the theatrical profession who wanted to check acting and presentation styles of companies they had heard about but had not, until now, had a chance to see.

So began for me many visits to Heathrow Airport to greet various companies, all so excited, nervous, and proud to be appearing in London as representatives of their country. Until the M4 motorway was opened, journeys via the Great West Road took an intolerable time, and I used to be ashamed at how backward Britain seemed in not providing a desperately needed speedy road to the busy airport.

Often it was extremely difficult to recognise a company as they came into the arrivals section of an airport. When I was waiting for the Schiller Theatre Company from Berlin to arrive, an agent, Adza Vincent, joined me. She was carrying several very attractive posies, and as the actresses of the company came through, she handed one to each. They were surprised but touched by this friendly gesture and everything seemed to be going well as we walked towards the coach until Adza, talking to one of the company, found to her horror that one girl into whose hands she had thrust a posy was just a student who happened to be passing by at the time. "Oh, really!" cried Adza, grumpily and a trifle unkindly. She snatched the posy back from the startled girl, and then looked wildly round for the actress who had missed out in the floral distribution stakes.

The most delightful company of that first season was the Greek Art Theatre under Karolos Koun, who was the father figure to a group of young people who played a chirpy musical version of Aristophanes' *The*

*Birds* and *The Persians,* an attractive play, over two weeks. The public adored them. It was an amazing contrast when they were followed by the Moscow Art Theatre with three productions, the first of which was entitled *Dead Souls.* This lugubrious title hid an excellent play by Gorki that was memorable in many ways, not least for the performance by an actress of greatly advanced years who had apparently been playing the same role since she was a young woman. Her character was a rich landowner whose one scene consisted of an interview she gave to another landowner (who was trying to buy up, illegally, the names of her deceased serfs), so it was perfectly legitimate for the actress to be any age.

This production had another memorable moment. A dinner party attended by twenty-six guests had to be staged. This scene had to be struck in a matter of seconds, and in spite of the offstage space restrictions, this was accomplished. As with all quick changes, it was brilliantly choreographed: every diner took his or her chair and somehow made a speedy exit to the wings through two groups of stagehands who were coming onstage. The first group had to strike the fully laden tabletops on which, securely fixed, were all the necessary signs of the end of a substantial meal, and the second group struck the two huge tables from their V-shape setting.

In repertory with *Dead Souls* was a modern play, *Kremlin Chimes,* which the Moscow Art Theatre had insisted must be shown in spite of strong protests from Peter Daubeny, and *The Cherry Orchard.* Many were hoping that at last the Moscow Art Company would show how the extraordinary sound was made that the family hear when they are in the open air in the second act of the play. But it didn't turn out that way. They had a small box set up in the wing space, stage left, but they would not allow any of the local staff, or myself, to see what caused that weird, otherworldly noise to come out of the box.

Privately I had hoped that the presence of this company in London would somehow draw attention to the fact that the correct title for the company is the Moscow Art Theatre and that the word *Art* does not have the letter *s* attached to it — but no, the error still persists. This comes in the same category as the Shakespeare Memorial Theatre, which is often referred to as the Stratford Memorial Theatre.

## Scene 17 ✏ Simultaneous translation in action

Many an evening I cursed my stupidity in giving the World Theatre Seasons audiences the choice of listening to the play as spoken by the actors onstage or via simultaneous translation. This self-cursing started from day one.

While the first production of the Comédie Française, *Tartuffe*, was being set up, the firm equipping the theatre with simultaneous translation was building the soundproof cabin that would house the translators. There was no run-through of *Tartuffe* before its first performance, so this was going to be a real test of the system from the outset. Two readers, Susan Field and Adrian Brine, would have to fit the English words to the actors whose style, speed of delivery, accents, and actions would be unknown to them until the performance started. Only a short time before the curtain rose, we shut the two of them into their glass-fronted cage and saw them seated at the table, each with a microphone, the French and English texts, a glass of water, and a shaded table lamp. We mimed good wishes through the thick glass and left them to get on with it.

The incoming audience held long discussions as to how many in the various groups wanted a simultaneous translation baton. These were on hire in the foyer with staff specially engaged for the job of handing out the instruments. There were plenty of comments such as, "I know the play so well, I certainly don't want one of those things," to the more truthful "I know I shan't understand a word without help," and so the performance began with a capacity house.

It wasn't long before Peter Sibley found me and said that there was unrest at the back of the stalls because the audience sitting near the translators' box could hear them speaking: the sound was anything but proofed. I decided that there was nothing to be done during the first half of the evening, so I told Peter I would look for alternative accommodation, and he was to try, heavens knew how, to calm the protestors.

At last the blessed interval arrived, and I went into the back of the stalls where there was mayhem. Anyone who looked as if they were in any way remotely connected with the theatre was attacked verbally and, at times, I thought it was going to be physically too. I managed to get Susan and Adrian out of the box, from which they willingly fled, taking their scripts with them. As soon as they left, the technicians, who were standing by, moved in and connected extensions to the input and output wires. They then followed us, amidst roaring, angry patrons, through the door at the back of the stalls, luckily very close to the now ignominiously deserted cabin, past the stalls bar, and into the catering storeroom situated under the Aldwych pavement. The area was chilly and damp, but waiting for our two intrepid translators were two chairs, the flat top of a deep freeze, suitably lit, and no members of the audience shouting abuse.

The main obstacle, of course, was that Susan and Adrian would not be able to see the stage, but they were both quite superb in the way they accepted their change of locale, settling down as comfortably as they could, knowing that Peter Sibley was already on his way to give the word to Naomi Dunning, the liaison officer, that the front-of-house was clear and the curtain could rise on the second act. The insurgents in the stalls had been told, if they could hear above the hubbub, that the translators had been moved to another area, and certainly their anger abated somewhat when they saw the empty cabin, but this uneasy calm did not remain for long.

Few rented the batons, compared to performances later in the season. More batons were rented at later performances when the theatre company was one whose native tongue was more alien to British ears than French. Those renting these little instruments always managed to make the worst of them. They all seemed determined to hold the instruments incorrectly. If the tiny loudspeaker at the top of the baton could be held so that the sound was directed out into the auditorium and not into the holder's ear, then that is how it was held. The holder, not hearing the actors very clearly because he or she was listening through the plastic cover and not the speaker, would then decide to cure the lack of volume by turning the sound up to full. Those having the misfortune of sitting near the baton user would then get the translation at full blast. They were always the ones (taking the Comédie Française as an example) who wanted to drink in the beauty of the French language spoken by French actors, but instead got Adrian and Susan speaking impeccable English.

I still feel quite sick at the remembrance of that ghastly evening, which somehow managed to reach the final curtain. But it was not until the reception for the company much later that evening that I was able to apologise to the actors, who had also been disturbed by the chatter coming from the auditorium. They had been warned about the simultaneous translation, of course, because of being asked for a copy of the text, but, like us, they were not prepared for the sounds winging their way up from the audience.

Next day, Mr. Montague arrived with a much more solid-looking and allegedly truly soundproof cabin, which, having got permission all round, was placed in the audience left dress circle box. It was angled towards the stage as much as the design of the box would allow, and it was in there, from the second night of the visit by the Comédie Française onwards, that all the translators were seated. Certainly, a faint murmur still reached a few seats near the box, but we never had any more complaints. It was the translators who suffered from the move, for although the cabin certainly allowed a view of the stage, it was from an awkward angle, which did not cover the entire area.

The next question to arise was exactly how the translators should speak the lines. Should they act the speeches or should they be delivered flat? The arguments for and against continued day after day, usually depending on who had been tackled the previous evening by a friend or an unknown member of the public. They were genuinely trying to help, but no one method ever came out firmly on top. Part of the problem lay with the translators themselves, for even if I asked them to try and keep the dialogue as flat as possible ("as if it were a stream of consciousness" was a favourite phrase of the Flat Delivery School), it was not only extremely difficult but well nigh impossible to stop some of them from taking the tone and the volume of an actor onstage when delivering a passionate speech. If a piece of dialogue such as: "No, no. Please don't leave me! You mustn't go!" reached a translator through the headphones, then his or her flat voice vanished and an agonised, pleading one took its place. I often felt that the translators didn't realise their pitch had changed and they had started to act the scene.

It fell to an Italian company to present a hazard that we had not foreseen, not that we could have done anything about it if we had. Geoffrey Dunn was quite brilliant as the sole translator for Peppino de Filippo's *Metamorphoses of a Wandering Minstrel,* but even he had great difficulty on the opening night. He was faced, as ever, with a production he had never seen, during which one of the actors dried. No one onstage tried to help their fellow in his hour of need, so, following a sudden pause in the dialogue, this poor actor obviously decided that it was up to him to continue. On he ploughed as best as he could, but unfortunately the next line he chose happened to be five pages ahead. This bold but misguided attempt totally confused those onstage with him, but they had all been playing this particular play for a long time, so, once it dawned on them that a big chunk of text had been skipped, they rallied round and, shakily at first, the scene continued. Poor Geoffrey was doing wonderfully well until this incident, when suddenly what he was hearing did not match up in any way with what was on the page in front of him.

He quickly realised what had happened, but he also realised that if he were to keep the dialogue going, he had literally to translate simultaneously with no text to help him. Not an easy task, for, even when the actors were speaking the lines in the correct order, they were going at great speed. Geoffrey had been having difficulty enough, even with the translation in front of him, trying to fit the longer English sentences to the economical Italian ones. He managed to achieve a most superb feat of translation; no one in the audience commented on the short break when the actor dried or on the matching of English to Italian.

Perhaps the most successful timing was achieved when the Schiller Theatre, from what was then known as West Berlin, came with Max Frisch's *Andorra* and Goethe's *Clavigo*. At last the balance was reversed, with an English sentence being shorter than the German. It was a real joy to hear the translator starting a sentence in English exactly at the moment that the German actor opened his mouth, and then to hear the actor and the translator finishing at exactly the same time.

But, however adept the audience became at controlling the batons, there was no getting away from the major problem that hovered over the dress circle. As soon as the batons were switched on, an unseen group of men, somewhere near the chandelier, started chattering away in some unknown tongue. No one was able to explain how the sound collected in that area nor how it could be eradicated, but there those men were. They haunted me throughout the season, which makes me wonder if they are still up there, enjoying an animated conversation that can now only be heard in the dead of night.

I fervently wished that I could find an alternative to the baton, but however much I asked and searched around, I had to accept that it was Mr. Montague's batons or nothing, and we had gone too far for it to be nothing. Many were not returned at the end of a performance, the reason for which, we decided, was probably one of thrift. Many of our patrons came to a very credible number of performances during a World Theatre Season so, in spite of the hire charge being the extremely reasonable sum of two shillings and sixpence, many of them must have reckoned that to keep a baton for future use made good economic sense. At the same time, we came to realise that many other patrons erroneously thought that they were renting tiny radios, which would come in very handy at home. The sad side to this latter group's action was that when at home it was found to be useless as a radio, the baton would be thrown away rather than returned on a future visit — if such a visit were made. We lost a large number of batons during the season.

We did our best to ensure that at each performance the batons hired out contained a well-charged little battery. Even so, some when checked worked perfectly but when handed to a patron failed to produce a sound. Our elder son, Guy, as he was leaving the theatre one evening, handed his baton to the usherette on collecting-the-batons duty and said, with no hint of complaint, "I wasn't able to get this one to work." The usherette took the baton as she thanked him for mentioning the fact, and Guy moved on to the exit. Just before he went through the doorway, he glanced back to see her throwing the baton into the large container already half full. I have a nasty feeling that this scene must have, unfortunately, been repeated many times.

## Scene 18 ❧ The National anthems at World Theatre Season performances

At the first performance of the first play by each of the World Theatre Season companies, as soon as the royal party, always accompanied by the visiting company's ambassador, had reached their seats, the national anthem of our visitor's country and then our own national anthem would be played over the auditorium speakers. The BBC was very helpful in supplying recordings of our visitors' anthems, and this it did for the first visit by Karolos Koun and his young actors of the Greek Art Theatre Company.

The guest of honour that evening was Princess Margaret, who was accompanied by her husband, our photographer friend of the Royal Court days, Tony Armstrong-Jones, now Lord Snowdon. When they and the Greek ambassador had reached their seats in the stalls, the Greek national anthem was played. It was the first time there had been a chance for the sound operator to play it, and it proved a jaunty little tune, which, compared to many anthems, was enjoyable. The music came to a climax, and there was a moment's silence after which the audience expected "God Save the Queen." But no. To its amazement, the jaunty little tune was played again.

Everyone was very well behaved, and we all stood upright at attention. At last, the anthem reached the end once more, and I breathed a sigh of relief that it had passed off as if it had been intended. But I was feeling relieved too soon, for over the air once more came the, by now, extremely well known melody. This third appearance was too much for the audience who simply burst out laughing. Princess Margaret stared ahead, even though she must have felt Lord Snowdon's head turn towards her. From where I was in the row behind him, I could see the twinkle in his eye. The ambassador, towering over the Princess, was ramrod stiff, also staring straight ahead.

At last the anthem came to its finale, and the whole house was dead quiet. Would it be the roll of the drums to signal the start of our own anthem or would it be the little tune? The explosion of laughter when the little tune came round again was, from one point of view, a joyous sound, but from the point of view of many in the house, including myself, it was awful. I was at the end of a row, so it wouldn't have been impossible for me to walk up the new centre aisle I had created for this evening, across to the side of the theatre, down to the door of the box that housed the sound equipment, and tear out all the wires that came to hand. I decided that such a move would only make matters worse, so I stayed and suffered.

At length — and it was strange how the Greek anthem seemed to last longer each time it was played — it came to an end, and once more the audience fell silent. And then the roll of drums? But the embarrassment wasn't over yet. This particular version of our national anthem had an extremely discreet drum roll followed by a stately silence before, and very very quietly, the first notes of the anthem could just, and only just, be heard. I am sure it was a brilliant arrangement, but in a tinderbox situation, the pause after the drum roll meant to our patrons — or to most of them — that there was now the glorious possibility it would be followed by that seemingly inevitable Greek tune. By the time those first gentle notes of "God Save the Queen" arrived, the audience was beside itself, and many were helpless with laughter. It seemed an age before the military band worked itself up to its crescendo, and it was only then the audience realised that, after all, it really was our own national anthem that was being played this time.

As soon as the last note sounded, the audience flopped down into their seats, happy and exhausted, and the house rang out with conversations and the sound of further merriment. Understandably, there was a little island of ice down in the centre front of the stalls, but Karolos's company, from the moment the curtain was taken up, couldn't have wished for a more receptive audience for their enchanting, merry production of Aristophanes' *The Birds*.

## Scene 19 ❧ The Royal Shakespeare Company performs *The Comedy of Errors*, Windsor Castle, 1964

While the World Theatre Season was playing at the Aldwych, *King Lear* and *The Comedy of Errors* were on a world tour at the end of which the company was due to break up. But fate decided otherwise for Peter Hall. In another meeting with Prince Philip, he was asked if it would be possible for the Royal Shakespeare Company to present a production in the Waterloo Chamber at Windsor Castle during Ascot Week in mid-June. It seemed that the after-dinner entertainment for Her Majesty's guests at Windsor Castle during that week had been arranged except for one evening, and Prince Philip had decided it should be filled with a Shakespeare production played on his home ground. The season at Stratford was well under way, while at the Aldwych the month of June would see two productions being given their first performances, so the choice could fall on nothing better nor more fortuitous than *The Comedy of Errors,* which would just have returned to Britain.

Two days before the Windsor performance, I took a small group of the necessary staff to the castle for a very brief reconnaissance, and then, on a really wet and chilly June evening, Elizabeth and I drove down for the performance. The setting of three raked and stepped rostra had been set up at one end of the long, very high-ceilinged but comparatively narrow Waterloo Chamber, with two large adjoining rooms allocated as dressing rooms.

The company arrived by coach in good spirits that were raised even higher when several castle staff appeared unannounced in the dressing-room doorways bearing trays of smoked salmon and champagne. There was also amazement at what the temporary dressing rooms contained, with Diana Rigg rushing next door to ask Alec McCowen, "We've got two Rembrandts in our dressing room. What have you got in yours?" Soon Sir Fordham and Lady Flower arrived, so the four of us went through to the chamber where we found our seats to be part of a single line of chairs placed alongside stage left. This meant that we would be watching, as it were, from the wings of a proscenium theatre. On the other side of the stage was a similar line of chairs occupied by boys from nearby Eton College.

If we looked to our left, we looked down the length of the chamber, which was filled with row after row of individual chairs, placed neatly one behind another, on the level floor. It was lucky for the guests sitting in those seats, I decided, that the production was played on those three levels, for even the front of the lowest level was at least eighteen inches above the floor. The many chairs in the very front row would be occupied by the Queen and her guests.

As soon as the royal party was seated — a very neat manoeuvre as if the guests, taking their places with Her Majesty and Prince Philip in the centre, had entered the chamber in the order in which they were to sit — the performance began. Although the company had played the production many times, it was a special night, and this affected several of the actors, who stood just in front of us with legs ashiver. If nerves attack hands or legs, nothing can be done to control them, and it always seems unfair, especially on Lady Macbeth, for example, who first appears reading a letter, which can flutter wildly if the hands are taken over by nerves.

The first scene of *The Comedy of Errors* is long on serious speeches but short on laughs. Prince Philip was obviously determined that the Queen should enjoy this play, even though, as was generally accepted, theatre was not to her taste. Whenever there was the chance of a smile, he laughed heartily, turning to Her Majesty as if to say "That was good, wasn't it?" For a long time it was obvious she didn't agree with him since she was concentrating on the story that Tony Church as Aegeon was telling.

However, once the plot developed, the royal party got caught up in the identity problems caused by two sets of identical twins. Her Majesty's gloriously infectious laugh was heard, and the front row relaxed and enjoyed itself. The biggest laugh of all came during the scene when goods and chattels belonging to Antipholus of Syracuse were being taken to the quayside. Atop the highest rostrum, an official with a clipboard was waiting to be shown each item separately so that he could tick it off his list. Most items were greeted by a murmur or a laugh until a large gold picture frame was carried on. The official indicated that he wished to see the actual picture. The actor swung the frame round so that it faced the audience. In the frame was a large portrait of Queen Victoria. This totally unexpected object nearly brought the Waterloo Chamber down.

The production, brilliantly directed by Clifford Williams, hurtled to its end, which was greeted with tremendous but not prolonged applause, after which the royal party moved into an adjoining chamber for refreshment, and soon the company and staff followed them. There were no presentations, and the company mixed with their hosts and the other guests as if they had all been invited to join a neighbour's family at a buffet supper.

While Elizabeth and I were talking to the Queen Mother, I noticed that two of our dressers were standing alone out of the mainstream. I pointed them out to Her Majesty and explained that they had been with the company for a long time and I was sure they would be honoured to be presented and might I bring them across. "Of course," said the Queen Mother, so I excused myself and went over to the two ladies. I told them what the Queen Mother had said, so that if they came over with me, I would present them. At once they said that they wouldn't want that, thank you very much. They were very happy watching all the guests and eating the delicious food. I returned and reported that they would rather not come over whereupon Her Majesty said, "They're shy," and at once crossed the room and chatted to the two totally stunned members of our staff.

# Scene 20 ❦ Pinter and Beckett, Aldwych Theatre, 1964

Peter Hall's determination to celebrate Shakespeare's 400th birthday by pouring productions into the Aldwych really got under way as soon as all the bag and baggage belonging to the last of our World Theatre Season guests were packed, got out into Drury Lane, loaded into the waiting trucks, and were gone. What proved to be the first of the World Theatre Seasons at the Aldwych was reckoned to have been a success.

The first production to follow our multilingual visitors was Harold Pinter's *The Birthday Party*. This was directed by Harold himself, whereas when another of his plays, *The Collection*, had joined the rep at the Aldwych in June 1962, the direction was by Peter Hall and Harold. Although *The Birthday Party* was extremely strongly cast and given a wonderful production, it didn't draw the crowds it deserved. It seemed that once again, London audiences were not yet ready for either Harold or Samuel Beckett, but thank heavens they both held on and soon I was welcoming Beckett's *endgame* back to London. When we presented it with its French cast at the Royal Court in 1957, it had been titled *Fin de Partie,* while towards the end of 1958 it became, with the English cast and still at the Court, *End-game*, but at the Aldwych we went into the e. e. cummings mode so there were no capital letters and no hyphen.

Once again, the casting was strong with Patrick Magee and Jack MacGowran at their peaks of form. Physically, they were perfect in the style to which we had become accustomed for this play: the heavily built Pat as Hamm, blind and short-tempered, shouting orders in his unique rasping voice to the gnomelike, thin-as-a-rake Jackie as Clov. The two characters were also quite different in what they could and could not do. Hamm was imprisoned in his chair, while Clov dashed hither and yon around the stage, as well as up and down a ladder, looking out through the paneless windows to nothingness.

*The Birthday Party,* one of Harold's masterpieces of menace, relied as ever on the Pinter pause, during which an audience wondered which way the plot would turn when the silence was broken. This must have been one of the reasons why Harold, strongly backed by Peter Hall, told me that I must ensure absolute silence once the play had started. This meant that the practice of letting latecomers stand at the back of the circle behind the glass screen until (as stated in the programme) "a suitable break in the performance" would not be allowed. No suitable breaks in future; they would have to wait in the foyer until the interval.

"It won't be easy . . ." I started. But Harold cut in with, "Easy or not, that is what has to happen." I went to Peter Sibley to alert him to this new rule, for he would be the one who would have to explain it to latecomers. At once he prepared and, using a Roneo duplicator, ran off many copies of a *précis* of Act I so that the latecomers would have something to read while waiting for the act to finish. It would, he hoped, give them some idea of what had gone on during the act they were missing. He also arranged for a notice about the restriction to be put up at the box office, where the staff were primed to tell all those who booked. It was our public's bad luck that a television camera, relaying the scene onstage to monitors in the front-of-house, had not reached inside theatre buildings at that time, for it would have made the new rule a little easier to bear.

As ever, the public responded to this refusal to allow admission in a variety of ways. There were the Bad Luck stories (obviously true), such as those whose baby-sitter had arrived late or those who had faced parking difficulty. But there were also the Belligerents. Peter came close to being physically assaulted at every performance. One evening, an extreme example of a Belligerent stormed up to Peter and told him in no uncertain terms that he could keep his tickets. While speaking, he stuffed them into the breast pocket of Peter's dinner jacket. Unfortunately for Peter, the complainant didn't then lift his fingers out, but pulled them directly towards himself, which meant he tore the pocket from its moorings. We were sure it must have been very satisfactory for the man but not so good for Peter's suit.

If the Aldwych had been the Royal Opera House, audiences would know they would not be let in if they arrived late, but the Aldwych was a West End theatre where one could come and go as one liked, as Peter was being informed daily. After all, one had paid for one's seat, so it was there to be occupied or not as one wished — and not, absolutely not, as the management wished.

Peter and I agreed with the new rule, but we knew there would be many problems. We both knew from experience how some patrons — not the majority, thank goodness — would always try to beat a system, no matter in which area of the theatre it applied. In pre–*The Birthday Party* days, there were those latecomers who, in spite of repeated requests to be as quiet as possible while waiting at the back of the dress circle to be seated, sprang into action as soon as the usherette had left them. Although they were standing behind the glass screen, they would discuss, not too quietly, how they were to reach their seats. If a couple could see two empty seats placed more or less where they thought theirs should be, they didn't wait to be ushered to them, but off they went, causing total disruption for many in that area of the circle. Even if an usherette stayed with the latecomers, it was only too easy for several pairs — and sometimes more — to wait for her to be coping with a new influx from the foyer, and then make a lightning dash for seats. More bedlam ensued when two latecomers sat in the first empty pair of seats they could see, only to find a second pair of latecomers arriving in the same row a few seconds later to claim the seats, quite legitimately, as theirs.

It was great for me to meet up once more with Harold and with Sam, although I had to learn to call Harold by this, his real name. During his days at the Royal Court, he was an actor and his name for that activity was David Barron. It was also great to feel that Peter Hall's faith in the two of them would surely mean another necessary step for both towards acceptance, understanding, and appreciation of their enormous talents by the public.

It was interesting to watch the faces of Harold and Sam while they listened. Both faces gave nothing away; no hint from either as to how the information was being received. But both, in their own very different way, changed completely when they smiled or laughed. It didn't seem possible that either would allow such emotions to affect their faces.

Yet Harold's dark and extremely stern stare would totally disappear, his eyes that had locked onto one's own and had stayed stock still, would light up, and his expression would change to merriment and friendliness.

Sam's kind and heavily lined face looked as if it held infinite sorrows, cares, and worries, which he would never be able to cast off. But unexpectedly, like Harold, they disappeared in a moment. The lines remained, they were too deep, but they became laugh lines, while his eyes twinkled with happiness and pleasure, and one knew at once where the humour in his spare grey plays came from. It fact, when chatting to him, I often felt that his plays gently mocked us and that he enjoyed observing how seriously so many of them were taken.

## Scene 21 ❧ *Afore Night Come*, Aldwych Theatre, 1964

David Rudkin's play, *Afore Night Come*, had started life during the Royal Shakespeare Company's experimental season at the little Arts Theatre, which is conveniently set in the centre of the West End, close to Leicester Square. The thirteen characters offered excellent chances to Peter Hall's company of actors to present ensemble playing at its best.

The interesting thing about this play and Clifford Williams's atmospheric production was the way the climax was directed. The core conflict was between a team of annual pear pickers and the introduction to this team, amongst others, of an Irish vagrant played by Patrick Magee. The old hands suspected that in some way he was up to no good. With every word he spoke and every move he made, the tension and the mistrust amongst the men grew greater and greater, although a Birmingham student (Peter McEnery) tried to diffuse it.

John Bury's setting of the orchard managed, even on the narrow Aldwych stage, to show two small hills with a pathway between. It was up that pathway towards the end of the play that the Irishman went, followed by the foreman leading the pack. One knew that something very unpleasant was going to happen, and every member of the audience must have been picturing what he or she thought might be going on once the little party disappeared behind one of the hills. There was silence and then came a most unpleasant sound followed by another short silence before a dark ball appeared at the further end of the centre path. This rolled thumpingly downstage, fast at first then slowing until finally it stopped. If one hadn't guessed by then, it was at this point that one knew for certain that it was a human head, followed immediately by the certainty that it was the head of the vagrant.

## Scene 22 ✑ *The Marat/Sade* included in productions for Shakespeare's 400th birthday

*The Birthday Party, Afore Night Come,* and *endgame,* plus a few performances of a programme of one-act plays entitled *Expeditions One,* built up the repertoire at the Aldwych very quickly. The next scheduled production, to be directed by Trevor Nunn, was a Tirso de Molina play, *Don Gil in the Green Stockings.* Somehow that play got lost on the way, and it was replaced by Robin Midgley's production of *Victor or The Children Take Over* by Roger Vitrac. Hardly had the children taken over before a new play by Peter Weiss, *The Murder of Marat,* was scheduled to join a repertoire of six productions. Of those six, three had a single word for their titles, the shortest of which was *Eh?* by Henry Livings; the other four had three or four words, but Peter Weiss's play had twenty-four. The full title, proudly heading the list of Aldwych productions on the front of the leaflet that covered May 18 to September 5, 1964, was *The Persecution and Assassination of Marat as Performed by the Inmates of the Asylum of Charenton under the Direction of the Marquis de Sade.*

This title, in itself, couldn't fail to make one curious. However, although it gave a prospective playgoer a fair idea of what he was going to see, for use in publicity, in newspaper advertisements, and even in the detailing of the repertoire in that same first leaflet, a shorter version had to be displayed, and it became *The Murder of Marat.* Thus it stayed until the leaflet, covering October 19, 1964 to January 23, 1965, was printed. It then became and remained *The Marat/Sade.* Also in this leaflet, six more lines carrying the names of the remainder of the production team were added to the original credit "directed by Peter Brook." This play was obviously going to be challenging, fascinating, and exciting, and as obviously it was going to be one of those plays that would be widely discussed. I was also certain that it would attract publicity to itself for I was sure that at dinner tables there would be those who would try to outshine their friends by not only boasting that they had seen the production but also by reciting the full title.

As with Peter Brook's production of *The Physicists,* the house curtain would not be used at all during the evening, so the audience would come into the auditorium and be faced with a totally grey stage — grey wooden, steeply raked flooring and a grey surround — wonderfully designed by Sally Jacobs. The skillfulness of the setting was not apparent immediately to the audience until a scene change, which demanded the stage to be full one moment and empty the next. This Sally Jacobs achieved by having the stage floor honeycombed with traps. At the end of a scene when all Charenton's inmates were present, Peter Brook positioned them so that none was standing on a trap and thus those detailed to open them were able to do this swiftly and silently, and as swiftly and silently they all slid from sight down under the stage flooring. The covers were lowered by the last actor of each trap and the stage was cleared ready for the next scene.

The text had been cleverly translated by Geoffrey Skelton while Adrian Mitchell added an equally clever adaptation of the verse. Richard Peaslee, a quiet American, wrote the haunting, exciting music of which there was much throughout the evening.

The casting came from what I might call the company-in-residence at the Aldwych. There were many good speaking parts, while the nonspeaking roles were those of the lunatics who were incarcerated in the asylum at Charenton. Early in rehearsals Peter told the nine inmates that when they came for rehearsal the next morning, he expected them all to tell him what afflicted their characters, which had resulted in them being sent to Charenton, and how they would show this during the play.

Meeting one of the inmates, Mary Allen, by chance that evening, I asked her what she had chosen to be the matter with her character, and she said that hers was very worried that the clouds would fall on her head, so she intended to tell Peter that she would be holding up her hands to save herself from such a terrible fate. The suggestions many inmates made were passed by Peter, including Mary Allen's, but others were not so fortunate. Peter would simply say that the idea put forward was not acceptable, although he would never give a hint why he did not approve. The actor had to work this out for himself so that all the afflictions were homegrown and wisely were not imposed on the actors by the director.

Peter directed the very end of the play by making the whole cast, singing one of Richard Peaslee's most insistent, pounding, and catchy songs, march menacingly downstage in a mass. At the first rehearsal, when the front line reached the front of the fore-stage, they were forced to stop with the result that those behind bumped into those ahead. Of course, the leaders at once asked Peter, "How do we know when to stop, or should we jump down into the stalls?" There seemed no immediate answer until Ruth Atkinson, the excellent stage manager, who had come out of the prompt corner and was leaning against the proscenium arch, said that she had a whistle permanently hanging round her neck during rehearsals, so perhaps she should let out a goodly blast. Peter accepted this at once, adding that Ruth was to appear, as she had just done, and not be an unseen whistler in the wings.

The production was a sensation, and the Aldwych was full at all its performances. The press acknowledged the strength of the production and praised the ensemble work of the company, while picking out Glenda Jackson, who played Charlotte Corday, as an "actress to watch." Many theatregoers had already had the opportunity to watch her work for she had appeared in Peter Brook's productions for the Royal Shakespeare Company of the *Theatre of Cruelty* and *The Screens*.

## Scene 23 ✏ The Actors Studio Theatre at the Aldwych Theatre, 1965

When Peter Daubeny let us know he had arranged with Lee Strasberg for his Actors Studio Theatre to be part of the 1965 World Theatre Season, we knew that he had got hold of a company that would be of enormous interest to the public, and we looked forward eagerly to their arrival. Any number of interesting names were being bandied about such as Paul Newman, Joanne Woodward, Shelley Winters, and Geraldine Page, but as the months went by, the starry names seemed to melt away. However, the company would be here, and that continued to cheer us. I was doubly cheered for it would mean that during three weeks of the season, there would be no need for simultaneous translation.

Of their two plays, perhaps the keenest interest was in *The Three Sisters* (with the company neatly choosing to insert the definite article in the title) with Kim Stanley, playing Olga; Nan Martin, Masha; and Sandy Dennis, Irina. Lee Strasberg directed the production, his wife

Paula was very much on hand, and his son John was the assistant stage manager. Paula, always dressed in black, had a big say in everything to do with the production, while it seemed that John must have come to keep the family together, since the poor chap seemed to know little or nothing about the play or the setting.

The press night did not go well, but then it was difficult to concentrate on the play when Sandy Dennis was on the stage. Top of the list were her lines, which came out in fits and starts with lots of umm's and err's, and while she was onstage, though not participating in the scene, it seemed that nothing could stop her from acting and reacting in her own private world. She sighed, she twirled a lock of hair, she grimaced, she smiled and laughed. During the run, I was chatting to her and mentioned how struck I was by the way she delivered her lines, whereupon her face lit up (not difficult for her to achieve since it was always prepared for such an effect), and she said, using that wonderfully American phrase that is so sincerely insincere and is always spoken slowly with heavy emphasis on the second word, "Why, thank you." She paused briefly so that the gracious acceptance of my compliment should be recognised, and then she continued, "Yes, I learn my lines and then I forget them, so that when I am given my cue, it seems as if I am really speaking them for the first time and I have only just thought of what I would say." I didn't feel that I should follow this by enquiring where the lines came from if she really had forgotten them for she was so securely certain that her method was right for her and right for the play.

On the press night, she certainly gave us her all and perhaps a little bit more, but it wasn't enough to save the show. When the company lined up for the curtain call, all the actors faced the audience, but in the middle of that line, the leading lady, Kim Stanley, faced upstage. There wasn't time to warn Peter Sibley, who was in the prompt corner, as was usual on all World Theatre Season press nights, waiting to take sufficient bouquets onto the stage to enable him to hand one to each lady in the cast.

On this particular evening, he stepped out at the appropriate time but when he reached the centre of this line, he was certainly not prepared to find an actress's back towards him rather than a pair of hands eager to take the flowers. With his usual aplomb, he paused fractionally, and then continued along the line arriving at the farther end still holding the uncollected bunch. The applause was maintained so while her companions — or, should I say, while the remainder of the cast — bowed and smiled, Kim, with a sudden movement, began to walk, very slowly, upstage until she reached the big tree that had dominated the final scene. There she remained, still facing upstage, until the curtain finally fell.

One evening during *The Three Sisters* run, I chanced to go backstage to be met by an agitated Lee. "Oh, there you are, Michael," he said, as if I were there by invitation and was slightly late. "George has gone!" I translated this quickly to mean that George C. Scott, the Vershinin, was not in the theatre. "Gone where?" I not unnaturally asked. "To Spain!" Lee croaked. I am not inquisitive by nature but to get the full story before deciding on a plan of action, I felt impelled to ask a second question. "But why has he gone to Spain?" "Because Ava's gone to Spain, so of course George has gone after her." Well, that seemed pretty understandable, especially when I realised that Ava was Ava Gardner, the big, very big, Hollywood movie star.

"So who's the understudy?" was my next question, although I felt sure I knew the answer. "There isn't one," Lee confessed. He then told me that Robert Loggia had played Vershinin in New York at one time and had wanted to repeat the performance in London, but Lee had, unwisely as it turned out, chosen George. However, he had offered Bob the part of Solyony, which he accepted because he wanted to appear on a London stage, but it was on the understanding that he would not be asked to play for George should the latter be off at any time. What did Bob know that Lee did not, I wondered.

"Well, we must go and see Bob," I said to Lee, once I had heard the full story. But Lee said, "Oh, I can't do that, after my promise." "Well, I can," I said, and we went to Bob's dressing room. Lee stayed close to the door for a quick getaway, while I talked to the taciturn Bob. It took longer — like twenty minutes in all — than I would have wished to get him to agree to go on that evening, but he finally and grudgingly said that he would, providing that an announcement, which he must vet, was made before the play began and providing he could take the book onstage and read the part.

I worked out a sentence that he liked and that I promised Peter Sibley would read out from the stage, and I then raced downstairs to hand the paper to Peter. He had already twice told the audience that there was a slight delay but the curtain would go up as soon as possible. On he went again and read out the piece about Bob taking over at short notice due to the unavailability of George, and the curtain rose about fifteen minutes late. When at last Vershinin appeared, sure enough Bob carried the script and was perhaps rather too obviously reading his lines. I didn't blame him, and soon I had occasion to be utterly grateful to him, for, as I had reckoned and hoped, during the passage of his first scene he looked less and less at the script, and finally, as he passed the end of the grand piano, he unobtrusively put the script down on it and proceeded to give an extremely good performance.

## Scene 24   The Lord Chamberlain's Office: Jean-Louis Barrault and James Baldwin

At this time, and for over two hundred years before, every play that was presented to a paying public had to have the seal of approval from the Lord Chamberlain's Office, situated in St. James's Palace, before a word of it might be spoken from the stage. His officers had to ensure that certain rules of conduct on a stage were strictly observed. After a script was despatched, I had to wait for a letter that would thank me for submitting such-and-such a play and would I note that the following actions were not permitted in this or that scene, and the following words must not be spoken. If alternative actions, words, or phrases replaced the original, then these must be sent to the Lord Chamberlain for his inspection. If a playwright or director found the Lord Chamberlain's comments unacceptable, then I would arrange a meeting at St. James's Palace where either I would go by myself on behalf of the director or playwright to argue the case — having been duly primed — or I would go with one or both of them.

The World Theatre Seasons' texts also had to be submitted, and these caused one or two problems. Jean-Louis Barrault, leading his Théâtre de France company, sent the text of *Le Piéton de L'Air*, which included a stage direction to the effect that a character, having fallen overboard, is seen in the water clinging to a log. "Would he be swimming in the nude?" was the curious question from the Lord Chamberlain's officer. Jean-Louis, who would be playing the part concerned, managed, with no difficulty, to be amused, outraged and disbelieving all at the same time. "Of course not," he sneered. "How could anyone think such a thing?" The scene turned out to be a miraculous example of his brilliance as a mime artist, for, fully dressed and with the log across his shoulders and his arms grasping each end, it was possible to believe totally that he was breasting wave after wave as he slowly crossed the empty stage.

Another visitor, who simply could not understand that we had a censor, was James Baldwin, whose play *Blues for Mr. Charlie* was the second of the two productions brought over from New York by Lee Strasberg's Actors Studio Theatre. The letter from the Lord Chamberlain concerning this play contained several pages of words that would have to be omitted before a licence could be granted. Jimmy objected strongly, simply because, as he said, "We have been playing my play in New York, and no one has objected to these words or expressions, so why should they be objected to here?" He then added, "Especially when the public here hasn't seen the play yet!" I told him that I had made an appointment with Colonel Johnston at St. James's Palace, so pleased at the thought that he was going to set foot in a palace, we made our way. As we approached the low, red-brick building, he became more excited, in fact I got the impression that he would have inserted doubtful words and expressions into a completely innocent text if it would mean he would be invited to a real palace. I only wished we were able to enter through the main gates, but it had to be through a door on the further side of the building.

Because Jimmy had the endearing habit of always addressing me as "Mr. Hallifax baby," and because of the very considerable difference in height between us, we made a strange duo as we were ushered into the office with its huge desk, behind which Colonel Johnston politely stood to greet his guests. He indicated a mammoth leather armchair to Jimmy, who went over to it and clambered into its seat. For him to sit comfortably with his back against the back of the chair, it meant that his little legs stuck out into the room, but he seemed at ease and as soon as Colonel Johnston asked how he could help with regard to the text of his play, Jimmy started to speak.

For about five minutes, he gave the most fascinating story of his life, of the manner in which blacks were treated and the language they used in his country, of Malcolm X and of his play and its reception in New York. As soon as he had finished, he shot out of the chair with such force that it resulted in him crossing the room at quite a speed. When he jumped up to sit on the desk, his momentum didn't allow him to stop on the edge, as he had obviously intended, for he slid across the desk towards Colonel Johnston. The Colonel leaned back quickly in his chair so that he would not get the full force of this engaging and brilliant little man as he hurtled towards him.

He needn't have worried. Jimmy came to a halt before he reached the other side where he found himself in the perfect position. Between himself and the Colonel was the script of *Blues for Mister Charlie,* and he then went through the script page by page, pointing to word after word that had the censor's blue pencil line through it and saying, "All right, Colonel, I'll cut that out, but here, d'you see, three lines later, I want that to stay. It's important and really, Colonel, that is what they say in New York because there's no other way to say it."

And so between them they haggled over the words that had to go and the ones that, after all, would be allowed, and eventually a very satisfied Jimmy and I left the palace from where he went happily up St. James Street, and I returned to the real world.

## Scene 25   The National Theatre of Greece at the Aldwych Theatre, 1966

The artistic director of the National Theatre of Greece was Alexis Minotis who brought to the Aldwych three of his productions, *Hecuba, Oedipus Rex,* and *Oedipus at Colonus.* He also brought his wife, Katina Paxinou, who was to play Hecuba. She soon established herself as the powerhouse of the company and also appeared to be cast in the same mould as Paula Strasberg, although, on reflection, I think Mme. Paxinou just had the edge over Paula. After Paula, I suppose I could say we were able to accept bossy ladies dressed in what seemed to be the obligatory black outfit but the imperious manner Katina used to deal with underlings, such as the (literally) Greek chorus, was something to be believed only when experienced. I would not care to be lashed by that tongue, but they all took it like men as they moved as one with their green pleated skirts swaying and swooping for all the world as if they were dancing girls in Hawaii. Not a sign did they give, as they tried for the umpteenth time to speak the speeches in absolute unison, that she was going perhaps a touch too far. After all, she put bread in their mouths, even if it was not buttered. That evening, watching Katina as Hecuba taking her revenge on Polymnestor, it seemed as if what I had witnessed some hours earlier had been a warm-up for the tremendous performance she was now giving us.

It was not an evening of pure magic for Elizabeth and myself, for when the anthems — no problem here with the Greek national anthem for the tape had now been docked of the many verses that had thoughtfully been supplied by the BBC just in case we would all be singing the full anthem — had been played and we had seated ourselves in the row behind Princess Marina, our royal visitor for this company, I turned to Elizabeth and whispered, "May I have a baton, please?" She immediately whispered back, "I thought you had collected them." This meant over an hour of unadulterated Greek.

Alex had directed all three plays and appeared in all of them; although, of course, his main role was Oedipus, and it was during a matinee of *Oedipus at Colonus* that I had to go backstage. When I reached the prompt corner, I heard a chilling, eerie sound. I was standing close to Alex's amanuensis, who was obviously following the text that was placed on a lectern before him, while Alex was on a high rostrum centre stage pouring out his words. This strange sound reminded me of the one in the Moscow Art Theatre's *The Cherry Orchard*. I caught the eye of Richard York, the excellent liaison officer for the World Theatre Season that year, and he crept towards me. I indicated the sound, and he whispered, "This guy here," pointing towards the man standing at the lectern, "is a ventriloquist, and he is throwing the lines to Alex." I went on up to the green room, where I was due to see Maggie Roy, who was coping marvellously as ever with the curious requests from our visitors, leaving the simultaneous prompter to continue his good work.

# Scene 26 &#8758; Leningrad Gorki Theatre at the Aldwych Theatre, 1966

The Leningrad Gorki Theatre was the final company in my last World Theatre Season. We were due to present Dostoyevsky's *The Idiot, The Barbarians* by Gorki, and *Grandma, Uncle Iliko, Hilarion and I* by two contemporary Georgian playwrights, N. Dumbadze and G. Lordkipanidze. But *The Barbarians* had had to be dropped due to the illness of the leading actor, so we made up with two extra performances of *The Idiot* and *Grandma* et al. But that hiccup was nothing compared to the arrival — or rather the almost nonarrival — of the scenery, which was coming by sea. The Aldwych staff was at the docks ready to pick up the off-loaded goods when they learned that a threatened dockers' strike was no longer threatened but had started. Twenty-four hours were lost before the trucks arrived at the Aldwych dock doors. By that time, the company's chief director, Georgi Tovstonogov, was completely convinced that this was a plot by the Aldwych staff to jeopardise the Monday evening performance of *The Idiot*.

Alf Davis, the master carpenter, and his excellent hardworking staff had no time for such delusions and worked with a will, and with as much speed as the language barrier would allow, to set up the various scenes, while David Read, the chief electrician, and his dedicated staff managed somehow to light each set at enormous speed before it was dismantled to set up the next set.

Much later in the day, I warned Peter Sibley not to let the audience in to the auditorium until he got the go-ahead from me, after which I went up and changed into a dinner jacket. It was one of those performances when royalty was present, this evening's guest being Princess Margaret. Luckily, I had just finished changing when a phone call summoned me to the stalls where I found David Read uncharacteristically greatly put out. "Mr. Tovstonogov says that the curtain may not go up this evening unless he has seen every lighting cue in its correct order from start to finish. With well over a hundred cues, we cannot possibly do that and get the curtain up at any sort of reasonable time."

Georgi was in the stalls, so I went to him, icy calm but seething inside, and said "I do understand why you are asking to check all the lighting cues, and I only wish I could allow this to happen, but the first members of the audience are already being held back in the foyer and in under twenty minutes, Princess Margaret will be here. I can promise you that David Read is one of the finest chief electricians in the profession, and if he guarantees to me that every cue will be as you would want it, I can accept his word. I ask you also to accept his word and place in him the trust that I have in his capability and professionalism."

It came pouring out. Over the years, when addressing foreign visitors, I always tried to use straightforward words in plain sentences, with no little local allusions and jokes. This time, however, my first approach to the angry Russian director did not get my usual careful attention. Sure enough, my statement did nothing to help the situation. Instead, they brought forth a stream of broken English, the gist of which was, as David had reported, that he would not allow the curtain to go up without every lighting cue being shown to him, and not to mince words in whatever language, that was that.

By this time, the physical distance between us was also widening, so when Peter Sibley appeared at the back of the auditorium to report that he was finding it hard to keep the audience out any longer and the foyer was bulging, I called out to Mr. Tovstonogov across the wastes of the stalls seating that I was sorry, but I was allowing the audience to come in, and the curtain would go up at 7:30. At once, I gave the go-ahead to Peter, and I raced upstairs to the office where I dialled Clarence House. Princess Margaret's personal assistant answered at once. "There's a slight holdup here," I began. "So I was just wondering if Her Royal Highness had left yet for the Aldwych." "Oh, yes," was the cheerful yet unwanted reply. "She's on her way." She had a comforting tone in her voice as if she thought I was concerned that H.R.H. might be a little late. "That's good," I lied. "Thanks so much." Down went the phone and down the stairs went I. Lickety-split.

Molly and Peter Daubeny, looking elegant and cool as cucumbers, were correctly in the foyer in front of and with their backs to the box office, which was our usual place for presentations and as I approached them from one side, from the other I could see Princess Margaret coming up the steps into the foyer. I wouldn't have worried the Daubenys anyway, but I wasn't given the opportunity to consider whether I said anything to them or not, for it was time for me to make the presentations and then, with a hissed, "You take Princess Margaret," from Peter, the Princess and I climbed the stairs to the dress circle. After a politeness or two, I said, "Ma'am, I am sorry to say we have been having a little trouble with the director of the company, and this may mean that the curtain will have to be held for a few minutes." I don't know what I was expecting, but I was certainly taken aback when Princess Margaret said, "Oh, that's all right. We'll just sit in our seats until you are ready." Fantastic. As soon as I could, I signalled another go-ahead to Peter Sibley and sure enough the first of the two national anthems started as soon as Princess Margaret reached her seat. This was followed by our own anthem, and then the curtain rose — dead on time.

The role of the Idiot was played by Innokenti Smoktunovsky and that of Nastasya Filipovna by Tatyana Doronina. We never knew the reason why these two were at loggerheads but hate each other they patently did. The fact that they didn't speak offstage was acceptable, but they carried the mutual dislike onto the stage with the result that neither would look at the other. Those members of the audience who had read the plot in the programme might have wondered if the writer had got the story right, for it stated that "Mishkin and Nastasya meet for the first time and are immediately attracted to one another." Yet, there they were, just the two of them on the stage, but one was down right and the other down left, and the whole scene was played with each staring fixedly out front.

If the action onstage was unusual, the action of David Read on the lighting board was faultless. At the reception for the company after the first performance, I greeted Tovstonogov like an old friend and congratulated him on the production. He acknowledged this with a bow of his head. Neither of us mentioned the contretemps we had had a few hours earlier. Nor was it ever mentioned during the remainder of the company's stay. Nor did David receive any form of thanks from the Russians for his heroic work that evening.

# Act Five
## The National Theatre of Great Britain: 1966 to 1969

Chosen by Sir Laurence Olivier to be the executive company manager of the National Theatre of Great Britain. The company's many fine productions include *The Royal Hunt of the Sun, Much Ado About Nothing, Rosencrantz and Guildenstern are Dead,* and an all-male *As You Like It*. Sir Laurence is diagnosed with cancer, which changes plans for a tour across Canada.

### Scene 1 ⚭ A vacancy at the National Theatre, 1966

At the beginning of August 1966, I was invited by George Rowbottom, the general manager of the National Theatre, to go to the offices in Aquinas Street to have a meeting with the director, Sir Laurence Olivier. "Sir Laurence," said George, "is looking for a company manager, and since he has known you for some time and you have worked together, I am hopeful he will appreciate why I have asked you to come along."

Sir Laurence said that he wanted a company manager who could be the link between the acting company and those who worked in administration. "I don't want there to be a 'them and us' situation. I want them to know that we are all on the same side and they must understand that we care about them. There must be no 'front office' mentality." He continued to talk about the company and his pride in what they had achieved so far. We chatted for some time before I left him to continue interviews with other contenders for the post.

The following day, George phoned to say that Sir Laurence had asked him to let me know that if I wanted the job it was mine. After I had accepted — even though it meant a considerable drop in salary — we worked out when I could start, and it wasn't long before I was having another meeting with Sir Laurence. "You will have to do the contracts for the acting company and the stage management," he said. "And you will find we have two teachers, Kate Fleming for voice and William Hobbs for fencing, so they must be dealt with separately. Kenneth Tynan, our literary manager, talks to authors, but he will pass details to you of those he wishes to be contracted, and you will take over from there. Of course, there are also composers, musicians, and choreographers. Then there is the touring. By arrangement with the Arts Council of Great Britain, we have to perform within the United Kingdom for ten weeks each year, and the first tour you will be involved with goes out at the end of October, so you must set that up at once."

I said that all that was fine, but my only concern was the title of the job. I didn't like the thought of being called company manager. Was it possible for me to have another? "I don't mind what you call yourself, dear boy," he said. "Just let me know what you choose, and I'm sure I'll approve." That evening we spent a happy time at home with everyone suggesting brilliantly funny titles until one of Elizabeth's brothers-in-law, over from Canada, mentioned that many businessmen in his country now sported the word *executive* in their title, and maybe we could get something from that thought. "What about executive company manager?" asked Elizabeth, taking up Douglas's suggestion — and so a new title was born. When I took it to Sir Laurence at our next meeting, he said, "I don't know what it means, but if it's what you want, then that's what it shall be."

As executive company manager, I came under the overall command of the general manager — or general administrator, as the title became in time — and certainly whenever the general manager needed to consult with his heads of departments (company, financial, press and public relations, and technical), I attended under the company heading. But in the main, I went ahead on the artistic side, responsible to the director, Sir Laurence Olivier.

## Scene 2 ✑ The huts in Aquinas Street, Waterloo

In 1962 when Sir Laurence was appointed director of a yet-to-be-formed National Theatre, there was no building in which the company could perform. But by the time of the opening of the first production,

*Hamlet*, an arrangement had been made with the governors of the Old Vic Theatre on Waterloo Road. The arrangement was for the company to take over the beautiful, old (it was opened in 1818) theatre until the time came for a move into its own specially designed building on the South Bank. Thus was a home provided for the artistic side of the company, but there was still the question of a home for the administration. This remarkably small group could not possibly fit into the extremely limited office space at the Old Vic, and so a number of Terrapin huts, left over from the Second World War, were brought into service once more.

It was an eight-minute walk from the Old Vic Theatre to reach the huts in Aquinas Street. Halfway along this short street was a brick arch housing an imposing pair of wooden gates. This was the splendid entrance to the compound housing the huts, but the view ahead from the entrance was not so imposing. There they were — the huts. At first, a high brick wall hid the greater length of the huts from view, but walking down the slope from the gates produced a most depressing sight. A long row of single-storey wooden huts placed end to end formed a seemingly endless wooden wall, broken only by evenly spaced windows and one set of double doors. The only redeeming feature, from a practical point of view, was a parking space for many cars.

Each hut consisted of four small offices, two on each side of a central corridor. When a number of these huts were placed end to end, they formed a single building with a very long corridor off which on both sides were a number of doors. Opposite the door in each office was a window. However, some occupants, such as Sir Laurence, had two doors and two windows because the partition between two offices had been removed. If you entered by the main door, marked reception, and turned down the left-hand long corridor, the first two doors on the left led into Sir Laurence's office. If you had turned to the right from reception, the first door on the right was the office of Sir Laurence's associate director, John Dexter. The second door was my office, and continuing past this, one would find on one side Virginia Fairweather (press and publicity) and further on, on the other side, Kenneth Tynan (literary manager). Beyond their offices were the washrooms, and then a large rehearsal room. Because of its size, it had two relatively slim pillars supporting the roof, but as with all such obstructions in rehearsal rooms, the pillars always seemed to get in the way of an important part of a set, no matter what production was rehearsed there.

Also at the far end, jutting out towards the Aquinas Street entrance, was the canteen. This room, with space for a fair number of tables, was divided from the kitchen by a wall containing a large hatch through which, Rose, the cook, handed out excellent meals. The kitchen was Rose's kingdom, and how she managed to produce the meals that she did with the equipment and the space that was provided for her was impossible to understand: but meals always appeared on time, and they were hot and varied. She never wanted to let her customers down, and this caused her one morning to tell me how worried she had been that day when some drama had meant she was late getting to her kitchen. "I didn't get here until nine-thirty," she said, adding, "so I went straight in and put on the greens." No wonder they were sometimes more the browns than the greens. But no one complained.

Rose was a great chatterbox and a glorious Mrs. Malaprop, which one enjoyed but one would never think of laughing at her. At one time I was having difficulty with the daily journey from Barnes to Waterloo because the railway workers were on strike. In her kind way, she was very concerned for me, and as the days went by this concern grew. One day, she blurted out, "Oh, those railway men. They're holding the whole country to random." Rose's kindness and concern also encompassed our dog, Andrew. She knew that he liked to get the marrow out of a certain type of bone, and when she had used one in her cooking, she would offer it to me. Once when I was collecting a mid-afternoon cup of tea, she said that later she would have such a bone ready for me to take back for Andrew. It chanced that that same day, an actor's agent, with whom I had been having protracted telephone conversations concerning his client, phoned to say that he would be passing through Waterloo that evening and might he call in. He was sure a face-to-face chat would quickly settle the matter. I had never met this particular man, although we had been talking over the phone for years, and I had a very clear picture in my mind as to how he would look. Sure enough he looked exactly the same as he had sounded, but I hadn't reckoned on a camel-hair coat hanging free from his shoulders. He was unbelievably smart with everything of the best, and, of course, he arrived — no, swept through the gates — in the most chic of modern cars.

My office only had room for a good-sized desk, which I put end on to the single window, with my rather grand chair (inherited from my predecessor) on one side and a chair for a visitor on the other. Just inside the door was a filing cabinet. Unless I was discussing a contract with someone in person or over the phone, I always had my office door open, but on this occasion, because of the subject of our meeting, I had ushered the agent to the visitor's chair and closed the door. As he forecast, our conversation did not take long, and the result was satisfactory to both of us, but there was a very slight pause during our discussion when there was a very discreet tap on the door. Since I did not answer it, in the hope that the caller would realise I did not wish to be interrupted, there came a second little tap. Another pause, during which we continued what we were saying, when very, very slowly the door opened a very small way, and a hand appeared holding something wrapped in a crumpled page torn from a newspaper. This disgusting looking object was gradually lifted up until it could be placed on the very top and on the very edge of the filing cabinet. As soon as it was safely perched there, the hand withdrew and the door was desperately slowly and noiselessly closed. Rose had delivered a bone. Neither my visitor nor I mentioned this delivery service, but he couldn't fail to be aware of the bundle as he passed within inches of it on his way out.

Rose's assistant was the patient, uncomplaining Nellie. She did all the dirty work, cleaning the kitchen and the pots and pans and doing all the washing up. She was not allowed any contact with Rose's customers. When Maggie Smith was queuing one lunchtime, she watched the activities of Rose and Nellie and then commented, "Rose has got the most lines but Nellie has the better part."

The huts being single storey meant that the elements were not so far overhead. The roof became very hot when the sun beat down while the arrival of rain meant that in almost all the offices receptacles of one kind or another had to be deployed to catch the rain drops that unerringly found a way down. It was sometimes difficult to hear what was being said if a phone call came through during a storm, for not only was the rain battering at the thin roof, but there was strong competition from the sound of water plopping into waste bins. I was one of the very few fortunates whose offices were weatherproof.

Many visitors, especially those from a foreign national theatre, were shocked at the conditions under which we worked. There were many I took in for a meeting with Sir Laurence only to have them splutter, "How can the greatest actor in the world and the man who is the director of the National Theatre of Great Britain be allowed to work in such a terrible place." Of course, I understood their concern, but on the other hand, I never worked with so many people who were so near at hand. We all saved so much time when, needing a reply to a question that couldn't be dealt with easily over the phone, it only meant a few steps and one had the answer.

For many of those who worked in the Aquinas Street offices there was no reason for them to make their way to the Old Vic Theatre, or to the workshops that were just a side street away from the theatre, but that didn't apply to myself. I had to make endless journeys along Stamford Street and up and down Cornwell Street. Apart from having to suffer blazing summer sun with absolutely no chance of any shade along Stamford Street, I found these walks useful: not only was I having a short walk but I was also away from my desk and I could use the time to think things over away from the telephone. Once down at the theatre, I could speak to the house manager and the box office manager in the front-of-house, while backstage, I could find the general stage manager or any of the heads of the technical departments, stage, electrics, properties, and wardrobe. Crossing Webber Street to the workshops meant I could talk to the production manager and the various heads of departments, carpenters, paint frame, property, and armoury, as well as to the costume supervisor in the making wardrobe.

On many occasions when backstage at the theatre, I found myself using a half-landing on one of the dressing-room staircases as my second office, for so often as I reached this vantage point, many of the actors with whom I wished to have a word, chanced to pass, and I was able to catch them for a quick chat. Many of the quick chats would have been even quicker if I had not passed greetings to others in the cast as they passed up or down the stairs.

## Scene 3 ⊗ Sir Laurence Olivier

When Sir Laurence came to the Royal Court Theatre in 1957, we all seemed automatically to call him Sir. His knighthood, bestowed on him in 1947, demanded that he be addressed either in this way or the longer Sir Laurence, but we used Sir affectionately as if it were his first name or even a nickname. Thus, if I came into the theatre and saw a member of *The Entertainer* stage management, I could ask, "Has Sir arrived yet?" and there was never any doubt as to whom I meant. Curiously, Sir Laurence was the only theatrical knight with whom I worked to be thought of in this way. Sir Ralph Richardson, Sir Lewis Casson, and Sir Tyrone Guthrie were always addressed by their title followed by the first name.

One of the first things that struck me when I started working with Sir was his insistence that no actor, unknown to him, was engaged to join the National Theatre Company unless he or she had been auditioned by him. At these auditions, he would do his best to establish a calm and friendly atmosphere for he knew that auditions are nerve-wracking affairs at the best of times, but auditioning before the man many considered the greatest actor of his age — or, as some would have it, of any age — must score ten out of ten for sheer terror. It stood to reason then that very few who appeared before him would be able to give of their best unless he could put them at their ease, and this he tried to do by having a friendly chat before the actor got up to deliver the first of his or her three chosen speeches. Often Sir would not let an auditionee leave once the pieces were over, for if some word or phrase caught his attention he would become a director. He would discuss a point with the actor, even asking for a speech to be given again, this time with some variation of pace or stress, or understanding of a sentence perhaps, that he felt would help the actor to realise totally what Shakespeare intended, as well as helping the actor at future auditions.

If an actor was being considered for a role and Sir knew the actor's work, he or she would be asked to come to the huts for a talk about the part and the play: this was sometimes with and sometimes without the director of the play. Martin Shaw came to Aquinas Street for one of these chats, and he mentioned that he had recently played Laertes in a production of *Hamlet* at Birmingham Rep, where the American actor, Richard Chamberlain, played Hamlet. "What about his American accent?" enquired Sir immediately. "His English was perfect," said Martin, "except for the word *flourish*. At every performance, this word came out sounding something like 'fleur-rish.'" Sir knew for certain that he himself was always perfect in any accent he adopted, so he was fascinated to hear of a word that appeared to beat the American.

Another side of Sir Laurence that had struck me on joining was his devotion to his actors. He knew very well what he could expect from those with whom he had worked previously and also those who had been with the company from or near the start in 1963. Even so he was always keen to see the members of that group being given roles that would stretch them just that little bit further. This approach applied even more to those who had joined recently, especially the young ones. If there were one or two in this group who appeared suitable for a small but important part, he used to ask who had been waiting the longest for just such an opportunity — or, "Whose turn is it next?" — and he or she would then be offered the part. Sometimes he broke this system, knowingly. He would say, "Yes, yes, I understand that we ought really to offer this part to X but I am very interested in Y. He has been doing very well and it is time he got pushed, and this is just the role that will do that."

I found Sir Laurence's performance as James Tyrone in *Long Day's Journey into Night* mesmerising, as with the whole of Michael Blakemore's superb production, but there was something that worried me about his Irish-American accent. I am assured it was wonderfully accurate, but it didn't seem to lie comfortably on his tongue. In one small respect I was not alone for it would seem that he was not backed by the remainder of the cast when he told them the pronunciation, as used in the days in which the play was set, of the name of the motorcar, Mercedes. He insisted that the stress lay on the first syllable, thus *Mer*-cedes, and not Mer-*ce*-des. Mary Tyrone was played by the American actress Constance Cummings and although she gently protested, Sir had his way. He also allowed his Shylock to say "May-hee-coh" when he had to mention Mexico. Doubtless again quite correct, but the word spoken in this way could cause the listener to wonder what this word was and so concentration was lost for a moment.

In one scene in *Long Day's Journey*, Sir Laurence, as James Tyrone, climbed onto the round table downstage centre so that he could unscrew all but one of the lightbulbs in the hanging lamp in order to save money on electricity. For the early performances, he jumped backwards off the table, but he was soon persuaded that he really shouldn't continue with this bit of business — one of those that could be recorded in "The Book of Extraordinary Moments in Olivier Performances," sadly never written — and he stopped.

One day when he was in rehearsal for *The Dance of Death*, I needed to speak to him urgently, so I went along the corridor and asked his secretary, Peggy Gilson, if he was alone. As with all good secretaries of busy bosses, she guarded him zealously, some would say too zealously, but on this occasion, albeit unwillingly, she allowed me to tap on his second door, the one furthest from his desk. I heard a faint "come in." He was standing in the narrow space behind his desk in his shirtsleeves and sporting his favourite scarlet braces. As I entered, he looked across the room with a strange vague look on his face. He said nothing for a moment as he examined the floor once more but then he looked up. His greeting was also vague. "Ah. Michael . . ." He seemed to have run out of steam and I said nothing until at last I tried, "Are you all right, Sir?" "Yes. Oh, yes." Another pause. "It's just that I'm checking what I'm doing in this production. It's very hard. Often I instinctively do or say something in a way I know is interesting and exactly right, but then I think, I've used that bit of business before. And that's when I have to start thinking of something new. You see, I know there are people out there who are watching everything I do in the hope that they can say to their friends [and here he put on a very exaggerated upper-class accent]: 'Oh, yes, Larry was very good, but you remember what he did at the end of the first act? Well, I saw him do exactly the same thing in the third act of . . . [and here Sir named one of the many productions in which he had appeared].' I am determined not to give anyone the chance to say that about this performance."

When I joined the National, Sir's repertory manager was a lovely person from New Zealand, Sunny Amey. On her first arriving in England, she made straight for the Royal Court and was soon in my office explaining that she knew all about us. She said she had read everything she could find about the English Stage Company when she was at home and how she had come over to England with the firm intention of working in this exciting-sounding theatre. What could I do but invite her to join us as an assistant stage manager? It was a wise move, but now she had preceded me to the National Theatre where, although titled repertory manager, she was, in effect, Sir's amanuensis. She had an office on the other side of the corridor from mine and slightly nearer to Sir's.

It wasn't long before Sir suggested that when he sent for Sunny, I should also go along to his office, for she and I had to work closely together. Sunny would have the schedules that covered rehearsals, performances, and the timings of such activities, as well as details of the setting up of tours, while I was concerned with the actors who would be involved in all that was being planned. If Sir had not got an evening performance, he would often stay working in his office after most of the occupants of the other offices up and down the corridor had gone home at six o'clock, and it was then that he took to calling us in. These were useful times when we could brief him on some subject for which he had had only sketchy details, or when we could put a few questions to him so that we could get his reactions. All this helped us work out whether we should go ahead with a scheme or shelve it. The added bonus of these evening meetings was that there were no telephones ringing or cars sweeping in and out to distract us.

I used to have a folder with all my cribs in it, for, when called, I never knew what the subjects for the evening would be, and although these times were very productive, there would be some evenings when Sunny and I hoped that he would get tired around seven-thirty. We knew that that was about the last moment to give time for his car to be summoned, and he could be taken off to Victoria Station to catch the eight o'clock train home to Brighton. There were also many evenings when we wouldn't get called, so Sunny and I used the time to catch up on some of our work in our own offices, although part of my mind was waiting for a shout from Sunny. This came when she heard Sir take his coat off the back of his office door, a movement that used to leave the hanger swinging wildly, making a distinctive sound that reached her office but not mine. Then Sunny would call out, "The hanger!" and I would start to put my papers in a drawer and so be ready for an instant getaway once Sir's car had passed my window.

If he was in rehearsal as an actor, then these were usually held in the rehearsal room at the huts. This meant that if a scene in which he didn't appear was about to be rehearsed, he could go along to his office where he could study his role or, if any pressing business had sprung up, he and Peggy Gilson could deal with it. She said that sometimes she was even lucky enough to be able to talk over with him at these snatched moments some of the many other items she would have on a list. I too had my "Sir list" that sometimes became dangerously long.

One morning, to my surprise, I was asked by Sir to see him during a rehearsal lunch break at Aquinas Street. I had often seen him queuing in the canteen for his daily lunch — always the same, an apple and a chunk of Cheddar cheese — but now I was apparently going to be present at the eating thereof. This proved to be the case, for as we talked he started eating. He began with the cheese, large pieces being bitten off and then slowly chewed. The cheese course finished, there was a slight pause and then the apple was attacked. Again, large pieces were bitten off, but this time the chewing was exceptionally noisy, similar to a horse eating a lump of sugar.

As the months went by and I saw the disposal of much cheese and many apples, I realised that we both gained a lot from these meetings. I used to go in with a series of questions, all of which were pared to the bone, although I hoped with just enough detail for him to get a clear understanding of the various problems or suggestions. On the other side of the desk, Sir used his mouthfuls as marvellous times for thought. A tricky question was followed by a grunt, and then a piece of food was delivered to the mouth. Good manners took over at once, which meant no more talk until the mouth was empty. It was surprising how long it sometimes took him to swallow a piece of cheese.

He liked to know everything that went on in my area. We checked over the salary list as the end of a season drew near, examining both the basic salary and the performance fee. We discussed the allocation of dressing rooms. Would I be able to give X a room closer to the stage than his current one, now that he will be playing a leading role in the next production? Would the colour of the next leaflet herald the change to spring? Sir was insistent on the leaflets being given seasonal colours. Early in the year, which encompassed Lent, it had to be religious purple. Spring was recognised with bright green to match the new leaves. Summer mirrored (hopefully) the summer sky and so was bright blue.

The autumn of course was brown to indicate the dying leaves, while Christmas burst out with two colours, dark green and bright red, honouring the holly.

It wasn't too long before the day that I feared might come actually did come — when Sunny said she had to return to New Zealand. We all missed her a lot, especially myself, and not only for the pleasure of her company nor that, once she had gone, all her jobs would come my way, but more that I would have to do them on my own. Now it was up to me to go through with Sir the performance schedule that would end up in a leaflet: how long the gaps were between appearances of each play and how many plays were being presented each week; how many changeovers would occur between matinee and evening shows; how many performances were given of each production each week and what the total number of those performances at the end of the leaflet's time span would be. If a new play appeared, Sir studied the number of performances I had allocated it at the start of its existence before it became just part of the repertoire. This was always a difficult balancing act for a new production needed as many performances as possible at the start of its life so that it became firmly fixed in the minds of all involved, whereas I knew that there might be perhaps three or four productions waiting offstage, longing to be played as soon as we returned to a normal weekly repertoire.

By the time Sir Laurence was planning the repertoire for the newly formed National Theatre, he knew that Peter Hall was not only filling the Royal Shakespeare Company's London theatre, the Aldwych, with classic and new plays but also with Shakespeare productions brought down from Stratford. Sir Laurence was determined that in no way was the National Theatre to be seen as being in competition with the Royal Shakespeare Company over Shakespeare, and yet the National Theatre would not be carrying out its avowed intent, "to present the whole spectrum of world theatre," if it did not include Shakespeare in its repertoire. Therefore he declared that his first production would be *Hamlet,* after which there would be one Shakespeare in the National Theatre's repertoire each year. At the same time, he determined that on Shakespeare's birthday, April 23, the National Theatre would always stage one of his plays. It never mattered what it did to the rhythm of the repertoire at that time, how long since it had last been played, or even whether it meant recasting, the order was firm: "Only Shakespeare on the Birthday."

Sir also checked his performances to ensure that the rep was not too reliant on his pulling power at the box office. He never baulked at the number of performances allotted to the plays in which he appeared, but he had one quirk. He relished playing the matinee on a Saturday. His wicked joy was to meet the actors coming to the theatre for the evening show as he was on his way to the stage door for the start of his journey home. "Have a lovely evening," he would call out. "I'm just off for the weekend."

Finally, the overall picture and the variety in the repertoire had to be scrutinised. There were endless questions and sometimes these were hard to answer. By the time Sir saw a final draft of the leaflet, it had gone through so many versions that the reason for playing, or not playing, a certain production on a particular day, could get lost in the mists of drafts. As the years passed and the renown of the National Theatre spread, the number of National Theatre players (Sir always referred to his actors as "players") being sought by television and film directors increased. Some actors, with or without the help of an agent, managed to get work on a television commercial. Agents were apt to frown on such activity since at that time it was considered not the sort of work one of their actors should be seen doing. Voice-overs, yes; an appearance, no. It was not difficult for me to give permission for any of this work providing it was local and providing the actor was not in rehearsal at the National Theatre, but films on location were more of a problem. This nearly always meant the actor being away for several days, so firstly I had to get a very firm assurance from the film company that the agreed number of days away would be rigidly observed and secondly I had to keep that actor's plays at the Old Vic out of the schedule for those particular days. This second point must seem obvious and easy to arrange, and so it would have been if one or two actors only were involved, but often there were more than two asking for a release that covered the same days and all the time I was trying to keep a good balance of performances.

I don't quite know why, but in the early days I felt that Sir would not like to think that his actors were away from the Vic using their energies in television or in films, so I never told him if I had given a release. This meant I had to play a private game whereby I could make it possible for Colin Blakely, for instance, to go to Ireland for a film without eagle-eyed Sir noticing that there was a dearth of Colin's performances over more days than usual. I took another risk with Robert Stephens when he was wanted for the film of *The Prime of Miss Jean Brodie*. This was being shot in Edinburgh, and he would be needed for a week. As with Colin, this was an important film for Robert, and I knew that I had to make it possible for both to accept the offers. Because Robert Stephens was cast in so many productions at that time, Sir homed in on that one, but I managed to prove that there were legitimate reasons for the repertoire to be as I had arranged it — filming, of course, did not figure in these reasons — and he accepted it. Both Colin and Robert made their films and were back in good time for their next performances. I have no doubt that both of them, and certainly Robert, would have mentioned to Sir their involvement with the film world, but if they did, he never gave any indication that he knew they had been away.

I also had to watch those productions that had not pleased the critics or, more worryingly, the public. Travelling up by train, surrounded by daily commuters, often used to give me a very good idea how a production was generally regarded. Sitting in a compartment mainly filled with bowler-hatted city gentlemen, it was impossible not to overhear their conversation, which was usually carried out in short, sharp sentences. "Went to the Old Vic last night." Pause. "Saw *The National Health*." Pause. "Seen it?" These snippets would only be interesting comments, for my true source as to the state of advance booking, once a production had opened, came to me from the box office manager, Pat Layton. As soon as he warned me that the advance for a production was not good, I would "nurse" it in the leaflet I was preparing: this meant I would ease down on the number of its performances so that it only appeared in the rep occasionally. I had to make sure they weren't too occasional, for this would make it difficult for the actors to maintain a momentum. Thankfully, the few performances I allocated, in what I called a "ticking-over" situation, could nearly always be relied on to draw in audiences of a very reasonable size. My aim was to entice audiences that were large enough, I hoped, not only to encourage the actors, who would be playing to a well-filled house, but also to make the audiences feel comfortable by being surrounded by others and not by rows of empty seats.

With Sunny gone, there was no longer the triumphant shout of "the hanger" down the corridor, and often when the coat was taken off its hanger, it didn't mean that he was going home. Usually he had phoned me earlier asking if I would like to accompany him to a West End show. "We'll have supper at Overton's in Victoria and Joanie will join us there after her show, then she and I can travel home to Brighton together." Sir's phone call always meant I had to get in touch with Elizabeth and tell her the bad news that I was off to a theatre with Sir. Often I would have to say to myself, "Here you are being taken to a theatre by this fantastic actor. You will be given supper with him and your old friend Joan Plowright, and when, after a good meal and wonderful company, they have left to catch a train, you can go home — so why are you complaining?"

When I was asked to accompany him to a dress rehearsal at the Vic, we would have supper on the way, usually at a little Italian café under one of Waterloo Road's railway bridges. Wherever we went, he was always recognised. Once when we went to *Hair*, he said at the interval that he couldn't stay any longer for some reason. As we left our seats, I murmured to those in the seats behind us (who seemed to be staying there simply to watch him), "He loved the show, but he's got to get back to work." At least the first part of this statement was true, but mainly I said this because I didn't want them telling anyone that Sir Laurence had walked out of the show at the interval.

If there was one subject, outside the theatre, that he had mastered thoroughly, it was medical knowledge. My introduction to his ability to diagnose an illness and then prescribe for it was at the Royal Court. During the rehearsals of *The Entertainer* there was a widespread and severe epidemic of influenza. It provided a great opportunity for him, something he could really get his teeth into. No one in his cast was going to go down with the flu, so he made sure of this by advising all and sundry to follow his preventive plan. "Keep your bowels open," he would cheerily and loudly announce to all and sundry. "The flu will never get you if you keep your bowels open."

If he learnt of anyone being ill or having a fracture or a broken bone, he would immediately point out where the seat of the ailment or the location of a bone would be and what the patient should do to improve the condition at once. Ken Tynan's emphysema brought forth graphic descriptions about the poor chap's affliction — poor chap, I find myself saying, although his chain-smoking habit must have exacerbated his condition. Sir really enjoyed playing on home ground when his appendix was removed (in February 1968) and then a thrombosis (in August 1970), both of which brought forth the most detailed descriptions of how, why, and where.

## Scene 4 ⟨ Auditions and casting

I had only been with the company a couple of days when Sir sent for me and told me that his casting manager was leaving to make a film. "So I would like you to take over her job, dear boy," he said. "Of course," I said, for there was nothing else to say. But it proved to be an extremely time-consuming job, and so with permission granted, I phoned Ann Robinson and asked if she could possibly come in on a part-time basis to cope with the enormous amount of mail directed at the casting department. In the early 1950s, Ann had been my assistant stage manager on H. M. Tennent's production of Dodie Smith's *Letter from Paris* and later my co-stage manager on another Tennent production, R. C. Sherriff's *The White Carnation*. I couldn't have asked for an assistant who was so good at her job, who never got upset or riled, and who had a great sense of humour. Her promotion to stage manager was fully justified.

Having at first a very attractive assistant who then became a co-stage manager for whom everything seemed fun meant that stage staff in the many theatres we played up and down the country would do anything for her, and we never had any complaints from the actors. All of them, like myself, enjoyed having her around. She worked the same magic when she joined the casting department. Her two half-days soon spread to four half-days, and then they became four full days and so to a full week. The letters continued to pour in, yet she managed to carry out our aim, which was to make every actor aware that if he or she wrote to the National, the letter wouldn't go off into the blue and never receive a reply — not even an acknowledgment and certainly not the offer of an audition. Ann saw to it that all letters were answered and that everyone got an audition. At first, we roped in the associate producers for the auditions, the young directors who assisted a director during the rehearsal period as well as finding time to take rehearsals of the understudies. Then Robert Stephens became interested, and he joined the panel at the auditions. I always felt guilty that Ann could not be one of those watching the auditions, but she was so good at dealing with the actors as they waited for their turn to audition, as well as learning so much about each person as they sat and chatted, that it seemed we gained more by her being outside the door rather than in the room. Of course, she was really wanted on both sides at the same time.

Auditions were held in the rehearsal room at the top of the dressing-room area in the Old Vic. It was not a user-friendly room in summer. It had large windows, but if they were opened, the noise of the traffic on Waterloo Road made it almost impossible to hear what was being said. If they were kept closed, the heat became intolerable, with the skylight section of the roof letting in much sunshine and therefore heat. Auditions with Sir were held in the rehearsal room at Aquinas Street so that he was away from the office for the shortest time.

## Scene 5 ❦ A and B Companies within the National Theatre Company

I am sure that George Devine must have advised Sir Laurence in the bow-fronted dressing room at the Royal Court that the soon-to-be-announced National Theatre Company should not be made up of one large group of actors from which every play could be cast. Instead, there must be two distinct companies. When one company went on tour, the other would remain at the base theatre with a reasonable repertoire. George and Sir did not know at that time that the theatre would be the Old Vic. Doubtless, they would have discussed how there must also be a summer break, when visiting companies — such as we had at the Royal Court in 1957 — could save the Old Vic from going dark. Sir was insistent that his actors must get away for three weeks each summer and have a holiday with their families, as he intended to do. This meant that the company would play at the Old Vic for definite seasons, opening in September and closing the following August.

The two companies became A and B. Sir announced that, since he didn't want the public to think the A Company was the better because it was given the first letter in the alphabet, he would always play with the B Company. There were about thirty-five actors in each company, staying around this number for several years. Very few of the actors left at the end of a season, and this allowed strong ensembles to grow, which was clearly shown in the number of remarkable and excellent productions.

Sir Laurence was the only actor who, for many years, had a dressing room to himself at the Old Vic until Paul Scofield joined the company in 1971. They were never in the same production, so, though they shared the dressing room, they never met in it. This dressing room had played a large part in the history of the Old Vic. It had been the office of the legendary Lilian Baylis, and about half the room was taken up with Miss Baylis's huge rolltop desk. The other dressing rooms had a mix of actors from both companies, and I had to ensure that an actor from one company did not have to put away his or her personal effects to clear a space for an occupant from the other. There was a shower room at the top of the building. Sir's room also had a shower en suite (essential for *Othello*), but otherwise washing facilities consisted of one basin for each room.

Three small dressing rooms on stage level faced Webber Street, which meant they were on the opposite side of the building from the stage door on Waterloo Road. One of these dressing rooms had identical-sized square marks, one on the inner wall and, directly opposite, one on the outer. The marks clearly indicated holes that had been filled in. Across the narrow corridor and in the wall that divided the corridor from the stage was a mark similar to those in the dressing room. These three holes had once been covered with hinged flaps. It soon became clear that in those days rolled-up cloths (backcloths, stage cloths, etc.) were passed from Webber Street through the holes to the stage without hindering the unloading of scenery through the dock doors across the stage on the other side of the building.

The Grand Theatre in Leeds, to which theatre the National often toured, went several points better than the Old Vic regarding cloths. Because the stage of the Grand was two floors above ground level, a rickety old lift had to be used for getting scenery in and out, but the cloths had a special trap upstage, which, when opened, revealed a slide. A cloth placed on the slide disappeared from view as it travelled directly down to the street.

In the days when scenery was transported each Sunday from town to town by train, a carter would bring his horse and cart to the same Grand Theatre in Leeds on a Saturday night for loading the outgoing scenery. After the flats — and they were flat, seldom any built pieces — were tied down, the carter gave instructions to his horse to go to the railway station while he repaired to a local pub. After a while, he would rejoin his horse, which by then was waiting for him at the station.

The National's actors were paid on a system not used before in a drama company. In addition to a basic salary, each actor received a performance fee every time a production with which he or she was involved was presented to a paying public. This applied to both an actor who appeared in the production as well as to understudies. Both payments varied with the actor's standing in the company. In the 1960s, basic salaries ranged from £10 to £60 a week, whilst performance fees were on a scale of £1 to £15. This meant that the several leading actors who headed the National Theatre when it was formed were not paid the relatively large sums they could command when appearing in an eight-performance week in a West End play. Instead, they received a reasonable basic salary plus the extra performance fees for what, at the Old Vic, might be only two or three performances a week.

As soon as the productions for both companies in the next season became firm and roles were allocated, I had a long session each year with Sir in which we talked over every actor in the two companies. We discussed roles played or understudied, what would be on offer in the early part of the next season and, finally, salaries. Sir always viewed these, where appropriate, from a family point of view. He had to be assured that the basic salary for each actor would be sufficient for his or her family to live on from week to week, while the amount from the performance fees would come to the family as a blessed bonus. And the performance fees for the younger members of the company certainly did mount up, even when an actor was on the lowest salary level. For four performances in a week, the pay packet would be filled with £14 (basic of £10 plus performance fees of £4). While on tour, if one company stayed in a town for a full week with two productions, the packet would hold a princely £18 (basic of £10 plus performance fees of £8). At the top end of the scale, a leading player on £60 with a performance fee of £15 would be given a pay packet holding a kingly £105 for a week of three performances.

My next move, once Sir and I had mapped out salaries for the next season for every actor, was to invite all the actors, one by one, to talk over the current season—the highs and lows, hopes realised or dashed—and, most importantly, what the next season might hold. One bizarre event occurred an hour or two after I had had a session with Edward Petherbridge. He was an actor in whom Sir had great faith and for whom Sir was always looking for a chance to "stretch," even if it meant giving him a role that should, under Sir's normal policy, have gone to the next in line of those actors who would usually be playing very small or walk-on parts plus large understudies. After Edward left my office, I saw one or two more of the company, and then started to phone their agents (most members of the company had an agent) to tell them what had transpired at my meetings with their clients. I would leave until last the subject of salary (which I would not have mentioned to the actor) and what I could offer for the next season. When I phoned Edward's agent, I dialled the number and was rather surprised when the bell at his end didn't ring and yet, recognising his voice, I found I had somehow got through to him direct. I was about to speak, but before I could get out a greeting, I heard the agent already talking. For a fleeting moment, I imagined he was concluding a conversation with someone in his office before he turned to the phone to speak to me, yet it proved not to be this at all. Obviously I was on a crossed line (not uncommon then) but a crossed line par excellence. I heard the voice of Edward's agent, and then I heard the unmistakable voice of Edward himself, saying, "Hello, Ken, I have just been to see Michael Hallifax . . ." I put the phone down immediately and never mentioned the event to either about what, with luck, would be a unique event. I decided that if I mentioned this extraordinary coincidence to them, and even if I added that I had replaced the telephone at once, one or the other might think I had actually heard more than I admitted, and then there could have started a nagging thought, "What might he have heard? What did we say at the beginning of our conversation?"

I always hoped that the representatives of organisations such as British Actors Equity, the Musicians Union, and the Arts Council and also the agents of actors and playwrights would reckon that the person at the National Theatre with whom they were dealing was straightforward and honest. I may have been fooling myself, but I felt, especially when money, for instance, was under discussion with agents, that when I said I was sorry but I could go no higher, the other side realised I was speaking the truth; what was on offer was fair and that, indeed, was as far as I could go.

I had learnt very early on when I first had to go to negotiation meetings, where the majority of those round the table represented West End managements, that if Union leaders, Equity representatives, or whoever were told at the beginning that such-and-such a figure was the percentage increase on offer, take it or leave it, this was a challenge and hostilities could break out. When I spoke to the agents, I would name the increases to the basic salary and the performance fee, which sometimes, along with the prospective roles, we would discuss at length. In the main, the agents would come back to me saying that their client had accepted. Occasionally, an agent would phone to say that his or her client was not happy with the money, even though the agent had considered the increases to be fair. I knew then that, if I felt the actor deserved it, I had to help the agent by increasing the fee a very small amount, thereby making it possible for the agent to get back to the client and show that, however small, he or she had been able to get more than had been originally offered.

## Scene 6 ❧ Kenneth Tynan

Kenneth Tynan didn't turn up at the huts every day but came punctually to meetings and went to dress rehearsals, during and after which he would give notes to directors in addition to chatting to authors if they were present. At planning meetings, he was hugely helpful to Sir

Laurence. As literary manager, he was the one who would suggest plays, both new and classic, and the breadth of each company's repertoire was his responsibility in the first instance.

He came to planning meetings very well organised. He sat contentedly at the small table at the other end of Sir's office. He chain-smoked with the charming affectation of holding the cigarette between the second and third fingers, rather than the plebeian habit of employing the first and second. When the meeting began, we would soon discover he had either come with a broad outlook, such as, "Isn't it time we turned to the Scandinavian Tundra?" (William Gaskill's evocative term for plays by Ibsen and Strindberg), or he would come with specifics: "Larry, I think you should play Edgar in *The Dance of Death*." But that wouldn't be the end. He would continue by suggesting possible casting for the other two main roles in the Strindberg and would then go further still and put forward his ideas as to what those two actors could play in following productions.

Sometimes, having suggested a play, he would turn to Sir and enquire, "What do you think of that play, Larry?" Like Tony Richardson, he was a great one for using the first name. Often the reply would be, "It's a long time since I read it. I'll read it again and let you know." If Sir professed to know a play Ken had just suggested, I often felt that Ken then enjoyed himself by asking a supplementary question that needed a fairly deep knowledge of the play and its characters. When Sir was really caught out, and this was seldom for he could be wily too, he would turn to me and say, "I don't think we got a very good education at our school, did we?" This always managed to ease the line of questioning out of the way.

Sir and I had been to the same school, though not, I should add, at the same time, and it was there, one bleak afternoon in 1935, that the buzz flashed around that an Old Boy of the school, Laurence Olivier, was in the Quad with Dorothy Hyson and Jill Esmond. They were all appearing in *The Ringmaster* in Oxford's large touring theatre, the New, and it must have been a remarkably boring week if his companions had agreed to come a mile or two up the road to visit his old school. Jill Esmond, his wife, was dark and very attractive while Dorothy Hyson was very fair and was popularly known as "the most ravishing beauty in England" and "the perfect English rose." It was amazing how many

St. Edward's schoolboys that afternoon suddenly had to go and check items on the notice boards, which also happened to be the first port of call for the trio. The post-visit chatter did not contain mention of Mr. Olivier. He was just a peg on which to hang those two lovely ladies.

I sometimes felt that Kenneth Tynan was the administrative side of the Demon in a pantomime. All quiet down the end of the corridor, and then, whoosh, the star trap opens up, and there, shooting up from under the stage and appearing out of a cloud of green smoke, was Kenneth. He would talk with his literary assistant, the perfectly cast Rosina Adler, give instructions to be passed to me regarding a contract for a playwright, pick up scripts that had landed on his desk — scripts addressed to Ken were never given to him or put in his in tray or anything banal, they always "landed on his desk" as if delivered personally by a messenger from the gods — and then he was gone. Life went on at its busy pace whether he appeared or not, yet there was something strange about those visits. For a long time he would come by taxi, then out of the blue one day he arrived in a cute little car, a Mini. This couldn't, of course, be painted in a single colour, it had to be slightly unusual, and this he achieved by having a basket-weave pattern on the panels. "I thought I ought to learn to drive," he announced, as if he had thought of it one day and passed the driving test the next. The delightful Rosina must have had a busy, but fascinating, time keeping up with her butterfly boss.

## Scene 7 ❧ Sir Laurence's production of *Three Sisters*, July 1967

Early summer 1967 saw the start of rehearsals of Chekhov's *Three Sisters*. A new translation was prepared by Baroness Moura Budberg. Moura was a large Russian lady who, as soon as possible after being introduced, would tell her new acquaintance that she used to be Gorki's mistress. Few of those to whom she gave this snippet of news knew how to react. Most just stared while they quickly wondered whether one said "Well done," or perhaps, "How fascinating," or even, "Bad luck." At various times I noticed that when she was mentioned in a normal conversation, her name had become linked with Gorki, giving her an extended surname.

On June 15, I was phoned from the Old Vic, where the production was being rehearsed, asking me to meet Sir in his dressing room in half an hour's time. When the few who were summoned had gathered, Sir said he had bad news for us. He had been diagnosed with prostate cancer, and he had to go into St. Thomas's Hospital at once for chemotherapy. There were therefore two major points to be considered, he continued: firstly, *The Three Sisters* and secondly, the six-week tour across Canada scheduled to start at the end of September.

He said that he was not worried about *The Three Sisters,* for he reckoned it to be in very good shape. He had absolute faith in Mark Cullingham, his assistant, who would be able to carry on with great competence. The pre-pre-production weekend was in three days time, with the first night on Tuesday, July 4, just under three weeks. Sir Laurence said he had been told that his treatment was going to be very tiring, but during the two-week period between one treatment and the next, he would be getting stronger each day. The end of his first two-week period fortuitously coincided with the production weekend (July 2 and 3), so he planned to come to the Old Vic on Saturday, July 1, when he would watch a run-through and give notes before returning to the hospital.

Sure enough he turned up at the theatre in a wheelchair and professed himself delighted with what he saw before, very tired, he was taken back to St. Thomas's. The production, with amazing settings by the Czech designer, Josef Svoboda, needed six miles of stout twine, which, when stretched with one strand beside the next from floor to ceiling, gave the impression of the solid walls in the Prosorov's house as well as magically creating the trees in the final exterior scene.

Sir Laurence wanted to give the audience the feeling at the very end of the play that the Revolution was not all that far off. Therefore, as many of the company as could be mustered went to a recording studio where we all learnt the Russian words and music of the "Internationale." Marc Wilkinson, the National Theatre's music director, was in charge of the recording, with which Sir professed himself more than pleased. He arranged for it to be introduced into the dying moments of Act IV, at first hardly audible but with the volume steadily increasing until the final curtain fell with the music filling the theatre at full blast.

The play was extremely well received by the press, and the public and it was happily absorbed into the repertoire.

## Scene 8 ❧ Preparing for the Canadian tour, 1967

Sir's illness created complications with the Canadian tour, and these were twofold. Firstly, would Sir Laurence be able to stand the strain of flying out to Vancouver? The week's performances in that city were to be followed by a journey across Canada to Toronto, with shows at Edmonton, Winnipeg, and Montreal en route. Secondly, what three productions should B Company take? The original choices were *Othello* and *Love for Love* in which Sir Laurence would appear and *A Flea in Her Ear* in which he would not. At our Old Vic meeting, Sir had said the doctors were confident that he would be able to go but he must not play the role of Othello. The two to three hours he had to spend making up for every performance (he had seven layers of black makeup applied to his body so that he would never have to worry that, if he were touched onstage, white skin would be revealed), followed by a long and tiring role, to say nothing of the hour or so it took him to wash himself clean after a performance, would be too much for him.

The British Council advised us that the cities in which the National Theatre would be appearing were agog at the news that Sir Laurence would be leading the company. It was obvious that somehow he had to go on the tour and that *Othello* had to be replaced by another production in which he played. This wasn't a problem for there was only one — Strindberg's *The Dance of Death*. It was certainly not the production that one would choose to play in the vasty theatres of Canada, for an audience needed to be up close to watch the reactions of the three main protagonists. But it could boast an excellent production by Glen Byam Shaw and stunning performances by Sir, Geraldine McEwan and Robert Lang, the three B Company stalwarts.

He had strict orders from his doctors that he must rest as much as possible — and already plans were well advanced for Joan to come out for short visits to watch over him. Nonetheless, I worried about those nights when *A Flea in Her Ear* was playing, thus giving Sir a free evening. I especially looked at Winnipeg, for we were only taking one production, *A Flea in her Ear*, to that city. He would be fair game for all and sundry to extend hospitality to him and invite him to give a talk, attend a dinner, go to a fundraising event, and so on. I was also certain he would appear rude if he refused with what might seem the lame excuse of, "My doctors say I must rest." I therefore went to him and suggested that, in addition to *Love for Love* and *The Dance of Death*, he should also appear in *A Flea in Her Ear*. The only role not cast was Etienne Plucheux, the butler, a role initially played by Robert Lang, who, when Albert Finney left the cast, moved into Albert's dual role of Chande-bise/Poche, and Anthony Hopkins took over as the butler. Robert would be playing his dual role for the tour, but Anthony Hopkins, luckily as far as my plan was concerned, was not going.

As soon as Sir accepted my suggestion, he went to Paris for a discussion with Jacques Charon, the director of this glorious French farce. Jacques was a long-serving leading actor and director with the Comédie Française. Near the time for our departure to Canada, he was able to come over from Paris for a few days to concentrate on Sir's new role. Jacques also used the time to help those who had come into the production since its first appearance in the National repertoire. I was so sorry for them since Jacques would watch a scene and then say, "That's very good, but I wonder if you could just be a little more . . ." As the cast started the scene again, Jacques would leap up and play the part himself, while the actor concerned was required to watch. *Concerned* is perhaps the correct word, for, male or female, Jacques was not averse to acting out every role, endowing each with a gloriously funny characterisation. I often felt that each actor must have been thinking, "If only I could go away and think about how I can translate what Jacques has shown me into my own way. But no, I have to get up there and immediately try to copy him, without looking as if I am copying him."

There wasn't much either Jacques or Sir Laurence could do with the role I had wished on the latter. It was a typical butler's role of announcing guests as they burst into the drawing room in Act I. he did not appear in the frenetic Act II, but was back at the opening of Act III when he and Sheila Reid, a delicious *poule* of a maid, let the audience know what had been happening during the Interval. Sir wore the same livery as his predecessor, but he insisted on adding white gloves.

A few weeks before the company, with myself as manager, was due to fly out on September 30 direct to Vancouver, I appealed to George

Rowbottom to be allowed to take an assistant. I could foresee that there would be many occasions when a team of two was essential. George said there was no money available for such a person, but if I could find someone who would go for a daily subsistence allowance only, then he would give his permission. There was no one from the staff in the huts who could be spared for over six weeks, so, remembering the superb team Paddy Donnell and his wife, Floy, made when they toured with the Shakespeare Memorial Theatre on its overseas tours, I appealed to Elizabeth and another husband-and-wife team hit the road. It wasn't easy for her to organise affairs at home when she would be away for so long, but somehow she arranged it. I know that I could never have managed the tour without her company and her wonderful help.

## Scene 9 ⚭ Vancouver and Edmonton, September 30 to October 11, 1967

*Love for Love* was to be the only offering in Vancouver's Queen Elizabeth Hall. Sir would be playing Tattle, which meant he had some good scenes but nothing too tiring. The company was spread over the city in three hotels, which was certainly not what I would have chosen, but I just had to accept what had been planned for us. I put Elizabeth and myself in the Georgia Hotel where Sir also stayed so that I was on hand. Apart from the weather breaking the day we arrived ("We haven't had any rain for weeks and weeks . . ."), all went well. The reception of the play was always excellent. When Sir came into our office one evening and flopped down onto my much-travelled office box, Elizabeth said, "You didn't get your usual exit round after that scene." He turned his face, with its white makeup and black beauty spots and framed by a long curly wig, towards her, cast his eyes upwards, and commented, "They were stunned by my beauty."

We certainly had three beauties also staying at the Georgia. They were a singing trio, little known to us, called The Supremes, and their leader, Diana Ross, and Sir quickly became acquainted. Very soon, Diana was insisting that Sir go to the nightclub where they were performing. He didn't need any persuasion, and the next thing I knew, he was telling the company that he was off to hear The Supremes after the show that evening and was anyone going with him. "You mustn't go, Sir," I said. "You're meant to be resting." "Quite right," said Sir. "I have been resting all day, so after the show I'm entitled to a little relaxation." That evening's visit to the nightclub proved to be the first of several, with Sir showing no sign of fatigue, so that was a relief. As for The Supremes, they asked me to arrange three seats for the Saturday matinee of *Love for Love*. It seems they had promised Sir that if he came to their show, they would come to his. I never saw them to ask how they had enjoyed it, which I am sure they did, for Peter Wood, the director, had ensured there was plenty to watch even if the plot was not always easy to understand.

We moved on to Edmonton where the company played in a huge theatre with every seat sold for every performance. During the half on the first evening, I went to see Sir and mentioned that the box office manager had told me that he was amazed at the distances many had travelled to see Sir Laurence and his company. I added that some of the names of the towns, such as Slave Lake, Vermilion, and Black Diamond, were wonderfully evocative, so he asked if I could get him a list of these faraway places. I took this list to him as soon as I could and was at the back of the stalls at the end of the performance. After several curtain calls, Sir stepped forward and thanked everyone for coming to the theatre that evening, adding that he especially wanted to thank those who had come from, and here he named one of the towns on my list even though he had no list in his hand. Tremendous applause, especially from one block not too far in front of me. When it died down, he went on: "And those from . . ." and again he named another town, which brought forth further frantic applause from another part of the house. And so the towns were named until he reached the sixteenth and final one. A great feat of memory, and although it doesn't sound as if he would have had too many names to remember, they were of towns he had not come across before. Again, it wasn't as if he could just rattle off a list of names, for he had to wait for the applause before he could move on to the next and that pause made it very special. The audience certainly knew it was very special, and the hundreds as they left the building were all aglow.

The box office manager also told me that his theatre and the one in Calgary, some two hundred miles or more directly south, were identical. Many times he had overheard patrons in the large, wide foyer asking another member of a group, "Are we in Edmonton or is this Calgary?"

When Elizabeth and I were checking out the dressing rooms before allocating them, under the stage we found one with the name of the occupant in a special holder on the door — obviously a permanent member of the staff. The name was Brian Priestman. We knew he had left the Royal Shakespeare Company (memories of Brian, the Royal Shakespeare Theatre's music director, conducting Handel on the barge came floating back), but we had no idea where he had gone. When we checked the number on the door, we found that this was the room the theatre had chosen for us. Brian appeared and seemed pleased to find we had taken over his office for he had arranged for this, and soon he whisked us off to lunch in one of those slowly revolving restaurants atop a pencil-slim tower.

The next day, declaring that he was certain we could leave the theatre for an hour, he drove us to a remarkable house on the outskirts of the town, whose owner, he assured us, was a great friend of his and we were expected. The house covered a goodly amount of land (not that Canada is short of land, as we were discovering) for it was single storey and all the rooms faced a large central square. The drive led up to the only gap in the square, and into this gap Brian drove with great flourish (all his driving was with great flourish, and sitting beside him as he whirled, at great speed, round and round and round down from a remarkably high level of a multistorey car park was an experience I wouldn't want to repeat), skidding to a halt beside a door on the further side of the square. He then guided us into the living room of the house. Our hostess appeared at once, while we gasped at the room: it was rectangular, very large and had a monster in-the-round fireplace in the very centre. A huge fire was burning, while over it hung a large shiny metal cone. The thick carpet was white, and not only did it cover the entire floor, it ran up the walls until it met the ceiling. I was almost surprised it had stopped there. There were no windows on the square side of the room, but the outer wall was entirely glass, and one looked onto a lawn that quickly sloped away, presumably down a ravine, for the tops of great trees filled the gap beyond the end of the lawn.

When touring, one sees the interiors of many public and official buildings, so it is always very good to see a person's home. On the way back, Brian made us get out and stand on one of the roads we had just crossed, for he said this was the road that went directly from Edmonton to Fairbanks, many, many miles away to the north in Alaska.

## Scene 10 ◎ Last night of the 1955 Shakespeare Memorial Theatre Season

Sir Laurence's feat of memory in Edmonton reminded me of the last night of the 1955 season at the Shakespeare Memorial Theatre, Stratford-upon-Avon. It was the custom at this theatre, in the days when there was a definite season, that at the curtain call at the end of the performance on the last night, the leading actor would step forward and thank the audience for their warm reception that evening and the townsfolk of Stratford-upon-Avon for the kind way in which they had supported the company and made all of them feel so welcome in this beautiful town. Then followed other such expected platitudes, and when duly delivered, that would be the end of the evening.

In 1955, it was Sir Laurence who stepped forward, but instead of ending the normal short speech in the usual manner, he said he would like to thank his leading lady, Miss Vivien Leigh, for her wonderful performances in — and here he named her plays and her characters. This gesture he repeated with the other leading players, Anthony Quayle, Angela Baddeley, Joyce Redman, and Alan Webb. At this point, the applause indicated that the audience had decided that this must be end of the speech, but it was not so. Sir Laurence then moved to the second row where thirteen actors stood, and although he didn't name their roles, he named every actor. And so he came to thirty-four actors placed in two rows where once again he named every one. He never paused for a name. When he reached the final actor, the audience thought "This really must be the end" and applauded more fervently than before. But it was not the end. Sir Laurence returned to the front of the company and said that none of them must forget those who had worked tirelessly backstage all season to make sure the season ran smoothly and efficiently. Here he named the master carpenter and his staff, the chief electrician and his staff, the wardrobe mistress and her staff, and so it went on and on. At last, after more than twenty minutes, all were thanked, the audience was exhausted with applauding and thrilled that they had been there on this very special night, and everyone had nothing but praise for the man who had such a prodigious memory. The only group that was perhaps not quite so ecstatic as everyone else were those in the press and public relations under the brilliant leadership of John Goodwin. Their work had been exemplary, but their department was the only one not mentioned.

When I think about Sir Laurence's extended speech of thanks, I wonder whether he had decided to make sure the audience remembered all the roles Vivien Leigh had played during the season. But if he picked her out and named those roles, he was courteous enough to know that he couldn't stop there; the other leading actors must be treated in the same way. And so it would go on. Wherever the idea sprang from, it was a noble effort.

## Scene 11 ❧ Montreal and Toronto, October 15 to November 12, 1967

One had to keep one's wits about one in the two-theatre building in Montreal. Just as in Copenhagen, where I went with *Hedda Gabler*, one theatre was built directly over the other. It was all too easy for an actor to take the wrong turning from his dressing room and, on opening the door onto the stage area, find he was faced with the back of a set that did not relate in any way to the one that, in his eyes, should be there. If an actor did not immediately react to his call over the Tannoy, which meant he was a moment or two later than usual leaving his dressing room, it was always the occasion that he found himself in the wrong theatre. This shock, as well as the ghastly realization that the time to reach the correct theatre via the correct route was already tight, caused instant panic and loss of reason. Suddenly, the actor couldn't remember whether *A Flea in Her Ear* was above or below where he had found himself, and the situation at once became akin to a nightmare from which he was not going to wake and find all was well. He was only too aware that all was very much not well, and it was getting worse every moment. Luckily, the corridors usually had locals scurrying along, going to goodness knows where, and, on occasions such as these, they were able to calm a lost actor and take him briskly upstairs (or down) and show him the back of the familiar *Flea* scenery. No entrances were ever missed, but several heartbeats were.

It was in Montreal that I was standing next to Sir at the back of the stage. Robert Lang and Geraldine McEwan were playing a scene, with Sir watching intently. "Aren't these young actors amazing?" he whispered. "Take Bob. He's just had a long scene as Monsieur Chandebise with Geraldine, then we heard him thundering up the stairs. He appears briefly at the top before racing at perilous speed down the steep lead-off treads and into the quick-change room. A moment later he reappears in the uniform of Poche. And now here he is tearing up the lead-off steps, down the stairs on the other side, and he's back on the stage starting another scene with Geraldine, this time as his other character. Brilliant." Sir meant every word as he stood there slowly shaking his head with pleasure and admiration.

## Scene 12 ❧ Social engagements in Canada

Joan came out to join Sir Laurence twice in Canada, and I know it was very good for him to have someone to keep him from doing too much. We presumed she kept him on a tight rein during her visits, which would have been very good for his recuperation. We saw little of him when she was in Canada. When she went home, he resumed the way he had been living. In fact, his touring days seemed very much like his days in England, except that he got up later. So he may have gained a few hours of rest in the mornings, but that only meant he added that time to the end of his day, which would continue until the early hours. Whatever the role, like most actors, he needed to wind down for a considerable time after evening performances. Winding down for Sir Laurence didn't mean that he sat quietly sipping a glass or two of wine before eating a simple supper: One evening, he hosted a splendid birthday party for the assistant producer, Louisa Browne. He also went to all the after-the-show supper parties whenever the company was invited. In Montreal, he took the company to a magnificent affair in the British Pavilion at Expo 67, while on many occasions he would look in at the office during a show and say to Elizabeth and myself, "My dears, we three are going out for supper this evening." Eventually, long after curtain down, out we went. He had the edge over us, although we never pointed this out, for our days used to start around 6:30 AM. So when at two o'clock in the morning he ordered, "Just one more brandy, and then we must retire," we could have done without that brandy — or two. But as always, at whatever time and wherever we were, he was the perfect host or the perfect guest, whichever role he had to play. Amazingly and wonderfully, he never flagged.

Daytime events he kept to the minimum, so he didn't come to Niagara Falls. The technical staff had asked Elizabeth to arrange this outing. It was a day full of little events such as Anthony Nicholls deciding not to come with us, although he had put his name on the list, and failing to let us know. The coach's departure was badly held up while Elizabeth and I raced around the vast Royal York Hotel in Toronto searching for a man who was not in his room, nor in any of the restaurants or coffee bars, and certainly not at the meeting point in the main lobby. In the end, we left him a message and raced to the coach. We next saw him in the hotel that evening when he explained that he had "wandered out to do a little shopping."

At last we arrived at the falls where we all had to don black boots, long black raincoats, and black sou'westers in a special changing room from which Elizabeth and I were the last to leave. This meant that we were able to get the full glorious picture of what ahead of us looked exactly like a large group of chatty penguins as they waddled, black from head to foot, down the corridor towards the viewing platform. There we were able to stare at that unbelievable mass of water thundering down in front of us.

We were as late leaving the site at the end of this fantastic day's outing as we had been in the morning, with poor Geraldine getting worried that she wouldn't have time for an essential rest before going to the theatre for *Flea* that evening. This was all due to our two props, who, like Anthony Nicholls, had decided to wander off at the very time they were due to board the coach. In order to check that the pair hadn't managed to sneak back up to the top of the viewing tower, one of us scoured the grounds, while the other made occasional trips up the tower in case, by some coincidence, they were going up or down in one elevator while one of us was down or up in the other. Neither of us liked this job, for the lift was the first of its kind we had met. All seemed normal when one got in at ground level, but as the lift rose, one was suddenly no longer in a box with solid walls, but in a box with glass walls. There was the ground, but it was receding at a frighteningly fast pace. The tower seemed to be taller each time we made the journey, but the boys weren't up there after all for, just as we were reckoning that we would have to abandon the search, they meandered into view, never having been in either lift.

We made it back to Toronto, but soon gathered we had only just made it. On television and radio shortly before we went to the theatre, we learned that there had been an accident on the bridge that we had had to cross on our way back from the falls. This apparently resulted in a total holdup of all traffic, with no vehicle able to cross from either side. What made it scary in retrospect was that the accident occurred only a very short time after we had crossed without difficulty. Geraldine got her rest.

In Montreal, one visitor to Sir Laurence's dressing room was so over-awed that he used the name of the mighty local river when addressing the great man. Sir Laurence gently reproached him by echoing his visitor. "Saint Laurence," he said. "Thank you very much for the thought, but I'm no saint." That was true.

## Scene 13 ⊛ Kim Goodman — child actor on the Canadian tour

Kim Goodman and I had to check in at Bow Street Magistrate's Office before we went to Canada. He was fourteen and so under age to travel alone, and I was to be his chaperon for the tour. Bow Street professed themselves satisfied that, on leaving England, he looked well, but we were to check with the local police at all our Canada dates, and on return, we were to report once more to Bow Street.

As requested, Kim and I used to trek off to a specified police station at every town we visited so that he could be seen to be still in good health and apparently well looked after. The chosen police stations always proved to be as far from the theatre as could be arranged, but we dutifully went and at each place we got our papers signed. In one police station, we stood in awe behind a typist who was using a "golf ball" typewriter, which neither Kim nor myself had seen before. We hadn't time to check how it worked, but it appeared that instead of keys rising up and making an arc before hitting the paper, this had a ball in the centre of the machine that, we thought, contained all the letters, numbers, and so on. When in action, the ball whizzed around to bring the required letter close to the paper. The speed with which the secretary who was typing with this revolutionary piece of equipment was amazing. Nowadays, such machines must be exhibits in museums.

At another police station, we were amongst the Mounties, and this impressed Kim for he was interrogated by a splendid chap in a scarlet tunic, black trousers, and shiny boots. The questions Kim was asked were always the same. Was he being well looked after? Was he eating well? Was he feeling well? Was he getting enough rest? And on and on. Four days after our return to London, he and I met up for the last time when we returned to Bow Street Magistrate's Court. They were very pleased with Kim's verbal report of his wonderful time in Canada and pleased with how well he looked. Our papers were signed, and my responsibility for Kim was at an end.

## Scene 14 ❧ *Rosencrantz and Guildenstern are Dead*, 1966/1967

The announcement by Kenneth Tynan that he had found a new play in which he was extremely interested was not given in the usual way — it had not landed on his desk. This play was *Rosencrantz and Guildenstern are Dead*, the first play by a young journalist on a Bristol newspaper, Tom Stoppard. Ken had gone to the 1966 Edinburgh Festival, and he was really excited by Tom's play, which he had seen there in a production on the fringe (not yet honoured with a capital *F*) by the Oxford Theatre Group. "This is Tom's first play," reported Ken to Sir, as soon as he got back from Scotland. "There is some work to be done on the script, but Tom says he will be happy to work with me on it. We must schedule it as soon as possible." Ken had warned me of this, so I was able to show Sir that it certainly would be possible to fit in a production in April the next year, 1967, just seven months away.

Sir was happy to go along with such a headlong dash, although he said that he didn't think it would be possible to get a first-class director on such short notice, and therefore he would hand the production to one of the assistant producers, Derek Goldby. The company would be B, and the leading roles would go to John Stride (Rosencrantz) and Edward Petherbridge (Guildenstern).

Very early on in the planning, with Tom Stoppard working closely with Derek, I was asked if it would be possible to have at least twenty courtiers. Derek explained that he wanted to have as complete a contrast as possible between the times when the King and Queen and the court were onstage (very full) and when they were not (all but empty). I therefore brought into being a C Company, which was a mixture of actors from A and B. Ann Robinson had to be very careful whom she chose to play these nonspeaking courtiers, for when Tom Stoppard's play went out on tour, it had to leave behind a strong repertoire and not one weakened by the absence of several productions because some of the cast were in *Rosencrantz*. In the end we provided Derek with a court of seventeen.

The staging of the scenes with the King and Queen in Act I worked brilliantly in Desmond Heeley's simple but attractive set of a castle's antechamber — empty and cold, with granite walls and a row of arches upstage. In this room, Rosencrantz and Guildenstern play games, verbal and physical, while they wait for news as to why they are there. Suddenly the court arrives. The King and Queen sweep in from stage left at great speed with the courtiers directly behind them. The room is all at once chock-a-block with people and colour and bustle. The dialogue is also played at speed, and then, as suddenly as they had come, the King and Queen, moving very quickly once more, exit stage right. The courtiers follow the King and Queen at once, and within seconds the room is empty — except for the two young men. They seem even more lost and lonely than before this whirlwind scene took place.

Tom was present at all rehearsals. When Derek was taken ill and couldn't get to rehearsals, Tom took over the direction, with the company gratefully feeling they were still in safe hands. The production work, spread over three consecutive weekends, as had always been the practice used by the company, went well as did the final dress rehearsal on the Monday before the play opened to the press the next evening. It proved to be one of those evenings that gave no indication what the reviews would be like in the morning papers: There had certainly been a lot of laughter but from the first scene, with its tossing-the-coin game in progress, the audience seemed not quite to know how they should be reacting. Of course, this reminded me of *Look Back in Anger* in New York. At the end, I felt the reviews could go either way but whichever way they went, it would be total. Love it or hate it. The press notices proved conclusively that it was love it — with a vengeance.

## Scene 15 ❧ The Brighton Festival, April 1967

Soon after rehearsals for *Rosencrantz and Guildenstern are Dead* began, the director of the Brighton Festival got in touch to say how delighted he was that the National Theatre was to be part of the festival that year, but now he said that he would like up to three actors to take part in another festival activity — a Questions and Answers Evening in Brighton on Sunday, April 16, 1967. This would be the day before the start of the week when *The Dance of Death* and *A Flea in Her Ear* would each be playing for three days in the attractive Theatre Royal. I replied by saying that by chance, Tom Stoppard's play was opening at the Old Vic on Tuesday, April 11, and I felt that the offer sounded like something Tom Stoppard, John Stride, and Edward Petherbridge would like to do. Each would receive an honorarium, and I didn't think that would come amiss for any of them. All three agreed, and I set plans in motion.

I had never thought of the play or the players not being successful, so I was taken aback when, at one of Sir's meetings, I was asked, "What sort of greeting are these three going to get if the play is a huge flop?" But the notices that came out two days before the evening in Brighton ensured a full and excited house, and the trio received a rapturous reception when they came onto the platform. After an evening when they all spoke well, interestingly and amusingly, the three left the platform to thunderous applause and cheers after a thoroughly entertaining and fun evening.

It could have been in Brighton that the engaging Tom gave his immortal answer to a journalist who posed the question, "But what is your play about, Mr. Stoppard?" At once came the reply. "It's about [pause] to make me very rich."

It was to the Old Vic Theatre box office that a lady came to book tickets for Tom's play. Leaning over the counter, she got in a muddle when giving the name of the play. She tried variations such as "Rosenguild" before the box office clerk helped her by giving the full title: "*Rosencrantz and Guildenstern are Dead*, madam."

"Oh, dear," said the lady. "I am sorry." Whereupon she turned round and left.

## Scene 16 ❧ Repertory at the Old Vic Theatre 1967

When *Rosencrantz and Guildenstern are Dead* (*R & G*) opened at the Old Vic, it joined a six-play repertoire, five of which played in that theatre during the week prior to *R & G*'s opening. The five plays were: *The Storm, The Royal Hunt of the Sun, The Dance of Death, A Flea in Her Ear,* and *Much Ado About Nothing.* Except for *The Storm*, which left the rep soon after *R & G* opened, it was an extremely good clutch of productions, and in spite of *R & G* being C Company, it was possible from mid-April to mid-May 1967 for four weeks touring. These weeks included the Brighton week with *The Dance of Death* and *A Flea in Her Ear,* which pair later played in Liverpool. *The Royal Hunt of the Sun* could also share weeks with *A Flea in Her Ear* playing in Oxford and Nottingham. Left behind at the Vic were *R & G, Much Ado,* and *Love for Love.*

Three other productions were presented during 1967: *Three Sisters, As You Like It,* and *Tartuffe.* Sir Tyrone Guthrie was engaged to direct both *Tartuffe* and *Volpone,* and they straddled the turn of the year. Both were good, but they both lacked the final spark. When the very tall, craggy Sir Tyrone came to London in advance of his first rehearsals to discuss casting with Sir, he seemed as direct and organised as he must always have been. But he grew tired doing the two back-to-back productions. Because he had done them both at least once before — somewhere in the world — there was no excitement for him as there would have been if he were working on a fresh text. I realised this when I went to a rehearsal of *Volpone* to get an immediate answer from him — which he was very good at doing. There was never any question of his saying, "Ask me after rehearsal." As I crept into the back of the Old Vic, I heard him call from the stage across the stalls to Tanya Moiseiwitsch, his designer, with whom he had worked so often. "What did we use to do with these people up here?" he said, pointing to a huddle of actors upstage. He was trying to re-create a carbon copy of a previous success.

It hadn't taken me long before I found myself a seat in the Old Vic that no one else used, so I knew that whatever performance I went to, such as a preview of a new production or an understudy playing for a principal, I wouldn't have to stand even when the house was full. My seat was at the back of the dress circle, very close to the double doors at the top of the stairs from the foyer, and although it wasn't upholstered, it proved amazingly comfortable. What I hated was the entrance into the circle of a perfectly legitimate visitor, such as a walking understudy checking on a scene, which made even one patron turn round to see who or what had made a distracting noise. I therefore used to make sure that when I went into the circle, there was no light spill from the landing and that, on my few steps to my seat, I didn't tread on any of the squeaky boards — of which there were plenty on that level. My seat was a wooden radiator cover. The radiators were chubby and tall, so the seat was about four feet from the floor and, presumably to cause the least obstruction, only about eight inches wide. It meant sitting in rather a strange angular way but at least I wasn't on my feet. It was warm (sometimes too warm), and I wasn't taking up a seat that could be sold. I could also slip out of the circle when I had watched whatever part of the play I had called in to see.

## Scene 17 ❧ Overseas tour of the all-male *As You Like It*, 1968

*As You Like It*'s overseas tour was sponsored by the British Council. This A Company production, directed by Clifford Williams and designed by Ralph Koltai, was having a huge success at the Old Vic, and I took it abroad with great pride in the work. We were due to play Stockholm, Copenhagen, Belgrade, and Venice. Jane Edgeworth from the British Council was accompanying the tour, which was just as well, for Stockholm proved to be a very much more expensive city than the council's local representative had led the British Council in London to believe. This meant the daily allowance or per diem, which was given to everyone in the company to cover the cost of a day's meals and refreshment, was inadequate. The actors complained that buying a drink for their opposite number in the Royal Dramatic Theatre's company cost them nearly the whole of their daily allowance. After much telephoning to London, Jane was able to increase the allowance. Even so, everyone had to be extremely careful about how they spent their money.

One day, the company was invited to visit the eighteenth-century theatre at the Royal Palace of Drottningholm. This theatre was closed and forgotten for well over a hundred years. How this came about is beyond me, for this reasonably large building sits almost next door to the Royal Palace. I cannot believe that someone didn't, at some point, ask a royal retainer, "What's inside that large building over there?" The company was very fortunate to be given the chance to visit it. Coaches were arranged to collect the company and transport us, as we imagined, to the Royal Palace. But no, off we went to the harbour where we were to board a couple of launches, our hosts rightly reckoning that this would be a speedy way to travel as well as giving everyone a different perspective of the city. This sounded excellent, but I hadn't reckoned on two members of the company who said that they couldn't travel on the flat harbour waters as they would be seasick. Luckily, I was able to persuade them that it would be very calm and the journey would be short. It really was not possible to arrange other transport at that time — and I certainly couldn't afford to send them in a taxi. The only advice I gave them was not to make the journey in the cabin. "Stay in the fresh air," I said. Looking as if they were being asked to walk the plank, they came aboard. Twenty minutes later they were happily on dry ground at the end of the voyage without any queasiness on the way.

The theatre was fascinating. We admired the pretty auditorium and gazed up at a box with a delicate wooden screen that could hide the occupant from clear view. This, we were told, was where the king's mistress sat to see the play, shielded from public gaze. On the stage we saw a series of wood and canvas rollers, of irregular size and shape, on which breaking waves were painted. When the big capstan under the stage was operated, which in turn made the rollers revolve, we could see how a brilliant effect of the tide rolling in was created. The idea doubtless came from the large capstans used on sailing ships, and they needed to be big, on ships or in the theatre. As the stagehands turned the great capstan by pushing on the wooden stakes sticking out from it, the hempen ropes, which could be of great length, were wound up or down.

How many stagehands (or were they actually sailors?) were needed to turn the capstan, I wondered.

Even more fascinating was the method of changing the stage scene. Upstage were several backcloths each painted with a different scene. Both wings housed six masking flats, each echoing the scene of one of the backcloths; just as these were hung one behind the other, so were the wing flats stacked. Another capstan was used to change the scenery. All the flats of one scene were linked with ropes, which went below stage to the second capstan. When the capstan turned, the flats that were on view to the audience slid offstage, and the next set of flats, bearing a portion of the same scene that was appearing on the next backcloth, came into view. The principle of this system had been used on the Old Vic stage for Franco Zeffirelli's glorious production of *Much Ado About Nothing* and I had thought what a brilliant invention — although being the twentieth century, there was no capstan to slide the flats on and off. But here in Drottningholm the same effect was in use two hundred years earlier. So much for the credit I had awarded Franco.

We played *As You Like It* at the Royal Dramatic Theatre in Stockholm, which was the first theatre where we encountered a closed circuit television control in the prompt corner. This meant that our stage manager, John Rothenberg, was able to focus a camera in the auditorium onto the royal box. Thus he was able to see the entrance of Princess Alexandra, Princess Marina's daughter and a guest of the Swedish royal family, and give the cue at the appropriate time for taking out the houselights. No national anthems, I was pleased to note.

I met another surprise at our next date in Copenhagen. The first evening was a very busy one; several of the company objected strongly to the hotel allocated to them, and Jane had to work hard to house them elsewhere. I had to deal with one actor, Frederick Pyne, who complained of feeling very unwell. I was given the telephone number of a doctor, and when I dialled, he answered at once. I explained the problem briefly and gave the address of the hotel where the patient could be found. "That is all clear and I understand," said the doctor, speaking perfect English. "I am driving along [here he named a street], so I can be with you in twenty minutes." Such service. Quite amazing. I found it unbelievable that at seven o'clock on a very wet evening my call had gone straight through to a doctor in his car who gave me his time of arrival.

The invalid seemed to get better just on hearing the news that the doc would be there in fifteen minutes. Whatever the doctor prescribed, it certainly seemed to be what the patient needed, for the next day he was completely well again.

From Copenhagen, we were due to fly out at 1:00 PM for Belgrade. The company was spread over six hotels, so it took a little working out how the three coaches allotted us could best be routed and what time the occupants of each hotel should be ready. I arranged with John Rothenberg that he would be in charge of one coach and a member of his very good stage management team would be in charge of the second. The third coach would report to the hotel where the majority of the company and myself had been staying. All coaches were to arrive at the airport at noon.

In spite of one of our party deciding to go out shopping (shades of Anthony Nicholls in Toronto) when he should have been lugging his baggage down to the lobby, as we circled a roundabout at the entrance to the airport, we were joined, each from a different offshoot road, by the other two coaches. That was a wonderful start. As ever, I had all the passports, so I went to check-in and announced, not without pride and certainly with relief, that we were all present: two women (wardrobe and wigs) and forty-nine men (actors, stage management, technicians, and myself). "I am sorry to have to tell you, Mr. Hallifax," the charming check-in girl said, "but the plane to take you to Belgrade has not yet left that airport. We are hoping it will leave soon. Will you please tell your company that they are now free to stay here in the airport or to go back into the city, but they will be required to report back here by eighteen hundred hours." I made the necessary announcement and stressed they must be back by six o'clock. I let them know that I would be staying at the airport and to page me if I was wanted for anything, otherwise to check in on return from their afternoon in Copenhagen, and we would all meet up at a point I had chosen.

Most of the company happily went back into town, while I organised meals for those who had elected to stay. It wasn't long before I was called over the Tannoy (or its Danish equivalent) and asked to go to a certain desk where I was told that the plane would be very late in, and it would be midnight before we could hope to leave. By this time, I had discovered that there were many cabins, like sleepers on a train, available for free to the public, so I booked all of those and said they would be occupied from 1800 hours. There weren't enough for the whole company, but then I made another discovery. I found a large area that included a huge dormitory with many beds, again available to the public for free. Once more I booked as many as I could, and by the time the company dribbled back at about six o'clock, I was able to send them off to claim their beds.

However, long before that time, I had been called over the Tannoy once more with the message that John McEnery, the actor playing Silvius, wanted to see me at passport control. I decided not to go out of the control area and join him to save myself the hassle of getting back once our conversation was over, so we talked through a thick-glass panel. At once, he reported that he had lost his passport. "How could you lose that hard-backed object?" I pointlessly asked, but I hadn't been prepared for the answer. "I was dancing down the street," he said. "Please go and find the airport police and report to them," I told him, "and let me know what they say. I will get on to the British Council." I went to a nearby phone and while talking, I could see John across the large hall, going in and out of offices. The British Council official, who likely thought he had seen the last of us, very nobly said he would come to the airport immediately. This was very good news, for any help would be gratefully received, and in time he turned up. We badgered the airport authorities over a long period of time. Our perseverance finally paid off for at last I was told that, as far as the airport was concerned, I could take John on the plane with us, but after that it was up to me. They could not help; in fact, they just wanted to get rid of him, and they would be glad when he was gone. I understood only too well how they felt.

It was long after midnight before we were gone. It was a singularly uncomfortable plane furnished with excessively small seats. Not having been able to take advantage of a rest on a bed at Copenhagen airport, I was looking forward to getting some sleep on the plane, but the back of the seat just about reached the top of my shoulder blades, and the seat back remained firmly upright. For compensation, I was sitting next to a charming Czech who practised his English on me. The whole journey.

We seemed to have been travelling for some time, when it was announced that we were landing at Prague. We all had to disembark, not that there was anything to disembark for. Nothing was open, and the whole airport appeared to be in darkness. The only good thought was that there seemed no possibility someone would suddenly ask what John was doing there. At last we continued our journey, but it was not Belgrade where we landed next, but in the north of Yugoslavia at Zagreb, and there we would have to go through passport control, we were told, before we made our weary way south to Belgrade.

We were guided into a huge corrugated shed and down a slope within it. Midway through the shed, at the foot of the slope, was a barrier manned by a large man in uniform. "Keep close to me," I hissed to John, and slowly the company went past the guard and into the freedom of Yugoslavia. At last John and I were left. Showing my passport, I walked past the guard, saying the while, "This is my friend whose passport has been lost in Copenhagen." Up went the arm of the guard and the owner grunted something that obviously could be translated as, "Where's his passport?" Jane joined us, and the company gathered round on their side of the barrier. At the same time, a neat little airline stewardess appeared from nowhere and in good English asked if she might help us. Gratefully I accepted and explained in a few words what our problem was. She turned to the guard and in some foreign language spoke at length, but his demeanour did not change a whit. Central casting had done their usual good job. He was perfect for the part. Now we had to charm him or wear him down. On second thoughts, I didn't think charm was going to get us anywhere.

After I had been through all the "these-are-actors" and similar speeches, nobly translated by our friend, I suddenly remembered that I had several large sheets on which all details of those travelling were recorded. I got out this document, opened it up until I came to the Mc's and then pointed out John's name. "There you are," I said, using a tone that I hoped would come across, even to our stolid friend, as being the clincher of the matter, "J-o-h-n M-c-E-n-e-r-y. And that's him." I pointed in triumph at John and then back to the paper.

Stolidly he stood there. No expression. No laughs. No permission to pass. Another brilliant idea struck me. The last thing I had done before leaving the theatre building in Copenhagen was to go to the deserted, dimly lit front-of-house and take down all the photographs of the production that had been placed there. Once more, a scrabble through all my papers until, at length, I found them. Thumbing through them quickly, I found one of John, as Silvius, with Gerald James, as Corin. I saw Gerald in the crowd and pointed him out to Stolid and then indicated which one he was in the photograph. I then put my hand on John's arm and again pointed to the other figure in the picture. This must be it, I thought. But no. It was then that Jane Edgeworth said, "Let's all sit down and let him know we're not going to move until John is let through." I asked the company to do this, while Jane made sure our kind interpreter understood what we were doing. Soon just the four of us were left standing, the remainder sitting, very close. Nearly fifty people take up a surprising amount of ground.

Jane had made a breakthrough. Stolid spoke for the first time, addressing his remarks, slowly, to the stewardess. She listened closely, and when Stolid stopped, she said, "He wants the young man to go with him. I will go too," she added quickly. And bravely, I thought, for the situation was really quite tense by now.

"Excellent, many thanks," I said, and the little party went up the slope to a small corrugated hut within the large shed. Like any good spy thriller, the two contestants stood in front of a small window fitted with opaque glass. Behind them was a bright light, so we saw the two of them in silhouette. There were muted calls of the "there's John, I think he moved a bit" kind, then silence. After not too long, although it seemed very long, all the shadows disappeared, and John came out of the door, making his way down the slope towards us. Stolid and the stewardess followed, so John was able to hold a hand close to his chest and give the thumbs-up sign.

At once, the company scrambled to its feet and talking broke what had become an eerie silence. The stewardess came up and said, "He wants to sign the large paper," so I produced that again, pointed out John's line and beside the name Stolid made a little squiggle. With the company all smiles and many thank you's being called to him, we parted from Stolid, whose expression still had not changed. The stewardess disappeared in the crowd, and we never saw her again.

With the triumph of getting John through passport control, we felt our journey was nearly over, but there was another surprise in store. As we flew down the length of Yugoslavia, our captain announced that

Belgrade was fog-bound and therefore we were going to Dubrovnik, where we would land and where we would stay until Belgrade was clear. "Not Dubrovnik!" exclaimed Derek Jacobi. "That's one of the most dangerous airports in the world for landing!" That cheered us all up, and we held our breaths until the plane started to bounce, but at least we had passed the encircling mountains and were bouncing on and off the land.

We were told we had to go into the airport buildings, which had still not opened. It was about five-thirty on a dry misty morning, and although members of the airport staff were gradually arriving, there was no one to make even a cup of coffee. Back to the plane, with the captain telling us that Belgrade was now clear, and at about seven-thirty we reached our destination. Unbelievably, waiting to greet us were actors from the Yugoslav National Theatre in whose house the company was to play. These kind souls had doggedly stayed up the whole night since they were never quite sure when we were going to touch down. As the company came through the barrier, the local actors handed out a single rose to everyone. The roses, after their long exposure, were quite dead. The British council representative was there with the coaches, and we were driven at speed into the city. On the way, he told me that the British Council's office in Belgrade had already been alerted to the problem of the passport, and with the greatest help from the British consul, a new one was issued to John shortly before we left for Italy. At the same time, we learned that the original passport had indeed been found in a Copenhagen street.

As the coach roared towards Belgrade, the British council representative produced a bag containing envelopes filled with the per diems. As company members drooped into the lobby of our high-rise hotel, I told them that I would stay in the lobby so that if anyone had any room or other problems, he or she should contact me, and I would sort it out. I added that I had the per diems and would be grateful if they could come and collect as soon as they had checked into their rooms.

It wasn't long before one of the young actors appeared, looking surprisingly fresh. He said that his room was fine, but would I please tell him the way to the post office. There's nothing like having faith in your leader, I thought. Much later when I got in the lift to go up to my room, I saw a charming notice in English giving advice on using the lift. The first instruction was: "To move the cabin press the button of wishing floor." This was followed by: "If the cabin enter more persons each one should press the button of wishing floor. Driving is then going automatically of natural order." They made perfect sense.

For the first two days in Belgrade, all I saw of the town was the road between the hotel and the theatre. Mainly modern and very depressing, but then Jeremy Brett (Orlando) and Sydney Edwards (drama critic on the *Evening Standard*) invited me to join them for lunch. This time we went down the hill past the stage door instead of my usual route heading straight on past the front-of-house. The hill was quite steep, and soon we were in the old Belgrade. The difference from what I had been used to was quite dramatic, and Jeremy and Sydney were pleased at my reaction as if they had set up this area especially to amaze me. We had a good lunch in a long, low building that had a narrow frontage onto the ancient road; no tarmac here but large old and worn paving stones.

The reception of the production at each of the packed houses was excellent. The days in Belgrade went by very quickly, and soon it was time to move on to Italy. The first part of our journey to Venice meant we had a short stopover in the dreaded Dubrovnik. However, we landed safely once more but as I watched the company crossing the tarmac on their way to the transit lounge, I saw Ronald Pickup and Derek Jacobi carrying Harry Lomax, using the fireman's lift method. Before they reached me, I had started the search for a doctor and one appeared very quickly. He didn't speak any English but he seemed to understand Harry's problem and he gave him some medication to help him on the rest of the long day.

Our second stopver was in Rome where we gathered in the airport after we had been, without incident, through passport control, waiting for information about boarding our final flight to Venice. At last, as the time of departure came perilously close, and in spite of repeated requests for information from various officials whose only help was to indicate that we must listen to the speaker system, I tried another counter for news, only to be told that the plane was waiting for us to board, but it was at a neighbouring airport. I yelled to the company to pick up their traps, for we had to catch a bus that would take us to the other airport. There was a mad dash. Jeremy Brett stood in the middle of the road and flagged down a couple of buses, into which we hurled ourselves and our baggage. Off we went, the drivers being encouraged to ignore all speed limits. They were very happy to do this, and we skidded to a halt at the second airport after a record-breaking journey. I urged the company to make for the plane, while I took the passports to the counter. Off they dashed, assuring me that they wouldn't leave me behind. After what seemed like a long time for all the papers to be checked, I ran out to the tarmac to find that the company had strung themselves out in a long line from the airport building to the plane. Once on board, they told me that they would have used the Zagreb technique if I had been delayed any longer and the captain had decided to leave.

The exact timing of the get-in and get-out at Teatro La Fenice was a first for our production manager and our technical staff. The scenery had to be loaded onto boats to be brought from the mainland to the theatre, arriving at the time when the tide was at its highest. The distance between boat and dock doors was then the shortest possible, and therefore the time taken for get-in or get-out was at a minimum.

It was such an honour to be invited to play in the Teatro La Fenice in Venice. It was the most beautiful theatre, although the behaviour of the audiences was unusual. Early in the first performance, I heard talking in the auditorium, so I investigated and saw a group of latecomers taking their seats and being greeted by friends already seated. It was as if there was no show going on. Surely friends had to greet friends, and it never occurred to them to whisper. However, these interruptions didn't seem to upset the actors nor the other members of the audience.

During the dance at the end of the show, I was standing stage left and at one point as the actors whirled past, one of the younger ones, Peter Winter, disengaged himself from the others, spun off towards me, and fainted as I caught him. I collected the inert and, fortunately, light body and turned to find an Italian stagehand standing directly behind me. "*Il dottore?*" I asked in impeccable Italian. To my surprise, he nodded and said "*Si, si.*" He led the way offstage along a passage and down a flight of stairs. We walked down another endless corridor until he stopped outside a door and knocked. A nurse opened the door, and they exchanged some speedy dialogue. The stagehand withdrew, and I was ushered into a large, white room. It had a vaulted ceiling and was stocked with medical equipment and trays of instruments, which gave the room a general hospital air. Beside a trolley was a doctor to whom I spoke in English. He indicated I should put Peter, still apparently unconscious, on the trolley, and the nurse ushered me out. To find a fully staffed and equipped medical room in a theatre was certainly novel and exciting. Greville Poke, you should have been here. A first-aid box lurking somewhere in the props room was about the best a normal British theatre could provide in the way of medical care. Even then the box would most probably be empty, for there was never anyone in sole charge of it.

That evening the company had been invited to a restaurant very close to the theatre for supper after the show, so I went with them to make sure all was well there, and then returned to the theatre to find the patient was ready to be escorted to his hotel. He seemed much better but a little weak. As we walked slowly through the streets, he explained that the doctor, though kind, was brusque for he suspected, unnecessarily, that Peter had been taking drugs. Once he was settled in bed, declaring he didn't want any food, I left him and returned through the dark, quiet streets on a lovely, balmy night to the restaurant. The party was going well, and so was the food — in fact, as I soon discovered, it had gone so well there was none left. Peter was quite recovered the next day. I realise now I never asked him what had been the matter. So long as he was well, I didn't care what the cause had been.

As usual, I had no time for sightseeing in this beautiful, fascinating city, except for the day when Philip Locke, who had taken over Jaques from Robert Stephens, sent a message to say he was not feeling at all well and could I get a doctor. Since he was mobile and there was a good doctor only a short distance from the theatre, we set off on foot. Our route took us nowhere near the usual tourist areas, but through the backstreets, across a large square, and over a bridge. After a little concern as to whether we were at the correct house, we reached the doctor's waiting room. At once we realised that no one spoke English and this realisation worried an already extremely nervous Philip even more. After a short wait, his name was called. As he stood up, I wished him good luck, whereupon he said, "Oh, no. You must come in with me." Not the sort of invitation I wanted, to say the least, but I could see it was a case of my going in with him or no treatment, so in we went.

With sign language and a mixture of English and Italian, the doctor seemed to know what was wrong, and thank goodness, it wasn't long before I was paying the doctor's bill and we were out in the sun once more. I soon realised that finding our way back along the route that we had come was not the easiest thing to do in Venice, but when we chanced upon the large square, we knew all was well. All was even better when we saw a chemist's shop on one side of the square, towards which Philip, waving his prescription, dashed as if he had just seen the Holy Grail and might get to it first. The prescription eventually produced a huge bottle of white liquid, for which I paid. I thought we could now go back into the square and then aim for Philip's hotel, but hardly had we got out of the chemist's shop, then Philip tore the wrapping off the bottle and started swigging the contents. If the pharmacist had looked up and seen what he was doing, I think he would have yelled at Philip to stop. Instead, I firmly took his arm, and he got the message. Certain that he was already cured, he took the remaining half of the bottle back to the hotel. That evening he played Jaques as interestingly and as intriguingly as ever. As with Peter, by the next day Philip was very much better.

Two weeks after the company returned to England, the production was on the move again. This time it was to the Empire Theatre, Sunderland. Not a town that made one think of the arts, but the theatre had had a face-lift that, unusually for theatre face-lifts, included the dressing rooms as well as the front-of-house. I was particularly grateful for the latter changes since they included an excellent restaurant, in what had been the circle bar, where good and varied types of meals were served all day. This meant that each morning I was able to get to work in the theatre around nine o'clock and not have to leave the building until after the evening show.

During one performance the rain came and soon some of it — as with the huts in Aquinas Street — had found a way through the roof. The spot it chose, unfortunately, was centre stage exactly where poor Derek Jacobi, as Touchstone, had to give the "retort courteous . . . quip modest . . ." speech. Trying and failing to miss the raindrops must have been bad enough, but he was facing downstage, whereas six of the cast were sitting on the floor in a semicircle with their backs to the audience listening to him, so their enjoyment of the situation did not need to be too restrained. When Touchstone was requested by Jaques to "nominate in order the degrees of the lie," Derek always took his next speech at tremendous speed and with brio. But on this occasion, as he became more and more wet, he somehow managed to get through the speech even faster. The next line from Jaques now seemed even more appropriate than usual, "Is this not a rare fellow, my lord?" It was a pity he did not have an additional question on this occasion, such as, "And is he not exceeding wet?"

## Scene 18 ❦ Receptions when touring abroad with the National Theatre

On any tour with which I was involved, there was always an understanding that no invitation would be accepted unless it applied to the entire company. For our kind hosts, during the 1954 *Hedda Gabler* tour, to invite twelve seemed not too heavy a burden, but to invite fifty or sixty must have seemed a very tall order. However, there were many receptions where food and drink were in plentiful supply and where we answered endless questions from our hosts and their local guests.

In Vienna, during the 1955 Shakespeare Memorial Theatre's *Much Ado About Nothing/King Lear* Tour, we were ushered into a large room where those we were to meet were at the far end. They surged forward to greet us, but it was not long before the buzz went surreptitiously round the company that no one was talking to Sir John Gielgud the leading actor, in addition to being the director of *Much Ado*. It was thought that his arrival in a beautiful grey dinner jacket, rather than black as worn by all the gentlemen present, meant that he was "one of those," as one man was heard to say. The company made sure that, once it was aware of the situation, he was not alone from then on.

For many of the younger members of big companies, a reception meant not having to spend a per diem on a lot of food during the day since they could make up at the affair in the evening — or rather, the late evening, for the hospitality always had to be after an evening performance. This was not always the way it worked out in practice, however. At the Vienna reception, there was plenty of drink, which was fine, but we were all, whether we had starved during the day or not, hungry by now, and yet there was no sign of a meal. Actors have a nose for food, and although it took some time, word spread around that if one went into an adjoining corridor and made for a certain door, one would find the food. The main room emptied quite quickly, and soon waiters, who had at last started to bring out trays of dainty canapés (no buffet as anticipated), found that their trays were emptied long before they reached the reception. The kitchen staff didn't know how close they had come to having their premises invaded.

It is often difficult to recognise an actor offstage even if one has just seen him or her onstage. I met this several times when *As You Like It* toured. I soon realised that Philip Locke and myself must be a pair not easily distinguishable at a reception. Many a time, I was approached by a fellow guest who greeted me with, "What a lovely show that was. We did enjoy it, and we never for a moment thought that the girls were not girls. We thought you were so good as Jaques. How did you learn all those lines?" And on it would go at breakneck speed so that when the outpouring finally came to an end, there was then the difficult choice. Did I confess that, sadly, I was not the one who played Jaques, which, I knew, would cause great embarrassment and neither of us would know the balm to apply? Or should I let it go and pray that Philip didn't wander up and expose my apparent duplicity? I always chose the latter course and was never found out even though it was often touch and go.

Perhaps the greatest of all invitations was to the Carlsberg Brewery in Copenhagen, again on the *As You Like It* tour. It was incredibly and embarrassingly late before we arrived at the brewery, where we were taken through the visitors' area, eventually reaching the room where we were to have supper. This proved to be a banquet, with something in the order of fourteen courses, each accompanied by a different drink.

At the end of this vast repast, and after much drink had been quaffed, the representative of the brewery rose and gave the most brilliantly witty speech, which lasted for some time. I am sure it was the "Speech for Evening Visitors," but whatever it was, it was an enormous pleasure to listen to. Many of us likened the speaker to a huge favourite around the world at that time, his fellow countryman, Victor Borge.

It was then incumbent on a leading member of the company to

reply, but after such lavish hospitality to expect an actor to stand up for a reasonable amount of time, let alone deliver a brilliant speech of thanks, was a tall order. One of our leading actors made a brave attempt, but singularly failed, and it fell to Derek Jacobi to save the evening by rising to his feet, standing steady on them, and delivering a very good, neat, and exactly right speech. No rain on his head at the brewery, needless to say.

## Scene 19 ❦ National Theatre productions at the Old Vic, 1968

Productions were not consistently good during 1968, but certainly the repertoire could not be accused of being unadventurous. In March 1968, Peter Brook's exciting production of Seneca's *Oedipus* came into the Old Vic, both onto the stage and into the auditorium. Audiences were surprised on reaching their seats to notice actors standing on narrow pedestals or plinths at the base of all the pillars in the stalls and in the dress circle. Then they noticed that these actors were making sounds. "They must be doing voice exercises," came the comments from the know-alls. Some of the audience were more concerned about the actors' welfare than their voices. One of the seventeen spread around the auditorium felt a slight pressure on a foot, so he stopped his voice work, looked down, and there was an elderly lady well settled in a seat at his feet. Having gained his attention, she pointed to a wrapped chocolate that she had placed on his plinth. "For you," she whispered. Another on reading her programme found small photographs of the thirty-six members of the cast. She held the programme open at the page of pictures and quietly enquired, "Which one is you?"

During one rehearsal, Peter Brook was about to work on a scene during which Irene Worth as Jocasta would be standing on the plinth. When she said that it would help if she could have the actual plinth, Sir John was heard to murmur, "Plinth Philip or Plinth Charles?"

Peter Brook decided that there should be, as there would have been in Seneca's time, an antimasque to conclude the evening. This started with the unveiling centre stage of an enormous golden phallus. On the first night, as soon as it was revealed, Coral Browne (still two years before she, too, would be playing at the Old Vic as Mrs. Warren in *Mrs. Warren's Profession*) turned to her female companion sitting beside her in the stalls and commented in tones that were anything but hushed, "It's all right, dear. It's no one we know."

The antimasque also involved the actors and the band marching round the auditorium. The free-and-easy style made me think of a village band, and all professionalism seemed lost. It may have been necessary in Greece about two thousand years ago, but I felt no need for such a diversion at the Old Vic in 1968. I wanted to retain the impact of the play with its two powerful performances by Irene Worth and Sir John Gielgud, backed by the strength of the other thirty-four National Theatre players.

*Oedipus* was followed by another production for C Company, *Edward II*. Frank Dunlop, the director, wanted this play by Bertolt Brecht to have crowds that looked like crowds so once again, as with *Rosencrantz and Guildenstern are Dead*, Ann Robinson sought for a crowd throughout A and B Companies and was able to offer Frank a cast of forty-seven. Twenty-five of these were peasants, soldiers, servants, and such like, although many of them also had small roles in addition to the mass menial ones.

Two months later came — and sadly, soon went — three short plays under the explanatory title of Triple Bill. The bill was made up of *The Covent Garden Tragedy* by Henry Fielding, *A Most Unwarrantable Intrusion* by John Maddison Morton, and *In His Own Write* by John Lennon. The interesting part of these short plays was that the directors were Robert Lang (one of the longtime leading actors of B Company) for the Fielding, Robert Stephens (by then, Sir Laurence's associate director) for the Morton, and Victor Spinetti (a very witty and entertaining man and a former member of Joan Littlewood's Theatre Workshop at Stratford East) for the Lennon. Tony Walton designed all the beautiful sets and costumes. Each play was well directed and excellently played by the company, several of whom were in two of the plays, while Mary Griffiths played in all three. Some of the cast in the Lennon play had a variety of parts: Oliver Cotton, for example, was cast as Elepoon Pill, TV Camera, Danoota, Monster, Radio Actor 3, Reverend Felix Hyacinth Smythe, A Cab, Radio Padre, and Fieldmarcher Loud Mount

Gammery. It would be hard to beat that for versatility in a short play. The only newcomer was Angela Baddeley, an actress of great experience in all the media and the wife of Glen Byam Shaw. As an evening, however, the plays did not make for satisfaction. I wanted the delightful characters in the first piece to reappear in the second, but no, I had to get to know and love an entirely new lot, great fun though they were, only to have them also disappear, and after the interval, I started again with a third group.

Just before Christmas, 1968, Sir Laurence's production of *Love's Labour Lost* opened after the, until then, unknown luxury of two preview performances before the press night. The set was most exquisitely designed by Carl Toms. He had based his designs on the fifteenth-century French school with ravishing results. But though visually beautiful, the setting presented difficulties during dress rehearsals. His setting included many trees, which could be strung out across the stage or reined back to allow more acting space, and it often seemed during technical and dress rehearsals that the position of these trees, as they were made to traverse back and forth across the stage, were having more time spent on them than should have been necessary. At the same time, there was a problem with the sound quality of the band, which played the haunting music from the *Songs of the Auvergne*. They, too, at one rehearsal kept appearing from one side of the stage and tramping across it with their instruments to set up shop on the other. But after playing on that side, it was up sticks and back they went once more to their original site. Having seen the trees and the band ever criss-crossing, it was no wonder I felt it appropriate to comment, "I can't see the woodwind for the trees."

I had never seen *Love Labour's Lost* before, so I was glad Sir Laurence had chosen this to be one of the six productions he directed for the National Theatre between *Hamlet* in 1963 and *Amphitryon 38* in 1971. Once again A Company actors seemed tailor-made for their roles, and I loved watching them playing as a team so brilliantly. The play? This was another matter. The speeches of Don Armado (Ronald Pickup) and Holofernes (Paul Curran) I found difficult to understand at first hearing, and I am not sure I really understood completely after the umpteenth.

## Scene 20 ❦ National Theatre productions at the Old Vic, 1969

The year 1969 proved to be another one of fascinating productions, although only one was a success — a huge success. This was Peter Nichols's excellent *The National Health or Nurse Norton's Affair*. It was a play that managed, extremely subtly, to engage all one's emotions, but because it was so interesting and enjoyable and the characters so recognisable, it was not easy to realise how one was being manipulated. There were scenes that raised laughter, others that touched one. There was drama and tension, and all made so real and totally believable in Michael Blakemore's ace production that it was no wonder it drew the public in shoals. Once more with a National Theatre company, the ensemble playing was of the very highest order. *The National Health* was also an excellent example of senior actors, who would normally expect to support those to whom the plum parts had gone, being given really good leading roles. The wealth of experience of these senior players was more than evident in Peter Nichols's wonderful play.

For most of my career, I had been with companies that, as a result of working together over several weeks, turned themselves into ensembles. Each had its leading actors, and although the younger members might wish to play a role that was given to another, most accepted that repertory companies in the regions are the places in which to learn. Learning certainly came through the experience of playing increasingly important roles, but an actor can learn by watching and listening during rehearsals, even if not appearing in that particular scene.

At the National, the younger members were able to watch those who were always cast in the leading roles knowing that they too had been young actors who through talent and hard work, and often long years, had reached the positions they were now in. Many had risen within the ranks of the National Theatre itself, for by October 1969, the theatre had been in existence for six years, and many of Sir Laurence's players had appeared in a great number of major productions. The cast lists not only listed the casts, but also listed the National Theatre productions in which the leading players had appeared. In one programme, I chanced on the name of Louise Purnell, and noted with interest that, from Lady in Waiting in the opening production of *Hamlet* in October 1963 to

Eve, Zoe, Cleopatra-Semiramis in *Back to Methuselah* in August 1969, she had played in sixteen productions at the Old Vic.

In 1969, an interesting group of directors came to the National. Geoffrey Reeves was handed Charles Wood's play with the title of *H or Monologues at Front of Burning Cities* — but I never heard the play referred to as such nor would I think it would have helped over much if it had been. We all called it *H*. I liked it. A period of British history, the India Mutiny of 1856, centred on General Havelock of whom, until the play, I knew nothing except that there was a public house in Battersea bearing his name — and no wonder when I learned that, at news of his death, there had never been such national mourning since the death of Nelson. Because of this, I was sorry when the pub ceased trading under the name of General Havelock, which it must have borne since the 1850s.

Then Michael Langham came to direct Congreve's *The Way of the World*, after which Frank Dunlop teamed up with Robert Stephens on John Spurling's *Macrune's Guevara*, which was one half of a double bill, the other half being Maureen Duffy's *Rites* directed by Joan Plowright.

These last two productions had first been shown during the National Theatre's Workshop Season, at a little Holborn theatre, the Jeannetta Cochrane. The season played for three weeks from February 9, 1969.

Two directors again, when Clifford Williams and Donald Mac-Kechnie miraculously put the two parts of Bernard Shaw's *Back to Methuselah* onto the Old Vic stage, with brilliant designs by Ralph Koltai. Plays one, two, and three, which made up part one, played for three hours and eight minutes, including two intervals of fifteen minutes each, while part two, which contained plays four and five, played for two hours fifty minutes with one interval of nineteen minutes. These two parts took over the Old Vic for a season, which began on Tuesday, July 22, with part one. It was played again the following night, after which there were no public performances until Tuesday, July 29, when part two played its first performance, followed by its second on the following night. Part one's press night was on Thursday, July 31, with the press for part two on Friday, August 1. After that, for its three-week run in repertory, the plays more or less alternated the evening performances. On matinee days (Thursdays and Saturdays), part one played the matinee and part two the evening, except on the middle Saturday, when the plays were reversed. This was to allow those, who could only get to matinees on a Saturday, to see both parts and in the correct order.

Towards the end of the year, Frank Dunlop, solo this time, directed *The White Devil* before another duo, Donald MacKechnie and Joan Plowright directed *The Travails of Sancho Panza*.

## Scene 21 ◎ New buildings for the Royal Shakespeare Company and for the National Theatre

In 1963, when Peter Hall asked me to transfer to the Royal Shakespeare Company's London theatre, the Aldwych, he explained that this was only a temporary base, for plans were well in hand for a new theatre to be built specifically for the Royal Shakespeare Company at Notting Hill. The little Mercury Theatre in Ladbroke Road would be replaced with this new building, the only stumbling block being a pub that was within the site, and the owners of this pub did not intend that it should be removed along with the Mercury. However, this did not deter the architects, for soon the plans for the new theatre showed it wrapping itself around the pub. Gently the heat was taken off Notting Hill, and it became accepted that the company would stay at the Aldwych until a new theatre was built, but this would not be on the Notting Hill site.

When in 1962, the National Theatre Board appointed Sir Laurence as the first director of the National Theatre, he too was promised that a theatre would be built for his company and that it would be ready for occupation in 1969. In 1963, the architect Denys Lasdun was appointed to the project, but six years later the theatre was not ready for occupation. One reason for this apparent dilatoriness in starting building was a 1961 plan put to the Chancellor of the Exchequer by the London County Council that both the National Theatre and Sadler's Wells Opera should be housed on the same site on the South Bank. Denys Lasdun obligingly designed two handsome buildings that would sit side-by-side. By 1967, the dual idea was dropped, mainly due to the funding bodies not wishing to spend the amount these two buildings would cost, although the commitment to build a National Theatre remained.

The actual site for the National Theatre had had a chequered career. At first, it was destined to be built on a small grassy island plot opposite the Victoria and Albert Museum in South Kensington, but the planners changed their minds and decided it should be on the other side of the river. So a site was found for it close to Waterloo Bridge, but the Royal Festival Hall edged it out from there. It was then that the idea of the two theatres beside County Hall was mooted. When that came to nothing, a site on the downstream side of Waterloo Bridge was suggested and was accepted, and this is where it now stands.

Thus it was that the year 1969 did not see the National Theatre Company taking over its new home, but at least the splendid arts minister, Jennie Lee, was able to "turn the first sod," with, I hope, a suitably inscribed spade. When this customary duty had been carried out, building work could begin. The first true home for the National Theatre would open in 1973. So they said.

## Scene 22 ⟨ℒ⟩ National Theatre touring throughout the United Kingdom

Touring the National Theatre was very important to Sir Laurence. For himself, I think he enjoyed going out on tour for it was a short break, and he could delay (perhaps permanently) dealing with an awkward matter by writing to the person concerned to say that he was sorry he was off on tour and was therefore "in purdah," a favourite expression. He was always adamant that any production taken to the regions, as the provinces were wishing to be named, had to be as close to the way it was presented at the Old Vic as possible. The days of moving the physical productions from town to town by rail had gone; now it was taken by road, so the National Theatre bought two pantechnicons or vans. This remarkable word used to refer to a furniture warehouse, but over the years its meaning has changed from the storing to the transporting of furniture. The vast vans used by the National Theatre, like any company moving large productions, had to transport far more than just furntiure. These great beasts had to carry scenery, lighting rigs and lamps, props, wardrobe, and everything else connected with a show.

Sunday and Monday, the production's personnel would arrive. In addition to the cast, the staff director, the stage management, and all the staff from every technical department, there would also be the original lighting designer and a scenic painter who would stand by to repair any damage caused by the loading and unloading from the trucks. The wardrobe would be fully staffed, and a member of the National Theatre's wig department, with the appropriate drying cabinets, also went out — so unlike my touring days in the 1930s, 1940s, and 1950s, when wigs were sent to be dressed by a local hairdresser on a Monday, after which the actor concerned had to care for his or her wig for the rest of the week.

Again, unlike that long-ago touring, the National Theatre sent out a repertoire of plays. It was not very often that one production played eight performances in a town. The norm was that two plays would go out, each playing three evenings and one matinee. When *The Advertisement* and *Home and Beauty* were in the rep, however, they often shared four of the eight performances, thus making it a three-play week. There was also a notable exception towards the end of the 1966 Autumn Tour. We were scheduled to play three weeks at the Royal Shakespeare Theatre. The National had never played in that theatre, and Sir was determined that the Midlands should be shown what the National could do and the style in which it was done. He therefore announced that five productions would go there.

The first week would be the two productions, *The Royal Hunt of the Sun* and *Much Ado About Nothing*, that had been sharing the tour until then. The second week would be *The Storm* (which had opened at the Old Vic, not very successfully, five weeks previously) and *A Flea in Her Ear*. This glorious farce would be held over into the last week until the Thursday, with the final three performances taken by *Love for Love*.

Sadly, *The Storm*'s reputation must have reached the Midlands, for audience figures for its four performances totalled only one hundred fifty patrons more than came to *A Flea in Her Ear* on the Saturday night. It was a pity also that *A Flea in Her Ear* was given the extra performance during the final week, for the local audiences did not approve of this saucy French farce (as they referred to it in and around the town), and audience figures for its five performances were only fair. Audience reactions were tepid and scenes that would be greeted with the proverbial gales of laughter elsewhere were watched in almost dead silence. What they wanted was *Love for Love*, but this had only three performances when all seats were sold and only a few standing tickets were left unsold.

It might seem that with these productions on tour, there could be little left for the Old Vic, but during the Stratford weeks, five productions could be seen in London. Not only was it possible for all of those presented at the Royal Shakespeare Theatre to play in London, but there were two other productions available to the Old Vic rep that were not taken to Stratford. These were *Trelawny of the "Wells"* and the double bill of John Osborne's *Bond Honoured* and Peter Shaffer's *Black Comedy*. Stratford and District missed a lot by not seeing two of these three. *Trelawny* was quite delicious and Peter Shaffer's *Black Comedy* could make audiences laugh until they just couldn't laugh any more. It was quite brilliant. The short opening scene was played in blackness although the actors' conversation, which came out of the dark, showed that they were experiencing nothing unusual. Suddenly, full lighting comes up at which the actors exclaim that all the lights had gone out. The lighting stays up for the remainder of the play, although the actors behave as if they are in total darkness.

Not only was there much travelling to and fro by the actors to appear in productions on tour and in the same week at the Old Vic, but they also took part in talks, workshops, and special performances that were usually connected with the plays being presented in the local theatre. The majority of this extracurricular activity was carried out by the actors on the tour, but sometimes casting made it necessary to send out others who were not playing at the Old Vic on the days when they were needed for these extra activities out of town.

Arranging a tour meant talking with Jack Phipps, head of the Touring Department at the Arts Council of Great Britain, for he was the mastermind behind DALTA, an acronym standing for Dramatic And Lyric Theatres Association. This had been formed by the Arts Council so that touring by the big subsidised companies to regional towns or cities could be scheduled to form seasons rather than occasional, and seemingly haphazard, visits throughout the year.

As an example, from February 26 to April 13, 1968, DALTA arranged a five-week season at the Grand Theatre, Leeds. The National Theatre took week one with four performances of *Rosencrantz and*

*Guildenstern are Dead* at the start of the week and four performances of *The Dance of Death* at the end. Weeks two and three saw the Royal Ballet in occupation, with three full-length and three programmes of shorter ballets, while, during the final weeks, four and five, Sadler's Wells Opera presented eight of their productions. This latter opera company took its name from, and was based at, Sadler's Wells, and this is the "Wells" that *Trelawny* was of.

On paper, these seasons made great sense, but they didn't take into account the financial burden it placed on those patrons who would have difficulty finding the necessary cash to come to both National Theatre offerings. But if these patrons also had a great love for either or both of the other two visiting companies, what chance did many have to afford tickets for all that they wished to see within such a short space of time? When I visited the company in Leeds, so many of the public commented to me, "If the visits by these great companies could be spread over six months, then our coffers would have a chance to be filled up again before we need to start booking for the next visit." I don't know how the other two companies fared during their weeks in Leeds that season, but the Grand Theatre, with a capacity for four performances of 6,256 seats, attracted 6,054 patrons for four performances of *Rosencrantz*, while 6,235 came to *The Dance of Death*.

Between October 1966 and June 1971, the Company toured the United Kingdom for thirty-two weeks and took productions overseas for fourteen weeks. I acted as the manager for all that touring, which meant that I had the usual chores associated with taking a company out of London. I started by asking the company and staff to let me know whether they would be travelling by train or individually. If the former was chosen, which proved to be the majority, I then purchased tickets and reserved seats or compartments. If the latter, then those individuals would be paid the cost of the rail fare. Company members also had to advise me of any theatre tickets they wished to buy so that I could ask the local theatre manager in advance to reserve them. At the same time, I would ask for six house seats to be allocated to the company for each of their performances, the distribution of which I would control when we arrived at the theatre. These would not be complimentary, so I had to collect the cost of any seats I allocated and pay it in to the box office.

The accounts department would send me out with details of how much I would be putting into each person's weekly pay packet, so these packets had to be prepared during the week with the amount the packet contained written on the outside. Early in the week, I would have informed the bank as to the breakdown of the total sum I would be collecting on Friday, having worked out how much I would need in the various denominations. In paper money, there would be notes to the value of one pound and of ten shillings. Then in silver, I would ask for half-crowns (an easy term for two shillings and sixpence), florins (two shillings), shillings, and sixpenny pieces; and finally in copper, pennies and halfpennies. On Friday morning, it would be time to visit the local bank with a cheque for the total amount, and within minutes, my briefcase would be full of the notes, held together with elastic bands, and the coins suitably bagged.

Back to the theatre, having walked out of the bank trying to look as if I had just paid some money in rather than having taken a considerable amount out, and so to the dressing room that served as my office. There I would put the appropriate notes and coins into each of the prepared envelopes. I always made sure not to seal any envelope until I had finished the whole operation, for however carefully I would count out the various coins and however diligently I made sure no note was sticking to another, there were times when too few notes were left on the table and yet one more envelope to be filled. Then started the lengthy task of checking the contents of each of the filled envelopes until the culprit was found. The missing money always turned up, and I could never blame anyone but myself. It was either lack of concentration or because I had started the work late for some reason or other. I would have posted a call on the board at the stage door during the week announcing that treasury would be at noon on Friday. This would allow me just about enough time to make up the weekly wage packets and also the extra ones that contained payments to those in the various departments who had made purchases during the week. It was often at least ten minutes before midday on a Friday that I would hear conversations going on just outside the office, and although I never used this as an excuse to myself, the chatter was often distracting if I was rushing to finish the work. Those outside were at the head of the treasury queue, and doubtless they were broke. Their presence meant that at noon precisely — or a little before if possible — I had to open the door and start handing out the envelopes, which had to be signed for. The pub beckoned.

Very few of the company would use the old theatrical expression for enquiring the time of a treasury call, which was, "When does the Ghost walk?" In those far-off days, the Ghost usually walked as late as possible on a Saturday night. Experience had taught the managers that paying treasury on a Thursday or even a Friday meant that an actor could then vanish into the night with several performances still to be given but a full week paid for.

My contacts at the theatre would principally be the theatre manager and the box office manager. It was important to hear from the former the reaction of his public to what we had brought and what was the standing of the National Theatre amongst the local theatregoers. It was galling to be told how many knew of the Royal Shakespeare Company but not so many knew of the National Theatre. The box office manager had to be consulted over the tickets the members of the company had said they wished to buy for friends or relatives, and there were contacts to be made with the organisations where the extra activities would take place. So there was plenty to keep me occupied all day every day. In the evenings, there was always the first performance of each play to be watched and commented on where necessary. Again, it was good to be close to the public and to note their reactions.

During a performance of *The Royal Hunt of the Sun*, I could always rely on a massive reaction at the same place at each performance. Michael Annals's large golden circle hanging at the back of the empty stage would unexpectedly fracture and six jagged gold pieces, opening like petals on a flower, would reveal Robert Stephens as Atahualpa, standing motionless in the centre, completely clad in white feathers from his tall headdress to his feet. It was the most stunning moment.

On the Saturday night after the evening performance, I would go to the manager's office where we worked out the settlement: This was the division of the week's total amount taken at the box office. The National's share would be eroded by local costs, which either had been or would be paid by the manager on the National's behalf.

Ordinary office work didn't stop during these weeks, and I had to take out, in my faithful and much-travelled office box, the necessary papers and folders that I reckoned I would be needing. The tours I found most difficult were those when I was negotiating contracts for a new season with artists' agents for the actors and literary agents for playwrights. Since it was cheaper to telephone from a public call box rather than a hotel room (if, indeed, it boasted a telephone), I would find a public phone in a quiet street, and there I would set up office with a mass of coins to make sure I was not cut off. Of flat surfaces, these call boxes had two, a very small shelf and, smaller still, the top of the coin box, so the placing of an open file became a matter of a delicate balance. Even so, it always took me by surprise when a file, sitting apparently quite contentedly on the shelf for five minutes, suddenly flipped over the edge and landed on the filthy floor, spilling out its papers, which a second before had been neatly encased and in the correct order.

My travel charts covered acres of paper. The name of each person taking part in a tour was written down the left-hand side of the paper, while across the top would be the headings showing the considerable number of train journeys that were necessary to transport groups or individuals whisking to and fro, not only from one tour date to another but journeys back to London for a few performances before returning, probably to the tour's next date. At the line where a name met a train, I would put down the number of the ticket that would be given out to that person.

There was a ten-year gap in my U.K. touring between 1956 and 1966, but even so I was able to find my way around regional cities and towns as easily as if the gap had been one year. Yet there was one puzzle in most towns that at first I could not solve. This was the curious feeling I had when, glancing down a small street or lane close to a city's centre, I was certain I had been along there before, yet, on exploring, I could find no reason for this recognition. I could have found the answer in any big city, but by chance, I was in Liverpool when I happened to walk along a narrow road in the centre of town and, passing a newsagent, it suddenly hit me. Of course, it was the morning newspaper. In the late 1940s and early 1950s, newsprint was in short supply, so the number of copies of a daily paper delivered to a newsagent was very small. It was hopeless to imagine that a newsagent on a railway station would have a copy for sale, for their stocks disappeared in a flash. Similarly, newsagents in suburban areas would not be able to display any for sale since their supplies went via delivery boys to their regular customers. But the little tobacconist-cum-newsagent in one of these small side streets that were close enough to the centre of a big town not to be surrounded by housing was the place that held out the most hope. During those post-war years, I spent many months on tour, so I soon knew where I might buy a morning paper in all the major cities. No wonder all those years later that I could recall the little streets. As I thought of them, I could also recall that even when one could get a copy of a daily newspaper (I never minded what paper it was, any paper was good enough), it was often only a four-sided affair, but it did contain news even if nothing else.

## Scene 23 ⌘ Theatrical Digs

The neat word *digs* is a shortened form of diggings or lodgings, and it would seem that it might have come from the army expression of "digging in." This would mean digging a trench or a foxhole. In other words, making oneself a temporary shelter.

Good theatre digs started with the landladies. They had to love the company of theatre people; they had to be good cooks and be willing to provide at least two substantial meals a day; they had to have a large house or apartment so that they had plenty of bedrooms (they were adept at putting beds in the most unlikely places if the demand was heavy — this sometimes meant one had to go through another's room to reach one's own). And all this for a ridiculously low cost for a week's stay.

Good digs soon became known, and it was necessary to find out where one's tour was going so that one could quickly book rooms. Even good digs could have a snag. There would only be one bathroom and very few bedrooms would have a washbasin. For myself, if I were in crowded digs, I used to get up very early to make sure I didn't have to queue in a chilly corridor waiting for the bathroom to become free.

I used to relish the suppertime chatter as my fellow residents returned from the local repertory theatre or from a number 2 or number 3 touring date. Early in the 1950s, I had moved up from little tours playing in number 2 or number 3 dates to the dizzy heights of the number 1 touring circuit. But whatever type of theatre housed one's show, one had to find a place to stay. I was always delighted to find that I was often sharing the house with artists from at least one music hall. As the supper table filled up, so theatre chat started to flow freely with the best stories usually coming from the Archie Rices from the local music hall. They were superb storytellers whose lives seemed to be peopled with extraordinary characters, although I found that I was sorry for the curious way many were forced to live. They told how they would have a ten-minute spot in each half of the evening's bill, with nothing to do in between except to go to the local bar. Seldom, they would say, was there any linking with others on the same bill. In fact, many would tell us that some artists would not allow their fellows to watch their acts from the wings. I could learn so much from the recounting of incidents in these other theatres. I never wondered that landladies used to produce an excellent supper, and then come in and join the chatter. It was also no wonder that most of their lodgers went to bed very late.

My first experience of digs was in 1939 when, as stage manager for the Wilson Barrett and Esmond Knight Company, we played a season at the Empire Theatre, Edinburgh (now the Festival Theatre). I stayed with dear Miss Howie at 58 Arden Street in one of her many, very pleasant bedrooms. Meals were taken in the large room off which was the kitchen, and it was from there that many meals would appear. A large, cooked breakfast, before going to the theatre for rehearsal, then back for lunch. Up to the theatre again for the afternoon session followed by another walk back to be offered high tea. This proved to be a light cooked meal accompanied by baps (those delicious Scottish soft rolls), scones, and cakes. Suitably prepared for the evening show, I crossed the Meadows once more and walked up to the Empire. After the show, I would find a hot supper waiting. As a tall and still growing teenager, these many meals were very welcome and very necessary.

Miss Howie couldn't go to bed until all her lodgers had left the large, friendly communal room in which we ate, read, chatted, or listened to my portable radio (the only contact at number 58 with the outside world), for this was also her bedroom. It took me some time to work this out. Looking at the inside wall in the room, I thought that behind two large doors, always closed, was a cupboard. But one day, one of the doors was open revealing a bed. My Scottish friends soon told me that this was quite common. How sensible I thought, but I was never sure how little Miss Howie managed to clamber up into her cosy bedroom.

If I were lucky in my early touring days, the management would add perhaps one pound (twenty shillings) to the weekly salary. This was their contribution towards the extra cost of living away from home. By the time I reached the National Theatre, everyone going out on a U.K. tour was paid a touring allowance, which often didn't cover the cost of a reasonable hotel room, let alone pay for meals as well. One of Sir Laurence's players was Alan Adams. In the alphabetical list of his players that Sir Laurence liked to appear on the backs of the leaflets, Alan stayed at the top for many years. Amongst his many talents, he was very adept at winkling out the cheapest digs in a town. It was not unusual for him to share a room, which kept the cost to the minimum. The downside to this arrangement was that he was permitted to sleep in the bed overnight, but he had to leave the room, and the digs, very early in the morning. This system was necessary for the room had to be ready when the daytime occupant returned from his night shift. Although this meant that Alan had no daytime base apart from the theatre, and even that would be closed during the afternoons (he must have blessed the matinees), at least it gave him enough money from his touring allowance to pay for the bed by night and, if thrifty, food by day.

# Act Six

## The National Theatre of Great Britain, 1970 to 1973

*The Beaux' Stratagem* and *Three Sisters* play a season in Los Angeles. The National Theatre continues to present productions at the Old Vic, such as *Long Day's Journey into Night, The Misanthrope, The Front Page,* and *Equus,* but also undertakes *Seasons* in West End theatres. The Young Vic opens. Sir Laurence relinquishes the position of artistic director of the National Theatre.

### Scene 1 ⊕ The Bryson Hotel, Los Angeles, 1970

On January 16, 1970, the first National Theatre company from the Old Vic to play in America left London for Los Angeles. *The Beaux" Stratagem*, wonderfully directed by William Gaskill, was to be the first production playing at the Ahmanson Theatre for three weeks, after which *Three Sisters*, also playing for three weeks, would complete the season. Each would play eight performances a week following the British pattern of Monday to Saturday inclusive, rather than the American style, Tuesday to Sunday inclusive.

Except for Ronald Pickup who stayed with friends, Gerald James who stayed in an hotel apart from the company, and Robert Stephens and his wife Maggie Smith (with their small son and their assistant, Chris) who had been offered a house in Malibu by Robert Fryer (the producer of the movie *The Prime of Miss Jean Brodie* in which Maggie had scored a huge success playing Jean Brodie), we all lived in an apartment hotel, the Bryson. This was owned by the movie star Fred MacMurray, who, according to his charming manager, Mrs. Brown, was very pleased that actors would be in his hotel. It was situated at the junction of Rampart and Wilshire Boulevard.

A total surprise hit me on the first morning at the Bryson. Like all the company, I'm sure I was not able to sleep much the first night, and I got up with the dawn. I wandered round the apartment opening up the shades, starting in the bedroom, and there, high up on a faraway hill, was a huge sign: Hollywood. I certainly knew that such a sign existed, but somehow I had never thought of Los Angeles and Hollywood as being neighbours, but there it was.

I was allotted an extremely pleasant apartment on the ground floor just off the lobby. This was presumably where all managers of large companies would be placed so that they would be easy to get hold of when wanted by their own charges or by the hotel staff. I had a large sitting-room, from which I could just see Wilshire beyond the trees that lined the hotel's gardens, bedroom, bathroom, and a galley-type kitchen. This latter would be a huge boon for there would be no question of having to go out for breakfast, and I could cook an evening meal when I got back from the theatre. Preparing for that meant I went off very early each morning to the local supermarket, and there, with my Elizabeth David book *Cooking for One* very much in evidence, I would choose what I would eat that evening. The store was not too large, and there was seldom more than one or two other customers, so the local staff got to know of my daily visit, and I used to be greeted with, "Well, sir, what are you having today?" I would show them the book, and they would come to the meat counter to make sure I had exactly what Mrs. David recommended.

## Scene 2 ✆ The Ahmanson Theatre in the Music Center, Los Angeles, 1970

The Bryson Hotel was only about a twenty-minute walk away from the Ahmanson Theatre, and since the temperature early in the day was comfortably around the 56-degree mark, although it rose quite rapidly during the morning, I used to spurn the convenient bus and walked in. At least I had some exercise before going into the theatre, which, apart from its front-of-house, was windowless. Even the Ahmanson and Mark Taper Forum offices, several floors above the Ahmanson stage door and dressing room area, were windowless. This seemed unfair to the occupants, especially since so many rooms had one wall that was against the outside of the building, and windows would have given them spectacular views. However, the lighting of the offices was excellent, and it took me a visit or two to realise that there actually were no windows, the overhead lights produced such an impression of daylight.

The production of *The Beaux' Stratagem* had an unusual start. It was given two previews in the Old Vic Theatre on January 6 and 7, 1970, after which the scenery was flown to Los Angeles. It didn't meet up with the actors again until a dress rehearsal on Monday, January 19. The first night was the next evening, with an 8:30 PM start. The 2,800-seat theatre was packed with a glittering audience. We had got so used in London to audiences coming to a first or any night in whatever clothes they happened to be wearing that day or what was most comfortable, that it was a real surprise to see that the Los Angeles public didn't do it that way. All the ladies not only looked as if they had spent the last couple of days at the hairdresser's, but all were wearing elaborate gowns with their escorts dressed to the nines to complement them.

The evening was a sensation with Maggie Smith as Mrs. Sullen at her most brilliant best. Ronald Pickup as Aimwell and Robert Stephens as Archer were in great form, as indeed was the rest of a marvellous cast. The critics were full of praise for the production, with Maggie getting the lion's share. One would have to be leading an extremely enclosed life not to know the name of Maggie Smith in Los Angeles at that time. Not only from the notices for *The Beaux' Stratagem,* but also because Robert Fryer had cleverly arranged that almost every movie house in and around Los Angeles was showing a double bill of re-runs, the smash hit *Butch Cassidy and the Sundance Kid* teamed with *The Prime of Miss Jean Brodie.* So there on nearly every marquee was the name of Maggie Smith.

Once the first show was on, it was time to think of the second, *Three Sisters.* The company that went out to Los Angeles appeared in both plays, but *Three Sisters* needed an extra actress to play Anfisa, the old nurse. So Daphne Heard, who had been playing that part at the Old Vic, came out to Los Angeles towards the end of the run of *The Beaux' Stratagem.* In the normal way of things, this changeover at the Ahmanson from one production to another would present no problem. But

Joan Plowright was not able to be away from home for what would be nearly four weeks, so Sir Laurence asked Maggie if she would take over Joan's role of Masha, and very reluctantly, she agreed.

Sir Laurence came over briefly for the start of the season. He arrived on Saturday, a day after the company, and flew out the following Tuesday at midnight after watching the first performance of The *Beaux' Stratagem*. He returned two and a half weeks later, so he was able to take the final rehearsals for Maggie's move into *Three Sisters*. The *Beaux' Stratagem*'s last performance was played before an ecstatic audience, and the ladies' hairstyles and dresses were even more extravagant than usual. *Three Sisters* got excellent reviews with a rave from the *Herald Examiner*.

Sir went back to London the following Wednesday, the day after *Three Sisters* opened. It should have been a tiring few weeks, and I don't know his state when he got back home in the middle of February, but he was certainly in fine fettle while in Los Angeles on both his visits.

On Sir Laurence's return to Los Angeles, Dale Olsen, the Music Center's press representative, said that he would be going to the airport to greet the great man and would I join him so that I could make the introductions. In the car, Dale was a mixture of excitement and nervousness. On the way, I saw a movie-house marquee where one of Sir's films of long ago was playing and pointed out that his first name had been spelled with a *w* and not a *u*. Dale didn't want Sir Laurence to be irritated at the start of his visit, so he leaned forward — quite some lean in that long car — and instructed the driver not to come back along this road but to take a diversionary route. The driver nodded. Yet on the return journey, he calmly drove down the forbidden road where, sure enough, to Dale's great discomfort, Sir noticed the offending marquee. However, he only sighed and said, "They never could get my name right," and we sped on with Dale relaxed once more.

Sir was given the use of a limousine and chauffeur, and it was in that large car that we finally left the Ahmanson stage door after a *Beaux' Stratagem* performance during the rehearsals for *Three Sisters*. The show came down about eleven-thirty, after which he had to go round to the front-of-house to say good-bye to the wife and family of the late Tyrone Power (one of whose sons was Sir's godson) before we got into the car, which sped off along Grand Avenue. "We just want somewhere to eat,"

Sir cheerfully called to the driver, who immediately replied, "There's nowhere open at this time of night." Disbelief for a while, followed by, "Well, we must eat — but where?" At that, I was forced to admit that I had something in the fridge at the Bryson, so should we go back there. Sir readily agreed, and soon he was settled with a drink in the living room, while I was in the kitchen. There was a large opening between the two rooms, so we were able to chat as I decided what we should eat. I found some chops and vegetables, but I chickened out and offered him bacon and eggs.

## Scene 3 ⚘ Sir Laurence's party in the Dorothy Chandler Pavilion's Restaurant

As soon as he had arrived in Los Angeles, Sir Laurence said he wanted to give a party, and this was to be in the restaurant on top of the Dorothy Chandler Pavilion. Of the three theatres of the Music Center, the Ahmanson was at one end with a little round theatre, the Mark Taper Forum, where Gordon Davidson was the extremely successful artistic director, nestling close to it. At the other end stood the Dorothy Chandler Pavilion, which one reached after crossing a large piazza.

The company had been told how to get from the Ahmanson to the party in the Pavilion. Even so, that evening I was hanging around in the dressing room area in case anyone was suddenly struck by amnesia. I was shortly joined by a friend, Richard Gregson, a London theatrical agent, who said that he had been going to guide his wife and a friend over, but he had to go ahead, so would I please take them, and he would meet us there. He indicated they were in the ladies powder room and left.

Soon two attractive, petite young American women appeared, and we wandered, chatting the while, over the piazza and up to the restaurant on the top floor of the Pavilion. Richard met us, and eventually we went into the party and mingled. Later I was congratulated on bringing in such an illustrious pair of American film actresses, for they turned out to be Natalie Wood (Richard's wife) and Jane Fonda. Another of Sir's guests was Kirk Douglas, who stayed firmly on a settee all evening and didn't mix, while Greer Garson was very good at being a welcoming local friendly celebrity. From the height angle, Kirk was on a level with my new friends, Jane and Natalie, but things looked up when I found myself, while queuing for a superb buffet supper, between and on a level with Gregory Peck and Charlton Heston. It was impossible not to recognise them, while I found it impossible to know what to say when I found myself the filling in a sandwich made up of these two giants of the movies.

## Scene 4 ❦ Norman Macdonald and the Ahmanson's green room

I was very lucky to be working at the Ahmanson during the time when Norman MacDonald was the theatre manager. A real man of the theatre who was as caring about the many sides of the theatre, in which he had been involved over the years, as he was about his current work at the Ahmanson. The theatre was kept incredibly clean, which was laudable. Not so laudable was the mass of locked doors: This system was obviously in force so that, once the cleaners had finished their work, as few parts of the theatre as possible would be sullied by staff and visitors until an audience arrived. Anyone would think it was owned by Mr. Wingate of the Comedy, for he certainly would have approved of the "no one allowed in the auditorium until the performance" rule — except he would have removed the last three words. At the top of the building were the offices, and again, the elevators only went to that floor and were programmed, during the day, not to stop at any floor that gave access to the actual theatre.

After we had been there for a few days, some of the women in the cast asked me if it were possible to have a green room in which they could rest during breaks in rehearsals or between matinee and evening shows. I went at once to Norman and he twinkled and said, "But we've got a green room. Let me show it you." Murmuring "That's wonderful," I followed him on the long journey through numerous doors, that had to be unlocked and relocked, to the dressing-room area.

Guiding me down a corridor I hadn't used before, we came to a door, which, of course, was locked. Norman seemed to know exactly which key out of an enormous bundle fitted which door, so very soon he flung the door open, switched on a blaze of lights, and stood back to watch my reaction. It was a large square room and it was certainly green. Green walls, green ceiling, green carpet, and all the furniture was green, including the banquette seating along every wall. Totally overpowered, as Norman knew I would be, I could only blurt out, "Well, it is quite ghastly, but at least it is in a quiet area and there are some comfortable-looking chairs. Well, thanks, Norman, this will do fine." "Oh, you can't use it," said Norman, as he switched off the blinding lights. "The board doesn't allow anyone to use this room because the leather for the banquettes and chairs was very expensive, and they don't wish to risk them being cut or marked." He was duly locking up as he spoke, and off we went, leaving the Rip Van Winkle room to continue its undisturbed existence.

"However," said Norman, "there is a dressing room along this passage that you haven't used, in fact you may not know it's there. If the girls would like that room, we can get some daybeds and hand it over to them. But it must be well looked after." I assured him it would be, and so off he went, while I made out a notice that, to me, explained exactly the purpose of the room: "Ladies Rest Room." That evening the local stagehands thought this was extremely funny. "We didn't know there was a john in that room, for that's what your notice says." The laughter went on and on. I couldn't wait to get back to the room, take down the misleading (to American eyes only) notice, and replace it with the simple, "Ladies." They could work it out.

## Scene 5 ❧ The Ahmanson box office

Each of the three Music Center theatres had its own box office, but until an hour or so before a performance, the three operated from one large underground room — at least it was underground when one knew it was under the Dorothy Chandler Pavilion and it had no windows (not that that meant anything as I knew from the offices). But walking along Grand, it was a surprise to find that the entrance was on street level. A few steps further on was the entrance to the car park — all seven levels of this enormous space under the Piazza.

As often as I could before a performance, I would go through to the Ahmanson's own box office and watch not only the clerks at work but the patrons as they came up to the window. Once the clerks had got my measure, they started telling me about those who were booking, such as, "She's the oldest student in town. She's eighty-four and is currently studying such-and-such a subject. She's a regular here because she gets in at the special student rate." But they really enjoyed pointing out the celebrities. "Hey, come over here quick — here's Lee J. Cobb," or "Look, here's husband and wife, Shirley Jones and Jack Cassidy." This bit of information was followed, as the pair left the window and were out of earshot, by the wicked comment, "I'm not sure who was wearing the most makeup."

Because of the three Music Center's theatres being so close together, many patrons bought tickets only to return later complaining that they had really wanted to see Yves Montand in the pavilion. So when the clerks were asked, "Have you any seats for this evening?" they quickly learned during our first three weeks to answer with the question, "For *The Beaux' Stratagem*?" If the answer was no, then they were directed to the correct theatre and no time was wasted. For the second half of our season, the clerk's question had to be changed, so when a small neat man came to the window at a matinee and asked if there were any tickets, the clerk automatically said, "For *Three Sisters*?" to which the man, with more than a touch of surprise in his voice, answered, "No, for my wife and myself."

## Scene 6 ✆ The visit to the *Queen Mary*, Long Beach

The company in Los Angeles were very well treated and much hospitality was offered. The invitations were made to the whole company who were asked to put their name on a list at the stage door against the offers to which they would like to go. Some invites worked out well, others were not so good. The worst was a publicity affair of the "British actors visit the veteran liner *Queen Mary* in her new home in America" type, and it sounded as if it would prove to be an interesting day. We would be driven to Long Beach, have lunch, and be taken round the liner, returning to the Bryson in plenty of time for a break before being taken to the theatre.

The first surprise was that our transport was a London bus and when we got aboard, our "conductor" announced that he was from Yorkshire. As he entertained us with the story of his life, he handed round fish and chips, wrapped in a reproduction, on shiny paper, of a page from the *Times* of London newspaper. We could have done without all this, especially the fish, which was lukewarm, and the chips, which were limp and soggy. The food was accompanied by bottles of root beer, which our guide told us was beer, but the company soon found that it was not beer as they knew it. Grumbles increased during the long journey in an uncomfortable bus and the endless Yorkshire chatter.

At last we arrived at a quayside, and there was an enormous ship tied alongside: it was extremely drab, dirty, and stained, and it had no superstructure. The funnels were lying on the quayside in sections, also looking very much the worse for wear. Ever-cheerful female guides, impeccably made up and costumed, greeted us as we disembarked. At once, the bejewelled finger of one attractive young woman delicately pointed at the hulk and told us that this was what was once the magnificent ocean liner, the *Queen Mary*.

We were divided into groups and taken aboard. Everywhere work was in progress. There were cables snaking along corridors and in all the main rooms. The floors were wet and the whole atmosphere was damp, chilly, and extremely noisy. We were taken from saloons to bars to restaurants, all in a state of utter chaos. No room were we shown was in any way finished until we came to the cabins: unbelievably, one of these was actually furnished. It was so sad that in the whole ship, there was only this one small room that we could glance into from the doorway and admire very briefly before we had to move on. Otherwise it was, "This will be the bar and you can see how beautiful the wood panelling is: it will be polished soon and returned to its former glory." Everything was going to be returned to its former glory, but there was no sign of it so far.

With the disappointment of the ship, the next question everyone started to ask was, "Where do we have lunch in this battered wreck and when will it be served?" I sought out our guide and put the question to her. "Why," she said, her eyes opening wider, "surely you were given your lunch on the bus?" The cold fish and the soggy chips was lunch. We couldn't wait to get back on the bus, even though it meant suffering further streams of an unwanted monologue from the Man from Yorkshire. The sight of the Bryson never looked so welcoming.

On reflection, this was a press photo opportunity, yet I never saw a photographer nor was I given any newspaper clippings of the visit. The press obviously knew something that we didn't — until too late.

## Scene 7 ⟡ Invitations when in Los Angeles

Invitations to supper after a show were all good and very much appreciated. We were jealous of the amazing views over the city from houses that were perched on the sides of hills. In the case of Dale Olsen's house, it was curious to enter through the front door and immediately go down a flight of stairs with the first room to be seen being a bedroom. On down, and into a huge living room with vast windows looking out over the city. At this affair, I found myself engaged in a long conversation with an actor I had admired over the years, Henry Fonda, who told me all about the problem of bringing up children in the Hollywood atmosphere.

One Sunday evening, we were invited by Peggy Webster, a friend of Gerald James, to be her guests at her dinner-theatre restaurant in Santa Monica. On arrival, we were greeted by Peggy who introduced us to another of our hosts, Lee Marvin. I began to feel that wherever I went, I would catch a glimpse of this actor with red socks. I had seen him on one of my many visits to the airport and also in the theatre and now here he was again. I began to wonder if there were a number of look-alikes around town at that time.

Drinks were awaiting us, and then we were encouraged to sit where we wished at the dining tables. My companions were a delightful family all of whom were acting in a long-running television Western so that was a good start. But at the end of the meal we were asked to reseat ourselves in preparation for the evening's entertainment. This dinner-theatre location was well known for its Sunday evening shows, and we were told it had proved to be an excellent showcase for out-of-work actors waiting for the Big Chance. Tonight's show was to be Dylan Thomas's *Under Milk Wood*. I would much have preferred an American play especially if it were new, but I am certain the Dylan Thomas had been chosen on purpose to make us feel at home.

I was chatting with Karl Malden and his wife at a table very close to the acting area, when the show suddenly started, and I got caught there. Strangely, there was no stage, not even a rostrum, the actors simply standing at one end of the not very long room. I certainly wished I hadn't been so embarrassingly close when, about ten minutes into the show, an English voice, some way behind me, made an audible comment on the lines that the show wasn't very good. The play went on, and then the critic gave his opinion once more, this time a little louder and a little more critical of the actors. The small size of the room meant that anyone speaking, even softly, could be heard by both actors and audience. After the third comment — this one was given with still more vocal force as the critic became more and more incensed by what he was hearing — the actors stopped, and those in the acting area, led by the actor playing Captain Cat, all directed black looks in the direction of the voice. It was rather like the last scene of John Dexter's superb production of *The Royal Hunt of the Sun,* when all the masked heads slowly turned in unison.

By now, the speaker had the floor, and he gave it full force, criticising the acting, the accents, and any other angle of the presentation that deserved his attention. I knew only too well who the speaker was, for he had been an actor with the National Theatre for some years. Captain Cat then made an announcement to the effect that the performance would be stopped unless this outrageous interruption ceased at once. This was pouring petrol on the fire, and the language heated up. I was considering going to deal with the actor, but it would mean my walking through the audience towards the back of the room. I decided that my appearance would only pinpoint the fact that it was a member of the National Theatre and not a local, although all the locals there must have been aware that it was not one of them.

Then I heard the voices of two of the company's senior actors, Kenneth Mackintosh and Paul Curran, trying to calm the outraged actor, but this only made matters worse still, if that were possible. He was proving to be one of those drunks who, when appealed to in a quiet voice, respond by shouting louder. I couldn't see how Kenneth and Paul dealt with the offender, but they obviously took him to a nearby exit door and left the restaurant. Unfortunately, the outer walls must have been paper-thin, for the exchange of words on the pavement could easily be heard inside. There was a terrible hush for a while before the American actors, in an understandable state of high dudgeon, trooped off never to reappear. At the same time, with the scraping of many chairs, the audience got to its feet and the evening was over. I rounded up the company, and we got into the coach and returned to the Bryson.

Not the National Theatre at its best. It's sad how the offer of free and limitless drinks can take away the ability of so many to refuse yet another glass. It must have taken Peggy and Lee a long time to recover from this disgraceful display. The sad thing about the whole affair was that the critical actor was absolutely right, and if he could have held his hush until we got back into the coach, we could all have had a great time on the return journey working our way through the cast and commenting on each.

## Scene 8 ❧ The "Laugh-In" recording and Vice President Spiro Agnew

I had heard of the American comedy TV programme, "Rowan & Martin's Laugh-In," for most people in England seemed to watch its weekly screening, knowing all the characters and recognising the running gags. But I had never been lucky enough to catch it, so although I was interested to go with the company, when we were invited to join an audience at the filming of an episode, it wasn't one of the outings I really looked forward to.

As ever, the filming seemed a very slow process. The set was the wall of a house with shuttered openings at various levels and of various sizes. Through these, the obviously much-loved members of the cast popped their heads to a round of applause and a burst of laughter from a predominately American audience. In fact, most of what was said was greeted with these bursts of laughter, which were more, perhaps, than the lines deserved.

Because of the long gaps between takes, there was much wandering in and out, so I left the studio after a short while and meandered round the lot before I came to a door leading to the outside world with its brilliant sunshine. I had reached a road that ran along the side of the studios, and there was a chuck wagon selling coffee, sandwiches, and suchlike joys.

I drank my coffee with pleasure at being in the open air when I could feel a sense of bustle and controlled excitement. On asking one huge friendly fellow beside me what was going to happen, he at once replied, "Spiro Agnew, the vice president, is visiting. He should be arriving any minute." We all gazed down the road, and sure enough a vast black limo appeared at the far end of the studio building and made its way slowly towards us. As soon as it cleared the corner, the nose of a second, a third, and then a fourth limo came steadily behind the leader, all absolutely evenly spaced, one behind the other. In the end, the motorcade consisted of seven cars.

When the first stopped just short of the chuck wagon, so, too, did all the following cars. They had been travelling so slowly that it was possible for the next startling effect to take place. A second or two before each car came to an absolute stop, all the car doors, and there seemed to be three down each side of each car, shot open and out leapt one large, tall, black-suited man from each car. In unison their eyes immediately raked both sides of the road and the building. The effect was stunning: The timing and the precision was reminiscent of a Busby Berkley routine in a Hollywood movie. No girls though.

I didn't have long to wait before I saw the vice president. He was as tall as his bodyguards, who really were guarding him, for a selected group had somehow managed to surround him very closely, and this tight bundle of men came towards the chuck wagon. Was he going to be given a cup of coffee, I had time to wonder, before they swung to the left and went into a building behind the chuck wagon and were gone. If I had put out an arm, I would have been able to touch him which caused another wonder as the last of the surround team disappeared from sight. I wouldn't have been able to get away with it, but if I had really wanted to harm him, it would have been incredibly easy. I decided I didn't want to be a vice president or anyone in the position of having to travel with a bodyguard.

## Scene 9 ◎ King Farouk drives through Cairo, 1944

When I was thinking back to this extraordinary arrival of Spiro Agnew and close friends, the whole occasion made me remember the time I witnessed a scene to rival Agnew's. Together with several officers from my battery, I was on leave in Cairo during the Second World War. It was our first morning in the town, and we had naturally found our way to the world-famous hotel, Shepheard's, which had been taken over as an officers' club. The hotel had a large open-air terrace, one floor above the entrance hall at the front of the hotel. It was now furnished with tables and chairs, and we were sitting there relaxing in the winter sun, when we heard the sound of a commotion coming up from the road.

There were suddenly many police down below us who started shouting and indicating to those in cars and those on foot to leave the street. The populace too were shouting to each other so that the noise was considerable but in a remarkably short time the man in the street had become the man up an alleyway. The street was totally empty.

There followed one of those pauses when the world seems to be holding its breath, but it was not for long, for the noise of motorcycles could be heard and into view came the first of the outriders. They wore scarlet uniforms and their machines were scarlet. There were at least twelve travelling in pairs and moving fast. Then came the bodyguards in the Spiro Agnew mould although Farouk got there first. The king was alone in the back seat of a scarlet Rolls-Royce with an open top. He, too, was in scarlet with a scarlet fez atop a full face which in turn was above a full body. A great sense of majesty, quite appropriately, and of opulence. Clustered around the car were many more motorcyclists — too many to count in the short space of time we could see them. Following the car came the rearguard, like their comrades out in front, several pairs of scarlet riders on scarlet motorbikes.

It must have taken only a few seconds for the whole parade to pass us, but such a flamboyant sight has stayed with me firmly. If you've got it, flaunt it and King Farouk certainly had it and he certainly flaunted it. If Spiro Agnew had it, he certainly didn't flaunt it. But each, in their own way, made both of those days very special.

## Scene 10 ◌ The end of the season in Los Angeles

Our weeks in Los Angeles went all too quickly. There was much to be done in the matter of the Internal Revenue Service — it didn't take us long to know all too well what those initials, IRS, stood for. There was a Sunday matinee of *Hair* that had to be arranged. It was liked by Daphne Heard, our octogenarian, whereas it was disliked by young

Helen Fraser, who left at the interval. There was the daily booking of a coach to collect the company at the Bryson for a performance, once I had worked out how many would be travelling to the theatre in it and, since I would be at the theatre, who would be able to check them in at the hotel. Also a booking for the reverse journey, when, most days, I was travelling in it.

Soon it was time for the good-byes. The patient clerk who took those coach bookings with whom I had established a telephonic friendship. The box office staffs at the Music Center, whether they worked at the Ahmanson or the other two theatres. The staff at the theatre itself, not forgetting the guards, one of whom (with revolver in holster) was always on stage door duty. The tremendous group who worked in the theatre offices who were always fun to visit and with whom it was always so easy to do business. And, of course, my good friend, Norman MacDonald. Then there was my last shopping trip to the supermarket where there was a very touching farewell with all the staff coming to the door to wave as I walked back to the Bryson.

That final day went so quickly and soon it was the last curtain call and the get-out. Stage manager John Rothenberg and I stayed in the theatre until we saw the last piece loaded (and had been duly impressed by the ability of the trucks to come into the building so that the doors could be closed while the get-out was taking place). We got back to the hotel towards morning, so he helped finish off a bottle of whisky as we watched the arrival of dawn. Suddenly it was almost time to assemble in the lobby, so packing had to be done at breakneck speed.

My good-byes at the supermarket didn't come up to the farewell that Mrs. Brown gave the whole company when, early on March 1, we came staggering into the lobby with all our luggage (much more than on the outward journey). We found that she had arranged a special breakfast. The whole of her staff seemed to be there, fussing over us, giving us coffee and muffins as well as mementoes, and saying how much they had enjoyed having the company in the hotel, and they really looked forward to the day when we returned. Sadly, that day never came.

We boarded the coach for the last time and went off to the airport for the long journey home. As with the outward leg, our journey included an hour-long, tiring stopover in San Francisco. We were travelling at a time when jumbo jets were just about to be introduced — in fact we saw one of the first on the tarmac at Heathrow when we arrived the next morning. We were on the old type plane with three seats either side of a central gangway. This gave a feeling of claustrophobia, especially when, for both trans-Atlantic flights, the planes were full.

## Scene 11 ❧ The Young Vic opens August 12, 1970

About one hundred fifty yards along The Cut from the Old Vic, a new theatre was being built. This would be used as a branch of the National Theatre and would be named the Young Vic. What had been a butcher's shop was being turned into the central portion of the new building with a small foyer on street level and offices on the two upper floors. On one side of the foyer would be the theatre and on the other a snack bar. At the back would be a good-sized space that would be divided to form a studio theatre and the dressing rooms. Frank Dunlop, then one of Sir Laurence's associate directors, became director of the Young Vic Theatre, and it was his production, *The Cheats of Scapino,* that opened the theatre on Wednesday, August 12, 1970 with huge success. Jim Dale gave a gloriously fast, friendly, and funny performance as Scapino.

The Young Vic became at once enormously popular with local children for there was an air of great freedom about the whole place, especially in the auditorium: wooden benches painted scarlet and tickets that let one sit where one liked. If a young person saw a friend several rows in front, there would at once be a yell of recognition and the immediate clambering from bench to bench until the friend was reached. If that particular row had seemed full before the arrival of the newcomer, then everyone just shuffled along and a space was found.

## Scene 12 ❧ The season at the Cambridge Theatre, London, June 1970 to January 1971

On Monday, June 8, the National Theatre started a season at the Cambridge Theatre in the Seven Dials area on the edge of the West End. This meant that the company of seventy-eight players was appearing in three London theatres with many, such as Jim Dale (Barnet in *The National Health* at the Old Vic, Launcelot Gobbo in *The Merchant of Venice* at the Cambridge Theatre, and Scapino at the Young Vic), playing in all three. Soon it was not unknown for an actor to act in a play for children at the Young Vic on a Saturday morning, and then go off, either to the Cambridge or the Old Vic, for a matinee and an evening performance.

The season at the Cambridge had started with a very attractive repertoire of two plays: the first, a new look by Jonathan Miller at *The Merchant of Venice*, in which Sir Laurence played Shylock, and the second, Ingmar Bergman's *Hedda Gabler* with Maggie Smith as Hedda. Both excellent productions with excellent casts. It isn't easy to forget the trial scene in *The Merchant of Venice,* which was played at a table placed up- and downstage. The Duke sat at its head with Portia (Joan Plowright) and Shylock (Laurence Olivier) on either side of him. Jonathan Miller allowed no Old Bailey–style confrontation, as I had witnessed at Stratford in 1960, when Dorothy Tutin was Portia and Peter O'Toole was Shylock.

At the Old Vic, the arguments in the case were delivered in almost conversational yet determined tones across the table until each time the Duke spoke, whereupon all contestants would turn upstage to face him. A moment to savour in that scene was shortly after Shylock entered the Venetian Court of Justice when Benjamin Whitrow, as a firm but in no way a dictatorial duke, very quietly said, "Shylock, the world thinks —" Here he paused before continuing the sentence in an even quieter voice: "and I think so too . . ." It was tremendously effective.

Joan Plowright adopted the same style when, as a believable "young and learned doctor," she entered the court, and the trial proper began. Nor can one forget the end of the scene with the exit of Shylock, who gave a terrible cry offstage followed by the sound of someone apparently stumbling down a flight of stairs.

The opening moments in *Hedda Gabler* were certainly unforgettable. Maggie Smith, as Hedda, dressed in a white peignoir standing silently centre stage in a totally red room, studying with disgust the outline of her body in a pier glass. Immediately we know she is checking as to whether her pregnancy is visible yet, although she is to allow no hint of such a condition to be given to her aunt-in-law, Miss Tesman, who breaks into this scene when paying an unexpected and unwanted call on Hedda. The silent start to the play was stunning.

## Scene 13 ❧ Sir Laurence becomes Lord Olivier, June 1970

The baronetcy conferred on Sir Laurence was announced on Saturday, June 14, 1970. It was a day on which he had two performances of *The Merchant of Venice* at the Cambridge Theatre. I arrived at the theatre at the start of the half and went in to his dressing room to congratulate him, and I then went into the auditorium to see how the audience would react. The honour seemed to be on everyone's lips, and I got the firm impression that the members of the audience were delighted that they would be at the first performance following the announcement.

I am sure these patrons did not listen too closely to the first two scenes that afternoon: They wanted the actor playing Shylock, and it must have seemed a long time before Jeremy Brett as Bassanio reappeared but this time not with Antonio but with Shylock. I had heard many an audience erupt with applause and cheers directed at this great actor, but somehow this afternoon's eruption seemed just that different. Shylock in his frock coat, with lips that barely covered the specially made, slightly protruding false teeth, stood quite still. There was no acknowledgment of any kind. It was Shylock standing there, not Lord Olivier. The greeting died down, and the play went on.

He made a brief curtain speech, but as soon as the curtain divided him from the audience, he gathered the company around him, thanked them for their congratulations, and said, in his often-used humble mode, that no one was to feel that anything would change with the arrival of this new honour. "You must all go on calling me whatever you have been calling me." This was a wise instruction for many had been asking each other how to address him. So the usual greetings remained — the Sir's, the Larry's, the Sir Laurence's and even the Slorence's. It reminded me of the story that came back from a film studio in Paris, whither Sir went in 1967 to talk over his interpretation of Etienne Plucheux, the butler in *A Flea in Her Ear*, when he took over the role for the Canadian tour. Someone had telephoned the studio from London asking for Sir Laurence Olivier, so a messenger boy was despatched to roam the studios seeking the person whose name he had been told. How was the boy to know that the person he was paging was a man? The name he called out on his journey was, "Solange Olivier!"

So, twenty-three years after he became a knight, an honour reserved then for those at the very top of their business, trade, or profession, Sir moved up to become a Lord. This gave him the right to attend the House of Lords (the upper house in the Houses of Parliament) and speak on his own or the profession's behalf.

## Scene 14 ❧ Maggie Smith

When I joined the National Theatre in 1966, at the Old Vic, Maggie Smith was playing Beatrice in *Much Ado About Nothing,* Avonia Bunn in *Trelawny of the "Wells,"* Desdemona in *Othello*, Marcela in *A Bond Honoured,* which John Osborne based on a Lope de Vega play, and Clea in *Black Comedy.* She continued to play Desdemona when *Othello* moved over the river and joined the repertoire at the Queen's Theatre in Shaftesbury Avenue. I had seen her in the West End before this, and although I thought she was just brilliant, to see her playing this range of parts over a matter of a few nights was quite staggering. Effortlessly, it seemed, she could make me crumple up with laughter in *Black Comedy* and *Trelawny,* while fascinating and then saddening me at the end of *Othello.*

I was told that Maggie was "difficult," but I remembered the so-called difficult Ann Todd all those years ago when she was the leading actress and I was company manager on Mary Hayley Bell's *Foreign Field.* As Sam Wanamaker, the director, then foretold, providing the company and staff gave a clean show each performance (which they did), the word would not apply to her. So I made no comment at this revelation about Maggie, for up to then I had experienced nothing but friendliness and cooperation. It wasn't until *The Beaux' Stratagem* at the Cambridge Theatre did I meet her in a difficult frame of mind.

One day, knowing there was a matinee of *The Beaux' Stratagem,* I had gone over to the West End to see how the company was faring in the Cambridge Theatre. I was greeted with the news that Maggie was being difficult, so beware. I went to her dressing room to find her in a high old rage. She then explained the reason for it. The play, designed by Rene Allio, opened with an empty stage into which a series of painted borders were lowered from the flies, one by one. Each border had a definite stopping place — known as a "dead"— on its downward journey, starting about fifteen feet above the stage. This allowed the audience to see the design on the first border of the edge of a field and a hedgerow before the second border, stopping just above the first, appeared. On this was painted a row of cottages, larger houses, and trees. A third border arrived, once more reaching a dead just above the second, and on which one saw a church and more houses.

With all the borders in place, the audience realised they were being shown a view of the little town of Lichfield where the action would take place. Enter the actors, who at once drew the focus of the audience down from the borders, and the play itself began.

On the day in question, the curtain rose on Act 1, and after a pause, the first of the borders came into view. Down it came, passed its dead, thus exposing the ropes from which it hung, and made its way shakily towards the stage, which it hit with a loud thud. The audience thought this very amusing, and while they laughed, the ropes were pulled and the border shot up until, with much up-a-bit and down-a-bit, it settled on an arbitrary stopping place. After another pause, the second border appeared, it too haring past its dead before it stopped, then went up a short way and came to a halt.

The audience by this time thought this was wildly funny with the initial gentle laughter having given way to guffaws, until at last, with the borders more or less in their correct positions, the play began. When I went to see Maggie, she reported this series of disasters, ending by asking, "Who are these men in the flies? If they can't do their job properly, they shouldn't be working in a West End theatre, ruining a good production. They are professionals, aren't they? What they did this afternoon meant that I had to go onto that stage and calm that audience into a state where they started to listen to the play — and that's not why I'm here."

I knew I was dealing with a perfectionist and not with a temperamental actress. I said that I would investigate at once, but as a guess, I thought that the local management, who engage stage staff in the West End, may have been short staffed that day and had called in inexperienced staff from a theatre that didn't have a matinee. Another thought was that the markings of the deads for those new to the fly gallery were not very clear. When I asked the stage manager how the performance progressed after such a start, I was told me that within minutes Maggie had wrought her magic. The audience quietened at once and concentrated on the play, which continued as if there been no incident.

I never heard of another such occurrence during the remainder of the season at the Cambridge. It is ironic, however, that the cover photograph on the leaflet for the period September 14 to October 24, 1970, which set out the repertoire for both the Cambridge Theatre, where *The Beaux' Stratagem* was playing, and the Old Vic, should show a flyman in the fly gallery. His hands, one up and the other down, are confidently holding one of the ropes, ready at a moment's notice to carry out his cue.

## Scene 15 ଚ Ingmar Bergman

When the great Swedish director, Ingmar Bergman, came to us to direct a production of *Hedda Gabler*, he paid an advance visit to discuss casting, rehearsals, and all other aspects of the production and to be taken round the Old Vic Theatre, bringing with him Mago, his designer. A few months before he was due to come over, Sir Laurence had had a new car delivered. It was a large Daimler in which at least six passengers could sit in comfort. Shortly before Ingmar arrived, I was in my office and, happening to look out onto the parking area, I saw Sir's chauffeur drive past in a small box of a car. When I later asked him what had happened to the new car, he said that one particular part had failed, and it was in the garage where a new one would be fitted. Although I merely murmured, "Oh yes," with a slight upward inflection on the *yes*, I kept to myself the thought that this was a strange thing to happen to such a prestigious and, for goodness sake, new luxury car.

Thus it was that Ingmar, Mago, and their host, Sir Laurence, had to squeeze into the unpleasant little replacement car to be ferried from the huts to the Old Vic and back. The huts must have had the same horrifying effect on our Swedish guests as they did on most of our visitors, but this was nothing compared to the shock of the Aquinas Street rehearsal room. Ingmar could not get over the depressing look of the room with its two roof supports and, perhaps worst of all, the liberal supply of water pipes that were fixed to the walls. It wasn't any noise the pipes might make, it was simply the run-down, uncared-for look, exacerbated by the pipes, to which he objected. Surely the actors of the National Theatre of Great Britain deserved better than such depressing premises to create works of art and beauty.

He beat the pipes by working in a very detailed way for a week with his outstanding cast, for, in addition to Maggie Smith as Hedda, there was Robert Stephens, Jeremy Brett, Jeanne Watts, Sheila Reid, John Moffatt, and Julia McCarthy. At the end of the week, he said that they were doing very well, that they fully understood the lines along which he wanted them to develop their characters, and he was going back to Sweden. He would return to London, he said, in plenty of time to rehearse with the company before the move into the Old Vic Theatre. As promised, he came back a short while before the production went onstage when, after watching a run-through, he announced he was delighted with what the cast had given him and the trust he had placed in them was fully justified. It became a huge success, with public and critics alike commenting on the business of Hedda's pregnancy, whereas in previous productions an audience could make up its own mind as to whether she was or not.

## Scene 16 ⋐ Robert Stephens

When the Shakespeare Memorial Company's *King Lear* tour reached Manchester in the autumn of 1955, George Devine asked me if I would like to join a small group that was going to the Library Theatre to see a matinee performance of Arthur Miller's *Death of a Salesman*. Playing the role of Biff was Robert Stephens, and he became one of the first actors to be cast at the start of the English Stage Company at the Royal Court Theatre. Out of the eight productions presented in 1956, he appeared in six, the last of which was *The Country Wife,* which transferred in February 1957 to the Adelphi Theatre in the Strand. But as soon as that run in the West End finished, he was back at the Court. John Dexter was directing the second play in the Sunday night "production without décor" series, *Yes — and After* by Michael Hastings and Robert was in it.

When I moved to the National Theatre, I was so pleased to know that he was with the company. If one was forced to choose the leading actor in A Company during the 1960s, it would have to be Robert Stephens. During the 1967 to 1968 season, for example, he was in all the A Company productions, playing Benedick in *Much Ado About Nothing*, Tartuffe in *Tartuffe*, Jaques in *As You Like It* (the Cambridge Theatre programme for *Hedda Gabler*, in its notes on Robert's roles with the National Theatre, gives this character a *c* in his name, which the original production's programmes at the Old Vic did not grant him), and Vershinin in *Three Sisters*.

During that same season, Sir Laurence appointed Robert, together with Frank Dunlop, as associate directors, but after a few months, Frank became administrative director, leaving Robert as the sole associate. This he remained until Paul Scofield joined the company. At the very end of 1970, for a short while, both Paul and Robert were associate directors, but on January 2, 1971, Robert left the company. It was a sad day indeed, for on that same day, his wife, Maggie Smith, also left.

Sir Laurence quite rightly placed great faith in Robert Stephens especially after he became an associate. Robert took that position very seriously, and he attended as many meetings as his acting and his directorial duties (in 1968, he directed one of the plays in Triple Bill) would allow. The new position for Robert meant that Sir Laurence at last had someone alongside him who could consider whatever was discussed from the actor's viewpoint as well as that of the administrative side.

It was always good for Ann Robinson, still running the casting department with great charm and ability, and myself that Robert came to so many auditions. Still, working on the system of auditioning for future reference, it meant a lot to those actors whose request for an audition was not only granted, but who then learnt that Robert Stephens would be on the audition panel.

## Scene 17 ✆ Forging links with the inhabitants of the Borough of Lambeth

In the late summer of 1970, I was asked to work with a representative from Lambeth Borough Council. The council wanted people in their borough to be given the opportunity of hearing talks by the chief practitioners from the worlds of sport and the arts so that a link would be formed between those who lived and those who worked in the borough. The previous year it seemed that football was the chosen subject, but for 1970 it had been decided that it should be theatre. The venue for the talks would be the Nautical School, which is in Stamford Street and only a long throw of a stone from the National Theatre's offices in Aquinas Street.

Barry Anderson, the borough's representative, asked me to supply a speaker on one evening a week for six weeks and said that each evening, starting at seven o'clock and ending at nine, should be split into two halves with a fifteen-minute coffee break in the middle. I suggested that I would aim to arrange for all sides of theatre work to be covered, which would probably mean one speaker before the break and another after. He thought this sounded good, so I set about the task of filling what, at first, seemed like twelve slots. However, the first two I got in touch with — who, to my delight, accepted on the spot — both said they would like to speak for the whole evening, and this suited me very well. One, to represent playwrights, was Tom Stoppard, and the other, to represent directors, was Jonathan Miller.

I wanted the series to start with a general talk about the National Theatre. In spite of the company being based in the borough, and in spite of our illustrious director, I knew there must be many out in the Great Beyond who would never have heard of the company's existence nor would Sir Laurence be associated in their minds with it. This opportunity of talking to local folk seemed to offer the hope that we might hook a few more patrons, providing that what we did and where we did it was made very clear at the outset. So for this first evening, Kenneth Rae, secretary to the board, and Anthony Easterbrook, general manager, both kindly accepted the invitation to be the speakers and were very happy to share the evening. We had a good house, both speakers did very well, and it was agreed that the series had got off to a really good start.

The next week was a solo, and the speaker could have gone on for much longer than the two halves of the evening allowed. Jonathan Miller was as wonderful, as I knew he would be, and his wise and witty talk ensured a splendid evening. Jonathan was followed the next week by the great designer, Ralph Koltai, with a talk that complemented so well what the audience had heard from Jonathan.

The fourth week, the audience was given Robert Ornbo and Douglas Cornelissen. It was back to a shared evening, with Bob Ornbo talking about lighting National Theatre productions and how his work was not confined only to the Old Vic Theatre but how he went on tour, around the United Kingdom and abroad, with the company. Douglas Cornelissen as general stage manager was able to discuss his own job as well as talking about his stage managers and the general work backstage.

The penultimate week was another shared evening with Marc Wilkinson speaking about writing music for many and varied National Theatre productions. He especially dwelt on the extraordinary and apt music and eerie sounds for *The Royal Hunt of the Sun* and how his musicians produced the sound effects that John Dexter, as director, required. After the coffee break, Malcolm Goddard, who had arranged many fights for National Theatre productions, spoke of those fights and how he rehearsed them with the actors.

The final evening was, as with all these special evenings, extremely well attended and, by reactions and comments, very much appreciated. In spite of Tom Stoppard's offer to be the only speaker, once again, the evening was shared, this time between Frank Barrie who spoke for actors and Tom Stoppard who spoke for playwrights. Frank gave a very good talk, making the audience realise what an actor had to endure before his performance was finally presented to the public, while Tom spoke about the journey of his first play, *Rosencrantz and Guildenstern are Dead*, from his writing of it to the amateur production by Oxford undergraduates during the 1967 Edinburgh Festival. He then spoke of the presentation by the National Theatre at the Old Vic Theatre the following year. His talk was full of jokes and the warmth of his personality allied to the fascinating tales he told impressed his audience mightily.

At one point, Tom compared his writing of a play to his going on holiday. He said he would pack his suitcase himself, being fully aware of all that he was putting in, but that when he unpacked at his destination, he would be amazed to find items that he was sure he had not put in his case. He said it was the same with his plays in performance, for he would hear lines he could not remember writing, and audiences would find laughs that he had not expected.

Some while later, when a totally recast production of *Rosencrantz and Guildenstern are Dead* went to New York, I got word back about the audiences laughing in places that had not raised laughs in England. One of these was when Rosencrantz was telling Guildenstern about fingernails. He explained that fingernails go on growing after death, but, on the other hand, toenails do not grow at all. New Yorkers, unlike the audiences at the Old Vic, were very quick to find a good laugh in the phrase, "on the other hand, toenails . . ."

## Scene 18 ✎ Superstitions, customs, and other oddities

During the coffee breaks at the Nautical School, I talked to members of the audiences and was surprised how many, having made comments about the speakers and the talks, asked about theatre superstitions. The lead-in was usually the one connected with *Macbeth*. They knew that one must never mention the play's title but use the alternative, *The Scottish Play*. How did this come about, they wanted to know. I said that I believed that the play had attracted many more accidents and incidents than other plays, and so a way had to be found to fool whoever, or whatever, wished these accidents upon a production of *Macbeth*. The method chosen was to pretend that the play in rehearsal was not *Macbeth* but *The Scottish Play*. I added that actors still do not entirely trust this deception and to this day are cautious when cast in the play. I also told my enquirers that I understood that the superstition only works when one mentions the title within a theatre, especially a dressing room. If it is inadvertently used there, I have heard it said that the culprit has to leave the room, turn round three times outside the door before knocking to gain re-admittance.

*Macbeth* came into the repertoire when I was at Stratford with Eric Porter and Irene Worth performing. Nothing untoward happened, I am glad to report. At the Old Vic in 1972, the play started out with Anthony Hopkins and Diana Rigg, but Anthony as Macbeth walked out, so Denis Quilley relinquished Banquo and took over. Before this occurred, Denis had objected to the staging of his appearance at the banquet. Michael Annals's set had a high rostrum upstage, and Banquo had to be shot up through the floor of the rostrum — exactly as the Demon King should appear in a pantomime — and Denis didn't trust the mechanism. This dramatic entrance was scrapped. Just as well, perhaps, for anyone might have said the dreaded word at that time.

My companions pressed me to tell about other superstitions. I said that in my early days, when rehearsing a new play, the last line was never spoken until the play's first public performance, which would usually have been its first night. It was so unlucky to say this line, that during rehearsals, I have heard a director cut in during the penultimate line with an instruction such as, "And that's as far as we go," to make quite sure that not one syllable of the last line would be uttered. If the actor concerned could be trusted, he or she could often be heard replacing the line with "Tum-ti-tum ti-tum-ti-tum." That seemed a good alternative. Those who had to use that phrase many times during rehearsal often made me wonder whether they might not use it at the first night.

I wasn't let off the hook, however; my superstition seekers appeared at the end of the evening, begging for one more. So I told them about whistling in a theatre. Again, this was terribly unlucky. My first stage director, George Larchet, was very firm on this. On reflection, whistling in the home and particularly in the street was rife at that time. Delivery boys, especially, would whistle happily as they cycled around the neighbourhood delivering goods stacked in baskets attached to their handlebars. When I dared to ask Mr. Larchet why he was determined not to allow whistling, he explained that in the days of sailing ships, because of the noise of the sails, the wind, and the sea, officers gave orders to the sailors by whistling. At that time, many sailors worked in theatres between voyages, and the theatre professionals were always worried that if someone whistled, a sailor might take it as a cue. I didn't think we had any sailors around, but I think George just liked to carry on a tradition.

As ever with these superstitions, one takes as true the version one fancies or finds the most acceptable. A member of the company who was passing as George was giving his explanation of the whistle stopped and said, "Oh, I'd heard it was because a whistle was used by the stage director for the carrying out of cues, and nothing to do with sailors." This exchange was then extended to the colour green. Neither of my informants could tell me why the colour green was considered unlucky, but it was thought that, with the stage being called "the green" and if it actually was green (the village green?), an actor wearing green might "disappear" into his surroundings. The only agreement was that the green room would be a room beside the green. At least that sounded correct. I cannot think that the stage is still referred to as the green, even though it wasn't too long ago that I overhead an actor say to another as they went to their respective dressing rooms, "See you on the green."

News of this conversation zipped round the company, and many more customs and oddities came to light. No real flowers must ever be brought onstage; they must be artificial. Flowers and leaves would be made of material and attached to wire stems. But there was a trap into which many an actress fell. The lady of the house would come through the French windows carrying a trug or basket of splendidly authenic-looking flowers, which she had to arrange in a vase — no water, of course — during the scene. The actress would bend each wire to get the most attractive display, forgetting that such treatment would break real flower stems. I decided this superstition was invented by some cunning managers for the cost of buying or hiring artificial flowers would be negligible compared to replacing real flowers every few days.

## Scene 19 ⚭ The National Theatre Company, 1970

During the booking period that covered June 8 to August 1, 1970, the company presented five plays in repertoire at the Old Vic and two at the Cambridge Theatre. Once *The Beaux' Stratagem* had to leave the rep at the Old Vic because Sheila Reid, Maggie Smith, Robert Stephens, and Jeanne Watts were needed at the Cambridge Theatre for *Hedda Gabler*, so a certain sparkle seemed to go with them. Business at the Cambridge was brisk with *The Merchant of Venice* sharing the eight performances a week. The next leaflet for that theatre, which covered the weeks from August 3 to September 26, showed *The Merchant* playing until August 13, when it was replaced by *The Beaux' Stratagem* crossing the river to join *Hedda*. The last week of the Cambridge Theatre leaflet showed *The Dance of Death* being seen again after a two-month layoff.

## Scene 20 ⚭ More medical information dispensed, 1970

The summer of 1970 seemed set fair until we learned at the beginning of August that Sir had pleurisy. It was not long before a thrombosis of the right leg was added to the tally. When he returned to the office, having recovered very quickly, we were treated to graphic descriptions of each part of his body that had been affected and infected. No detail was ignored. All appeared to get equal billing.

Needless to say, his absence caused huge problems. First there was a leaflet that was already printed and distributed. This showed performance details of *The Dance of Death* at the Cambridge and also the last nine performances of *The Merchant* (August 6 to 13). This problem had to be resolved at once and this was done by casting Robert Lang as Shylock, which he played exceedingly well. Although he had been playing leading roles with B Company for many years and would have been seen playing Kurt in *The Dance of Death* if it had made it to the Cambridge stage, to the public he was not Sir Laurence Olivier.

## Scene 21 ❧ The box office at the Old Vic Theatre

On April 10, 1971, a box office for both the Old and the Young Vic Theatres opened in a new building attached to the Young Vic Theatre. This meant that a large counter was up for grabs in the small Old Vic foyer, so the book-counter moved there from its cramped quarters in the corridor at the back of the stalls. However, space was left for a section of the box office to return to the theatre an hour before a performance, as with the theatres of the Music Center in Los Angeles, solely to deal with that performance.

Pat Layton was the box office manager, and his extremely well-run box office at the Old Vic must have been one of the first in London for the public to be able to look over a counter and see the colourful performance plans. Doubtless, many would idly wonder which colour pencil would be used to mark off the seats that had just been booked. This open-plan counter was a huge advance from the days when patrons had to talk to a clerk through a narrow grill, behind which the plans, impossible for the public to see, were zealously guarded

At the Old Vic during 1971, the price of a seat in the stalls ranged from £1.90 down to 90 pence, although for the Thursday matinee they dropped from a top price of £1 scaling down to 50 pence. On the day of a performance, thirty-three seats were on sale at the cut-down price of 75 pence with the cheapest seats down to 50 pence. The snag here was that all thirty-three seats had a restricted view. This meant for many that a pillar got in the way of a clear view of the stage, but they were slim pillars, and it was not impossible to get a reasonable view with a little shifting of the head as the actors moved across the stage. Standing tickets were also available and these cost 20 pence for the stalls or dress circle and 10 pence in the gallery.

For the season in the New Theatre that opened on June 15, 1971, prices were a little higher: £2 and £1.50 in the stalls and the royal circle (one floor above the stalls), while in the balcony (one floor above the royal circle) seats were 60 pence and 40 pence.

As with all theatres presenting repertoire, the Old Vic box office was kept continuously busy. With five productions available for booking, even if one or two were slow, there would always be others where the demand far outstripped the number of seats available. In the West End, theatres normally presented one production at a time, and although this would mean the staff were intensely busy during most of the run of a smash hit, for the production that had bad reviews or for which word of mouth was poor, there was little for the staff to do — except hope that the particular piece would soon leave the theatre and something with more appeal would follow immediately.

## Scene 22 ℘ The National Theatre at the Old Vic, 1971

During 1971, the National Theatre presented ten productions, shared between the Old Vic and the New Theatre (now the Albery Theatre) in St. Martin's Lane. There were some that blazed and some that fizzled and went out. It was always sad when that happened. I could look at the author, the director, the cast, and the production team, and all would signal that this play could do really well. But as happens all too often in the theatre, the various components do not connect and the production may send off a few sparks before sputtering out.

At the Old Vic, one that blazed early in the year was Zuckmeyer's *The Captain of Kopenick* in a wonderful translation by John Mortimer. As with his miraculous translation of *A Flea in Her Ear*, so John treated the Zuckmeyer. With Paul Scofield in tremendous form as the Captain and a cast of thirty-eight, most of whom had been National Theatre players for several years, it seemed exactly the sort of play that a National Theatre should have in its repertoire. Audiences of any age loved it, and I longed to be able to play it as much as possible, but the repertoire system prevented this. Paul was next due to play Leone Gala in Pirandello's *The Rules of the Game* in a translation by David Hare and Robert Rietty. The production opened for a week's run at the Theatre Royal, Newcastle-upon-Tyne, before moving into the New Theatre the following week. This meant that, with five plays in the repertoire at the Old Vic and Paul Scofield in rehearsal for the Pirandello, *The Captain of Köpenick* had to be spread out much too thinly. Worse still, while the repertoire at the New Theatre was being established, there were no performances at the Old Vic of this great success for seven weeks.

## Scene 23 ⊗ *Long Day's Journey into Night,* December 1971

The first preview of *Long Day's Journey into Night* was at the New Theatre on Tuesday, December 14, 1971. Many months before, I had gone to Sir and advised him that with a large number of special Christmas shows opening around that time, and because it was essential that critics were not given the opportunity to choose which of two clashing press nights they would review, the first date that was clear for *Long Day's Journey* meant that there would have to be seven previews. "At least the show will be well run in by then," I offered as a consoling thought. "I wouldn't care if you scheduled seventy previews," Sir said. "I would still be dreading that night, in the same way that I would be if you only scheduled one." I was about to say that it sounded a bit like *Long Day's Journey into Press Night* but decided against it.

The play would not be anglicised so four of the cast would have to adopt American accents — Sir would without doubt have a ball — while the fifth could speak in her own accent. This was Constance Cummings, who had recently been playing Volumnia, the mother to Anthony Hopkins's Coriolanus. The director, Michael Blakemore, whose production of *The National Health* was still doing huge business in the rep at the Old Vic, once more cast extremely well. Constance as Mary Cavan Tyrone became mother to Denis Quilley as Jamie and Ronald Pickup as Edmund. Maureen Lipman completed the household in the small but important part of Cathleen.

Michael Annals, the designer, was sent over to America to visit the actual house in which the playwright, Eugene O'Neill, had lived and in which the play was set. He returned to design a room that presented a beautiful but run-down part of a well-lived-in house where the four main characters could play out a portion of their lives.

It was superbly directed with all five actors giving outstanding performances. I was so sad for Mary, and one of her lines, the final line of the play, remains with me: "I fell in love with James Tyrone and I was happy for a time." Constance paused for a moment before, very quietly, saying the last three words.

## Scene 24 ❧ Production weekends

I had always been concerned that we lost a weekday evening's take at the Old Vic box office since we did not play the three Mondays before a new production opened. The first of these "weekends," made up of a Sunday and a Monday, would be purely technical, with the set put up for the first time: no actors would be called. Tuesday morning, the set would be taken down, carried across Webber Street and into the workshops in the annexe. The theatre then returned to playing the repertoire during the remainder of that week.

The second weekend would involve the new set being put up once more and as much lighting plotted as possible. This was in readiness for a technical rehearsal on the Monday afternoon and a dress rehearsal that evening. After that, down came the set again only to be put up once more for the third weekend when the play was nearing the final dress rehearsal on the Monday and the press night on the Tuesday. As the years went by, previews were introduced that would normally be on the Tuesday and Wednesday (following a dress rehearsal on the Monday) with the press night on the Thursday.

When I first mentioned my uncomplimentary opinion of this style of working, Sir said that he had always considered it was a good plan, especially for the workshops. They had the opportunity to check any faults that came to light during the first two weekends and then have a week each time in which they could be righted. I wasn't going to rush into making a change in spite of the fact that the production manager agreed with me. He said that the drawn-out system was not approved of by the stage staff, who each weekend spent much time setting up and then striking the set or sets. They did this almost every day with the normal repertoire. Now that I had broached the subject, the consensus was that it would be better by far to build the show on one weekend only and leave it there until the press night.

Sir listened to all this and said that he appreciated both sides but asked how and when could I make the change. I was ready for this and in fact had not brought the matter up until I could see a possible time. This came with the start of the Cambridge Theatre season. Because this was a West End theatre, automatically there were to be six evening performances and two matinees a week and so, with Sir's permission, I made the Old Vic fall into line.

## Scene 25 ⪼ The summer break, 1972

But it wasn't the end of getting more performances out of the company. I could see that it was good to have a season each year with a definite break between the end of one and the beginning of the next. It was also good that the company could go off for a holiday and once more it was good, in order that the Vic was not dark for too long, that it could present visiting companies from the regions or abroad during the break. What was not so good during visiting company weeks was that box office receipts had to be shared and therefore I had to find a way whereby, if we kept the Old Vic open, all receipts stayed with the National.

Then along came *Long Day's Journey,* and I saw that it could be possible for the Old Vic to be kept open during the summer while the majority of the company went off for holidays. *Long Day's Journey* was a production, like many over the years both with or without Sir Laurence in the cast, that could be played on any, and indeed every day of the week, and the theatre would be full. But this play had the advantage of a small cast, so once again I went to Sir to discuss this new idea.

Not only new, but he featured strongly in it. The plan was that the *Long Day's Journey* company should take their holidays during the first three weeks of August, after which they would return to the Vic to perform the play solidly for three consecutive weeks. That would be the time when the remainder (the majority) of the company went off for their holidays. The only snag was that *Long Day's Journey's* running time was three hours thirty-five minutes, including one eighteen-minute interval, so I would not be able to schedule matinees, but at least there would be six evenings a week.

There were several problems to be sorted out regarding the productions that would be needed to play during the *Long Days Journey* holidays. Firstly, *The Front Page*. Denis Quilley was playing Hildy Johnson, which was a long part to recast for a few performances over a three-week period, and Maureen Lipman was playing Mollie Malloy. I therefore decided that this excellent production should play in the rep right up to the night before the holiday break but then drop out. I would bring it back as the first production to start the full repertoire in early September. This was not my only problem as far as Denis and Maureen were concerned, for they were also in *The School for Scandal,* as indeed was Ronald Pickup, so these three roles were recast from within the company and the production was then ready to play in the slightly reduced rep at the Vic during *Long Day's Journey's* holidays.

Finally, there were the understudies in *Long Day's Journey.* They too needed a holiday but, because of their involvement with other productions, their holidays would have to be taken with the majority of the company. Ann Robinson and I thought it best to recast them, and in spite of the curious engagement, she brilliantly brought in five good new actors who came to see a performance of *Long Day's Journey* just before that company went on holiday. They then rehearsed the play, while their principals were away, as a totally separate production, and were therefore able confidently to cover them during the three-week run. As early as possible during those weeks, we gave them all the facilities of the production so that I could schedule a full run-through in the set and before a small audience.

Sir Laurence decided that he would be able to play all six evening performances in spite of having only one day off a week. His office work would continue as usual, although outside pressures were never so great during August. I then discussed the plan, firstly with the remainder of the *Long Day's Journey* company and then with the whole company, since so many of them would be involved with extra rehearsals and dress rehearsals.

The return from holidays saw the start of even more rehearsals, for every year at this time, several of the company would not only have gone away for their holiday but they went away for good. This meant, on return, the company would be faced with picking up the plays they had not performed for at least three weeks in addition to rehearsing the replacement actors.

The following year, 1973, I was able once more to repeat the 1972 system, so the company could again play at the Old Vic for fifty-two weeks. After this, I had to arrange for the actors to be given holidays when a break in their performances made this possible or they had to be paid in lieu. I hated this latter course for, with the amount of work they would have had during the year, to say nothing of what might be ahead, they needed the holiday. I could only hope that it must have been good to find an extra sum in one of their weekly pay packets.

## Scene 26 ❧ The National Theatre at the Old Vic, 1972

At the beginning of February 1972, it was a joy to welcome Tom Stoppard's *Jumpers* into the Old Vic. We needed something to give a lift to the repertoire. *Jumpers* played alongside the still ever-popular *The National Health* and Oliver Goldsmith's *The Good-Natured Man*. The latter play was announced as being a "long overdue for revival," but I could have done with its neglect being maintained for some years more. In spite of it appearing on paper to be one of those productions that had everything going for it — directed by John Dexter, setting by William Dudley, and cast with many National Theatre stalwart players — it was not liked. Over the river at the New Theatre, the repertoire system was dropped, and *Long Day's Journey* took over the theatre to play a special short season.

*Jumpers* opened on February 2, 1972, giving Tom Stoppard another huge success. Again directed by Peter Wood who had established a special relationship with the author in the same way that John Dexter had done with Peter Shaffer. Both teams produced excellent results. *Jumpers* brought us the remarkable Michael Hordern and the delicious Diana Rigg, both giving glorious performances. The first of the gymnasts, or jumpers as they were called in the play, to appear was Nicholas Clay, who spectacularly burst through a door made of paper, to be followed by his fellow jumpers. They were cast from our younger and, bravely, our not-quite-so-young actors, who managed to make simple gymnastic rolls and jumps appear, somehow, different.

Anna Carteret played the Secretary. A note in the script advised the actress playing this character, in so many Stoppardian words, not to look through the text for her lines, for the character did not speak. To compensate, perhaps, she got the chance to swing across the stage on a trapeze — in the nude — and to appear in many scenes with Michael Hordern. Diana Rigg, suitably costumed, was also hoisted aloft on a crescent moon where she sweetly sang "Sentimental Journey."

## Scene 27 ✒ Mobile productions, 1972

The National Theatre's credit to the director of a play would be "Production by . . ." or simply "Production," while the assistant would be "Assistant to the Producer." Apart from the time when they were allocated to an actual production, these assistants worked under the title of assistant producers while there was also a grade of staff producers, who could become an assistant to a producer. In 1972, I was considering the workload of the one remaining staff producer, Roland Joffé, and I decided that we were not taking the fullest advantage of his obvious talent, and this must be bad for him and bad for the company. So I went to him and suggested that he might like to consider organising lunchtime performances, providing, of course, that we first tracked down a suitable venue. Lunchtime theatre was becoming very popular, so I wasn't being very original, and certainly Ann Robinson had become a regular visitor to these worthwhile ventures, taking me along whenever I had the time. It was so much more satisfactory to see an actor working rather than at an audition.

Roland Joffé and I worked on the basis that, since it seemed every cellar under a pub, function room over a pub, church hall, and all similar spaces were occupied by adventurous companies, we needed to find our own. So we toured the district. I came across a warehouse over the river near Vauxhall Bridge, but when I started investigating, I realised that starting from scratch was out of the question. Heating, lighting, secondary lighting, emergency lighting, public access, dressing rooms, toilets (front-of-house and backstage), a licence from the council, and on and on, made this idea totally unworkable.

So the next best thing was to copy what Michael Kustow had organised so extremely well at the Aldwych. Under the title "Theatre-Go-Round," Royal Shakespeare Company productions were cast from the actors at the Aldwych and, with the minimum of settings, props, and costumes, would go out on one-night stands. These companies were enormously appreciated by audiences who couldn't get, or couldn't afford to get, to the Aldwych. It wasn't difficult to suggest to Roland that we copy this good example.

We chose to call these small-scale touring shows Mobile Productions, and Roland chose *'Tis Pity She's a Whore* by John Ford as the first production. Many of the cast came from *Jumpers* including Diana Rigg to play Hippolita, Anna Carteret as Annabella, and Nicholas Clay as Giovanni. Their first performance was at the Wyvern Theatre in Swindon on Monday, May 8, 1972, which I noticed nostalgically happened to be the sixteenth anniversary of *Look Back in Anger*'s opening at the Royal Court.

Once the scheme had official blessing, Yolande Bird, the assistant to the secretary to the National Theatre Board, joined as its administrator, and she was more than adept at arranging dates and finances with the venues, as well as booking the coaches for the company. There was separate transport for the production team, who would go, with the minimal sets, costumes, and so on, to the venue early in the morning of the visit to set up and generally prepare for the evening show.

Unlike the Royal Shakespeare Company's visits, which were planned to be not more than about an hour's drive from the Aldwych, Yolande spread her net much wider. This resulted in longer journeys and later back to London after the show. But it was very good for a National Theatre production to be seen in so many venues, which could not possibly accommodate shows from the Old Vic.

The coaches were not always the most luxurious and were, in fact, spartan but serviceable. The drivers were not always absolutely sure of the route or where the theatre or hall was situated once the town was reached. Perhaps the most bizarre example was when we set off for Newcastle-under-Lyme. This meant an early start but the driver said we would get there on time. Off we went up the M1, but the coach proved to be of advanced years and we suffered the indignity of smart new versions roaring past us with their occupants waving and cheering as we struggled along, with every gentle upward slope proving a real challenge.

At last some of the company felt that clinging to the M1 for too long was not going to bring us across to the Black Country, so when we were on a level with — but a long way from — Derby, we asked the driver if he thought it wasn't time to turn left. It was then we learned that he was mistakenly heading for Newcastle-upon-Tyne, a very long way from our under-Lyme version. An understandable but not very helpful mistake. There was only one map on the coach, and this was a very small one on the back page of a pocket diary. But it was enough for David Bradley brilliantly to guide the bemused driver up hill (just) and down dale across the Peak District. It was all so beautiful, but we were much too worried about the time to relish the views. We arrived during the half to find everything ready onstage and coffee and sandwiches available offstage. The curtain in the large town hall went up on time, and the company played as well as ever to a large, enthusiastic audience.

On January 4, 1973, Peter James's Mobile Production of *Twelfth Night* set off for its first date and, just over a year later, on January 17, 1974, Jonathan Miller's extremely fascinating and successful production of *Measure for Measure* opened at the Corn Exchange in King's Lynn. The setting was a series of street doors of all types, standing side by side, which was certainly striking and also useful to an audience. Very quickly, they realised that they would know exactly where the next scene was set by noting through which door the first actor in the scene made his entrance. The play was updated to the 1930s and set in Vienna. Both these changes worked wonderfully well, and because it seemed so long ago, the attitude of Isabella was just acceptable.

Later that same year, on September 13, Bill Bryden's clear and swift production of *Romeo and Juliet* opened at the Key Theatre in Peterborough, and the idea of Mobile Productions was truly under way.

## Scene 28 ⟋ *The Front Page*, July 6, 1972

Michael Blakemore's wonderful production of *The Front Page* presented the company with another huge hit. Once again the National was giving the public the sort of production that could be enjoyed by everyone, and it was yet another example of superb ensemble playing, but this time the cast had to use American accents. Denis Quilley had already proved in *Long Day's Journey* that he was totally at home with this accent, but there was a cast of twenty-seven in *The Front Page*. That made it all the more satisfying when American visitors came to the play and assured us that the accents were very good indeed.

Another bonus for this production was Michael Annals's setting. It was a single set of a newspaper office, foggy with cigarette smoke, that had to accommodate several desks, littered with papers and ever-ringing phones. There was a large window through which Clive Merrison as Earl Williams had to leap into the room and a large rolltop desk in which he had to hide. And a practical lift — or should it be elevator?

During the interval, the iron curtain had to be "lowered and raised in the presence of each audience" (as required in the theatre's licence), and of all the sets on the Old Vic stage into which this curtain had to appear, the set of *The Front Page* was the one that made me think "Look at all that furniture and general junk lying around. It isn't possible for the iron to come in." This thought did not allow for the brilliance of Michael Annals, however, for down came the iron, happily missing all the chairs, tables, and other clutter. I realised that although it seemed I had been looking square-on at a room, this was not the case. It was the room that had been craftily angled and not the iron, which was still moving down and up in its guide rails situated just upstage of the proscenium arch.

On the top of the rolltop desk was a wooden period calendar. The little box had three small windows on its face, one above the other, that showed the day, the date, and the month. This information could be changed by turning wooden rollers at the side of the frame, but I noticed that this prop calendar was never changed, with the date permanently set at Friday, September 22. Somehow this date stayed in my mind, so when I was preparing the schedules for the next leaflet, which included September, I was struck by the fact that the twenty-second fell on a

Friday. It needed a little juggling with the other plays, which eagle-eye Olivier noticed, but I didn't intend to tell him of my ludicrous plan. I had prepared a good reason for my playing *The Front Page* in a block that included Friday, September 22, which happily he accepted.

Thus, for one performance only, the calendar was telling the truth, though admittedly for 1972. When that performance arrived, I wondered whether any member of the audience noticed the calendar and, if so, whether he or she would think it was changed daily.

## Scene 29 ☙ Josef Svoboda

When I joined the National Theatre (August 1966), two of the five-play repertoire at the Old Vic, *Othello* and *Trelawny of the "Wells,"* were directed by John Dexter, as was *The Royal Hunt of the Sun* in the three-play rep at the Queen's Theatre, Shaftesbury Avenue. All were most wonderfully directed and hugely successful, so I was looking forward to the first play John was to direct soon after I joined. This was to be *The Storm.* I was particularly interested in this production since I had never heard of the playwright, Ostrovsky. I had another reason for great anticipation, for the designer was Josef Svoboda.

I had met him at the very end of 1965 when Molly and Peter Daubeny invited me to join them on a visit to Prague. We were to make detailed arrangements for the Czech National Theatre to take part in the 1966 World Theatre Season at the Aldwych. They were scheduled to bring Karel and Josef Capek's *The Insect Play.* In addition to meeting with the board of directors in the huge boardroom of the vast Czech National Theatre, sited on the banks of the Vitava, I also accepted an invitation to go out to Svoboda's workshop somewhere in the suburbs.

After he and I had dealt with the complexities of bringing over the expansive setting for *The Insect Play* with its two revolves (sadly, we were only able to fit one onto the Aldwych stage), he showed me model after model of the settings he had designed over the years. I was totally knocked out by them. Here was another of those designers who was approaching each play with a completely new vision as well as using materials I had never seen used on a stage before.

I only wished I could have seen the *Hamlet* for which he had designed a series of steps and had made use of vast mirrors hanging at various angles. At least I was able to see his designs for Arthur Miller's *After the Fall* at the Czech National Theatre that evening. There were many scene changes, and these were carried out without the curtain falling (unusual even in 1965), and yet the audience could not see the changes taking place. At the start of each scene change, upstage of one proscenium arch or the other, a pillar of extremely bright lights appeared and traversed the complete stage quite slowly from prompt corner to opposite to prompt or vice versa. These lights reached all levels of the auditorium and blinded the audience from seeing the activity onstage behind the moving pillar.

I found Prague to be a sad city, with its asleep-for-a-hundred-years aspect. The shop windows were all but empty, and every piece of timber was crying out for attention: priming and several coats of paint were desperately needed. But the buildings themselves were beautiful, and I felt we were in a fairy-tale city. It was a great pity that *The Insect Play* was not being performed during our brief stay. I wanted so much to see it presented in the way it should be seen, for there was no doubt that it was not at anywhere near its best when it came to the Aldwych. Even the cut-down version of the setting had to be shoehorned in, and because of that, all the magic was squeezed out.

## Scene 30 ❦ John Dexter

John was a great director and a great disciplinarian. If I saw an actor racing along the Waterloo Road between the station and the Old Vic, I knew that it must be nearly time for the start of a rehearsal. I also knew that John would be standing in the rehearsal room ready to give a lashing of the tongue to anyone arriving late. Rehearsals of any of his productions never started until the full company had had a half-hour voice class or, on alternate days, a movement class. Whatever time during the day an actor was called — or even if he or she did not have a call — the full company had to be at the morning classes. Once the rehearsal had begun, John expected every actor in his company to be in the room listening to and watching the rehearsal, even if not appearing in that scene. He hated seeing an actor reading, working on a crossword, or in any way not paying attention to what was going on. He worked on the principle that his actors should stay within the atmosphere of the play during rehearsals, rather than chatting in the canteen. He was also fully aware how much an actor could gain by listening carefully to what other characters were saying in scenes in which he or she was not involved. There was always the chance of picking up even the smallest clue to a situation or a mood that could affect him or her in a later scene.

He was really pleased when an actor came to him and said that overnight he had been considering such-and-such a scene, and it had suddenly come to him that there was another approach that might help him and perhaps help the scene. John's immediate reaction was always the same: "Show me!" He expected every member of his casts to work on the play at all times during the rehearsal period, and if he liked what an actor might bring to him as a suggestion, he would incorporate it and nurture the idea, for he knew that the actor's commitment to the play was total. That help and encouragement was always given unstintingly if the actor responded, but if it became clear that an actor switched off at the end of rehearsal one day and didn't switch on again until the start of the next day's work, then he was of no use to John.

To my sorrow, I never had time to sit in on any of his rehearsals, but I often had to creep into a rehearsal room at a moment when I hoped there would soon be a break so that I could talk to an actor or to John himself. If he saw me — or, I'm sure, any other unexpected visitor — trying to look as if I wasn't actually in the room, he would immediately send a very sharp comment winging across the room that, by experience, I knew had to be rebutted at once. He seemed to enjoy it if you stood up to him, and this was not difficult to do if you were prepared.

John would allocate one of his final rehearsals to the understudies. The staff director would have rehearsed them whenever possible during the rehearsal period, and John required them to play the whole play as if it were a performance. If it could be arranged, all the props were available and even costumes or parts of a costume, such as a sword and sword belt, were provided. Not only would he watch this performance, all the principals were called, and they were then able to see the play from the front, which many found immensely helpful.

## Scene 31 ⊛ *Equus*, July 1973

During Peter Shaffer's *The Royal Hunt of the Sun*, he and John Dexter established a wonderful working relationship, and this was seen again to enormous effect with Peter's third play for the National, *Equus*. If I saw Peter hurrying along a corridor, it was impossible to stop him even for the briefest of exchanges, since he would call, "Sorry. I can't stop. John wants me to rewrite a scene, and it must be ready for rehearsal tomorrow morning." And off he would go at a run. Next morning, amazingly, there would be the rewrite on several pages of coloured paper — a colour he had not used before, so that soon scripts became a mass of colours amongst the original white pages — and always the scene would have been improved.

John Napier designed the setting and the costumes for *Equus*. His setting needed permission from the Greater London Council, for the design showed a curving bank of seats for the audience on the stage and upstage of the acting area. This meant those members of the public who had bought tickets for these seats had to enter the theatre through the foyer, pass down the side of the stalls, through the pass door into the stage-left wing space, where they were directed to their seats. The scaffolding structure that held the rows of seats was tall and narrow so that it occupied as little of the acting area as possible. Sitting in those seats, especially on the higher levels, always made me think — as I am sure we, the audience, were meant to — that we were medical students looking down on a surgeon in an operating theatre.

Amongst the costumes that John Napier designed were those for the actors playing horses. No way must there be a hint of a pantomime horse and no way was there. The actors wore brown gloves and chestnut brown sweaters and corduroy trousers. On their heads they wore the outline of a horse's head made of light metal, and although one could see through these masks to the actor's head, for some reason I never found myself searching for the face beneath. I was looking at a horse.

There was more brilliance in the design of the horses' hooves, two for each actor. The hoof was created with two metal plates between which were four metal struts. This meant that when the actor's shoe was strapped to the upper plate, he was standing about a foot above the base plate of the hoof and thus, when Peter Firth, who created the role of the boy, Alan Strang, was amongst the horses, he had to reach up to touch their heads.

The hooves were also able to create the sound of real hooves, and when Alan went into the stable, the sound of stamping hoofs helped make the scene very real even though there no scenery at all to help the illusion of a stable building. When Alan rode a horse, played by Nicholas Clay, it was again remarkable how one could accept the fact, rather than thinking that it was just one actor sitting on another actor's back. The play opened at the Old Vic on July 26, 1973, and became an instant success.

## Scene 32 ❧ *The Misanthrope* and *The Cherry Orchard* at the Old Vic, 1973

The year 1973 was a wonderful one at the Old Vic. John Dexter not only directed *Equus* but earlier in the year, opening on February 22, he had directed *The Misanthrope.* Tony Harrison had translated Molière's French rhyming couplets into the most brilliant English rhyming couplets that allowed the actors to speak a sentence several lines long as if it were prose, and elegant rhythmic prose at that. If one did hear a couplet that rhymed, one could only marvel at its cunning and unexpectedness. He also updated the play by three hundred years to the 1960s, the France of General Charles de Gaulle, and this gave Tanya Moiseiwitsch the chance to design a stunning set in addition to providing exquisite dresses for Diana Rigg, at her most fascinating as Célimène, for Gillian Barge as Arsinoé, and Jeanne Watts as Eliante. The men, amongst them the excellent Alec McCowen playing Alceste, Alan Macnaughtan as Philinte, and Gawn Grainger as Oronte, were the best-dressed men about town.

On May 24, Michael Blakemore's production of *The Cherry Orchard,* with Constance Cummings as Madame Ranevsky, Michael Hordern as Gayev, and Denis Quilley as Lopakhin, in beautiful settings by Alan Tagg, joined the repertoire. Of all the very good things in this production, one remembers the performances of the two actors chosen by Sir Laurence to be his first staff directors, Kenneth Mackintosh and Harry Lomax. Sir Laurence declared that Kenneth's Pishchik was "definitive," while Harry, as Firs, towards the very end of the play, was able to open the door of what appeared to be a broom cupboard upstage centre and creep in almost unnoticed. When the family and staff had left the house and the room was absolutely quiet, many of the audience, seeing the play for the first time, must have thought that this was the end. But they would then have heard a clicking sound, repeated once or twice, and their gaze would have been drawn to the broom cupboard door. At once they would notice that the brass handle — not a knob — rose and fell a time or two before the door very slowly opened and out came the tiny figure of Firs. He looked about him, obviously not able to take in at once what had happened, and then slowly went to a settee, dust-sheeted as was all the remaining furniture, and, sitting on it carefully, he then lay back to rest after his exhausting journey of the few feet from the cupboard. After a moment, an arm slipped over the edge of the settee but was slowly drawn back: it fell again but this time it was not drawn back. From the orchard, which one could see through the windows at the back of the set, came the sound of the cherry trees being chopped down.

## Scene 33 ℭ Assistant producers and understudies

In the middle sixties, Sir Laurence was getting reports from some of his more senior players that they didn't feel they should be given notes during the run of a play by the younger members of the assistant producers' team. Sir could appreciate this comment, and at once he decided that in future he would appoint members of the company: these would be drawn from the group of mature character actors who had shown themselves to be not only good actors but good company members. Unlike the assistant producers at that time, these company members would not only accept the extra work and responsibility of the post, but they would also be able to continue their acting careers in the company. When Sir Laurence first discussed his idea with me, he said that he was certain that the many years in the profession of the two actors he had in mind and the excellent performances they had given would mean that they would have earned the respect of their fellow actors. He was also certain the appointment of this particular pair would mean that they would understand when a tactful suggestion to an actor would be taken as constructive and in no way would it be seen as the giving a note for sake of it or of trying to score a point. The company as a whole would also appreciate notes from these two staff producers, since it would be known that they would have witnessed a performance from the front.

The first two to be asked if they would like to be appointed to this new style of assistant producer were Harry Lomax and Kenneth Mackintosh. It is strange how automatic it is to write those names in alphabetical order. George Devine chose this way of setting out a list of actors in his company, and it became the style at Stratford-upon-Avon when Peter Hall took over the Shakespeare Memorial Theatre. Three years later, Sir Laurence agreed to listing his players this way, and so it has remained.

Harry Lomax was a National Theatre player from the start of the company in 1963 when he played the Player King in *Hamlet,* while Kenneth Mackintosh joined in 1964 to play Lodovico and to understudy Sir Laurence's Othello — a great honour, although one must wonder, as Kenneth must have wondered during the production's long stay in the repertoire, whether he would have been allowed to play for Sir Laurence should the chance have arisen.

With the National Theatre working on a repertory system, it was possible, when, for example, A Company was going into rehearsal, for Ann Robinson to cast the understudies from all members of A Company, whether they were in the production or not. This meant that the assistant producer could rehearse the understudies without any of them having to appear as more than one character in any one scene, no matter how many roles he or she might have within the whole play. This also meant that some actors would not appear onstage during the play but would be walking understudies, when they would spend the performances in a dressing room, in the canteen, or in the green room, well rehearsed and knowing their lines, just waiting for the chance to play for their principal. This was good for the actors in that they were involved with the production, rather than having a night off while their fellow company members were working. These understudies would get a performance fee for attending the theatre whether they appeared or not. If they played for their principal, their performance fee would be enhanced.

To Ann and myself, the ability the assistant producers had of rehearsing a play straight through, without having to go back on a scene to let an actor rehearse the other character or characters he or she was also understudying in the production, was an unbelievable luxury. When Ann and I had worked on plays for Tennent Productions in the early 1950s, we always had to understudy as well as being the stage management team. For R. C. Sherriff's *The White Carnation*, we were told that we would be understudying six "guests," three female for Ann and three male for me. During the once-a-week rehearsals, poor Rupert Marsh, the long-suffering and excellent company manager, needed all his patience while the two of us, usually trying in vain to control uncontrollable laughter, kept stopping the rehearsal to ask questions of each other, such as "Are you being Sally or Cynthia?" "Um. I think I was Sally, wasn't I?" "I couldn't tell. But if you were Sally, I should have been Major Howard for that bit of the scene, shouldn't I?" "Come on, you two," Rupert would implore, and the rehearsal would continue after a fashion. It was lucky we never had to go on, especially since Ann, during the whole scene, had to play the maid who stood upstage centre holding a large silver tray on which was a bowl of steaming punch (literally steaming but not literally punch) and, at the start of the scene, the appropriate number of glasses. Goodness knows who would have taken on that tray if Ann had had to appear as one of the guests. Perhaps Rupert?

## Scene 34 ❧ *Saturday Sunday Monday* at the Old Vic, 1973

It was Peter Daubeny who had brought Peppino de Filippo and his company from Italy to the Aldwych Theatre in London in 1964 as part of the first World Theatre Season, and it was Peter who brought Peppino's brother, Eduardo, with his company to the Aldwych for the 1972 World Theatre Season. That same year, Kenneth Tynan suggested to Sir Laurence that the National should stage one of Eduardo's plays, a suggestion Sir took up by inviting Franco Zeffirelli, an old friend of the Olivier family, to choose one of Eduardo's many plays and to direct it for the National. It would be Franco's first production for the company since *Much Ado About Nothing* in 1965.

He chose *Saturday Sunday Monday*, and an English adaptation was prepared by Keith Waterhouse and Willis Hall. Franco came over from Italy to talk to Sir about the casting. He arrived at the huts with a cast list of starry names which Sir listened to with patience before he asked Franco if he had seen any of the National Theatre's recent productions. He said he was sure that Franco would be surprised and delighted by the talent he saw there, even though the actors might not be known worldwide. Franco, having said that he hadn't seen any National Theatre productions lately, persisted with his preference for well-known actors when, for one role—and for some strange, unknown reason—Sir put forward the name of Franco Nero. Having mentioned him, he stuck with this actor until it would seem he was about the only actor outside the company who could play, well, practically any part. Zeffirelli in his turn remained fairly silent while the eulogies were heaped on Nero's head. At last he could stand it no longer. In desperation, it seemed, he suddenly burst out in his attractive accent, "Franco Nero! Franco Nero!" (There was the slightest of pauses between the *Fran* and the *co*, and all but none between the *co* and the *Nero*, all of which made the full name sound even more attractive). For a split second, it seemed that Sir was going to regain the higher ground with what could only have been a similar explosive comment, as signalled by a sharp intake of breath, but the Franco sitting opposite him was not finished. "Frank Black! Frank Black!" He was nearly shouting now. "Would you engage an English actor called Frank Black?!"

The haggling went on, but the fun had gone, and soon Franco was sent off with his promise that he would go to the Old Vic to see such-and-such a production when he said he would especially watch out for three actors named by Sir. Then he would go to another production and again especially watch out for others, who, once more, were named by Sir. All along, for some reason, Franco had been very insistent that the part of Rocco should come from outside the company, but he had to confess at a later meeting that seeing Nicholas Clay onstage and talking to him, he was quite satisfied that he would be ideal for that role.

Eduardo had been extremely pleased and honoured that one of his plays was to be included in the National Theatre's repertoire and even more honoured that Sir Laurence was to play in it. He took it for granted that the great British actor would play the part of Peppino, the father, that he, Eduardo, as was his wont, had written for himself. However, Sir did not want at that time to play a relatively large role nor did he want to play opposite his own wife, for Joan Plowright was to play Rosa, the wife of Peppino. When Eduardo heard that Sir Laurence had chosen to take the small role of Antonio, father to Peppino and a hat-maker, he became more angry than upset or disappointed. He could only regard Sir's choice as indicating that the role of Antonio was a better role than that of Peppino, although he knew from experience that this was not so. He just could not understand how any actor could turn down an important role for a minor one.

Nothing that anyone could say changed Sir Laurence's mind and soon the play, in its excellent adaptation, was in rehearsal with a cast of National Theatre players. There was some discussion as to what sort of accent the company should use: all were adamant that if it were to be Italian, it should not be the one known as the "ice cream vendor" type. They developed one that had a flavour or a hint of the way Neapolitans speak, and although Franco found it difficult to understand why this was approved of by the company, this was the one they all adopted.

Franco himself was not always popular with the company, for twice during rehearsals he disappeared. The first time was when his good friend, Anna Magnani, the great Italian actress, was killed in a car crash, and Franco went over to Italy at once. The company understood this journey, but all too soon, he vanished again — this time, for no known reason, he went to Paris. While he was away, rehearsals continued under Sir Laurence and Joan Plowright. However, Franco also disappeared during the first technical rehearsal. It seems that Joan had a quick-change, or quick costume change, that had not been rehearsed. This took longer at the first attempt than had been reckoned, so she missed her cue to re-enter the scene. Franco flared up and stormed out of the building— reverting to his other role of opera director, one might think. Sir Laurence sighed, and the rehearsal went on. This time Franco did not return until the press night.

The play was a spectacular success, and Franco was there to receive the plaudits. He really deserved a lot of praise but perhaps 75 percent, instead of the 100 percent that came his way, would be more fair. Once more, it was the perfect swan song of large-cast ensemble playing by Olivier's National Theatre players. Patrons of any age could enjoy it and could understand the emotions and the family problems presented by the various characters. During the first act, patrons could also understand why they felt hungry, for delicious cooking smells came drifting into the auditorium from the stage where Joan Plowright, giving a wonderful performance as the matriarch, was actually cooking ragout on a practical stove in the kitchen set.

## Scene 35 ⊘ British Actors Equity

I had two unions with whom I had to negotiate over the years: the Musicians Union and British Actors Equity. It was with the latter that I had the most contact. During my early days at the National Theatre, Equity's representative was Eddie Wyatt, who, at the start of any meeting, immediately set up a barrier between himself, halo aglow, as the representative of Us on one side, and myself, cast as the implacable Them, the enemy of the actor, on the other. Somewhere along the line, he had convinced himself that whatever I, as management, proposed could not possibly be to the actors' advantage. Sadly, this was his automatic reaction, and I used to find it hard to make him understand that we were really on the same side, both caring for the actors in our own particular way. I always hoped that when I put forward a proposal he would give it the consideration it deserved and not dismiss it immediately, simply because the idea had come from me.

It wasn't impossible, however, to bring in some practices that would, initially, apply only to National Theatre actors. One such, instigated by Sir Laurence, came about when he had one play in the rep while rehearsing another — a situation well known to anyone who has worked in the repertoire system. He said that he couldn't continue a rehearsal until, say, six o'clock if he had a performance that would be going up at seven-thirty. "I must have a two-hour break between the end of a day's rehearsal and curtain up on a performance of a different play," he said. "It is essential that I stop thinking about the play I have been working on all day and think about my character in the evening's performance. I want to have time for a steak and salad." This obviously made good sense, so it became a rule for the whole company to have the break, though not necessarily the steak and salad.

Another change to normal practice was the length of rest time that must be allowed to an actor between the end of an evening perform-ance, or the end of work at night such as a technical or a dress rehearsal, and the start of work the following day. Before the acceptance of this rule, that began at the National and then, sometimes with slight vari-ations, crept into general usage, it often was not a case of "at night" and "the following day," for the end of work was often not reached until the small hours of the following day, by which time everyone would be so tired that very little worthwhile work was done. When rehearsals were resumed later that morning, energy levels weren't too high, to say the least, for few would have had time for a reasonable rest.

So a definite break was instituted, which, for the National Theatre, became twelve hours. From then on, I very often found myself saying quietly to a director after a long day's work, "It's ten-forty-five now, and we've got to think of the twelve-hour-break rule. Why not give your-self another quarter of an hour and then call it a day for this will allow you to make the first call for tomorrow morning to be at eleven o'clock. The further you go after eleven this evening, the nearer to lunchtime your first call for tomorrow will become and soon you'll find yourself wondering if it's worth calling the company until early afternoon."

At the Royal Court, where so often we had to work right through the night, we used to take a break about 3:00 AM, when I would advise staff and stage management to have their cups of coffee or tea stand-ing up, or leaning back against a friendly piece of scenery, for once one sat down, it was extremely hard to get up and carry on with the same energy and determination as before the break. I often thought we each ought to be supplied with one of those wooden recliners that we saw being used by chorus girls in most of the marvellous film musicals that came pouring out of Hollywood, particularly in the 1930s. These appeared to be just a sloping plank with two shelves at elbow level on which the girls laid their forearms and two pieces of wood at the appro-priate angle at the base that supported and took some of the weight off those poor overworked tap-dancing feet.

# Scene 36 ❧ Scheduling

Scheduling performances and rehearsals when the National was at the Old Vic was reasonably straightforward for me at first, except when some of the company were out on tour.

That changed when the National Theatre was spread over three theatres. Starting on details for a new leaflet, I would begin with the intention of scheduling as many productions in each week as possible, which would be good for the public and for the company. However, I had to be careful that I did not do this in a way that would mean the stage staff spending each day and half the night changing one production to the next. Way back, I had checked with the actors as to what the maximum number of days a production could be out of the rep before it would become necessary for the cast to have a word rehearsal on its return. The answer was that ten days was the maximum, so I had to make sure I seldom exceeded that figure. If a word-run were necessary, it would take place as late as possible on the day when the production came back.

There was then the matter of productions that were needed in the rep but that were not exactly drawing the crowds. To nurse them along, I would never play them at the beginning of a week, and when they did appear, I would give them a block of just a few performances. This "delicate" scheduling nearly always paid off in that those few performances would be very well attended. At the other end of the scale were the productions in which Sir Laurence appeared. These could be scheduled on any day of the week — even a matinee on a Christmas Eve would result in a full house. From that point of view, scheduling was easy: all he and I had to do was to watch his workload.

Before I took a schedule to Sir, I would have checked a draft version with various groups and individuals, and not always in the same order. It was useful if I could talk to the director of a play that would be in rehearsal during the period in question, for it was important to see that his cast would not be called away to too many performances of their plays already in the rep. Evening performances meant stopping earlier than the director would perhaps wish, but it was the matinees that could decimate the cast — to say nothing of stage management

— of the play in rehearsal, so that no one was left with whom the director could work. There were also other areas to be looked at: Were there sufficient weeks of rehearsal overall? Did the balance of technical and dress rehearsals seem right? Were there enough previews? Was the night I had booked with the Society of West End Theatre as the press night best suited for the production?

A meeting with the production manager was vital. In this area, it was always a question of time. Not only the building and setting-up time, but were the actors going to need longer than normal to learn how to cope with unusual hazards in or around the set? Then the leading actors must be shown the rehearsal and performance schedules. I had to ensure that they would start rehearsals knowing they would have reasonable rehearsal time and that there would be a reasonable number of dress rehearsals and previews before the press night. If a leading actor had a particularly large role, I liked to point out the number of matinee days and also the approximate amount of time between curtain down on a matinee and curtain up for the evening performance.

I also allowed each new production to have several performances immediately following the press night, not only so that the second and third night press could be present at performances at the very start of a play's life, but also so that all the notices would appear in the press, both local and national, more or less at the same time. These performances were also necessary for the cast who could begin to become comfortable with their roles before these had to be put on one side while the old repertoire of plays was brought back for an airing. I was also well aware that sometimes a director could be making small changes to a new production up to and including the morning of the press night, and these must be allowed time to settle before the play was given its first break. Even after the first few performances, I would always let a new production have as many performances as I dared during the next week or two. I could argue with myself that this was to the detriment of the other plays in the rep, but I knew that if it could be arranged, it would be extremely beneficial to the new. There was also the thought that hopefully the extra performances would be building up the public's word of mouth, which could do more good to a play than notices in the press.

# Scene 37 ⍟ Changes 1970 to 1973

During 1970, the pace in the huts seemed very slowly to be increasing although the same could not be said for the pace at which the National Theatre was being built on the South Bank. Richard York would very kindly look in at my office to ask if I would like to be taken round the site, but I usually had to refuse owing to lack of time. Richard's title was South Bank Liaison Manager, which meant, as far as I was concerned, that he was the liaison between the huts and the Old Vic and the new building. It seemed that when I enquired of him how things were going, the answer was always "very slowly."

We never truly believed that it would — or rather that it could — be completed in 1973, and sure enough in 1971, we were told that the opening date would have to be put back a year. Would we now please work towards 1974? We were, perhaps, encouraged when, on May 3, 1973, there was a "topping-out" ceremony performed on the roof of the Olivier Theatre. It was a beautiful spring day, and there was a good turnout to see Lord Cottesloe and a fit and cheerful Sir Laurence ceremonially filling in a little hole in the roof to signify the end of the exterior building. "Oh, well," I heard someone say as we turned away and started our slow descent down the specially constructed stairway, "only the inside to finish off now." Irony hung in the still air.

As work on the new building continued, as we hoped it did, its occupation date kept doing a Cheshire cat act of almost seeming to be there and then disappearing. I felt it best to pretend that it might never happen and to carry on as if we would be at the Old Vic forever. Whenever a meeting on the other side of the river meant my walking over Waterloo Bridge, I would gaze down at what apparently was going to be the basement area and decide that it had looked exactly like this two months previously.

Even before I really knew it, the early 1970s brought a change in the air. First there was the news that Sir was to play Nathan Detroit in a production of *Guys and Dolls,* which resulted in the box office receiving shoals of enquiries, and even bookings, from all over the world. Then the production was cancelled due not only to Sir's illnesses but also, so rumour had it, to the board getting cold feet regarding cost. Then in

1971, we read that Peter Hall, just about to take over at the Royal Opera House as co-director with Colin Davis, had resigned. This at once led to many declaring with certain knowledge that he had done this to be ready to take over the National when Sir Laurence, either through further illness or fatigue, decided it was time to go.

The year 1972 brought more statements of fact, rather than rumours, from those who always seem to have second sight at their command. Now it was yes, definitely. Peter Hall would be taking over at the end of the year. Sir called a company meeting for April 12, 1972. He didn't enjoy company meetings, and he called them as seldom as possible. But this one was important. He told the company that he intended to stand down, but that he would see out the National Theatre's time at the Old Vic. He added that when the day for the move to the new building came, he would lead the company out of the Old Vic and march at its head down the Waterloo Road and straight on to the National Theatre. Once there, he said, he would not stop. He would walk in at the front and then go straight through the building and out of the back, leaving the company installed in its new home. A week later it was officially announced that Peter Hall would indeed be the new director, taking over from Sir Laurence towards the end of 1973, following a period of about six months when they would be joint directors.

On March 30, 1973, just before this arrangement started, Sir Laurence made a charming I-know-my-place gesture by leaving his double-sized office, in which he had been installed during his ten years as director, free for Peter. A smaller one was found for him much farther down the corridor, nearer to the rehearsal room and the canteen, and there he took up residence. But he didn't use it very often.

## Scene 38 ⚵ Sir Laurence's final years as director of the National Theatre

In 1971, in addition to directing *Amphitryon 38*, which opened at the New Theatre on June 23, Sir Laurence also appeared in two major movies (*Nicholas and Alexandra* and *Lady Caroline Lamb*) and played in *Long Day's Journey into Night*. This latter production became a TV film, directed by Peter Wood, in 1972. In this year he also played Andrew Wyck in the film version of *Sleuth* by Anthony Shaffer (twin brother of Peter), while 1973 saw him re-creating his Shylock when *The Merchant of Venice* was filmed for television. This was excellently directed, as it had been at the Old Vic, by Jonathan Miller.

On October 25, 1973, Sir appeared at the Old Vic in *Saturday Sunday Monday*, followed, on December 20, by his playing the role of John Tagg in Trevor Griffith's *The Party*. It seemed entirely appropriate that his last appearance in a play on any stage was at the Old Vic and that he was in a production directed by John Dexter, one of his original two associates. In this extremely good play, John Tagg was a retired trade union leader, a Trotskyite hailing from Glasgow. So, with the help of Paul Curran, a Scot who was a very longtime National Theatre player, Sir was able to play his final role using a strong Glaswegian accent. A modern play by a young British playwright and the chance to use an accent. No wonder he accepted the part.

This role was no delicious one in which he could quietly indulge himself, as he did when making hats in *Saturday Sunday Monday*, for during the course of Trevor's play, he had to deliver a seventeen-minute speech, which he painstakingly learnt over several weeks. I often wondered, listening to it several times when I went to the Old Vic for dress rehearsals, previews, and finally the press night, whether it was more difficult for Sir to remember the speech or for the actors onstage to keep awake while appearing to be hearing it for the first time.

Thursday, March 21, 1974, saw the last performance of *The Party*, so there was something very special about the curtain calls on this night. For the actors, they were now having to put aside a character that they, and nobody before them, had created. In the centre of the line was a superb actor, who had first appeared on that same stage in that same beautiful theatre thirty-seven years previously, and for him, this performance had been his last on that stage.

As the audience applauded the company, on one side of Sir Laurence a space appeared, and into this space, quite unexpectedly, stepped Peter Hall. When the applause died down, Peter paid a tribute to the great actor beside him, and as ever when Peter spoke in public, the words he chose and the length of the tribute were absolutely right. To end his speech, Peter asked the audience to "be upstanding," which they were at once, applauding and cheering.

At last the curtain fell and stayed down and the audience went home, but as soon as possible the actors of the company got together in the upstairs rehearsal room, and a wonderful party began. Joan and Sir appeared, and he was given a present from the actors, an ice-making machine, which was chosen to be a help at the house in Brighton where he and Joan were always such marvellous and generous hosts, dispensing endless hospitality that usually needed the addition of ice. There was a cake and champagne, and everyone sang while Denis Quilley accompanied brilliantly on the piano. Sir Laurence was in his element, relaxed and cheerful, surrounded by his company.

So ended for me more than seven years of working for this amazing man. It had been such an enormous honour, and it gave me such enormous pleasure, and yet even after all that time, I still found it very difficult to call him Larry, as he had unexpectedly asked Sunny and myself to do during one of our early evening discussions. At once I remembered how, in just the same way, I had found it almost impossible to call Mr. Devine George. But whatever I called Sir Laurence — or didn't call him, for it was easier that way — it was entirely due to him that, at the time of his leaving, I was able to think back over those years and realise how wonderful they had been.

# Act Seven
## The National Theatre of Great Britain, 1974 to 1976

The ever-changing date for the move to the new theatre complicates planning. The administration leaves Aquinas Street for the South Bank. Three fine productions among the last at the Old Vic. Reactions to the new building. Remembering Dame Peggy Ashcroft and Sir Ralph Richardson. The Lyttelton Theatre undergoes an acoustic test.

### Scene 1 ✆ A meeting with Peter Hall, January 1974

There were only three entries in my engagements diary for Tuesday, January 8, 1974, and these, written in different colours and entered in the order in which they came to hand rather than chronological, were:

*(in black)* 1. 6.30. Leave word at the box office re Dame Peggy [Ashcroft] meeting me to discuss *Happy Days*. Check use of an upstairs office for an hour.

*(in blue)* 2. 1 pm To see P. Hall at Donmar.

*(in green)* 3. Send B.P.'s 1 to 4 to Jack Phipps.

The choice of colour was determined by which pen I picked up first from the drawer that held pens of many colours, after which it didn't matter which colour was used so long as it was different from its predecessor.

Entry number one presented no problems. I always went through the rehearsal and performance draft schedules with leading actors, whether in the company or on the point of joining, as far ahead as possible before the start of rehearsals. Amongst many subjects, I needed to know if these actors had any outstanding commitments still to be honoured, if they foresaw any problem during rehearsals or during the run of the production, and, when playing certain roles, their assessment of their stamina. Did Albert Finney, as Hamlet, feel certain he could play a matinee followed by an evening performance? Albert gave this some thought and then said that, since it was to be an uncut version, he ought to say he was sorry, but one performance a day would probably be as much as he should risk.

I wasn't sure what entry number two would entail. Peter Hall, having taken over officially from Sir Laurence on November 1, 1973, had given me plans to work on during the six months when the two directors were working in tandem, though this appeared to mean not much more than that each had an office in the huts. I could only presume that at this meeting Peter wished to check on my progress. So, before I walked over Waterloo Bridge on my way to the Donmar rehearsal room, I collected a few *aides-memoire* that might be useful at our meeting.

Reaching Earlham Street and the entrance to Donmar, I climbed the long, single flight of stairs, remembering as I did that the name Donmar was a conjunction of three letters taken from the first names of Donald Albery, the very successful West End impresario, and Dame Margot Fonteyn, the glorious prima ballerina of the Royal Ballet, both of whom I knew and both of whom I admired enormously.

I reached the door of the rehearsal room and waited there until I could hear that there was no actual rehearsing taking place and therefore I should be able to slip in unnoticed. I had so often waited in this same place in the days when I was the London manager of the Royal Shakespeare Company at the Aldwych Theatre and the Donmar was one of the company's rehearsal rooms. At last the moment came, and I crept in and watched the last few moments of the morning rehearsal of *The Tempest*.

Another few minutes and the rehearsal ended, and after a while Peter came over to me and said, "That's been a good morning, so now let's go to lunch." I hadn't realised that the meeting would include lunch, but this was fine and I imagined we would be going to a pub or a nearby snack bar. But no, for we turned left out of the Donmar, crossed Neal Street, and went into Neal's, an extremely popular and chic restaurant. This wasn't the only surprise, for when we had ordered our simple dishes, Peter said that he was having to make changes in the managerial personnel of the company and he wanted me to be in charge of all the departments that dealt directly with the acting company. He then listed casting, touring, literary, and music and the general administration of the company itself, as well as continuing with planning and scheduling.

Since I had been intimately concerned with all these areas during Sir Laurence's reign, I was exceedingly pleased at this appointment. It not only meant that I could continue what I had been doing, but I would be allowed to appoint managers for any department that was currently without, if I considered such an appointment would be beneficial. It certainly would be beneficial to myself for it would mean I would have more time for all the additional work — and doubtless additional problems — that would come with the move from the Old Vic Theatre into the new National Theatre. Peter went on to say that he wanted me to maintain my contacts with both the Arts Council for Regional Touring and the British Council for Overseas Touring.

We finally talked about a title, which cheered me a lot for this would give me the chance to cast off the one I had had for many years of executive company manager. I disliked the word *manager*. I said that I would like to be an administrator, a title I used when I worked all too briefly with Tom Fleming, who was the director of the Royal Lyceum Theatre in Edinburgh. So we agreed on company administrator, which suited me very well.

I have never fully understood how big businessmen conclude mammoth deals over a meal when the participants number two. It is very difficult to chip in with a pertinent point when one has just taken a mouthful. Sometimes even the smallest bite can catch one out. Wanting to ensure that one can eat a reasonable amount, the moment comes at last when one asks a question that would seem to require an answer of a reasonable length. One's fork is loaded with a little more than has been possible so far, the question is asked, and the mouthful is taken. At this moment, one's guest (or host, it works either way) enquires, "What did you say?"

This didn't happen during the lunch with Peter, which progressed seamlessly, with one talking while the other had a mouthful. Knife-edge, though, at times. Peter finished our talk by saying what he had said to me when he appointed me the London manager at the Aldwych in 1963. "I shall leave you alone to get on at once with what we have been discussing, but of course come and see me if there is anything where you think I could offer advice or help. If I don't like what you're doing, I will let you know."

By the end of that day, my engagements diary showed ticks against numbers one and two, but a cross for number three. Entry number one had presented no problems. The initials B.P. mentioned in entry number three were my shortened form of "booking period." Each year was divided into five or six booking periods, which were sent out far and wide to the mailing list in the form of leaflets. These would contain information about performances, casting, booking procedures, and suchlike information, which would also be of interest to Jack Phipps, who was head of touring at the Arts Council. All U.K. touring was arranged after close consultation with Jack. I had to let him know as far ahead as I could what weeks I had marked for possible touring as well as what productions would be available to go out to the regions at those times. The B.P.s I would be sending him would not be printed in leaflet form, for they showed only performances covering, in this instance, April to December 1974, and these would be taken from the detailed day-to-day schedules, showing rehearsals and performances in the Old Vic that I had to prepare usually up to eighteen months ahead.

## Scene 2 ⊄ Another glance at the engagement diary

As I was wandering through my engagement diary for January 1974, I stopped at Monday, January 14. The entries on that day seemed to show a good example of the varied subjects that were dealt with by myself as the newly appointed company administrator. In brackets, I have added my comments and explanations (where possible) on what I put down all those years ago.

1. Speak to Cyril Cusack re his old Mrs. Wilkinson. [What can this mean?]
2. Phone Gerald Welch [agent] re Harry Waters [actor] & the Horses [*Equus*]
3. Do Calendar for B.P. 1. [First booking period: This would be for April 1 to June 8, 1974.]
4. Write confirmation to Peter Campbell [agent] re Arthur

Lowe [actor]: also OK for May 10, 11, and 13? [Arthur's agent had enquired whether he could be released on those dates in order to undertake outside work.]

5. Ask Tessa [my secretary] about releases. [This must refer to actors other than Arthur.]
6. Staff Director for *Eden End* — who is understudying in this play?
7. Check with Paddy Donnell [administrative director] on touring dates.
8. Check with Douglas Cornelissen [general stage manager] effects of 1st Jan '75 Bank Holiday on South Bank working.
9. Note changes made in B.P. 1 after checking with Peter Campbell re Arthur Lowe [as noted in number four above].
10. Check opening of *Happy Days* with Jules Boardman [marketing].

All these entries had ticks put beside them except for number seven, which was not urgent.

Continuing to look at entries for the remainder of that week, my eye was caught by Sunday, January 20. There was a short list, all ticked, that would seem to be notes for a phone call to Peter Hall for, opposite number three, I have put what must have been his reaction.

1. Recasting of *Heartbreak House* [to be directed by John Schlesinger].
2. Ending of contracts for those not in H.H. [*Heartbreak House*].
3. Does he need Stage Management for the prelim *Happy Days* rehearsal? No.
4. J. Dexter [John Dexter] available to direct *King Lear* in '75.
5. *Happy Days* cannot tour unless separate Stage Management.
6. *Happy Days* and K1. [K. Stream's first production] to be linked. [Since each play would have its own actors and

stage management team, *Happy Days* could play in the Lyttelton at the same time as K1 was playing in the Olivier.]

At the time these entries were written, it was understood that the National Theatre would have moved from the Old Vic into the new theatre in February 1975, with both the Lyttelton and the Olivier Theatres open to the public.

## Scene 3 ❧ Completion dates for the new theatre and forward planning

From early in 1973, Peter Hall was not idle on behalf of the National Theatre and it appeared that one of his early moves was to appoint a group of associate directors. The group's first meeting was on March 8, 1973, and present were Michael Blakemore, Jonathan Miller, Sir Laurence, Harold Pinter, and John Schlesinger. But he also had to check out the personnel and how the company was run to ensure that it was functioning in a way that would suit him when he took over total control as director in November. This held sway for some months, but by the end of December 1972, we were told to look to spring of 1975 as being the area we should be considering. It was not difficult for me to choose Wednesday, April 23, 1975, as being an appropriate day and date for the opening of the Olivier and the Lyttelton Theatres. A midweek day, on which one could celebrate Shakespeare's four hundred and eleventh birthday, St. George's Day, and the National Theatre officially opening its doors, seemed to have a good ring about it.

Peter called me in one day so that he could explain what he wanted for the company. He was sure he could attract major actors who would be willing to stay with the National Theatre for three years if it were possible, within that time, for them to be given a break. This could be used for appearing in the West End or making a film or working in television. Peter knew that Sir Laurence had started a three-year contract scheme some years previously, but this carried no automatic time-off period. The chosen few of his players to whom Sir offered such contracts were those who were being carefully cast in roles that would stretch them and make their performances increasingly stronger and assured. It could also have the added benefit that maybe they would not want, or even consider, a break within the three years, other than the usual summer holidays, because of the chance to play good roles.

Whenever Peter and I talked of an actor who would accept his three-year concept, I always thought of Diana Rigg. She was a member of the company at Stratford-upon-Avon when I went there as manager and licensee in 1960, and soon she was playing leading roles there. By 1972, when she joined the National Theatre to play Dottie in Tom Stoppard's *Jumpers*, she had starred in major movies and on television. I felt that if she were offered the chance of having six months away from the company during a three-year contract, and her agent knew a long way ahead, he would have no difficulty in finding roles for her in the theatre or another medium.

But Peter and I also hoped that these breaks would put a considerable amount of money in the pockets of all those who were given them. National Theatre salaries could not compare with what could be earned in films, television, and the West End. It was this problem of the time off that I knew I had to solve if the scheme could be adopted. Fine for my model, Diana Rigg, and other actors in the upper bracket to be offered work during the time off, but what about the lesser known actors? I hoped they would be proud and happy to be appearing at the National Theatre but to be told, "That's it. You've reached your break. Off you go and see you back at the end of six months." This was not going to be greeted with cheers.

At home we had a reasonably long dining-room table, so, since the producing of a plan was needed as soon as possible, my weekends were spent at the table on which was a large roll of graph paper. Before putting details on this paper, I ruled a column in the centre of the paper down which I entered every day and date from January 2, 1974 to the end of 1976. I then circled the Mondays: many of these would indicate public holidays, Easters, and Christmases. I would try not to schedule previews on those dates because of possible overtime.

Alongside the dates, I introduced more columns: one was for first nights and another, wider, in which to register which productions in the Olivier Theatre could play on the same nights as those in the Lyttelton. Finally, I gave each of these South Bank theatres four separate columns headed with the letters A, B, C, and D. These were for the four companies or streams, as Peter termed them, that I reckoned should provide sufficient productions for the initial months in the two theatres. It wasn't long before I found that a three-year span seemed to split comfortably into eight months on, six months off, eight on, six off, and a final eight on. During this time, the streams would each have plays one and two in the first eight months. When they returned, after their first six-month break, they would pick up play two to which would be added play three. These two plays would take them through to the end of their second eight-month stretch. When returning for their final eight months, they would return with play three and add play four. I didn't want to complicate matters at the start, but I had in mind that plays one and two could always return during the three-year span if either or both had been immensely popular.

By now, I had cut a long strip for each stream with the strips marked with the eight-on/six-off system. Then, holding A stream firm, I moved the other strips up and down until I could see not only a pattern but a way of solving the problem of those actors who wouldn't want time off. I felt I should be leaping out of the bath crying, "Eureka!"

If I started each new stream four weeks after the previous stream, at the end of eight months, I discovered it would be possible for an A stream actor, who didn't want a break, to hop streams. Not to slip sideways to join B stream but to hop over B and land on C, where rehearsals would just be starting for play C1. As C stream reached the end of its first eight months, so A stream was reassembling, which would enable the actor to rejoin. In the same way, B stream actors could hop across to join in rehearsals for D1, and so on.

When I started working out how to bring the three-year plan into being, I knew I had another hurdle to o'erleap. I was certain the scheme would work once we were in the two theatres on the South Bank, but during the course of 1974 and for a couple of months into 1975, I had to arrange for a buildup of productions. These must be shows that could not only play a reasonable number of performances at the Old Vic but could move over to the South Bank where they must instantly provide a good-sized repertoire in both the Olivier and the Lyttelton.

Back to the graph paper to work out how many productions we could open at the Old Vic and how many performances each would have given by the time of the move. It appeared that if I had four streams, and if both had two productions, those would be enough to allow each South Bank theatre to open with four plays. It was also obvious that all the 1974 productions would have to play for quite short spells at the Old Vic before being mothballed while new productions took over the single stage. And so it would continue throughout 1974 until the time came to recall the mothballed streams, give them short re-rehearsal periods and so be ready for two months of dress rehearsals and previews on the South Bank from February 1975. All this preparation culminating in the gala opening on April 23.

Peter, who was brilliant at understanding at amazing speed any papers I placed before him — whether plans, schedules, letters, memos, or whatever — quickly approved the outline of the three-year plan. I started at the beginning of 1974 and with my list of projected productions to hand, I entered the various plays under their code letter and number. When they were filled in, I was able to add the title of the plays to be set alongside the codes. Thus A1, A stream's first play and Peter Hall's first production for the National Theatre, had *The Tempest* placed beside it. Sir John Gielgud would be playing Prospero, and rehearsals would start at the beginning of January 1974. It would open in the Old Vic Theatre on March 5 and finish its run, in the 1974 special cut-down scheme, four months later on June 29.

A2 was J. B. Priestley's *Eden End,* directed by Sir Laurence. A1 should have been raided to provide at least some of A2's cast, but in the end, it became a one-off. This wasn't quite how the scheme was meant to work, but never mind, Sir was very keen to direct this play. It offered a good role, Stella Kirby, for Joan Plowright to follow her excellent and endearing Rosa in de Filippo's *Saturday Sunday Monday,* and the National Theatre had not yet presented any plays by J. B. Priestley. He was a prolific and successful dramatist who was also involved with theatre management during the 1930s, when *Eden End* was written. It would open at the Old Vic on April 4 and close after its allotted four-month run on August 1.

A3 was to be Bill Bryden's production of *Spring Awakening* by Wedekind. I have allied him with Ibsen and Strindberg so that he has a surname only, rather than calling him Frank Wedekind. This would start rehearsals on April 10, opening at the Vic on May 28, closing on October 5. These dates would have given A stream a nine-month run.

B stream's B1 would be John Hopkins's *Next of Kin*, directed by Harold Pinter. This would open at the Old Vic on May 2, closing on August 27, followed by B2, Jonathan Miller's production of *The Marriage of Figaro*, with the Beaumarchais text translated by John Wells. This would open on July 9, and I planned for it to stay in the rep until the beginning of December when it would be prepared for the South Bank. B3 was scheduled to be *The Diderot Readings*. This production would join the repertoire on July 24, closing on November 2. It was not scheduled for the South Bank.

C1 would start on September 10 and close on December 3. This would be a production of George Bernard Shaw's *Heartbreak House*, directed by John Schlesinger. C2, *The Jew of Mulhouse*, would open on November 10 and close on December 12 in readiness for the move. So to D stream, the last of these early streams, with D1 being Sir George Etherege's *She Would If She Could* opening on October 15 and closing at Christmas. Finally, D2 would be Ibsen's *John Gabriel Borkman* opening on December 12 and, after as many previews as possible, closing seven days later when it would be prepared for its appearance on the South Bank in the middle of February 1975.

Putting these together, it looked as if the two theatres would each have a strong repertoire:

LYTTELTON THEATRE
*She Would If She Could*
*The Jew of Mulhouse*
*Next of Kin*
*Spring Awakening*
*Eden End*

OLIVIER THEATRE
*The Tempest*
*The Marriage of Figaro*
*John Gabriel Borkman*
*Heartbreak House*

## Scene 4 ❦ The National Theatre's official opening date of April 23, 1975 confirmed

In March 1974, with the buildup of the four streams going ahead well, we learned that there would be a three-month handover of the building from September to November that year. This would be followed by a four-month period (December 1974 to March 1975) when the electrics could be checking out the new equipment and getting used to handling it. We would be able to have our dress rehearsals and previews as planned, and all seemed set fair. So confident was Peter that in May 1974 he announced to the press that the opening date would be April 23, 1975.

This proved to be a splendid occasion with the press invited to board a launch at Chelsea Pier from where we sailed down the Thames until our boat moored in the middle of the river opposite the National Theatre. There Peter Hall addressed his fellow passengers, telling them of the productions that would be lined up ready for the move into the magnificent concrete building that we faced across the Thames, finally giving them the opening date.

## Scene 5 ℰ The building of the National Theatre

In the mid-sixties, Denys Lasdun was chosen as the architect of the National Theatre to be built on the South Bank of the River Thames on the downstream side of Waterloo Bridge. In the early years of the 1970s I could look down from Waterloo Bridge onto what would be the lowest level, and this gave a good idea of how large the building would be. Considering that 1973 was to be the completion year, I was always surprised at how slowly the work was going. It was obviously a difficult job, for unlike, say, a hotel, where there are few curves and, once the bedroom levels are reached, the majority of the rooms are identical, a theatre building must have odd shapes and a huge open space for the stage and auditorium. In this instance, there were to be three such open spaces.

When at last the exterior was complete, I found it hard to cheer. It had to be built in concrete so that it matched the other arts buildings on this curve of the South Bank, but it seemed a pity that it was not possible, especially since Waterloo Bridge divided the new building from its nearest neighbours — the Queen Elizabeth Hall and the Purcell Room — for there to be some warm brick to take the curse off the seemingly endless grey.

It was some years before I was told there would be some bricks used in the building but sadly, when at last they were being laid, they looked pale grey, although I was assured they were technically white. They formed the wall that faces west towards Waterloo Bridge. On the inner side of this wall there would be the Lyttelton's scene dock and its large stage-left wing space. White bricks did not please me.

I was also told that a very special bricklayer had been called in to build this wall, and as he worked, it certainly looked as if he was doing a splendid job. There was a snag with the engagement of this man, however, for when he was called away for some reason, it seemed there was no one who could carry on the work. Given the slow rate of building on the site, the situation of the irreplaceable white-wall bricklayer must be repeated in many other areas of the building work, I reckoned.

The wide embankment between the front of the theatre and the river was extended, so that, having come from under Waterloo Bridge, it then passed the whole of the theatre's frontage before curving round to join the natural riverbank. When railings were put up on that curve, it was possible to lean on them and gaze downriver at the dome of St. Paul's Cathedral and the buildings and church spires in the City of London. To follow the style of the embankment, plane trees were planted in front of the theatre, which proved to be no dig a hole, pour in a lot of water, put the tree in, fill up the hole, and on to the next. Each tree had a very large and deep hole dug for it that was then lined on all four sides with white bricks. They were not laid to form a square of solid walls but were honeycombed. Maybe because it was so unexpected, I found these white honeycomb walls extremely attractive, and I was sorry when quite mature trees were lowered into the caverns that were then filled with earth.

I realised that these trees would somewhat obstruct a full view of the river and the magnificent Somerset House that lies directly across the water on the North Bank, but as the building rose, so, to my surprise, its river frontage proved to be not as I had imagined it. I had thought one would be standing in a foyer gazing out through acres of glass at the river. But what I wasn't told was that the foyer was below the level of the embankment so, although one could see the superstructure of some of the ships sailing past when the tide was high, one could never see the actual river.

At least those members of the public in the Lyttelton Foyer could look at it if they went up one floor, I reckoned, for there was a long space on the river side of the circle foyer that would become windows.

Once again I was disappointed. The South Bank was connected to Waterloo Station by an overhead concrete walkway that was now extended to reach the National Theatre. If only this walkway could have finished at that point, but, having come this far, it was not going to let go. It clung to the side of the National Theatre, eventually passing in front of the circle windows. Of course it had to have a balustrade, but it was a pity it had to be made of concrete. Result: no view.

It was soon possible to work out the geography of the Lyttelton. If one walked along the road that was at the back of the building, there was a huge hole in the wall and one could see over the stage of the Lyttelton right through to the back of the auditorium. We were told that this hole would eventually become the dock doors. These would open onto a road within the building that would connect with the Lyttelton and the Cottesloe theatres as well as the property shop, the paint frame, the carpenters' workshop, and the armoury. The Olivier also could be reached from this road, but, being forty-five feet above, scenery, props, and so on would be taken up to the Olivier by capacious lifts.

## Scene 6 ◎ *Tribute to the Lady,* Monday, May 6, 1974

Monday, May 6, was the one hundredth anniversary of the birth of Lilian Baylis, the remarkable lady whose work in presenting Shakespeare at the Old Vic, especially during the 1930s, laid the foundation for a National Theatre. To celebrate the centenary, the governors of the Royal Victoria Hall (one of the many names given to the Old Vic Theatre in its time) commissioned a gala evening entitled *Tribute to the Lady.*

Many who appeared in the gala had worked for Lilian Baylis and one of these was Dame Peggy Ashcroft who played Miss Baylis during the first part of the gala performance. I had never met or seen Miss Baylis in person, but the character that Dame Peggy portrayed was so absolute and so assured that, although I had worked on several productions in which Dame Peggy played the leading role, her Lilian Baylis was totally another person with not a hint of Peggy Ashcroft. It was quite remarkable and quite wonderful.

Episodes taken from Lilian Baylis's days at the Old Vic made up many of the scenes. Perhaps the one I enjoyed the most, even though I knew the tag line as I'm sure did most of the audience, was of the day she was bicycling between her two theatres, the Old Vic (for drama) and Sadler's Wells (for opera), when she was knocked off her machine. Passers-by stopped to give assistance to this unknown woman lying on the pavement, when a man in the crowd exclaimed, "I know her! That's Miss Baylis of the Old Vic!" At once she sat bolt upright and said very firmly, "*And* Sadler's Wells!"

Sir Laurence acted as narrator and the remainder of the distinguished cast comprised Anna Carteret, Sir John Clements, Gawn Grainger, Barbara Jefford, Robert Lang, Barbara Leigh-Hunt, Paul Scofield, and Nigel Stock. Except for the two Barbara's, we saw all the others in "Special Appearances," when onto the historic stage came Sir John Gielgud and Marius Goring and a quartet of supreme artists: Dame Ninette de Valois, Dame Edith Evans, Dame Flora Robson, and Dame Sybil Thorndike. Did they form a distaff of Dames?

I do hope Miss Baylis was watching. It was an evening to cherish, and she would have been proud to see to what heights in the profession many of her young acting company had achieved and to hear on one night on her stage Sir John's "O what a rogue and peasant slave . . . ," Sir Ralph Richardson's "Be not aferd; the isle is full of noises . . . ," and Sir Laurence's Saint Crispian's Day speech from *Henry V.* The evening was pure pleasure.

## Scene 7 ⟡ Activity and inactivity in 1974

We were all sure that Peter Hall's announcement to the press on the launch that the opening date would be April 23, 1975 prompted the contractors to agree, in July 1974, to this date. At the same time, I don't think any of us were really fooled by the contractors' optimism. Those of us who were able to visit the new building usually came back as concerned as everyone had been for a very long time. "I swear there were only two men and a dog on the site this afternoon — and the dog was asleep," was typical of site inspection reactions. Although the July pronouncement about the April 1975 date should have been reassuring, the building didn't look as if it could possibly be ready by then.

It was at a meeting on the last day of September 1974 that the many contractors concerned with the National Theatre, when pressed by Peter Hall for reports as to progress, began, one by one, to admit that there would be a delay. When pressed further, he was told that there was no possibility of the theatre being ready in 1975, but they were absolutely certain about spring 1976. Peter did not delay giving the news to the press that we would definitely open on the South Bank in March 1976. This was a calculated move to make the contractors realise that the company was not going to accept any longer the continual moving ahead of the opening date.

Nor did Peter delay in explaining the situation to the company. Many would continue within their streams up until the end of their first eight months, but there would not be a return after their six-month break as they, and we, had expected. The four-stream scheme would stand until *The Marriage of Figaro*, after which there would be a change from the original plan.

The change started with A stream, who presented *Romeo and Juliet* directed by Bill Bryden: this was a Mobile production although, as with Peter James's Mobile production of *Twelfth Night* at the beginning of 1974, a few performances were given at the Old Vic. The same opportunity to appear, even briefly, on the stage of the Vic was also given to Jonathan Miller's excellent Mobile production of *Measure for Measure*. By the end of 1974, in addition to the touring by the Mobile companies, eight productions had gone out from the Old Vic appearing in forty-three regional centres.

There were two more major productions before the end of 1974 and one more Mobile. At the Old Vic, Jonathan Miller directed Peter Nichols's *The Freeway* opening at the beginning of October, which was followed by A. E. Ellis's *Grand Manoeuvres* directed by Michael Blakemore. Sadly, neither drew the public, which was a great pity for both had so much to offer. The Mobile was David Hare's production of *The Party*, which was completely and successfully recast. From the middle of November until early in December, it visited eleven towns, usually playing two performances in each.

In spite of all that was happening in the offices in Aquinas Street and the changing of plans for the work at the Old Vic, National Theatre productions were not confined to that theatre. Besides the Mobiles, a recast production (mostly with actors who had been with the National Theatre or who were reaching the end of current National Theatre contracts) of *The Front Page* went out to Australia, while *The Tempest* toured in the United Kingdom. This latter production played at the Hippodrome in Bristol in mid-June 1974, where it was seen by 13,110 patrons: This meant a box office average of 82 percent for the eight-performance week. This average was brought down by a weak Saturday matinee of only 47 percent (an audience of 941), doubtless due to the absence of schools, which had helped produce a box office of 69 percent for the midweek matinee. The Tuesday evening's performance had been packed with an audience of 1959 and a box office of 98 percent.

Other productions that went on tour in the United Kingdom that year were *Eden End, Next of Kin, Spring Awakening,* and *The Marriage of Figaro. Eden End* did extremely well in Richmond but not so hot in Leeds, Cardiff, or Wolverhampton, but it had a smashing final week in Brighton. Neither *Next of Kin* nor *The Marriage of Figaro* was much appreciated in the regions, but *Spring Awakening* was a sensation at the New Theatre, Oxford. With the box office registering 100 percent for four of the performances and 99 percent for another, it produced a week's box office of 91 percent in spite of the weak Saturday matinee. Nottingham was even better with 98 percent for the week, doubtless reached because the Saturday matinee was 89 percent.

*Spring Awakening* was the first production for which the cast list, production credits, biographies, and suchlike information was printed as part of the Old Vic's programme. Up until this time, with financial restraints in mind, a considerable number of programmes — greatly admired — could confidently be printed for they contained nothing that would change during the run of a play. Cast lists were printed on a single piece of paper, for which there was no charge, and which were available in specially made boxes at every door into the auditorium. This system meant that any change of cast or other detail could be dealt with simply and speedily by reprinting these cheap cast lists with the new information.

## Scene 8 ❦ Sir Ralph Richardson

So 1975 was going to be another year of a one-theatre operation. New productions would be needed, and all of them would be putting themselves up for inclusion in the initial repertoire on the South Bank in 1976. The first of these, at the Old Vic Theatre, with previews starting on January 21, 1975, was Peter Hall's production of Ibsen's *John Gabriel Borkman* with Sir Ralph Richardson playing Borkman. I was so pleased to meet up with him again: I had first met him over twenty years previously when he was playing the leading role in R. C. Sherriff's *The White Carnation*. As the stage manager for that production, I was always down on the stage during the half, and whether we were at the Globe Theatre in Shaftesbury Avenue, or on lengthy tours both before and after our West End showing, Sir Ralph invariably came onto the stage before he went to his dressing room to prepare for a performance.

Often the first intimation I had that he was there was the cheery greeting, "Good evening, old fella." There he would be, slowly wandering about the stage before he made his way down to the front to gaze out at the auditorium, making little noises as if he were testing that he actually had a voice that evening and that it was working well. Sometimes he would enquire as to the size of the house for the evening's performance or ask if I knew why the audience at the previous night's show had reacted in a certain scene as they had done. Round the set he would wander, and then with a little wave, he was gone.

This reminding himself of the setting made me recall his performance as The Waiter in *You Never Can Tell*, which we saw at the Theatre Royal, Haymarket. In one scene, he was standing a little apart from a group that was seated down right. He was taking instructions from one of the group, and when that was given, he slowly withdrew from his position and very gradually backed towards a door in the wall stage left. As he reached the door, still not looking round, he put one hand behind him, and it exactly met the door handle. Although nothing was said about this, one knew that this old servant had been in that hotel for a very long time.

Offstage, Sir Ralph's head would often nod, almost imperceptibly. Once when Sir Laurence and I were chatting over an evening meal he mentioned this and asked if I had noticed. "I am sure that started during the war when we were both at Worthy Down in Hampshire," Sir said. "We used to ride motorcycles, always without helmets, and one day when Ralph was ahead of me, he skidded. He was thrown off his bike and slid across the road, only stopping when his head hit the kerb. He soon recovered from the shock and the crack on his head, but it seemed to me that those little nods started then."

During the rehearsals for *John Gabriel Borkman*, Sir Ralph had occasion to write to me when I was away from London with a touring production. Towards the end of the letter he mentioned that he was busy with rehearsals, adding that he had the John and he had the Borkman, but he was having a little difficulty finding the Gabriel. His letters were always brief and to the point and they were always written as if they were poems. He set the text in a block in the centre of the page, no matter the size of the writing paper, with the length of each line being almost exactly the same as the one above. On October 12, 1977, he wrote with a request, but he started the letter:

Dear Michael,
How are you?
I often think of
you.
You do remember
me — don't you?
I once played Borkman or
Hawkman or
Corkman, or
something like
that, with you in
kind management
of that affair,

In the next part of the letter he made his request before he closed it with:

I remain very sincerely
Yours,
Ralph Corkman

A year previously, on October 9, 1976, he had written to me from

Toronto where he was with Harold Pinter's wonderful play *No Man's Land* on its way to Broadway.

How are you?
I hope you are well?
The last I saw of you
was a flutter and a
flick at Heathrow
when we were off:
but I have been
thinking of you
and now when packing
up the traps to go from
here to Washington
remember how kind
and thoughtful you
have been to smooth
all our passage
and keep one's home. Are we all successful?
You have a great
Tamburlaine to put on
your time tables as
one gathers here in
Toronto — we are
pegging away — trying
so hard to get better
not knowing quite where
to dip the pan for a
grain of gold but
sometimes finding a
grain unexpectedly.

All affectionate
good wishes to you,
EVER,
TORONTO
Ralph

One of his last letters was written on June 27, 1983, when I was on tour but he knew when I was scheduled to return:

Hurry
up middle of
JULY — the place
has gone to
POT without you.

EVER
with LOVE
to you and
Elizabeth,
Ralph

Below this was his drawing of what looks like a cup with the letter *a* taking the place of a handle. The cup is on a saucer beside which is written A POT.

For *The White Carnation,* I was on the book for rehearsals, and I was most impressed that he came to the first rehearsal knowing his part. Although he had written out his lines in longhand, he never referred to them, and I very quickly learned that if he appeared to dry during a rehearsal, it was not that he had forgotten them but he was working something out. It was usually a comment about a move or the way a speech had been approached that could affect himself or another actor. After a silence, while everyone waited, he would put a suggestion to Noel Willman, the director. Very seldom was the suggestion challenged.

In one scene, he was seated at a table facing about half a dozen town hall officials. As each put his case, the actors changed places so that the scene was not totally static. On one occasion I was busy noting in the prompt script in which positions the actors were standing, when there was a silence. I had no idea where they had got to, so I said nothing, and sure enough a moment later, Sir Ralph looked at one of the actors facing him and asked, "Shouldn't you be over there by now, old fella?" "Oh, yes, Sir Ralph," stammered the veteran actor, "I'm sorry. Yes, yes. That's quite right. We changed it so often yesterday . . ." His speech trailed off as he realised he was compounding his felony.

As soon as he had scurried to his correct position, the rehearsal went on. I didn't need to check the move for I knew that Sir Ralph would have been right.

In his dressing room, he was a voracious reader, and usually he was ready to go onstage long before his call. This gave him time to sit in the armchair by the window and pick up a book from several on the table beside the chair. This was how I nearly always found him when I visited him before a performance. Unless he was making up, he would rise to his feet to greet me, which I found very touching, although I wished he would not use his energy for such an old-world show of manners. I also had to remember that when we shook hands, which was the next part of the ritual, he used the locking-of-thumbs greeting rather than the palm to palm.

## Scene 9 ✒ Dame Peggy Ashcroft

The autumn of 1974 saw another friend of mine join the company. I met Dame Peggy Ashcroft in 1954 at the start of rehearsals for the Tennent Productions presentation of Ibsen's *Hedda Gabler,* when she was to play Hedda and I was the stage manager. During the first week of rehearsals, she called me over and asked if I would go to her home in Hampstead on Saturday afternoon and hear her lines. A royal command indeed. As bidden, I reported to her house in Frognal and was ushered by a maid into the drawing room. Miss Ashcroft, as she was then, was lying back on a chaise longue, from where she greeted me. She indicated a chair, and we started the agonising job of hearing lines.

Though a great actress, she still stumbled over words or forgot lines and then reacted as many actors do when they make mistakes. The trick is to discover whether the person whose lines one is hearing wants to be stopped in full flight because of one word being wrong — a *shall* instead of a *will,* perhaps — or whether to note these small errors and mention them at a suitable break. When I started with the latter ploy, I soon realised I had made a grave mistake. "It's no good my saying these lines if you let me say them incorrectly," she said with great force and a touch of venom, perhaps. Wrong choice with a vengeance, I thought, as I apologised briefly — no wasting time giving explanations — and she began once more.

One might think that all would flow smoothly and sweetly from then on, but it wasn't as easy as that. Whenever I had to pull her up over some small point, even though she was rattling ahead, she would stop dead, glare at me, and sigh deeply before exhaling sharply to denote great displeasure. Then in a tone that indicated not only utter weariness but also clearly signaled that it was entirely my fault she had slipped up—for now she would have to go back and say the whole speech again — she would ask, "Where should I go back to?" She wanted to know where to pick up the speech to give herself a good run-up to the sentence in which she had made the mistake. My suggestion would at once be greeted incredulously with, "All the way back to *there?*" This was followed with another deep sigh before she set off once more. I knew all the time that she was annoyed with herself, but I was an easier target. I also knew that she would never make that mistake again.

In spite of the length of the role of Hedda, once it was secure, she could take any distraction. One such was when we were playing one-night stands in Holland. The theatre at Utrecht was extremely hot during our long day of getting-in, setting-up, and lighting but perhaps the management was compensating for the extreme cold outside. By the time the show was under way, I was very dry but there was nothing I could do about it. So I sat on the book, happy with each turn of the page, for that meant it was nearer the interval when I might, with luck, get some sort of liquid.

There then came that unmistakable sound of cup rattling on saucer, and sure enough, across the acres of wing space came a uniformed staff member. Coffee, I thought, how extremely thoughtful of someone, though, at the same time, I was willing him to stop the wretched china from making so much noise. He came straight towards me, and I was wondering where I could put the cup, when he not only came right up to me but went right on past. He squeezed neatly between the downstage flat and a set of black legs and disappeared from sight. Good grief, I thought, he's on the stage. The scene between Peggy and Rachel Kempson (as Thea) continued without a break, and soon I stopped worrying. As Peggy passed me at the start of the interval, I apologised for the intrusion, but she laughed and said, "Wasn't he sweet? He was obviously a fireman. He went round the proscenium arch and made for a chair that was set at the far end of the curved walkway that led to the stage box. There he settled himself, slowly drank his cup of coffee, and stayed for the rest of the act."

Our tour in Holland was followed by a brief visit to Copenhagen. I was not able to sit in a prompt corner but placed in a conductor's shell — a unique experience. This was cut out of the stage as far downstage centre as was possible. Below me and to my left was the chief electrician who could only carry out a cue, he told me firmly, when it had been given to him verbally. No light signals from the prompt corner for him.

When we started to dress the set, it suddenly hit me how awful my position in the prompter's box would be. The set demanded that a small settee be placed downstage centre with a rug before it so only the width of the rug separated me from those sitting on the settee. Since many scenes were played there, I was going to be within a few feet of the actors and only a fraction below their sight line. I decided that I must keep a very low profile, literally, and keep as still as possible, but there were those light cues to be given to the eager-faced man. I suggested to him that I gave a hand signal, but no, once more, that wasn't how we did it in that theatre. I had to look at him and speak to him. My main concern centred on the scenes between Dame Peggy and Rachel, but neither commented about my turning my head and whispering every now and then nor about my practically being in the scene with them. I was so thankful when we left that lovely city and made our way by train up the west coast of Sweden to Oslo.

There we played in Det Nye Teater (the New Theatre), which was housing a very successful long-running production of *White Horse Inn*, although it had been turned out briefly for our appearance. However, the decoration of the auditorium had not been removed, so the circle fronts, the walls, and the proscenium arch screamed the Tyrol, which was the setting for the musical. It was within this framework that the English version of *Hedda* was presented to the Norwegians in the dramatist's homeland.

On March 18, 1955, during our brief stay there, the company was invited to lunch with the leading members of the Oslo Kommune. This event was to take place in a beautiful restaurant, the Frognerseteren Hoved restaurant, high above and with a fabulous view of the city. We arrived to find a large room had been arranged with one very long table, obviously the high table, with four other tables at right angles to it. With so few of us and so many of them, we were spread among the local actors with Dame Peggy and the leading Norwegian actor sitting in the centre of the high table. At the end of the meal, the actor rose and, having welcomed the company, he offered his congratulations to the British actors. He then said that he had been instructed by the King of Norway to present Dame Peggy with a gold medal in recognition of her showing, in her performance as Hedda, the way that Ibsen should be played.

*Hedda Gabler* had had its first performance at the Lyric Theatre, Hammersmith, West London. This was the original Lyric, not the new version that is several floors above ground level. Much as I always enjoy going to performances in either the new Lyric's main theatre, whose auditorium exactly resembles the old, or the studio, it can never recapture for me the atmosphere that the old theatre enjoyed on street level.

Although the site allocated to the original theatre did not allow its frontage to be best placed, the building itself was in the very heart of Hammersmith. The short street on one side was filled each day by a street market, the many stalls of which backed onto the narrow pavement that ran past the stage door. The market was extremely popular, and on matinee days it was often difficult to reach the stage door. Not only was the pavement crowded with passers-by, but if the show was lucky enough to draw the public, there would be a queue down that pavement, past the stage door, and on to the junction with King Street. This was Hammersmith's main shopping street, and it was also part of the Great West Road that linked Southampton, where transatlantic Cunard liners docked, with London.

The dressing rooms and wardrobe of the Lyric were also on that side of the theatre, so their windows looked down onto the market from where not only the sounds of the general bustle of this lively area of London rose up but also the general market aromas. The street traders would have bought their baskets of produce very early in the morning from Covent Garden Market, still working in the heart of London. In high summer, it was no wonder that the stench of discarded outer cabbage leaves, or perhaps rotted fruit, drifted into the open windows of the Lyric.

One Saturday afternoon was particularly warm and oppressive, with not even a hint of a breeze to dispel the heat and the market smells.

Judging by the queue below the dressing-room windows, the house for the matinee that day was going to be very good. The queue was in the shade, but it was made up of several very hot and grumpy theatregoers. They saw me apparently trying to ease myself neatly into their midst, not realising I was aiming for the stage door, and greeted me with, "Hey, mister, this is a queue, you know."

However uncomfortable those in a building that had never heard of air-conditioning might have been, and in spite of the men in the company having to wear thick suits and the ladies having long skirts as well as being tightly corseted, the performances were as excellent as ever. All went smoothly until towards the end of the play. The scene was the battle of wills between Hedda and Judge Brack, the marvellous character that was played with a compelling blend of mischief and menace by Micheal MacLiammoir. He was standing centre stage with his back to me. I was on the book in the prompt corner on stage right. Downstage left was Dame Peggy sitting in a rocking chair that she used at times, by making it rock gently to and fro, to accentuate the words she was teasingly addressing to Brack.

Shortly after the scene began, I had a curious feeling that all was not well. Dame Peggy's performance seemed the same as ever, but there was something about her that made me send for the stagehand who, amongst other duties, was in charge of the house tabs, or more correctly, the house curtain. He appeared very quickly, and I whispered that I was worried about Dame Peggy, and he was to stand by the tabs and watch for a hand signal from me to lower them.

I couldn't believe that such a move was necessary, but I became increasingly concerned, and at last could stand it no more and I gave the signal. The tabs were brought in swiftly but not ridiculously so, and I raced across to Dame Peg. By the time I reached her, she had fainted. Micheal, greatly worried, sensibly moved upstage out of the way, and Dame Peggy was carried up to her dressing room. A doctor was sent for and, struggling through the market crowds, reached the stage door at last. I had no idea what had happened onstage so as soon as I could I ran down to find our superb company manager, Rupert Marsh, standing alone in the prompt corner. The tabs were still down, and there was silence in the house. "What's happened?" I asked him, adding, "Where's the audience?" "Oh, I decided not to put on the understudy at this late stage in the play," Rupert said with utter calm, "so I went in front of the curtain and told the audience that Dame Peggy had been taken ill and that it would not be possible for the play to continue. So they all left." "Didn't you tell them the end?" I asked. "Didn't you say that she was just about to —" "Oh, no," Rupert cut in. "Poor them," I murmured as we went upstairs for the latest report on our leading lady.

Because she wouldn't be able to play that evening, we arranged for wardrobe to check Hedda's costumes on Ruth Lodge, the understudy, after which we ran a few scenes as a warm-up for her. She gave an excellent and assured performance and received a rapturous reception. At the same time, I was sorry that the audience had not been able to see the highly praised performance for which they had undoubtedly booked tickets. Dame Peggy returned to the cast on the Monday.

By the time Dame Peggy joined the National, she and I had worked together (she the leading actress and myself in a variety of roles such as stage manager or theatre manager) many times. With the production of *Hedda Gabler*, with the Shakespeare Memorial Theatre at Stratford-upon-Avon and on a continental tour, the English Stage Company at the Royal Court Theatre, the Comedy Theatre, and the Royal Shakespeare Company at Stratford-upon-Avon and at the Aldwych. But I never heard her lines again.

Now here she was and here we were poring over schedules to see how her life, once she was in both *John Gabriel Borkman* and *Happy Days*, was going to work out. *Happy Days* was certainly her worry, for Sam Beckett had turned up and attended rehearsals, and she complained gently to me that he was being so pernickety. She was really worried and really put out. She said she could understand an author being concerned that every word should be the ones he had written, but the endless bits of business of which Winnie has so many, all these had to be exact. The way she took items out of her purse, how she placed them around her, the way she replaced them, the angle at which the parasol should be held, all these and many more had to be just as Sam wanted them. Even though Peter Hall was directing this production, he seemed quite content that the author should take over the direction of these bits of business.

At least Dame Peg was very pleased that, having decided to play Winnie with an Irish accent, she got approval for this decision from both Peter and Sam. Up to then she had been sure that Sam would not allow that accent, although she felt it would help her and the character. From what she said later, I felt she was quite sorry she didn't have to fight to get what she wanted.

## Scene 10 ✎ The curtain call for John Gabriel Borkman

John Bury designed a very austere drawing room for the opening of *John Gabriel Borkman* with a change to an exterior for the end of the play. This exterior showed an outside wall of Borkman's house on stage left while centre stage was a hill. Set into this hill on stage right were large steps that disappeared round the back, although one was sure they continued rising because there was a plain wooden bench on the top, and obviously that was where the steps led. The whole of the ground that the audience saw, including the steps, gave the effect of snow, for it was covered in white carpeting. The cold from the interior was repeated, in a different form, for the exterior.

Before the company played the final scene at the dress rehearsal, Peter Hall, as director and co-translator, told the cast that they were to play through the act and then rehearse the curtain call. At the very end of the play, Sir Ralph, as Borkman, lay dying on the bench on top of the hill, with Dame Peggy as Ella beside him. When the last line was spoken, the curtain fell, and Peter waited for it to rise and show him the cast lined up, as arranged, for the curtain call. But the curtain did not rise, and after a while, Peter called out, using that well-known question at times like these, "What's the holdup?" To those backstage, this cry from the darkened stalls can be intensely irritating for it always penetrates the curtain like shards of icicles (suitable in the case of Borkman) and hits the hearers' ears as, "What the hell are you doing backstage? Get it sorted at once." Even though those who hear it would know, if they could think of anything but sorting out, in the least possible time, whatever problem is causing the delay, that the second part of the question, kindly meant but never posed, is, "Is there anything I can do to help?"

There was silence for a moment following the hated question, and then the curtain rose to disclose Sir Ralph gallantly handing Dame Peggy down the steps. When they reached ground level, they hastened to their places in the centre of the six actors who had been awaiting their arrival. They were both obviously rather pleased with the way they had negotiated the descent so speedily, and their faces looked expectantly out into the auditorium, waiting for approval from Peter.

"That won't do at all," he said. Faces fell. "The audience will be on their way home if it takes that long for you to get down the hill," he added, rubbing salt into the wound. Then, because of who they were, he quickly went on, "I realise it is very difficult, but we must find a way to get you all together sooner."

The first idea was for those on ground level to go up the hill and the curtain call to be taken there, but this was immediately ruled out. Dame Wendy Hiller, playing Borkman's wife, Gunhild, would find it as hard to go up the hill as the others had found it coming down. While this suggestion was being considered and then discarded, Dame Peggy and Sir Ralph had been having a private conversation. When there was a pause in the general search for a solution, Sir Ralph said that he and Peggy had had an idea and could they show it to Peter for approval? Sir Ralph added that they would like to go from the very end of the play that would lead once more into the curtain call.

Peter agreed, so the two of them retraced their steps. Sir Ralph dutifully died and the final words were spoken and down came the curtain. About twenty seconds later, the curtain rose, and there was the whole cast, beaming and happy, strung out in the correct line. "How did you do that?" Peter called out with delight. Dame Peggy and Sir R.alph, looking like naughty schoolchildren, said they would show him if this time the curtain did not come down.

Having said this, they went up the hill once more and once more Borkman died, once more the last lines were spoken and the stage manager called out, "Curtain!" At once, Dame Peggy helped Sir Ralph get to his feet, and the pair of them moved to the front of the hill. There they sat down on the white carpet, held hands, and, pushing themselves off, slid down the hill and landed in the middle of the lineup that was hastily assembling. The laughing pair of elderly actors got to their feet and, peering into the auditorium once more, asked, "Will that do, Peter?"

## Scene 11 ❦ The first months of 1975

From the repertoire point of view, 1975 got off to a good start. Because of the delayed South Bank opening, Peter Hall's clear, clean, and incisive production of *John Gabriel Borkman* (although I always thought Dame Peggy's wig looked like a woolly tea cosy) was moved on several weeks so that its opening became January 28. The next production, opening on February 25, was an extremely good production of Bernard Shaw's *Heartbreak House*, directed by John Schlesinger. Captain Shotover was played by the excellent Colin Blakely. Although this character was a man many years older than Colin, I am certain that anyone who did not know him would simply accept that here was an actor of mature years acting his age.

Two weeks later, on Thursday, March 13, *Happy Days* joined the repertoire with Dame Peggy as Winnie and Alan Webb playing the long-suffering Willie. This was followed on April 23 by Peter Hall's third production of the year, Harold Pinter's *No Man's Land*.

When the leaflet for June/July 1975 is opened out, it shows, in a column down the right-hand side, the calendar for those two months followed by news of the cities to be visited by *Heartbreak House* (Norwich, Newcastle-upon-Tyne, and Birmingham). The remainder of the page gives brief details of the five plays that made up the current repertoire. At the very foot of the page is a neat paragraph in small print announcing: All the above productions were scheduled for the new National Theatre and are now staged at the Old Vic because of the South Bank delays.

From April 1, 1975, the cover of the repertory leaflets did not change its layout, but instead of covering the number of weeks that it was felt could safely be announced — around seven or eight — now each leaflet tidily showed the repertoire for two calendar months only. This arrangement continued during the last months at the Old Vic, until the final leaflet for that theatre. Just one month remained: February 1976.

## Scene 12 &#9775; Harold Pinter's *No Man's Land*

For Harold Pinter's *No Man's Land*, Sir John Gielgud returned to the National Theatre. He had agreed to play Spooner, a role that was to show this great actor's versatility once more. Here he created a character whose voice, walk, and appearance — especially the spectacles, the untidy clothes, and the socks and sandals — were totally unfamiliar even to playgoers who had been watching him with admiration playing a huge variety of roles over many years.

Spooner's adversary was Hirst played by Sir Ralph. Another remarkable performance, yet, sadly, many critics and public alike were so amazed at the character created by Sir John that the equally superb playing of Hirst by Sir Ralph was apt to be overlooked. The play was set in a room in Hirst's house with the main piece of furniture, his chair, placed appropriately downstage centre. John Bury designed an intriguing set. In spite of the sweeping curve of large windows, there was, for me, a prisonlike feeling about the room where Hirst did not seem aware of windows. It was almost as if, as he made his way to and from the large table, placed in front of the windows and liberally stocked with bottles, he felt curtains were drawn across them at all times.

As the play progresses, it becomes apparent that Hirst relies on the effects of the contents of the various bottles to help him through the day, although they also make him none too steady on his feet. I noticed that if a move brought him downstage towards his chair, he would put out a hand, and as soon as he was in striking distance, he'd slap it onto the high leather back. It was as if he had thrown the dice and got a six, so he was now home, and he could relax slightly. The chair would keep him upright until he lowered himself into the seat.

Later, I also noticed that Hirst's timing brought the audible slap so that it came a split second before the end of one of Spooner's lines. Whether one had been watching Hirst's slow, mesmerising advance or listening to Spooner prattling on about the early days, one's attention was at once drawn to Hirst. Then it dawned on me that the hand-on-leather slap was not only when he approached the chair, but there were other slaps on its arms, again usually given as he was about to get up. It could be accepted that he was aiding the rise, but again the sound of the slap certainly made one look at him.

Much of the floor was uncarpeted, which meant that if an actor crossing the stage were to put a foot down sharply, this could make a noise. This, too, could be timed to come just before a speech to be given by the actor whose shoes made the sound. Not only was the isle in *The Tempest* full of noises, so was Hirst's room. With Terence Rigby as Briggs and Michael Feast as Foster, both superbly sinister and suave, it was a stunning night in the theatre.

## Scene 13 ⦿ The offices in the new building

On June 23, 1975, I was invited once more to look round the new building. The invitation included a light lunch so instead of partaking of the excellent lunch that Rose produced in the canteen at Aquinas Street, I went over to meet Richard York on-site. After lunch in one of the offices in the southwest corner of the building with a view towards Waterloo Station, Richard took me down long corridors, and we eventually ended up outside a door, which he announced with a flourish, as he depressed the handle, "And this is your office." He fell against it, anticipating he would be proudly sweeping in, but the door did not move. He tried several ploys to get the door to open, and then went to the next door along the corridor and was soon speaking to me from the other side of the uncooperative door. "It's all right," he called, "just a bit of water." I followed where he had gone and found there was a communicating door between the offices, so I was now at last standing in my new home. "You see what has happened," said Richard, "the rain has got in along that line of expansion joint in your ceiling, but it has unfortunately decided to drop down into your office instead of going on a little further to the edge of the building. I must speak to them about this. I am sorry."

The office was about the same size as the totally dry one I had occupied in the Aquinas Street huts for many years. Room for a desk, with my chair behind it — perhaps a little more space here — and a visitor's chair the other side of the desk. There were two practical windows, for there would be no air-conditioning in the offices. Richard explained that each office would have a lockable cupboard, and mine would fit neatly behind the door. On the wall behind the visitor, a magnetised board would be fitted with little magnetised bars with the names of productions in various colours. I would be able to see what productions were playing, when, and where, without having to search through charts. With pleasure, I foresaw that I could amaze visitors with my ready knowledge of the repertoire without needing to check any papers.

This magnetised board was an advance on the four boards that Sir had at the "meetings" end of his office at the huts. Each board showed days and dates for a calendar month. Into the little squares, one a day, Sir would write in details of his and Joan's performances. As days passed, he would cross through the day or days that had gone, so the boards were more or less kept up-to-date. However, he was very cunning at using the crossing-off ceremony to his advantage. If, for any reason, a meeting was becoming difficult or if he had no immediate answer to a question, he would suddenly notice that he had not carried out his crossing-off duty for several days. He would get up, pick up a pen and a huge ruler, and cross the room to where we were sitting at the table, waiting for him to speak. Having reached the table in silence, he would lean over and very slowly and laboriously cross off the past days. The lines would be from bottom left to top right, and having drawn a line, he would step back, artist style, to make sure it was absolutely accurately drawn. Meanwhile, those sitting between him and the board had to lean over to make sure he had a clear run.

When at last he could find no more squares to be crossed through, he would go back to his desk, and as he sat, he would say, "Well, that's about it for today, I think." And the meeting was over.

## Scene 14 ✑ The summer of 1975 at the Old Vic Theatre

The summer of 1975 saw the Old Vic's strong repertoire of *No Man's Land, Happy Days, Heartbreak House* (recently back from a regional tour), and *John Gabriel Borkman*. Rejoining the rep was John Dexter's scintillating production of Molière's *The Misanthrope*. Its company had just returned from a very successful season on Broadway, and its reappearance at the Old Vic once more packed the theatre.

But the National Theatre company was not only busy at the Old

Vic, for July 30 saw the opening of a season of studio performances in the Institute of Contemporary Art in the Mall. Through August and September, seven new plays were presented of which two had follow-up performances. One was *The Man Himself* by Alan Drury, with Michael Feast (recently seen at the Old Vic as Ariel in *The Tempest*) playing the only character. This was presented for three lunchtime performances at the Young Vic Studio in November and December.

The other was *Judgement* by Barry Collins. This also was a one-man show with Colin Blakely (recently seen as a superb Captain Shotover in *Heartbreak House*). Unlike *The Man Himself*, which played for thirty-four minutes, *Judgement* ran for two hours and twenty minutes. Its first public performance was on August 28, 1975. It had been a blazingly hot summer day easing itself into a stifling evening. The house was full, with the audience sitting on unpadded moulded plastic seats — at £1 each. Colin's playing was absolutely remarkable and masterly, although he must have been suffering, as very soon was his audience, from the lack of air-conditioning or any form of ventilation.

So there most of us uncomfortably sat for at least two and a half hours, there being no interval, listening and watching one actor whose props were a chair, a table, and a glass of water. It wasn't as if we were going to be entertained with jokes and humorous stories, for Colin as Captain Vukhov was to tell us of his Second World War experience as one of several Russian soldiers imprisoned and then abandoned, still locked in their prison, by the Germans. The only means of staying alive until their hoped-for release was to resort to cannibalism, one by one.

Peter Hall directed the monologue, which, he commented, needed a different rehearsal technique from normal. "Now that Colin has learnt the play," he said, coming out of a run-through, "I cannot stop him to give him a note or make a suggestion or comment, for he has to drive right through to the end." The breaks during the performance, for both actor and audience, such as Colin taking a drink of water, or a move to illustrate some point or to indicate where another of the soldiers might be standing, were very well placed, timed, and motivated and not once during the evening did I feel fatigued and want to leave. It was riveting and a unique experience.

*Judgement*, too, was given three performances at the Young Vic Studio in November. Ten days later, early in December, the production joined the repertoire at the Old Vic.

## Scene 15 ✆ Sir Peter Daubeny

On September 2, 1975, a memorial service for Peter Daubeny was held in the church in Chester Square, which was only a hundred yards from where he and Molly had lived for many years. As we walked past the house, Elizabeth asked if I remembered the evening we had driven them to their home late one evening. Peter got out of the car and gazed around as if we had dropped him off on a particularly bleak part of the moon, but seeing Molly on the other side of the car, he called across, "Which is our house?" An unusual question perhaps, but she answered it as if it was quite a normal enquiry. "That one," she said, pointing across the road. "Then what are those lights?" was the next question. "That's the top floor," said Molly. "Who lives there?" asked Peter. "Your daughter," said Molly, kindly. Peter clutched the stump of his left arm and hurried over the road to the house he now knew for certain was theirs.

I had no idea in those days who was responsible for putting names forward for honours such as Commander of the British Empire (C.B.E) or knighthoods, but I decided very early on in the first World Theatre Season that if anyone deserved a knighthood for services to the theatre, it was Peter. To first nights during those seasons Peter would invite a member of the royal family and many of influence in the cabinet or the shadow cabinet. As often as I could, especially during intervals, I made sure that these guests knew what Peter had achieved in bringing to London these companies that so enriched the lives of theatregoers. Whether these prompts helped or not I cannot tell, but at last Peter was knighted.

The service for him was very moving, with many fine tributes. Perhaps the most unexpected part of the occasion was when, from the gallery high at the back of the church, a Zulu choir sang. They were one of the many companies whose visits to London Peter had engineered, and the sound they made was quite beautiful.

## Scene 16 ◈ The move to the National Theatre, September 1975

On Friday, September, 26, 1975, I walked out of Aquinas Street for the last time, and soon I was going in through the stage door of the National Theatre. Richard York had meticulously planned the transfer of personnel and equipment, and when I arrived at my open office door, the filing cabinet from my Aquinas Street office was being taken into my secretary's office next door.

I was pleased to notice that my door opened and shut with ease, there was no sign of damp, the carpet had dried out, and the desk, chairs, cupboard, and wallboard were all in place. I arranged to have my desk placed with one end hard up against the window ledge so that I could have a most wonderful view of the Thames and its northern bank, from Temple Gardens along the Embankment to Blackfriars Bridge. Standing magnificently between the three high-rise buildings in the City of London, in one of which Peter Hall had a penthouse, was the imposing dome of St. Paul's Cathedral. One of its towers on the West Side had a clock that proved very useful when I needed a quick time check.

Unlike Aquinas Street, where I looked out on the car parking area, and, interesting though it was during a telephone conversation to see who arrived and in what kind of car, it was not the greatest view. Now I would not see or hear any vehicles, for not only would I be two floors above them, but outside my windows was a reasonably wide terrace that would baffle any sound and preclude any sight. The only moving objects I would see were cars and trucks beyond the barges, tugs, pleasure boats, and other users of the great waterway. The pleasure boats all had commentators in the summer months, who, with the use of loudspeakers, told their captive audiences about the buildings and other items of interest as they journeyed leisurely up or down river. It was usually quite possible to hear the entire commentary as these boats passed by. Very shortly after we had taken possession of the theatre, one guide's booming voice came clearly across the water as he said, "On the right is the new National Theatre. This has just been voted by four hundred architects to be the ugliest building in London."

## Scene 17 ❧ Reactions to the move to the National Theatre's new home

I suppose I should have felt excited about being installed in the new building at last, but it was hard to have any real feeling since it was still in such an unfinished state. The only emotion I felt was of sorrow at leaving the Vic and, to an extent, even a slight regret at leaving our offices in the huts. It was, of course, impossible to judge like for like: the old buildings had character, they felt alive, and it was only too easy to believe that the venerable theatre cared what was put on its stage.

I would certainly miss my seemingly endless visits to the Old Vic to watch dress rehearsals, some of a production's previews, and finally the press nights of which there had been seventy since I joined. In addition, I also watched dress rehearsals and first performances at a change of cast or when an understudy was playing for a principal.

There would plainly not be any radiator covers in the Lyttelton on which I could perch to watch the plays as there had been at the Vic, but I found a director's box directly behind the back row of the stalls, and I soon learned that there would be a similar box in the Olivier, whenever that theatre was opened. But I decided that those boxes were certainly not for me, especially if the director of a production was in occupation, and soon I didn't even bother to consider that room when I went in to check on a performance.

When the Lyttelton first opened, I sometimes chose to stand at the back of the stalls, but that space was rather open. It was also rather tricky to enter the auditorium silently for the hermetically sealed doors refused to open without making a very audible sibilant sound. So I took to standing at the back of the circle where my entrances and exits were not so noticeable — especially when the doors had been cured of the all-too-audible hiss as they were wrenched apart.

Certainly a plus for the new building was the advantage of being able to consult the technical departments without having to make the eight-minute walk from Aquinas Street down to the annexe where the workshops, making wardrobe, and paint frame were situated. Although I would use the phone for many of my questions, usually it was much more productive to go down and speak directly to those in charge of the various departments that were concerned with putting the many productions onto the stage. Now in the new building they were only a few long corridors away. At last I was saved those walks, which always made me wonder under which conditions they were the worst: usually the hot, humid, and brilliantly sunny days won the prize for giving me the most uncomfortable journeys. It was impossible to find shade on the stretch along Stamford Street, but, on further consideration, trudging through snow came a very close second — especially when passing cars sent sprays of slush across the pavements.

Certainly heat, now I think of it, was again going to be something that we would very happily leave behind, for many areas in the new building would be air conditioned. The Old Vic could get very, very hot, not good for anyone, whichever side of the curtain.

I had been in my new office only a few weeks when I really longed to be back in the huts. Heavy rain one night meant my new office would be dripping in the morning. Once the autumnal rains came, they merrily plopped through. A helpful little Scotsman appeared in answer to my complaints and said that he would try and find out how the water found its way down. "But you must remember," he said, as if I had been told time and again, "there is a quarter of an acre of flat roof above us and the water may be coming though anywhere. Finding its way in is going to be very difficult and may take some time." That proved only too true.

## Scene 18 ❧ The naming of the three theatres in the National Theatre

The two main theatres in the National Theatre were named without difficulty. The larger of the two was named the Olivier in honour of Lord Olivier, who was the first director of the National Theatre, and the other was named the Lyttelton in honour of Lord Chandos (formerly Oliver Lyttelton), who was the first chairman of the National Theatre board. The spelling of Lyttelton was seldom correct when it appeared in newspapers and magazines in the early days, and even now the letters *e* and *l* are sometimes reversed.

The theatre that had no name initially was the smallest. It was referred to as the black box or the studio, when it really could have been given Peter Brook's title of "The Empty Space," for it was simply a hole within the building. And thus it would stay, it seemed, for there was no money to complete and then equip it.

However this did not stop John Bury producing designs for it. At one associates meeting he showed us a model, which was discussed at length and then accepted as the design that should be adopted once the money became available. But what should the theatre be called? There were several suggestions, but it was not until Guy Vaesen, who had recently joined the company as script department manager once Kenneth Tynan, the literary consultant, had left, said, "What about the Cottesloe, in honour of Lord Cottesloe? After all, he is the chairman of the South Bank board, which is responsible for the actual building of the National Theatre. And if he is asked whether he would like his name to be given to this theatre," continued Guy, "perhaps he might feel bound to give us the money so that it becomes a working theatre and not an unused space." Guy's idea was accepted at once, although his mischievous hope concerning finance was not realised.

## Scene 19 ⅊ Dressing rooms

It seemed very civilised to have a lift, situated just behind the stage door, to take us to our offices but it was a lift with a built-in puzzle. In the early days, we were told it was not possible to open the rooms that would become the canteen and the green room, but we were assured that indeed there were such rooms. They would be operational, they said, as soon as possible, and these rooms would be found on the second floor. This we could understand for the lift had a button marked 2. It also had buttons marked G for ground (and the stage door), 3 for two small rehearsal rooms and a small gymnasium, and 4 and 5 for the two floors of offices, but no button for a first floor. Supposing, as they might say in Belgrade, floor one was our wishing floor?

While we were trying to find explanations for the apparent unusual way of numbering levels in a lift, the puzzle was solved by Richard York, who, as ever, had answers to all our questions about this huge building. He had invited me to accompany him to the dressing-room block, saying, "Would you please number the rooms as soon as you can because we have to get on with the sign-posting." We met at the stage door, and he took me along a passage new to me that appeared to lead towards the centre of the building, if there were such a place. As we followed a curving, windowless corridor, I couldn't fail to notice that the corridor was sloping down. When it flattened out, Richard said, "We are still on the ground floor, but unlike the stage door area, where the floor above us was the second floor, here the level above is the first floor. It was possible for this 'extra' floor to be included in the back half of the building because of a slope in the ground."

Richard continued, "We are now facing the dressing-room block. The rooms are on four levels but only the lower two are usable at present." I then learned that they all shared the same outlook — or perhaps it should be inlook, for they all faced an inner well. As Richard was speaking, I remembered that one day some years earlier, Sir Laurence reported that he had been asked if he would like the centre of the dressing-room block to have a pool with a fountain. He told me that he'd immediately replied that he wouldn't want that at any price, thank you, for, he added, he would always be having to go to the nearest men's room if there was a continuous sound of running water. So there was no fountain but simply the roof of some underground space, though what it was I never knew — or cared. Richard continued with his description of the rooms: the first three floors had twelve dressing rooms each, but the fourth floor had thirteen, which was achieved by the extra room not being part of the square but the other side of the corridor.

The new building had many wonderful things about it, but there were also some dreadful areas, and one of these was the dressing-room block. Having come directly from the cosy but cramped Old Vic, it was good to feel the spaciousness on the South Bank. But to house about one hundred fifty actors and musicians, who must be able to reach any of the three theatres speedily, only a relatively small space could be allocated to the forty-eight dressing rooms. The idea of square rooms, in which several actors sat facing mirrors that not only reflected their own faces but also the backs of their fellows on the other side and where the conversation could be general, was obviously out of the question.

Now I was ushered into one of the largest rooms designed for six actors: each would have his or her own cubicle, but these were placed one behind the other, so there could be no direct contact.

Admittedly, each cubicle had a dressing table, good lighting fixtures, a central mirror, and two hinged side mirrors. There was a drawer, a washbasin, a curtain instead of a door and a speaker, or, as it was often called, a Tannoy. These speakers could be switched to bring a relay from any of the three theatres.

The six-person dressing room had a door at each end of the long, narrow room, one leading to the main corridor, the other to an identical (though back-to-front) six-person room. Almost half the fourth wall was given over to a wardrobe rail, which quickly proved to be fixed too low, resulting in cloaks, long dresses, and suchlike trailing on the carpeted floor. This hiccup was eventually solved by inserting a raised section into the original rail. The remainder of that wall was taken up with windows facing onto the central well. At first, these were sealed shut because of the air-conditioning, but it didn't take long for the occupants to decide they wanted to be in control of their own air-conditioning, thank you, and ways were found for them to be opened. At once it became possible to chat, send messages, mock, exchange banter, and generally communicate with others on the block.

This did not apply to the "extra" room on the third (and top) floor. This had no window, open or closed. I allocated this room to the musicians, for, unlike the actors, they were seldom in the building all day every day. Even so, I was always sorry that they had no outlook.

So now I was able to work on there being twelve rooms on the ground, first, and second floors, but thirteen on the third floor. At once, I could see the superstition of being in room 13 taking over, and the only way out of that was to start the numbering of all floors with 00, followed by 01, 02, and so on, as one walked round the block. This would make the musicians' room 12. So that was solved.

Then came the numbering of the floors. That was obvious for floors 1, 2, and 3 but what about the ground floor? Only one answer, it must be the useful 0. So the corner room on the ground floor became 000. On the floor above, the first floor, the same door in the same position became 100, and so on up the floors.

Placed between the six-person rooms, which were situated at each corner of the square, were rooms for two persons and rooms for one. The two-person rooms were my favourites. To a visitor, they somehow gave the illusion of being almost spacious: they weren't fitted with cubicles, the occupants sitting side-by-side. The one-person room had the privilege of a bath or a shower, but the "entertaining" area at the window end was very meagre. Each floor had large shower rooms.

I found the task that Richard York had set me extremely difficult. The top two floors were unfinished and so being able to check out only two levels of dressing rooms didn't help. The problem was compounded when I found that the layout of the single and double rooms was different on each floor, although at first glance they appeared the same. I dreaded to think what I would find when the upper two floors were handed over to us, let alone what the "extra" room would reveal.

At the Old Vic, I used to work out the allocation of dressing rooms. I would then take the list to Sir Laurence, who liked to know in which rooms his actors would be. I continued this tricky job when we moved to the South Bank, where, strangely, I found the additional number of rooms did not automatically ease the problems. The size of room I desperately needed was a room for four, but there was no way now, of course, that such a room would ever appear. If the two linked six-person rooms could have been divided to give me three rooms for four persons, I am sure the allocation would have been made much easier, and the actors would have been more pleased with where they were placed. But once we were in occupation, there was never the time or the money even to consider such alterations.

The only change I suggested in the whole building was a very simple one. Early in our occupation, I was walking through the ground floor passageway from the stage door to the dressing rooms with someone who seemed to have some authority in the builders' hierarchy and who had always been very helpful. As we reached the door leading to that much-used curving corridor on the ground floor, I commented that it seemed dangerous for that particular door not to be fitted with a glass panel. I added that I didn't think anyone would open the door gingerly on the off chance there might be someone approaching it from the other side. Within days, a glass panel was put in.

The other initial mammoth irritation was the Tannoy in the dressing-room corridors. Very sensible to be able to react to a call when one was on the way to or from a dressing room, but irritating to a degree to those actors trying to have a short sleep. They became incensed, especially by the calls from the stage door, which, for some reason, were always given in duplicate. "Mr. X, a visitor for you at the stage door. A visitor for you at the stage door, please, Mr. X." It was a struggle to get the excellent and patient staff at the stage door to change the way they put out their almost continual calls. I know they were correct when they explained that few reacted to a call that was only given once, so I suggested that maybe just the name of the person called should be given twice, at each end of the main information.

## Scene 20 ✆ The medical room

I had just planned who should be allotted which space in which dressing room, when I was told that, because of the ever-increasing number employed in the building, legislation demanded that (flashback to the Fenice) we had to provide a medical room. No empty sticking plaster tin somewhere in the prop room for us. There wasn't a suitable place front-of-house nor backstage, I was assured, except for a dressing room. And which room would I have to hand over? None other than one of the one-person rooms. Thanks a million. I complained, of course, but I knew that it was hopeless, so with my dressing-room allocation in tatters — even I found it strange that by having to move just one actor, a shudder went through the whole plan — I nominated room 002. This was very close to both the Lyttelton and the Cottesloe Theatres and the stage door and reasonably close to the kitchens, so it was the Olivier that lost out as far as easy access went.

Soon, into the canteen came Tony, our first medical attendant: a Canadian, young, black-haired, with big white teeth often on show. When I went to see him in his luxurious room, he said yes, he was very happy, and, no, he hadn't had any customers up to that time.

That was soon to change when a stage technician (I almost wrote stagehand, but that would look as if I were setting up a pun), working on the Lyttelton stage, gashed a hand, so he was helped at once to the medical room. When the party arrived, it seemed that Tony jumped up, put down the paper he was reading, and prepared to examine the injured man. The latter had been nursing his badly bleeding hand, but now he thrust it towards Tony, whose immediate reaction was to shoot his hands up, fingers extended, clasp his face, and exclaim, "Oh my Garrd!" Soon after this, Tony disappeared.

## Scene 21 ❦ The canteen

Until our canteen became operational, we were allowed to use the one in the National Film Theatre. The National Film Theatre was our next-door neighbour and, like us, fronted onto the Embankment, but unlike us, the view across the river was restricted since their building was under the road that led to Waterloo Bridge. We had to wait several weeks before we could discover what the view would be from our canteen, although, quite by chance, I had a slight inkling when I shared our lift with a workman employed by one of the building contractors. By the time he had hopped onto the lift, I had already pressed button 4, but he pressed button 2. I had never thought to do this for I knew it was a no-go floor for us, but now I would see what was happening on this floor. The door opened to reveal a lobby liberally supplied with doors, and with all its lights on, I felt as if I had reached El Dorado. This large very bright area reeked of exciting rooms that asked to be explored. Just as I was wondering which door led to where, the lift door closed and I was taken up two floors.

Soon after this day of discovery, the canteen and the green room were declared open. Both proved to have huge windows, the ones at the far end of the canteen faced directly north across the river to Somerset House, while the side wall, again made up mostly of windows, faced east. Our very close neighbour on that side housed the distribution point of the *Evening News*, one of the three London evening papers. Happily, its collection of buildings were low so one could look beyond them and be given a wonderful view down river towards the City of London.

The canteen had another advantage. The *Evening News* complex was built right up to the river's edge but this was the original riverbank, lying some way back from the front of the theatre. This meant that, standing in the canteen, one looked down onto the river towards the city with the *Evening News* on one's right, thus making it seem as if the river came right up to the stage door, tucked away one floor below. The same impression was there if one looked to the left, for the river, once again appeared to come right up to the front of the building. It was easy to imagine that one was on the prow of a ship.

The illusion would have been even better if silence accompanied the views, but the canteen was never silent. Any noise, coming from such items as crockery, cutlery, conversation, and calls over the Tannoy, was greatly amplified since the walls were faced with small, shiny pieces of mosaic and the floor was not carpeted.

When we first were allowed into the canteen, we found that it had been given a very smart title: "The Staff Restaurant." The staff would pay no attention to such a name and whatever the signposts might indicate, the canteen was the canteen and that was that. Of course, compared with Rose and Nellie's place at the huts and the basement gloom at the Old Vic, the large airy room by the river might easily be considered as having restaurant status, but theatre staff never ate in a restaurant. I don't think I was the only one who, while appreciating all that the catering staff was doing for us, missed Rose's greeting.

## Scene 22 ❧ The green room

Having established that one of the many doors in the El Dorado lobby led to the canteen, the next one to try, at the further end of the lobby, proved to lead to the green room. It was a pleasant enough, rectangular room of a reasonable size as rooms go, but with the possibility of a clientele of perhaps two hundred, it did not seem overgenerously proportioned. At least it shared with the canteen the splendid view to the east, with St. Paul's Cathedral still towering over the city buildings that surrounded it, while one could also see, dotted about the city, the spires of many churches designed by Sir Christopher Wren, as was St. Paul's.

Looking into the green room on its first day, one saw several armchairs, some long settees, and a table on which papers and magazines were set out neatly and orderly. Such precision was never attained again. The whole layout reminded me of the sets that I met so often in my repertory days but not, I am glad to say, in any of the productions in the West End with which I was involved. Often during a season at a local rep, one was presented with a set where, centre stage and facing square on to the audience, was a sofa behind and upstage of which was the obligatory sofa table. On this vital piece of furniture, one could be sure there would be a bowl of artificial flowers, a telephone, a cigarette box, and a cigarette lighter. There might have been a box of matches, of which two or three would be set sticking out at one end: This was to make it easy for an actor to pick out one, rather than having to fumble about in the box. Of course there would be an ashtray and one, sometimes two, rows of newspapers and magazines. These were always arranged with perfect symmetry, and if one of them had to be picked up and read during the action, after the interval it would be back where it belonged. This could vary if the next act started with the butler and the maid pushing the plot along with a little backstairs gossip while they tidied the room (much plumping of cushions). An example could be the third act of *A Flea in Her Ear.*

More or less in the centre of the green room was a tiny circular bar: a minute island that impeded the flow of traffic and that in no way allowed more than three to lean on the counter to order their drinks. Any idea of being able to stay there, chatting over a beer, was totally out of the question. At the back of the bar and completing the circle was a raised section about twice the height of the counter side: this was provided with shelving for bottles and glasses, but there was no space for extra supplies, such as crates of beer. These, therefore, had to be stored somewhere, and that somewhere was at the back and outside the circular structure. But that was the rub. Placing square wooden crates against a circle did not make for neat storage. However, they were more or less out of sight, even though they were an eyesore, and they didn't get in the way of those few who could stand at the counter. But they did get in the way of those using the further half of the room.

## Scene 23 ◎ Productions at the Old Vic from September 1975

During the time the huts in Aquinas Street were being vacated and the National Theatre began to come alive, productions were still arriving on the Old Vic stage. In September, a new version by Tony Harrison of Racine's *Phaedra* joined the repertoire. Tony chose the period to be the time of the British Raj in mid-nineteenth-century India and, as with his marvellous choice of Paris 1966 for *The Misanthrope,* I found *Phaedra Britannica* (as it was retitled) wonderfully satisfying. John Dexter directed as meticulously as ever, Tony's rhyming couplets sped along, and Michael Gough, Diana Rigg, and David Yelland as the Governor, the Governor's Wife, and the Governor's Son, respectively, were excellent.

*Phaedra Britannica* arrived on September 9 to be followed two weeks later by a production from the Nottingham Playhouse. This fascinating and really enjoyable visitor was *Comedians* by Trevor Griffiths. It was marvellously directed by Richard Eyre, who was the artistic director of the Playhouse. A great cast that included a stunning performance by Jonathan Pryce as one of the handful of would-be comics being taught their chosen profession by Jimmy Jewel. Jimmy, with his cousin Ben Warriss, had toured the music halls as Jewel & Warriss for many years with huge success before turning to radio and television. Also in the *Comedians* cast were Stephen Rea and Jim Norton, both of whom would be seen once more when Bill Bryden's production of *The Playboy of the Western World* — in which Jim would play Sean Keogh and Stephen Rea Christy Mahon, the playboy of the title — opened at the Old Vic on October 29. The cast was Irish except for Susan Fleetwood, who played Pegeen Mike. It must have been a great challenge for an English actress to go into the first rehearsal of an Irish play knowing she would be surrounded by Irish actors. Watching the play, one would have said that the entire cast was Irish.

On December 4, Peter Hall's production of *Hamlet* arrived. Albert Finney played the Prince, Roland Culver was Polonius, Angela Lansbury was Gertrude, and Susan Fleetwood was Ophelia. The full text of the play was used, which worried many when the news came out, for *Hamlet* is a very long play even when, in the accepted manner, it is cut. Without cuts, it obviously had the potential of being not just a long evening but an excessively long one. Peter had been reckoning that the performance would run for a total of 3 hours 15 minutes: this would be made up of 2 hours 15 minutes for the first act, an interval of 20 minutes, then 1 hour for the second act. However, when the production opened to the public, the first act exceeded hopes by 9 minutes, the second by 6, and the interval by 2, thus making a total of 3 hours

52 minutes. To allow for the length of the play, curtain up at evening performances was at seven o'clock (usually 7:30 PM) and matinees at two o'clock (usually 2:15 PM). *Hamlet* never played two performances on one day so, over a three-week period until January 3, 1976, *Judgement* played the evening performances after *Hamlet*'s matinees.

From January 17, *Happy Days* reappeared and took over the job from *Judgement* of pairing with *Hamlet*. Once more, this saved Albert having to play Hamlet twice in one day. John Bury's mound, in which Winnie would spend her happy days, could be comfortably set and lit during the break between the matinee and the evening show, especially when curtain up for *Happy Days* (with a playing time of only one and a half hours) was at eight o'clock.

## Scene 24 ❧ The acoustic test Lyttelton Theatre, Wednesday, February 4, 1976

It was early in December 1975 that Peter Hall told me that the Lyttelton Theatre, still unfinished, would have to be given an acoustic test. This apparently had to be set up for a date some weeks before the theatre opened officially to the public, so that if there were any improvements to be made, there would be time for them to be carried out. Peter asked if I would please organise this and if I needed his services on that evening in any capacity, he was very willing to be involved.

I had a meeting with the acoustic experts, who said that they would want to hear the spoken word from all over the Lyttelton's large acting area: well upstage, of course, as well as down. They would also want the solo voice and many actors speaking from all quarters. And finally, they would want to hear music, both vocal and instrumental.

As for the other side of the curtain, they would want some scenes watched by an audience seated only in the stalls, and others when only the circle would be filled. They would like several minutes when the auditorium would be empty. Maroons (small fireworks that explode loudly) would be let off and pistols would be fired, they said, and they would like the performance to last as long as a normal stage play, for they decided that would give them the time they needed for their various tests.

I am sure I was wrong, but from the way they spoke, I had a feeling that they knew as little about what their tests would tell them and what they must do with that information as we did. At once I was quite sure that what it seemed they wanted was an evening in the form of the old-fashioned music hall, lasting about two and a half hours.

I went round the company at once asking if anyone would like to be involved, and if so, in what way. I got a tremendous response with one exception, about which I was very sorry, although I quite understood. When I put my request to Angela Lansbury, she said that she would have to refuse. If she had to sing as part of a show, this presented no problem, but she couldn't stand at a piano and sing a song. She had to be in character. However, if I couldn't cajole Hamlet's Mother to take part, Hamlet himself, in the form of Albert Finney, immediately accepted my suggestion that he should be the master of ceremonies.

I then enlisted the help of one of the staff directors, Sebastian Graham-Jones, to be the director. Leonard Tucker, who had been responsible for the lighting for so many productions at the Old Vic, undertook the lighting of the show, and John Rothenberg, with Elizabeth Markham as his deputy, willingly agreed to head the stage management team of Angela Bisset, Jeremy Gadd, and Ernest Hall.

When my programme was just about filled, Gawn Grainger, already marked down for appearing in two of the items, asked if he and Albert could open the show with a sketch. He said they had worked out a little scene, and they would love it if it could be part of the show. Gawn then confessed that he had another request. If I agreed to them appearing in their sketch, would it be possible please for it to be at the top of the bill and might it please be played for the first time on the night of the test? "We don't want to do it even at the dress rehearsal," said Gawn. I immediately said, "Yes, that's fine. I want your sketch, and certainly it can be the first item that will follow the overture. As for not wanting to show it even at the dress rehearsal, that's also fine by me." He and I then had to work out what should appear in the programme and we came up with:

No. 2  The Comperes  Testing the Acoustics from    Albert Finney
                     an idea by Dinsdale Landen  Gawn Grainger

Dinsdale was currently helping to fill the Old Vic with glorious laughter with his performance as D'Arcy Tuck in Ben Travers's farce *Plunder*. This had opened on January 14 and had become an instant hit with the public. Michael Blakemore, in top form as ever, directed it to perfection. It was obviously going to be one of those productions that I would be able to schedule to play on any night and the house would be full.

As January wore on, so the word *acoustic* made more frequent appearances in the engagement diary:

January 19   See Dame P. re Acoustic and No Charity Collection
             Speak to Ivan re Acoustic Evening [Ivan Alderman was
             and had been for the whole of the National Theatre's
             existence the wonderful wardrobe supervisor.]
January 21   10.30: Acoustic Meeting
January 27   Ask Philip Locke to contact Dame Peg: see her at end
             of matinee on Thursday
February 2   Check on rehearsals for Acoustic [These rehearsals
             turn up the next day from 8 PM to 10 PM.]

Finally on the day of the test, I noted that the final rehearsal call would be from 3:30 to 5:30 PM, and against this note I wrote "Dame P—5.15."

She and Philip were each to read the John Donne sonnets "Song" and "Woman's Constancy." It was typical of this remarkable lady that as soon as I had told her about the test and asked if she would take part, she had at once said, "Of course I will so long as it doesn't clash with *Happy Days*." I had already scheduled *Phaedra Britannica* for the test evening, so Dame Peggy was free.

The audience was to be made up principally of staff from the architect's office, in addition to the contractors, subcontractors and their employees, so that they and their families could see the end product of their work. Well, more or less the end product in the case of the Lyttelton Theatre, but not for the Olivier or the Cottesloe.

February 4 finally arrived, and when I walked into the Lyttelton foyer, I wondered if the audience would smile wryly on arrival, for, in true new-building fashion, the carpet in the foyer was being laid as the first of them appeared. I didn't get upstairs to see whether the circle foyer was carpeted, but I suspect that it wasn't at that time.

The seats for the first four rows in the Lyttelton Theatre, unlike the majority in the house, were narrow and had no armrests. The other seating was designed so that it was possible, though not perhaps easy, for a patron to pass down a seated row without disturbing anyone. The first theatre in which I had met this great facility (in fact the space was so wide it was almost too great a facility) was the splendid Mermaid Theatre. This was situated on the fringe of the city in an area enticingly called Puddle Dock.

When the National Theatre was being built, Sir Laurence had asked that the first four rows in the stalls of the Olivier and Lyttelton Theatres should be sold as cheaply as possible. He was determined that this should be where young people, such as students, should sit. He said he didn't want those seats filled with members of society who could afford the usual high price of the front stalls and who were probably in the theatre because "one must be seen at the latest hit." He was also certain that that particular type of patron would be the first to go to sleep, whereas the students would be there because they were keen to see the play. He was also sure they wouldn't object to or even notice the size of the seats. Their enthusiasm and immediate response to the action would cause a ripple of excitement or laughter that would quickly spread to the remainder of the house. The seats were named the ripple seats.

On the night of the test, there were no students in those seats. Instead they were filled, apparently, by managerial staff, since there were many dinner jackets on view, looking quite out of place. Perhaps the wearers had thought they had given themselves the best seats in the house and not been told of the ripple.

The curtain went up more or less to time and, after an overture played by Matrix, onto an empty, and seemingly vast, stage came Albert and Gawn. They were deep in conversation as they walked at a comfortable pace from up left to down right, but it was not until they were halfway across before murmurs could be heard in the audience. And this was all that could be heard, for not one word of the conversation between the two actors came across the footlights, as one would have said in the old days.

The murmuring sound came from members of the audience who were asking each other if they could hear, and when many heads were shaken, so was the confidence in the acoustics. The theatre obviously had a disaster on its hands. Apparently unaware as to what was happening out front, the pair continued walking, and just before they disappeared offstage, they suddenly started speaking normally and everyone could hear them and there was a roar of laughter. The audience had been well and truly fooled, and the evening could not have got off to a better start. The starchiness and uncertainty, evidently due to so many not having been to a theatre before, disappeared, and there was total relaxation.

Dinsdale, who, with Sebastian, appeared next in a piece by Nicholas Tomalin that had been adapted by Sebastian and Michael Kustow, must have been encouraged by the success of his idea for Albie and Gawn, for the Tomalin went extremely well. Wherever the actors or musicians could, they roamed over the stage although that didn't apply to Gareth Hunt whose contribution, accompanied by Chuck Mallett, was "Songs at the Piano." Hardly had the last notes of "If I Were a Rich Man" faded, when our acoustic friends let off pistol shots and maroons, having, of course, warned the audience as to what they were going to do. By this time, the show was rolling along well. Oliver Cotton played three Spanish pieces most beautifully on his guitar, and Dame Peggy and Philip read their sonnets exquisitely.

At this point, the audience in the circle was asked to leave while first Albert Finney entertained and then Denise Myers, accompanied by Chuck, sang "Summertime." That brought us to the interval, although those in the stalls were asked to stay in their seats for five minutes. When they filed out, the auditorium was left totally empty for ten minutes.

The end of the interval was announced by the front-of-house management ringing handbells, there being no Tannoy, no electric bells, and no buzzers. The circle audience was invited to return to their seats. The second half started with the repeat of the arrangement for the end of the first half, except that this time it was the stalls who stayed outside while the circle first heard Denise sing "Summertime," and then Albie entertained as he had done before the interval. Most of the time, an expert on either side of the stalls walked up and down swinging some instrument. Very impressive. Denise and Albert didn't take long, and as soon as he finished, the stalls were invited to return and on with the show.

Peter Hall now made his entrance and seated himself at the piano ready to accompany Alexandra Denman, an usherette, and Pieter Serfontein, from accounts, as each sang a solo before they linked for the Rossini "A Duet for Two Cats," which was a great success with the audience. Immediately following the two cats came Keith Dewhurst's "The Last Acoustic Detail," directed by Bill Bryden and played by Andrew Byatt, Gareth Hunt, Michael Keating, Patrick Monkton, and Derek Newark. This was great as was the return of Matrix under Harrison Birtwistle again, this time playing his "La Plage," then a piece from *The Beggar's Opera* arranged by Carl Davis, and finally "Amazing Grace."

After more pistols shots and suchlike noise begetters, we reached the finale, and here was Hamlet's stepfather, Claudius, in the person of Denis Quilley, standing at the piano at which sat Chuck, ready as ever to accompany. Denis was well into his second number, "Bless Your Beautiful Hide," when all the lights went out. Chuck played on for a moment, but Denis stopped singing, and for a split second there was dead silence, broken only by the sound of running feet backstage, before the whole audience, it seemed, started talking at the same time while sitting in almost total darkness.

It was still the practice in some theatres (not the Aldwych) and cinemas at that time for usherettes to be equipped with flashlights for use when seating latecomers. As good fortune had it, on this evening and at this moment in the show, there were two usherettes in the circle, one on each side at the very front. Almost simultaneously, two beams of light were directed from their vantage points to the centre of the stage.

Again, by lucky chance, I was standing in the wings stage left and beside me was Albert. As soon as the beams of light appeared, I didn't wait to find out how and from where, I simply pushed Albie forward and said, "Please tell them some stories." He was marvellous, strolling nonchalantly to the middle of the stage as if he had been going to do that anyway, making sure the lights were on him and starting to chat.

Backstage all was controlled pandemonium. I could still hear hurrying footsteps, but there were definitely more now, dashing hither and yon all to no avail, while Albie continued to entertain the masses brilliantly. Roars of laughter greeted whatever it was he was saying, and it was a little while before I was able to return to the wings and listen. It took a moment to realise that the dear chap had run out of funny stories, and he was now beginning to treat the audience as if they were in a men-only club.

Having noticed several children in the audience, and because we were still in an age of comparative innocence, I called out, "Albie," very loudly. He must have heard, but he chose not to; he was enjoying himself much too much. I called again, but still getting no reaction, I went onstage. I wished I had the long staff with the hook at the top that used to be employed in the world of the music hall. When a manager decided that enough was enough, the offending artist was stopped by the simple means of hooking him by the neck and pulling. At least I had an arm, and this I employed successfully, and I managed to drag Albert offstage. He couldn't have made a better exit, and it was rightfully accompanied by the proverbial gales of laughter and tremendous applause.

Albie's exit was followed, almost as if it had been planned, by the return of the lights. More applause and cheers, and the audience left the first performance in the new National Theatre in high good humour. Whatever might be planned for the Lyttelton's opening in six weeks time, I felt that we had very successfully opened it with the acoustic test, and I was so very grateful to all those who had worked really hard to make it such a good show.

As the audience dispersed, I managed to track down Leonard (Lennie) Tucker, the long-serving chief electrician, and asked him what had happened to the lights. The first problem, he said, was that, after being in the building such a short time, no one had the slightest idea what might have happened, and even if they had, he didn't think they would then know how to rectify the problem. His staff had rushed around the area of the Lyttelton hoping to find a switch that might, with luck, restore the power. As often happens, the answer was much more simple than they had feared. It seems that there was an electrical firm's employee whose job at night was to be in control of the electricity supply to the as yet not fully occupied theatre. He was obviously not a theatre-minded person, and there was no reason why he should be, so it didn't matter to him what was happening on the floor above. He had his instructions, and he, rightly, was going to obey them. One of these was that, at 10:30 PM, he had to switch out the lights, and this is what he did. When someone found him in his quarters at the edge of the dressing-room block and had persuaded him to reverse his orders, all was well.

## Scene 25 ❧ The National Theatre leaves the Old Vic, February 28, 1976

While the audience in the National's new home had been experiencing an unusual and hopefully enjoyable evening on February 4, 1976, the audience in the National's old home was watching *Phaedra Britannica*. The National's stay in the Old Vic was running out fast, but audiences could still continue to come there to experience the repertoire for another nine days. During that time, it was possible to see two more perform-ances of *Phaedra Britannica* (although the second performance would be its last), as well as *Hamlet, Plunder,* and *Happy Days*. Once the last two of this quartet had played their final performances at the Old Vic, they were then ready to be transferred to the South Bank. *Hamlet* had six more performances before it too could be uprooted and taken to its new home, but before it played its last two, a new production came into the Old Vic. This was John Osborne's *Watch It Come Down*.

Everyone had to be funny about this title and the new theatre. I am sure when John chose the title, the last thing he would have had in mind was the hilarity it was going to cause vis-à-vis the new theatre in particular. It was too tempting for anyone not to point out that a few days after *Watch It Come Down* was put on the Old Vic stage, the National was leaving that theatre. Would they get out in time? The other side was that the National was moving into a new building with a play called *Watch It Come Down*: "Is this a prophetic title?" Ha, ha, ha.

Bill Bryden directed Jill Bennett, Michael Feast, Frank Finlay, Susan Fleetwood, and Michael Gough in a delightfully apt setting by Hay-den Griffin. The single scene was the booking hall of a railway station that was no longer used by the railway company, so it had been turned into a dwelling house. After five previews, it opened to the press on Tuesday, February 24, played three more performances during Wednesday and Thursday before being taken over to the new theatre.

This left *Hamlet* to play on Friday, February 27, and Saturday,

February 28, in that final week. Thus the first and the last performances by the National Theatre Company at the Old Vic were *Hamlet*. By the seventh week of the National's initial occupation of the Old Vic in 1963, a company of thirty-seven actors had a repertoire of four productions: *Hamlet, Saint Joan, Uncle Vanya,* and *The Recruiting Officer.* For the last seven weeks of the National's occupation of the Old Vic in 1976, a company of eighty-six actors had a repertoire of five productions: *Hamlet, Happy Days, Plunder, Watch It Come Down,* and *Phaedra Britannica.*

The moving of the National Theatre's repertoire from the Old Vic Theatre to the new building on the South Bank coincides with the end of the twenty years that this book set out to cover. I was really sad to have to say good-bye to the Old Vic for, although it had its disadvantages, the old theatre was warm and welcoming, it had dignity and friendliness, it had a sense of history, and it had a tremendous theatrical atmosphere.

The Lyttelton Theatre on the South Bank could not be called welcoming for the too too solid walls repelled more than welcomed. But the seats were wide and comfortable and the iron (or fire) curtain caught me out each time it split in the middle and half went up and the remainder down.

But this was only one theatre: there were two to come. Creeping in to the Olivier Theatre, unobserved by security, confirmed my most dire prediction that there would be more lashings of concrete and that the acting area would be absolutely vast. But the great sweep of the three levels of seating (the centre block of the stalls had raised sections either side) was exciting, and once more the seats, that apparently would be the same type as in the Lyttelton, would be comfortable.

But what of the Hole in the Building, that poor unfinished Cottesloe? Perhaps in the smallest of the three theatres, when eventually it was opened, there would be the warmth and the welcome that I sought. It was going to be a year before I would know but there would be no sitting around waiting to find out. As with the move into the Royal Court Theatre twenty years before, there was and there would be plenty to do. All I could hope was that the years ahead would be as wonderful as those through which I had just passed.

# ℚ EPILOGUE ℚ

I found it so interesting when writing this book the way that some events rushed back to mind immediately and some came wandering along, usually unsought and always out of chronological order. Inevitably, I suppose, the same is happening when I continue to look back but this time at my life following the move into the new National Theatre on the South Bank.

Those were great days with the unbelievable luxury of being able to look in briefly on three National Theatre productions in three different theatres, and yet the journey would only take five minutes. But strangely, once we had grown accustomed to the whole organisation being in one place, I found myself having to make more and more forays away from it.

Normal U.K. touring continued, but in addition I had to set up and organise annual two-week visits to Glasgow, based at the splendid Theatre Royal, which gave me enormous pleasure, and there was a memorable week when we took *Lark Rise* to Milton Keynes. This entailed re-creating the Cottesloe Theatre in a new building that would, the following week, become a light engineering factory.

Certainly, I spent much time travelling abroad, sometimes on my own (such as a fascinating trip to Venezuela that started with a request from the British Council, "I know you're in Denver, but I wonder if you could get away for a day or two and slip down to Caracas?"), but more usually with companies. We went to such countries as the United States, Germany, France, Mexico, Italy, and a fantastic visit to Epidaurus in Greece.

If there had been plenty to do when I was with the National Theatre, there seemed even more when retirement struck. At once, there was a three-month caretaker-administrator job at the Haymarket

Theatre, Leicester, followed by a four-month lecture tour, as part of the American College Theatre Festival, to universities and colleges across the United States. This led over several years to two more such tours in addition to one wonderful variation when I joined two delightful preofessors to form the American College Theatre Festival national judging panel. This meant over eight weeks assessing fifty-nine college and university productions across the country.

Back in the United Kingdom, for ten years I was London Weekend Television's adminstrator of the company's annual competition called Plays on Stage. LWT's excellent head of drama, Nick Elliott, had dreamed this up as one way of LWT thanking the world of theatre from where so many actors were taken to appear on television. For myself, the enormous pleasure was seeing, once a year, the artistic directors of three U.K. theatre companies leaving the award ceremony each with a cheque that was going to help their company put a play of their choice on a stage.

Overlapping with Plays on Stage, I organised a remarkable evening on the occasion of the twenty-fifth anniversary of the creation of the National Theatre, and I was also in charge of a special entertainment in the Olivier Theatre to celebrate Lord Olivier's eightieth birthday.

Somewhere amongst all this, I became overseas consultant for the International Theatre Festival of Chicago, I was on the board of the superb English Shakespeare Company, and I was twice involved with Shakespesare's Globe Theatre, first when I was the administrator of the 1995 Workshop Season and two years later when Her Majesty the Queen arrived by barge to open the complex. My link with Shakespeare's Globe was renewed when in 2001 I was very honoured to be invited to be a member of the board and also become the chairman of the artistic directorate.

Of the many joys of so much travelling around was watching productions in so many auditoriums. From the room above a pub in Bristol to the vast AuditoriumTheater in Chicago and all types in between. As the years went by, I found my preference was more and more for the smaller spaces. I can feel total involvement when sitting in the third row (that would probably be back row) in a tiny theatre, watching a play with no scenery and with the actors within a few feet. Much as I enjoy going into a large auditorium and seeing acres of stage filled with masses of scenery and lit by dozens of lamps, I find total involvement very hard to come by. However good the production and however brilliant the performances, all of which I can appreciate, I am constantly distracted by the size and, therefore, cost of it all.

Perhaps the most encouraging aspect of the past twenty years has been the emergence of so many excellent new and young playwrights, male and female, whose work can be seen during useful, short runs at the smaller theatres and the appearance of women in important posts in all sides of the business. A sensation was caused in the early fifties when a company, arriving for a week at the Theatre Royal, Newcastle-upon-Tyne, found that among the well-built, male stagehands was the splendid, similarly well-built female Lily.

I don't meet any of the Lily's now, for all my theatregoing is as a spectator, and although I may often be critical of what I am being shown, I still enormously enjoy the experience of being in a theatre. I count myself very fortunate to have been involved with theatre during a time when so many changes — in all departments — took place.

# ᘒ INDEX ᘒ

109–10, 316–19; directing *Hamlet*, 361; directing *Happy Days*, 341; directing *John Gabriel Borkman*, 332, 342–44; directing *Judgement*, 348; directing *No Man's Land*, 344; directing *Waiting for Godot*, 36; at farewell to Laurence Olivier, 314; listing actors alphabetically, 304; London home of, 350; and the Lord Chamberlain, 160–61; method of work of, 110; as new director National Theatre, 313; and new theatre for RSC, 248; and Peter Daubeny, 138, 140; and Peter O'Toole, 111; and Pinter and Beckett, 177; presenting Shakespeare plays, 202; presenting at Windsor Castle, 172; presenting World Theatre Season, 140; Riverside home of, 92–94, 115; at Shakespeare Memorial Theatre, 89, 91; and Shakespeare's 400th birthday, 158, 175; at State Gala, 142–43, 146, 149; Sunday phone call of, 320

Hall, Willis, 67, 306
Hallett, John, 136, 163
Hallifax, Clive, 4, 102, 138
Hallifax, Elizabeth: attending announcement of the bond winner, 100; attending fireworks, 97; buying a taxi, 18–19; at Coventry Cathedral Festival, 131; at farewell to the Court, 72, 74; finding a title, 192; illness of, 4; loaning a dog at the Royal Court, 158; making another move, 87; at mayoral reception, 108; with no *Hecuba* translation, 187; and Peter Daubeny, 138, 349; recounting a tale to

Laurence Olivier, 46; returning to London, 132, 134; at the Royal Opera House, 146; settling in, 95; touring Canada, 217; visiting a friend in Edmonton, 219; visiting Niagara Falls, 223; at Windsor Castle, 172

Hallifax, Guy, 4, 78, 102, 138, 170
Hamilton, Julie, 47
Handel, George Frederick, 95
Hans, the Zurich call boy, 120–21
Hare, David, 289, 330
Harris, Margaret (Percy): designing permanent surround for Royal Court, 29–30; as member of "Motley" design team, Royal Court, 15; as set designer of *The Country Wife*, 34; as set designer of *Hedda Gabler*, 139; as set designer of *Requiem for a Nun*, 63; as set designer of *Rosmersholm*, 85; visiting the Royal Court, 18

Harris, Sophie, 15, 16, 86
Harrison, Robin, 32
Harrison, Tony, 302, 360–61
Harvey, (Skikne) Laurence, 34, 37, 81
Harvey, Mr., Architect, 106
Hastings, Michael, 49, 280
Heard, Daphne, 261, 272
Heeley, Desmond, 226
Hellenes, the King and Queen of, 142–45
Henry, Victor, 158
Herbert, Jocelyn, 16, 18, 30, 48
Her Majesty the Queen: at Aldwych State Gala, 142–45, 152, 154; *The Comedy of Errors* at Windsor Castle, 173–74
Heston, Charlton, 264
Hewitson, Ian, 125

Montgomery, Lord, 102
Montini, G. B. Cardinal, 156
Mortimer, John, 288
Morton, John Maddison, 244
Muller, Robert, 23, 25
Myers, Denise, 366–67

Napier, John, 301
Negri, Richard, 116
Nellie, canteen assistant, 195, 359
Nero, Franco, 306–7
Newark, Derek, 131, 367
Nicholls, Anthony, 223, 232
Nichols, Peter, 246, 330
Nixon, David, 131
Noguchi, 119, 122
Norah, "Auntie," 130
Norton, Jim, 361
Nunn, Trevor, 179

O'Brien, David, 120–21
O'Casey, Sean, 154
Olivier, Sir Laurence: baronetcy of,
    276–77; casting, 206–9; 212,
    225, 306–7; in *The Dance of
    Death*, 199; in *Eden End*, 24;
    and end of 1955 Stratford Sea-
    son, 220–21; in *The Entertainer*,
    38–43, 197, 45–46; film roles
    of, 313–14; and Franco Nero,
    306–7; in *Guys and Dolls*, 312;
    illnesses of, 205–6, 286–87; in
    *Long Day's Journey*, 289, 313;
    directing *Love's Labours Lost*,
    245; last performances of,
    313–15; in *The Merchant of
    Venice*, 275, 314; as National
    Theatre director, 191–93, 196,
    197, 200–204, 248, 291–92,
    303, 308, 310, 347; and the new
    car, 279; and the new National
    Theatre, 312, 313; Olivier The-

atre named in honor of, 352; in
    *Saturday Sunday Monday*, 314;
    on Sir Ralph's accident, 332–33;
    and *Three Sisters*, 213–14; tour-
    ing, 215–18, 222–24, 249,
    262–63; in *Tribute to the Lady*,
    329; and use of accents, 198;
    visiting the old school, 212
Olsen, Dale, 262, 268
O'Neill, Eugene, 290
Ornbo, Robert, 282–83
Osborne, John, 7– 9: *Bond Hon-
    oured*, 251, 277; *The Entertainer*,
    35, 37–38, 40–41, 43; *Epitaph
    for George Dillon*, 64; *Look Back
    in Anger*, 9, 10, 20–21, 51, 56,
    58–50, 65; saying good-bye,
    61–62; *Watch It Come Down*,
    369
Ostrovsky, Alexander, 298
O'Toole, Peter, 67–70, 110–11,
    275
Owen, Alun, 49, 73

Pasco, Richard, 35, 45
Pavitt, G, 17
Paxinou, Katina, 186–87
Payne, B. Iden, 103
Pears, Peter, 32–33
Peaslee, Richard, 180
Peck, Gregory, 264
Pelham, David, 59–60
Petherbridge, Edward, 210, 226–27
Philip, Prince, the Duke of Edin-
    burgh: at Aldwych State Gala,
    142–43, 152, 154; at State Gala,
    Royal Opera House, 144, 147;
    at Windsor Castle, 172–73
Phipps, Jack, 251, 316, 319
Pickford, Miss, 13, 63
Pickup, Ronald: in *As You Like It*,
    237; in *The Beaux' Stratagem*,

Rigg, Diana (*continued*)
in *Macbeth*, 284; in *The Misan-*
*thrope*, 302; in *Phaedra Britan-*
*nica*, 361; at State Gala, 152;
and the three-year plan, 322; in
*'Tis Pity She's a Whore*, 295; at
Windsor Castle, 173
Roberts, John, 136–37
Robinson, Ann: attending audi-
tions, 281; attending lunchtime
performances, 294; casting,
206–7, 226, 244, 292, 304;
offering accommodation,
133–34; as understudy for *The*
*White Carnation*, 305
Robinson, Charles, 49
Robson, Dame Flora, 329
Rogers, Houston, 47
Rogers, Pieter, 74
Rose, the cook, 194, 346, 359
Ross, Diana, 217
Ross, Donald, 50
Rothenberg, John, 231–32, 273,
363
Rouse, Albert, 41
Rowbottom, George, 191, 217
Roy, Maggie, 136, 187
Rudkin, David, 178
Rye, Daphne, 8

Sales, Tom, 93, 106–7, 114,
129–30
Sallis, Peter, 134
Sass, Enid, 24
Schlesinger, John, 320–21, 325,
344
Schlissel, Jack, 59
Scofield, Paul: in *The Captain of*
*Kopenick*, 288; in *King Lear*,
125–27; as National Theatre
associate director, 281; and Old
Vic dressing room, 208; in *Rules*

of the Game, 289; in *Tribute to*
*the Lady*, 329
Scott, George C., 183
Scott, Zachary, 62–63
Sears, Heather, 35
Serfontein, Pieter, 367
Seneca, Lucius Annacus, 243
Shaffer, Anthony, 314
Shaffer, Peter: *Black Comedy*, 251;
*Equus*, 294–301; *Five Finger*
*Exercise*, 86; working with John
Dexter, 294, 301
Shakespeare, John, 108
Shakespeare, William, 108–9, 158,
202–3
Shaw, George Bernard, 130, 247,
325, 344
Shaw, Glen Byam, 92, 109–10, 215
Shaw, Martin, 197–98
Shaw, Robert, 67
Sherriff, R. C., 206, 305
Shorter, Eric, 157
Shulman, Milton, 157
Sibley, Peter: and Gorki Theatre
company problems, 188–90; and
latecomers to performances,
176–77; presenting bouquets,
163, 182; and Princess Marina,
160; and stage announcements,
184; and unrest in the stalls,
166–67
Sim, David, 47
Simpson, N.F., 50
Skelton, Geoffrey, 180
Smith, Dodie, 206
Smith, Maggie: in *The Beaux' Strata-*
*gem*, 261, 278–79; in *Hedda*
*Gabler*, 275, 280, 286; and the
huts canteen, 195; leaving the
National Theatre, 281; repertory
roles of, 277; in *Three Sisters*, 262
Smoktunovsky, Innokenti, 190

MICHAEL HALLIFAX's theater career began in 1939 as an A.S.M. for a repertory company at the King's Theatre in Hammersmith. From November 1939 to May 1946 he served in the Royal Artillery. Returning to the theatre, he became stage manager for several repertory companies until he was invited to join H. M. Tennent in 1950. For H.M.T., he stage managed six major West End productions until 1955. Over the next thirty years he worked as stage manager or administrator for several prestigious theatre companies.

Since 1985, he has managed two special events at the National Theatre and two at Shakespeare's Globe. For ten years he was the administrator of London Weekend Television's "Plays on Stage" competition. During the 1980s and 1990s he undertook three lecture tours to American colleges and universities, and in 1992, he was one of A.C.T.F.'s three national judges.